LETHAL
WITNESS

LETHAL WITNESS

SIR BERNARD SPILSBURY
HONORARY PATHOLOGIST

ANDREW ROSE

SUTTON PUBLISHING

First published in the United Kingdom in 2007 by
Sutton Publishing, an imprint of NPI Media Group Limited
Cirencester Road · Chalford · Stroud · Gloucestershire · GL6 8PE

British Library Cataloguing in Publication Data
A catalogue record for this book is available from the British Library.

Hardback ISBN 978-0-7509-4422-9
Paperback ISBN 978-0-7509-4423-6

Typeset in Photina MT.
Typesetting and origination by
NPI Media Group Limited.
Printed and bound in England.

To the memory of a surgeon,
Dr William Fiddes
of Belhelvie, Aberdeenshire,
who died on 15 April 1847, the result of septicaemia
contracted while performing a post-mortem

Contents

	Acknowledgements	ix
	Introduction	xv
One	An Unsentimental Education	1
Two	Dr Spilsbury	9
Three	Dr Crippen	21
Four	Moral High Ground	31
Five	Brides in the Bath	41
Six	Night of the Gothas	51
Seven	The Button and Badge Murder	63
Eight	Mid-Life Crisis	77
Nine	'Excuse Fingers'	85
Ten	'Arise, Sir Bernard'	97
Eleven	1924: Two Vintage Murders	111
Twelve	A Martyr to Spilsburyism	125
Thirteen	Not Proven	141
Fourteen	'Do you think I've come up here for fun?'	153
Fifteen	A Disappearing Bruise	163
Sixteen	The Blazing Car Murder	185
Seventeen	Murder Parade	199
Eighteen	Ghastly Speculation	211
Nineteen	'Laugh, baby, laugh for the last time!'	221
Twenty	Tony Mancini: The Brighton Trunk Murders	229
Twenty-one	Spilsbury in Decline	241
Twenty-two	Wartime	251
Twenty-three	Last Years	263
	Notes	271
	Select Bibliography	285
	Index	289

Acknowledgements

Professor Bernard Knight CBE, Emeritus Professor of Forensic Pathology, University of Wales College of Medicine, formerly Consultant Forensic Pathologist to the Home Office, and Barrister-at-Law, has been of immeasurable help for more than a decade. As the project for a life of Spilsbury has gradually taken shape, Professor Knight has always been ready, often at short notice, with help and advice on the more celebrated and difficult cases in which Spilsbury was involved. Professor Knight also lent me Spilsbury's 1944 engagement diary and address book, together with Alan Spilsbury's pocket diary for 1945, both of which shed valuable light on Spilsbury's last years.

I am most grateful to the late Rt Hon Sir Frederick Lawton QC, His Honour Judge Alan King-Hamilton QC, Dr Hazel Baker, Joy Cotton (Lady Spilsbury's niece), Dr David Foster, Dr Jean Gavin and Molly Lefebure for their personal recollections of Spilsbury. Dr Foster also made available to me records of *The Organon*, an academic dining club of which Spilsbury was a member.

Lord Hutchinson of Lullington QC (Jeremy Hutchinson) both wrote and spoke to me about aspects of Spilsbury's life, notably in relation to the Fox case. Mrs Susan Kittermaster and Mrs Daphne Torrie gave me useful information about the late Mrs Hilda Bainbridge. Dr Lewis Gavin gave me his memories of Professor Sir Sydney Smith and of Dr Gerald Roche Lynch, the Home Office analyst. The late Sir Geoffrey Wilson told me of his experiences as marshal to Mr Justice Rigby Swift, who presided at several trials in which Spilsbury gave evidence for the Crown. I am grateful to Dr Ian Wilson for family recollections of Spilsbury's work on the Tarrant Keyneston shooting mystery.

Sir Max Hastings allowed me to use material from his father's book *The Other Mr Churchill* (Harrap 1961), the biography of Robert Churchill, the gunsmith, who collaborated with Spilsbury in several murder trials. My thanks are due to Dr C.P.W. Willcox and Dr H.N.A. Willcox for allowing me to draw on material in *The Detective-Physician*, the biography of Sir William Willcox written by his son, the late Dr Philip Willcox. Bryan Senior, the distinguished artist and residuary legatee of Dick Spilsbury, gave me a number of photographs of Spilsbury family members, and I am most grateful to him for allowing me to quote from two letters in his possession written by Spilsbury during the Second World War. The late Professor Richard Cobb and

Mrs Margaret Cobb also spoke to me about Dick Spilsbury. Dr Robin Darwall-Smith, Archivist of Magdalen College, Oxford, allowed me to peruse documentation held in the college archives relevant to Spilsbury's academic record as an undergraduate. Dr Janet Jenkins supplied me with extracts from a diary describing conditions leading up to the air raid that killed Peter Spilsbury in September 1940.

Many thanks are also due to Kevin Brown, Trust Archivist and Alexander Fleming Museum Curator at St Mary's NHS Trust, Paddington, who permitted me to see archive material relating to Spilsbury held in his collection and who, with his unique knowledge of the hospital's history, provided me with valuable additional information about the background to Spilsbury's career at St Mary's.

Jonathan Evans, Archivist of the Royal London Hospital Archives and Museum, showed me material on the Crippen case, including a number of slides prepared by Spilsbury and other significant items. Diana Brahams, Secretary of the Medico-Legal Society, allowed me access to the society's annual records. I am grateful to Ms Kate Smith, of the Royal Society of Chemistry Library and Information Centre, for detail relating to James Spilsbury's fellowship of the Chemical Society.

My thanks are due to Mrs Elspeth Griffiths, Archivist at Sedbergh School, for information about Dick Spilsbury and in relation to Spilsbury's unsuccessful application to join the Methodist ministry. Gratitude also extends to John Bever, volunteer archivist of Manchester Grammar School, and to Helen Sender of University College School, for their assistance in relation to Spilsbury's attendance at their respective schools. Mrs K.A. Jowett, Assistant Librarian at the Library and Museum of the United Grand Lodge of England, sent me details of Spilsbury's membership of four Masonic lodges.

I am most grateful to Linda Steward for sending me a valuable collection of copy documents, including family charts, school records and newspaper extracts, relating to the life of Sydney Fox. Sir John Leslie Bt gave me important family recollections of the 'pocket cherub'. David J. Tolley has been an assiduous and most helpful correspondent, particularly in relation to Leamington Spa, Spilsbury's birthplace, and in relation to firearms issues.

Dr Gordon Ostlere (Richard Gordon) sent me a copy of his essay on Spilsbury in *Great Medical Disasters*. Jonathan Goodman, secretary of *Our Society* (of which Spilsbury was once a member), has been of inestimable help and drew my attention to the dubious career of Dr Massiah, linked to Brighton Trunk Murder Number One. My thanks are due to Robin Odell for lending me a file of press and personal photographs of Spilsbury and for allowing me to use material from the surviving case cards, placed on loan to the Galleries of Justice in Nottingham, which helpfully supplied me with photocopies. Richard Whittington-Egan, a good friend for a quarter of a century, has been a mine of information about Spilsbury's celebrated cases. Wilfred Gregg, author and member of *Our Society*, has long been a source of help and encouragement. My thanks also go to Loretta Lay, of Laybooks, an invaluable source of rare printed material and information on non-fiction crime.

My thanks are due to The National Archives, the British Library (and Newspaper Library), the Wellcome Medical Library, Manchester University Library, University College London Special Collections, the Royal College of Surgeons of Edinburgh, the Royal College of Physicians in London, the Medical Society of London, the North Dorset NHS Primary Care Trust and Devon County Record Office. Alan McCormick, Curator of the Metropolitan Police Crime Museum, allowed me to tour the collection and gave helpful information. Jacqueline Summers, of the Museum of Net Manufacture, Uploders, in Dorset, confirmed the use of Bridport rope at executions.

My gratitude also extends to Jaqueline Mitchell, former Senior Commissioning Editor, Sutton Publishing, to my agent, Andrew Lowrie, to Andrew Baker, Mrs Amy Glenister, Roy Gray, Professor Michael Green, Alan Hayhurst, Paul Jonsson, Chris King, David Machin (formerly Under-Treasurer, Gray's Inn), Huon Mallalieu, John March (Firearms) Ltd of Wimborne, John Meinhold, Mrs Janet Minister, Mrs Janet Morris, Dr Basil Purdue, Dr Andrew Scott Reid, Mrs Joan Smith, James Todd and Roger Wilkes.

. . . the chirurgeons have an useful practice, by which they put their apprentices and *tyrones* to work upon senseless dead bodies, to which, as they can do no good, so they certainly can do as little harm

(Sir Walter Scott, *Redgauntlet*)

The greatest experts are the crassest blunderers in life. Never trust an expert . . . God knows how many poor folk went to the gallows because of his ignorance and pig-headedness.

(Richard Gordon, *The Medical Witness*)

I am a martyr to Spilsburyism.
(Norman Thorne, executed at Wandsworth Prison on 22 April 1925)

Introduction

At 9 a.m. Wandsworth Prison lay in almost total silence, a rare event indeed. All prisoners had been confined to their cells. To preserve due order and decency among the inmates, the chime of the prison clock had been disconnected. The hour was not sounded. Two men, brought from the North of England, far away from south London and the risk of local recognition, were about to perform their duty.[1] The High Sheriff, the Prison Governor and the Chaplain stood by, perhaps glancing up momentarily at the massive wooden cross-beam supporting the rope, good Bridport cord.[2] Unusually, the Sheriff had allowed newspaper reporters to attend the scene, American-style.[3] The murder had been particularly gruesome and had attracted immense public interest. Secretly, during the previous evening, the appearance of the condemned man's neck had been carefully noted by his executioner, Tom Pierrepoint (uncle of Albert Pierrepoint, the last British hangman), scanning his subject through the tiny Judas hole in the door of the condemned cell.

The prisoner's neck was found to be 'long and loose-jointed', his body 'spare and muscular'.[4] The man was certainly not overweight. He had been under sentence of death for nearly two months. Men lose weight under such immense stress. The prisoner weighed just 141 pounds. From prison records, Tom knew that his client stood 5ft 11in tall. An executioner for nearly twenty years, Tom had carefully calculated the drop at 7ft 4in. Too short, the man might not die. Too long, and his head might be torn off his body. On the night before the execution, a weight equal to that of the condemned man had been suspended from the hangman's rope, so that it should be fully extended at the time of execution. Tom had checked that the rope had not become frayed. Rope was expensive. A good one might serve for several hangings, but cord would be replaced immediately after any sign of wear.[5]

The condemned man, held firmly by the arms, took his last, short walk. In a matter of seconds, Tom and his assistant had pinioned the prisoner's limbs, his feet directed to outlines drawn in chalk on the platform. The little group of spectators, all male, watched the brief dispatch from life to death. With his right hand, Tom pulled the soft white cotton hood swiftly over the head and, using his left hand, positioned the noose, which he secured by a simple slip-knot under the left side of the neck. Stepping aside, Tom released the execution lever.[6] The dull thud of the two falling trapdoors was heard well beyond the walls of the execution chamber, even by some prisoners in their cells.

By 10 a.m. that day, in the execution pit, a figure, white-hooded, legs bound, arms secured, had been hanging for an hour. The creaking of the rope and the swaying of the body that followed the sudden fall had now ceased. Tom and his assistant, Bill Willis from Manchester, were followed down the ladder by the prison doctor. Pierrepoint measured the drop from the level of the floor of the scaffold to the heels of the suspended body: 7ft 3in. Just one inch out. Not bad. Worth the ten guineas Tom was paid for the work – plus his third-class return fare to Bradford.[7]

The body was taken down. Dr Pearson, the prison medical officer, applied his stethoscope to the man's chest and felt for a pulse point. The hearts of hanged people can continue to beat for ten minutes or more,[8] but, after the prescribed hour of bodily suspension, the man's heart was stilled. The body was laid on a stretcher and wheeled to the prison mortuary. The mortuary was small, dark and smelt strongly of disinfectant. There the condemned man was stripped of his grey jacket, shirt, suit trousers, socks, vest and under-drawers. A small patch of urine at the crotch was the only evidence of traumatic incontinence.

Herbert 'Pat' Mahon, aged 34, now lay naked on a plain deal table, head steadied on two small wooden blocks, laid one on top of the other, awaiting the arrival of a Very Important Person indeed. Mahon and the VIP had already met each other before – in a manner of speaking – at Mahon's trial.

At 11 a.m. the VIP arrived, passing through the ranks of newspapermen and the morbidly curious who crowded round the prison entrance. The VIP raised his left arm repeatedly to shield his face from the gross intrusion of press photographers. Sir Bernard Spilsbury, elegantly tall in spats, striped trousers, grey waistcoat and black jacket, entered the mortuary. Spilsbury preferred to work alone, unaided by medically qualified assistants, unbothered by tiresome questions. He was followed, obediently, by the mortuary attendant, bearing Spilsbury's large black leather suitcase. Sponges, cloths, antiseptic liquid and enamel bowls were laid out in easy reach of the mortuary table. The attendant was accompanied by one of the detectives who had brought Patrick Mahon to justice for the murder of Emily Kaye, his discarded love.

Paradox was a hallmark of the Spilsbury phenomenon. The tone of his entrance was stylish and formal, but he did not behave like Sir Lancelot Spratt, the arrogant surgeon of *Doctor in the House*. Despite the aura of greatness, his manner was unassuming. He was calm, considerate, quiet and polite as he began the process of autopsy. Spilsbury discarded his jacket and put on a rubber apron and gloves. He removed the cuffs, made specially detachable, from his shirt. From the suitcase, he produced the tools of his trade: a large, sharp knife, scalpels and a handsaw. The knife, about 8in long, had a black handle, its surface already dull from use in hundreds of post-mortems. The suitcase, sometimes dubbed his 'murder bag', also contained bottles of formaldehyde and glass jars, ready to house selected body parts.

This was to be no ordinary post-mortem carried out after judicial execution. Normally, an autopsy, if held at all, was little more than a formality. Today Spilsbury had other ideas. He had persuaded the Coroner, Stephen Ingleby Oddie (a quaint name for a small, neurotic and still odder personality), to permit him full examination of the remains of a man at whose trial Spilsbury had been the principal expert witness for the Crown. There was other evidence of guilt, but Spilsbury's positive evidence had put the seal on the prosecution's case. He was to conduct a post-mortem on the body of a man his evidence had helped to hang.

Spilsbury had spent an intensely frustrating three days, working far into the night, in his laboratory at St Bartholomew's Hospital earlier that year, trying to re-assemble Emily's remains, which had been variously burnt, boiled, pulverised and cut up by her murderer into nearly one thousand evil-smelling fragments. Nevertheless, Spilsbury had been unable to determine the precise cause of the victim's death, even after a minutely detailed examination. She had probably died from a blow to the head, but the bones of her skull and upper neck were never found, despite all the solitary, painstaking work. In the prison mortuary, Spilsbury had her murderer's corpse, whole and entire, lying before him, there for him to work on as he saw fit, suitable revenge for all those long night hours at Bart's.

There was still warmth in the freshly hanged body on the mortuary table. Beginning his external examination,[9] Sir Bernard paid brief regard to the darkly handsome face of a psychotic murderer. The pupils of the dead man's eyes, eyelids lazily half-open, were seen to be dilated. Sir Bernard then turned his attention to the state of the dead man's penis. He noted that there was 'no priapism'. Damage to the spinal cord in hanging sometimes causes an involuntary erection (the subject of gross humour in Balzac's *Contes drolatiques*), even ejaculation, but here there was no evidence of seminal emission.

The skin of the body had reddened slightly, particularly on the fingers. Taking his knife, Spilsbury deftly sliced open the man's torso, cutting downwards from neck to groin. The liver, spleen and kidneys were found to be swollen with blood. Sir Bernard noted a slight abrasion and groove on the neck, with some haemorrhaging beneath both areas behind the jaw. In complete silence, Spilsbury worked fast, with his famed ambidexterity, sometimes flipping the scalpel between his hands. Turning the body over, Spilsbury cut into the skin of the back, exposing the spine, which was found to have been dislocated between the fourth and fifth vertebrae, and partially dislocated between the sixth and seventh. The spinal cord was 'soft and flattened' for ¾in at the level of the upper dislocation, an injury also marked by tiny burst blood vessels. There was slight laceration of the vertebral muscle.

Spilsbury extracted sections of the spine and, according to one report, using his handsaw (with its grim and unmistakable rasping sound), he sliced open the skull and took samples of brain tissue. These were the days of 'the criminal mind', the slightly crackpot theories of Cesare Lombroso, which verged on the fictional world of Baron Frankenstein. Spilsbury vainly hoped to find evidence that Mahon's notorious criminal propensities might be detectable by physical manifestations in his brain.

After less than an hour's work, Spilsbury resumed his formal daywear and left the mortuary, courteously thanking his assistant and acknowledging the police officer.

He made a telephone call to the Home Office from the prison, but was to be severely disappointed by the answer received.

Dr Pearson was at last able to conduct his own modest examination of the remains. He did not have much time for his work. The inquest was held just after midday, in a stuffy room elsewhere in the jail. Reporters crowded in to see the star of the show. Spilsbury, and not the prison doctor, would be topping the bill. The Coroner, anxious to show his own knowledge of pathology, put to Spilsbury that dislocation between the fourth and fifth vertebrae was 'unusually low'.[10] Sir Bernard obligingly agreed. Unconsciousness, added Spilsbury, stating the obvious with due solemnity, aware of the gaggle of reporters at the back of the tiny room, would come on 'quite instantly'.[11] Death was recorded as being due to 'unconsciousness followed by asphyxia' consequent upon judicial hanging.[12]

The Home Office was not so easily impressed by Spilsbury's evidence as the Coroner had been. The post-mortem, in the view of one senior civil servant, was 'probably unnecessary and also expensive'.[13] (Luckily, the cost would fall on London ratepayers, rather than on the Home Office budget.) The official noted, however (with satisfaction), that Sir Bernard's magisterial performance at inquest might have prevented something being 'hatched up' by the press. The next day, the formidable Legal Under-Secretary at the Home Office, Sir Ernley Blackwell, reviewed his subordinate's note in the Mahon file.

Blackwell was distinctly suspicious of Sir Bernard's real motives for performing the post-mortem. He had heard Sir Bernard's contributions at meetings of the prestigious Medico-Legal Society and was well aware of Spilsbury the Showman. In a fastidious hand, recording his thoughts in sharp black ink, he minuted: 'I think that Sir B. Spilsbury . . . offered to undertake it with the view to securing parts of the fractured vertebrae for anatomical demonstration purposes . . .'. Spilsbury might have been of use in averting unwanted press speculation, but he was not going to be allowed to promote his reputation with the help of the Home Office. 'He telephoned for permission to take away these,' wrote Blackwell. 'I absolutely forbade anything of the kind.'[14]

Spilsbury began the modern cult of forensic pathology. He gave pivotal evidence in nearly half a century of British murder trials, beginning in 1910 with Dr Crippen. *The Lancet*'s obituary claimed that Spilsbury 'stood alone and unchallenged as our greatest medico-legal expert'.[15]

Lethal Witness will tell his story and show how far the substance fell short of a carefully crafted image, taking a fresh look at murder trials in which Spilsbury was the star witness for the prosecution, as well as a selection of the more interesting capital and non-capital cases in his long career of over 20,000 autopsies.

Spilsbury – the 'Honorary Pathologist to the Home Office',[16] a title created specially for him – cultivated the manner and appearance of an English gentleman. He was tall, very handsome, aloof and faultlessly tailored. In murder trials, he appeared almost invariably for the Crown. He rarely travelled abroad, wrote no textbook, and for most of his professional career had no assistant, choosing to work alone.

Judges and prosecution barristers adored him. 'The leading detective-pathologist of the day,' enthused Christmas Humphreys QC.[17] Mr Justice Darling serenaded 'that incomparable witness . . . so fair, so clear'.[18] Mr Justice Finlay recommended him as 'really the very best opinion that can be obtained'. Lord Chief Justice Hewart led the judicial pack in saluting 'that wonderful witness. So fair. So clear.'[19] Spilsbury was the policeman's friend, too. This 'absolutely impartial' witness was 'to all intents and purposes an honorary member of the CID',[20] as well as pursuing a profound enthusiasm for Freemasonry, a leisure activity also popular with members of the Force.

Government revered his opinion. A Home Secretary secretly invited Spilsbury to a meeting that would determine the fate of a man condemned on Spilsbury's own evidence. He advised on the wartime ploy to create 'the Man Who Never Was'. He was happy to provide officialdom with answers to abstruse questions, such as the provenance of a woman's shoe found in the wreckage of an airship disaster. He would give his opinion on the mental and physical health of a brutally gang-raped teenage girl. Never mind that his advice was given on matters far beyond his professional expertise. 'His opinions were so impregnable', wrote Richard Gordon, in a mordant assessment,[21] 'he could achieve single-handed all the legal consequences of a homicide – arrest, prosecution, conviction, and final post-mortem – requiring only the brief assistance of the hangman.'

By the 1920s Spilsbury had become a media celebrity, but some people – outside the Establishment – were finding the Honorary Pathologist cold, stubborn, secretive and intolerant of opposition to his theories. The caustic pen of another distinguished pathologist adjudged Spilsbury 'very brilliant and very famous, but fallible . . . and very, very obstinate'.[22] Another colleague wrote of a man 'whose positive evidence had doubtless led to conviction at trials that might have ended with sufficient doubt for acquittal', and of a man 'unloved and unmourned' at his death.[23]

The classic murder trials between 1910 and 1947 illustrate Spilsbury's strengths and failings. On the credit side there was a minute attention to detail (a quality not always evinced by professional contemporaries); a dogged persistence in the face of the most daunting post-mortem conditions; and a rare ability to explain complex pathological and toxicological findings in ways that a lay jury could understand. Spilsbury was the first pathologist in England to become a public figure, and he broke through the prejudice and hostility that had, for half a century or more, beset practitioners of 'The Beastly Science'.[24]

On the debit side, Spilsbury's defects included a deep absorption in prosecution culture; a love of amateur detective work, leading to theories dangerously beyond his remit as medical witness; and an increasing tendency to play games with the truth. Spilsbury became arrogant. He worked so hard that, to his mind, no one could know more than he did about the causes and circumstances of a death. Professional and personal vanity refused to admit the possibility of error.

Several murder convictions based, directly or indirectly, on Spilsbury's evidence must now be regarded as unsafe. In particular, terrible miscarriages of justice have been exposed in the cases of David Greenwood and Sydney Fox, both of which demand an official pardon. The murder convictions of Norman Thorne, John Robinson and Henry Seymour are now in doubt. Likewise, Spilsbury's dogmatically expressed opinions in the Crippen and Armstrong trials can no longer be sustained. In the case of Linford Derrick, Spilsbury was shown to have made a fundamental error of fact. With Robert Churchill, in the trials of Donald Merrett and George Kitchen, Spilsbury put forward conclusions based on manifestly flawed experiments with firearms. He can be seen to have embellished his evidence in the cases of Rouse, Seymour and Mancini. Spilsbury's silence on a vital evidential issue almost cost the life of Drummer Dearnley.

Paradox was the hallmark of his career. Spilsbury, a plodding student, turned into a brilliant cross-examinee. Once a self-effacing junior doctor, he slyly overtook his teachers. Spilsbury's 'aloof . . . retiring . . . outwardly frigid'[25] personality concealed the intense ambition of a man who shrewdly manipulated the media and dominated entire trials. Although, in common with Greta Garbo in her later years, Spilsbury 'never abated his dislike of being photographed',[26] he would attend court immaculately dressed, flower in his buttonhole, a thorough extrovert in the witness box. Deeply conservative and a preacher of moral rectitude, Spilsbury seems to have failed in his marriage because of his association with another woman. His children suffered from lack of attention and, in the ultimate analysis, from lack of love.

Research into Spilsbury's life and times has taken more than a decade. I have accessed new material, beyond the well-thumbed pages of *Bernard Spilsbury: His Life and Cases* by Douglas Browne and E.V. Tullett, a fairly comprehensive, but largely uncritical, biography published in 1951. I looked for sources beyond printed trials and memoirs of the lawyers and medical men with whom Spilsbury had either cooperated or clashed.

I fought a small war of attrition with government departments, persuading them to open up files closed for 75 or even 100 years. The papers, often voluminous, have proved to be veritable bran-tubs of information, replete with confidential correspondence and reports, one even containing a rusty tin of abortionist's pills. These official files provide a unique insight into the ways in which the Establishment came to regard Spilsbury. In a few, exceptional, murder cases, the records cast doubt on the correctness of the original verdict.

The demands of time, space and publisher's costs have meant that many of Spilsbury's cases, interesting in their own right but not particularly illustrative of his gifts and failings, have been omitted. Further reading can be pursued with the help of the bibliography at the end of this book.

In my research, I studied the extant examples of Spilsbury's famous case cards, doing my best to decipher his almost impenetrable handwriting. I examined some of the large collection of histological slides that happily still survive at the Royal London Hospital. I sought out people who knew Spilsbury, who had studied under him and – perhaps most illuminating of all – who had heard him testify in court. Spilsbury, a very private man, left little in the way of memorabilia or academic literature, but surviving letters and diaries have helped to give a unique insight into the life of this strange, enigmatic, but ultimately remarkable personality, 'a *prima donna* . . . increasingly thought of as a bit of a rogue'.[27]

ONE

An Unsentimental Education

Sir Bernard Spilsbury possessed a profoundly English surname, whose origin lies in the Cotswold village of Spelsbury, standing between Chipping Campden and Woodstock, not many miles from the great university city of Oxford. The surname of Spilsbury is found throughout middle England.[1]

Although in later adult life he assumed the air and appearance of a country squire, Spilsbury came from a family of innkeepers in Stafford. At least since 1830 James Spilsbury was licensee of the Sun Inn in Foregate, an old coaching inn, which backed onto the town's cattle market.[2] By the mid-nineteenth century James was joined by his son Henry, who married a local girl, Mary Hopkinson, at Castlechurch in Stafford, in 1851. Their only child, James – Spilsbury's father – was born at the Sun Inn on 20 May 1852.

James Spilsbury senior and his son seem to have regarded themselves as a cut above the generality of Stafford's citizens. On official documents, each would describe himself as 'Gentleman', and Henry Spilsbury became a modest landowner.[3]

In 1856 the town was convulsed by the public execution, outside Stafford Gaol, of Dr William Palmer, convicted of poisoning John Parsons Cooke with strychnine and suspected of doing away with several other victims by similar methods.[4] Spilsbury senior and junior had a more than ordinary interest in the trial of Dr Palmer. They could well have served him over the bar counter. Palmer, who lived in Rugeley, had been a well-known character in the inns and pothouses. The doctor is credited with inventing the expression 'What's your poison?', a jolly question that might have been posed in the saloon bar or taproom of the Sun Inn.[5] Very probably, Bernard Spilsbury would have heard about the dramatic events of 1856 from his grandparents, and he certainly kept a letter from the doctor to his wife, Annie Brookes, which referred to medicines prescribed for her mother, said to have been one of Palmer's victims.

A principal prosecution witness at Palmer's Old Bailey trial was a pioneer of forensic pathology, Dr Alfred Swaine Taylor. Dr Taylor travelled extensively and studied abroad. In 1831 he was appointed professor of medical jurisprudence at Guy's Hospital, London, and lecturer in chemistry. His textbooks, including *A Manual of Medical Jurisprudence* and *Poisons in Relation to Medical Jurisprudence*, became standard texts throughout the world. Taylor's evidence in the Palmer trial, though accepted at the time, reads curiously today. He had detected antimony, another poison, in Cooke's remains, but was never able to prove that Cooke had taken strychnine. Indeed, it was only after hearing about the dramatic symptoms exhibited by Cooke that Taylor put forward his theory of strychnine poisoning.

Unhappily for Taylor, his reputation suffered a disastrous blow just three years after his triumph in the Palmer case. In 1859 yet another doctor stood in the dock at the Old Bailey. Dr Thomas Smethurst was charged with poisoning Isabella Bankes, his mistress, whom he had bigamously married. Taylor's evidence at committal proceedings appeared to show the presence of arsenic in the contents of a bottle owned by Smethurst. Taylor had not realised that the test he had used had itself contaminated the sample with arsenic. In the words of a fiercely critical editorial in *The Lancet*: 'The instrument employed for detection had itself furnished the poison!'[6] The murder verdict that arose out of this evidential muddle was heavily criticised not only in *The Lancet*, but – much more significantly – in *The Times*, virtually an organ of government in nineteenth-century Britain and a newspaper of immense influence. As a result of the Smethurst debacle, forensic pathology was dubbed the 'Beastly Science'. Public confidence in scientific evidence was badly shaken. It would take nearly half a century before the work of forensic pathologists and toxicologists would be taken seriously again.

James Spilsbury junior was not going to become a third-generation innkeeper in Stafford. Opportunities for studying chemistry were becoming available from the 1850s onwards, and he set up in business as an analytical chemist. In 1876, aged 24, James Spilsbury was confident enough in his commercial future to take the lease of premises at 35 Bath Street, Royal Leamington Spa. He also took a wife.

James Spilsbury and Marion (or Maria) Elizabeth Joy were married at St Anne's Church, Highgate, on 17 August 1876. On the marriage certificate, James, true to the Spilsbury tradition, described himself as 'Gentleman'. Social aspirations were also manifested in his choice of bride. Marion Joy was from a family of wealthy Oxford tradespeople. The fine interior of St Mary's Church, Oxford, boasts an elegant neo-classical *cartouche* dedicated to her ancestors, Thomas Joy, his first wife Martha, and second wife Maria. Her uncle, educated at Rugby and Trinity College, Cambridge, was a country parson, with a confortable living in East Anglia.

James Spilsbury took his young bride to live with him in Royal Leamington Spa, where 35 Bath Road still stands, an elegant four-storey Regency building, a corner property in a good trading position, midway between the railway station and the large, fashionable parish church. A large sign displayed on the frontage above the shop read:

SPILSBURY
Pharmaceutical & Analytical
CHYMIST

James Spilsbury advertised 'remedies of AMERICAN, CONTINENTAL & ENGLISH PHARMACY' and offered 'chemical and microscopic examination for all Sanitary, Medical, & Commercial purposes . . . Surgical Instruments, Invalid's Requirements, Electric Batteries & Appliances . . .'.[7] Exploiting Leamington's reputation as a spa, James offered his more hypochondriac customers a limitless supply of 'the genuine Leamington salts'. The ground floor was given over to business, including an analytical laboratory. The upper floors had a separate entrance in Regent Place, off Bath Road. The living quarters seem to become rather crowded. The couple shared their early married life with two male assistants and no fewer than three resident housemaids.

On 22 May 1877 a notice appeared in *The Times*: 'On the 16th inst. at 2 Regent Place, Leamington, the wife of JAMES SPILSBURY, of a son.' A boy, christened Bernard Henry and born above his father's shop, had joined this somewhat unusual ménage.

The Leamington in which Bernard Spilsbury would spent his first eleven years had grown rapidly since the latter part of the eighteenth century, after a Dr Allen had publicised his experiments with saline water in the *Coventry Mercury*. At least three major springs provided the famous waters. In 1855 a committee of local doctors attached to the Wharneford Hospital, no doubt mindful of the fees to be earned, solemnly claimed benefits for practically every known medical condition, including 'dyspepsia and consumption; derangement of the liver [and] spleen . . . jaundice, epilepsy, cholera, hysteria, and neuralgia'. Most forms of rheumatism could be alleviated, it seemed, together with 'many cases incidental to females', as well as scrofula, eczema, herpes, lepra and psoriasis.[8] Patients were advised to drink a pint of the water early in the morning to achieve what was euphemistically called the 'aperient effect'. In brief intervals between hurrying to the various public conveniences prudently dotted about the town, health-seekers could enjoy themselves in the Pump Room, which had a large swimming pool, in addition to hot and cold saline baths and a Turkish Bath, 'heated by Messrs Whitaker & Constantine's Patent Convulated Stove'.[9] Pleasure gardens, tennis and rackets courts, a free public library, a music hall and an institute equipped with reading, billiards and club rooms provided visitors with agreeable opportunities for relaxation, notwithstanding the dramatic effects that could result from over-indulgence in the Leamington waters.

In this genteel ambiance, Bernard Spilsbury grew up in an undemonstrative, rather puritanical, household. His father seems to have been professionally as well as socially ambitious and hard-working, with a detached, rather cold, personality. James Spilsbury's success as an analytical chemist was rewarded on 18 June 1885, when he was elected a Fellow of the Chemical Society, a considerable distinction. Little is known about Spilsbury's mother beyond the bare facts of her family background in Oxford. A daughter, Constance ('Connie'), was born in Leamington on 30 July 1878 and a second son,

Leonard, on 30 May 1884. Bernard is said to have been educated by a private tutor until the age of 9, when he was sent as a day-boy to Leamington College, which had been founded with the aim of rivalling the success of Rugby School.

Bernard had been at Leamington College for less than three years when his father decided to sell the Leamington business and move to north London, where he seems to have had commercial contacts. In 1889 James assigned the lease of 35 Bath Street to another Leamington chemist, and the family had to move into his widowed mother's house, Hough Villa at 35 Lichfield Road, Stafford. Eventually, James found a new home at 4 Lynton Road, Crouch End, not very far from Alexandra Palace.

As a result of the disturbance, Bernard was made to board for a while at Leamington, but in 1890 he was a day-boy again, this time at University College School (UCS), then situated at the side of University College in Gower Street, London. Each school day Bernard had to make the short journey by train, overground and underground, from Crouch End to Euston Square. Founded in 1830, UCS already sported a distinguished list of former pupils, including Joseph Chamberlain, John Morley (a future viscount), the painter Walter Sickert and Rufus Isaacs, lawyer and statesman. A non-denominational foundation, the school readily accepted new subjects, such as natural science and modern languages. A school magazine had appeared as early as 1869. By Spilsbury's time there was a Debating Society and a Scientific Society, and, true to its enlightment ideals, the school maintained a club for working lads in Clerkenwell. Despite the advantages offered by so progressive an education, there is no record of any achievements by Spilsbury, who seems to have had nothing to do with UCS in later life. A list of former pupils, published as late as 1937, when Spilsbury's name was a household word, simply records the attendance of 'Spilsbury B H' in 1890–1.[10]

Bernard's youngest sister, Gertrude ('Gertie'), born at 4 Lynton Road on 21 November 1890, completed the family, but, during the following year, James Spilsbury had decided to pursue business opportunities in Manchester. Retaining the house at Lynton Road, the family moved to a house, Evington, in Northumberland Street, Higher Broughton, a north-western suburb of Manchester. Speculation that the Spilsbury children 'probably thought it all rather fun'[11] seems wide of the mark as far as Bernard, the eldest child, was concerned.

Life at a day school, after several years' private tuition, must have been difficult enough for Bernard, but to have to become a boarder at the age of 12, on the verge of puberty, when many other boys would have been boarding since the age of 8 (or even younger), was a particularly insensitive decision by his father. Further uprooting to UCS, an institution set in a great city a hundred miles from Leamington, is likely to have compounded the feelings of isolation and introspection so evident in Spilsbury's later life. The constant changes in schooling meant that Bernard never had the opportunity to forge friendships during his formative years or to carve a niche in school life. The seeds of his mistrust of others, the characteristics of secrecy and the roots of a culture of betrayal may have arisen during this disturbed adolescence.

The move to Manchester occasioned yet another change of school. Manchester Grammar School, under High Master King, was justly famed as a centre of educational excellence in the great manufacturing north-west. Founded in 1515, the school could claim a roll drawn mostly from commercial and professional backgrounds, but with a leaven of scholarship boys drawn from the working-class areas of Salford, Ardwick and Hulme. Bernard Spilsbury attended Manchester Grammar School in 1892–3. Although he was now in his mid-teens, he seems to have shown no particular aptitude and certainly pocketed no prizes. The two annual assessments (the first records of his academic standing that survive) were each marked with a mediocre ß. He achieved no mention in the school magazine *Ulula*. As with UCS, Spilsbury seems to have had no love for his third school. At the time of his death, the school seems to have been unaware that he had ever been a pupil there, and no appreciation of its remarkable Old Boy appeared in the 1948 edition of *Ulula*.[12]

James Spilsbury was anxious, perhaps overly eager, to push his elder son, seemingly unaware of the difficulties Bernard was facing in the constant programme of removal. Bernard was expected to do better, and his lacklustre performance at school, perhaps understandable with the benefit of hindsight, seems to have irritated his father, who frequently lectured his son on his educational shortcomings. When Bernard, aged 16, reached the matriculation form at Manchester Grammar School, James decided that the boy needed a more practical education and sent him to Owen's College, where Bernard studied chemistry, physics and mechanics, and biology for the nine months between September 1893 and June 1894.

By early 1894 James Spilsbury had moved back to 4 Lynton Road in Crouch End. Bernard, left behind in Manchester, seems to have enjoyed his independence and had a measure of social life at Owen's College, even playing rugby there. Nevertheless – as earlier biographers have noted – he spent much of his leisure time in solitary fashion, walking, or skating alone during the exceptionally hard winter of 1895. An accident caused him to lose a joint of the index finger of his right hand, a loss supposed to have led later to his famed ambidexterity in the post-mortem room. For the time being, Bernard had little idea of which direction to take in life.

Early in 1895 James Spilsbury made the fateful decision to send his elder son to Magdalen College, Oxford. Bernard would try for a Demy (college term for a scholarship) in natural science, a major honour – if this could be achieved. In the year after leaving Owen's College, Bernard, who had given his father no real sign of the outstanding ability necessary to secure a scholarship at a prestigious Oxford college, probably received several months' worth of private coaching. His father had made his mind up that his wayward elder son should achieve what he had not been able to accomplish. James had not had the chance to join a profession. Bernard would become a medical doctor, whether he liked it or not.

Back in Stafford, Bernard's grandmother, Mary Spilsbury, was unimpressed. Probably Methodist by religion and suspicious of ostentatious ambition, the publican's widow thought that Bernard would be better employed in a steady trade. The old lady is said to have offered to set him up as a partner in Brookfields (Stafford's Victorian equivalent of a modern department store), if the Oxford idea were abandoned. Bernard could have spent his working life marketing merino and cashmere garments, walking the various Fancy Departments, and selling linoleum, cretonnes, carpets, rugs and brass bedsteads to his grandmother's dull, worthy and very provincial friends and neighbours.

Bernard rejected this banal option, and, in any case, his father was not to be diverted from his plans. In March 1895 Robert Günther, tutor at Magdalen College, received an unusual letter. Most enquiries about places and scholarships at his college would have been made by schoolmasters anxious to promote their pupils' careers. Bernard had long since left school and, bearing in mind his conspicuous lack of educational achievement thus far, a school-based reference was out of the question. 'My Dear Sir,' wrote James Spilsbury, in perhaps too familiar a style for a distinguished Oxford don whom he had never met, 'My son, who is entered as a Candidate for admission to the college, contemplates trying for a Natural Science Demyship.'[13]

In June 1895 Bernard at last managed to achieve an examination success, passing Responsions (the basic and relatively easy college entrance examination, known familiarly as 'Smalls'). In the end, however, the dream of a Demyship eluded young Bernard. Günther had sent James a letter breaking the news of failure. In his reply of 16 October 1895 the father offered excuses: 'Mechanics . . . is his acknowledged weak subject, but in theoretical Chemistry . . .' – a subject dear to James Spilsbury's heart – '. . . I fear he has not done justice to his knowledge.'[14]

Some students who have performed indifferently at school rise to the challenges posed by a university education, particularly at so famous an institution as Oxford. Bernard, however, was not such an achiever. On the other hand, although he could style himself only as an undergraduate 'Commoner', Bernard had secured a place at Magdalen College, founded in 1458, its ancient buildings impressively situated on the west bank of the River Cherwell. This was no rags-to-riches story. Bernard seems to have enjoyed a comfortable allowance from his father, whose business enterprises continued to thrive. Bernard personally filled in his entry in the college Matriculation Book. Adopting his father's archaic orthography, he described James Spilsbury as 'Chymist and Analyst'. Even more curiously, he gave the college an incomplete account of his educational background. In later years, Bernard would develop a well-publicised reputation for pinpoint accuracy and total probity. It is odd, therefore, to find that he omitted any mention of his year at UCS. The omission is particularly strange, because Robert Günther, his tutor, was himself an 'Old Gower', a former pupil of UCS.

In his first two years at Magdalen, Bernard occupied rooms on the ground floor of Staircase IV, New Buildings, a large and elegant Palladian structure designed in 1733. The rooms overlooked The Grove and the college deer park, where the handsome beasts could be seen, a peaceful spectacle until October, when the roarings of the rutting male deer would rival those of drunken undergraduates roaming the college quads. Bernard would have found himself in the company of young men from rather richer backgrounds, many from the great public schools. He became something of a dandy, exhibiting a taste for well-cut suits and fashion accessories that he retained to the end of his life. He does not seem to have had any particular vices during his undergraduate days, such as drinking, gambling and whoring, but his aloof, secretive, internalised character would cause problems with the college dons. Despite his father's hope that Bernard's interface with his tutors might be 'a mutual pleasure', surviving accounts show that this student could be both indolent and fractious. 'Mr Spilsbury', wrote one exasperated tutor, 'did not turn up' to a examination and had been 'taking it far too easy'. His preparatory work was especially bad.[15] Another commented that 'he writes badly . . . & I do not think that he has thrown himself heart and soul into his work'.[16] At about this time, Bernard gave himself a revealingly self-deprecating nickname – 'Buggins'.[17]

The most damning appraisal of Bernard's university career was given by a young Fellow of Magdalen, Horace Middleton Vernon. He was a shrewd commentator, and his reports reveal an almost uncanny prescience, pointing up many of Bernard's later character failings. On 16 March 1898 Bernard was in Vernon's charge for the 1st MB (Bachelor of Medicine) examinations that summer. Vernon's first impression of Bernard was that he had only a 'fair knowledge' of his work. He heard too many lectures, leaving insufficient time for reading. Vernon noted his pupil's interest in anatomy, but found that Bernard, already in his third year at Magdalen, 'had very incoherent ideas on the subject . . . he tries to read too fast'[18] and did not properly absorb facts. Vernon reported that Bernard 'occasionally seems quite ignorant of facts of fundamental importance'.[19]

Eventually, there were signs that the indolent dandy was beginning to apply himself to his studies, but Bernard's efforts were uneven. He had entered for his final Honour Schools examination, which he would sit in the summer of 1899. Perceptively, Vernon picked up an air of arrogance and pigheadedness on the part of a student with only moderate ability: 'He seemed confident that he knew well what he was reading, but, on questioning him, he proved himself to have by no means a clear knowledge of the subject.' Vernon bluntly attributed

Bernard's lack of good progress to 'sheer want of capacity'. He was 'too confident in his powers',[20] seeming to spend excessive time on practical work, leaving little time for reading.

As the final examinations approached, Vernon's negative opinion of the future Home Office pathologist did not alter significantly. In March 1899 he wrote that Bernard was 'likely not to get more than a 3rd', a situation largely due, he thought, to 'mere incapacity . . . his memory is very bad and he seems to read though pages of a book and scarcely remember a word'. Vernon did not like his pupil, whose character he found tiresome, offhand and generally irritating. 'He is not at all a satisfactory person to work with and he has cut me several times without any proper excuse . . . other than slackness.'[21]

In the event, Bernard obtained a second-class honours degree in natural science from Oxford University, rather better than Vernon had predicted, but by no means the achievement of a high-flyer. He was now able to proceed with his medical degree at London University. For this purpose, Bernard had to select a London teaching hospital. His choice could not have been better: he opted for St Mary's Hospital, Paddington.

TWO

Dr Spilsbury

In March 1899 the *St Mary's Hospital Gazette* carried an advertisement for scholarship examinations at the Medical School. Modest (and possibly unexpected) success in the Oxford finals seems to have prompted Spilsbury to redeem his failure to win a Demyship at his Oxford college. On 20 and 21 September 1899 he made his way via Praed Street to the hospital library, where, with a gaggle of other young hopefuls, he sat papers and answered questions *viva voce*. He did not win either of the two scholarships available, each worth £57 10s annually, but he headed the list of three Exhibitions, each worth £26 5s. With his father's continuing financial support, Spilsbury had no pressing need for money, but the award, though not of the first rank, was a significant career development. He was formally enrolled as a medical student on 2 October 1899.

By this time James Spilsbury had moved yet again, to Mayfield, a large house standing in Mayfield Road, Moseley, Birmingham. Leonard, now 15, was experiencing a less traumatic education than that experienced by his elder brother and was safely ensconced at Rugby. Connie and Gertie lived quietly at home, as they would continue to do for the lifetime of their parents.

Spilsbury's imaginative attitude to application forms was again shown when he provided the hospital's Dean with his personal details.[1] 'Mayfield', a comfortable villa in surburban Birmingham, had somehow assumed the grander title of 'Mayfield House'.

Although Spilsbury's relationship with his parents seems to have been formal, even cold, he made regular visits to the family home in Moseley, where in 1900 he met Edith Caroline Mary Horton, daughter of a Birmingham dentist, and the eldest of the three attractive Horton sisters. The Hortons were a well-established family in the area and, in social terms, resembled the Joys rather than the humbler Spilsburys, for among the ranks of Hortons could be found professional men, doctors and Anglican clergymen. Spilsbury and Edith became engaged that same year, but marriage was out of the question until Spilsbury had qualified, which he was in no hurry to do. Edith must have had great reserves of patience, for the wedding was not to take place until eight years later.

He took lodgings at 25 Cambridge Terrace, one among the warren of streets that surrounded the hospital buildings. St Mary's, founded in 1854, was going through an acute financial crisis at this time. The hospital was chronically understaffed and in dire need of new buildings. Despite these problems, St Mary's, at the dawn of the twentieth century, was assembling a remarkable team of physicians, surgeons, toxicologists, bacteriologists and – not least – pathologists, many of whom were to achieve the highest professional honours and international fame. At first, Spilsbury's ambition was only to become a GP, but the presence of so many able specialists at St Mary's, at such an exciting time in the development of so many specialities, must have caused the young student to reflect on his career path.

The most important influence on Spilsbury, in those early days at St Mary's, was the senior surgeon and pathologist Augustus John Pepper, an easy-going, friendly, short, dapper man, with a walrus moustache, often seen sporting a massive gold watch-chain on his waistcoat. The record of Pepper's academic achievement was in massive contrast to that of Spilsbury. Born in 1849, Pepper had enjoyed a student career at University College Hospital that was described as 'exceptionally brilliant'.[2] He won Gold Medals in anatomy, physiology, therapeutics, medicine, surgery, forensic medicine and obstetrics. He had been appointed to the surgical staff at St Mary's in 1882 and maintained a successful private practice in Harley Street. Pepper's unassuming manner ensured popularity with students, including Spilsbury, who crowded into his lectures, eagerly accompanied his surgical rounds and watched his operations. Surgery had moved on from the early Victorian days of keyhole incisions and blood-encrusted frock coats. Pepper, a surgeon of the first rank, was careful to employ the latest techniques, including antisepsis. Spilsbury recalled that, though Pepper was occasionally seen to stroke his luxuriant moustache during operations, post-operative infections were rare in his surgical ward.

Unusually for a surgeon of his calibre and practice, Pepper had developed an interest in pathology. Long after the Smethurst debacle, the 'Beastly Science' remained deeply unfashionable. In the course of his work as a surgeon, Pepper gave evidence at inquests in the Paddington area, and his abilities as a witness came to the notice of the Director of Public Prosecutions (DPP). From the mid-1880s onwards Pepper gave evidence for the Crown in serious criminal trials, eventually including cases of murder. During Spilsbury's early years at St Mary's, Pepper was already very much in the public eye. Even so august a newspaper as *The Times* would erroneously refer to him as 'Professor Pepper', the name of a well-known conjuror and popular music-hall entertainer.[3] Spilsbury may even have seen the distinguished surgeon's namesake, as he was fond of visiting 'the halls' from time to time, also enjoying concerts of classical music.

In an echo of his time at Oxford, Spilsbury's first two years at St Mary's passed unremarkably. Students had a choice of playing rugby, hockey or, in the summer, tennis. There was a swimming club, a chess club, a rifle club and a medical society. Spilsbury, at 22 older than the majority of his student peers and never much of a social animal, confined his activities to rugby (which he also played when at home in Moseley). No doubt with an eye to career prospects, he became a regular attender at the monthly meetings of the St Mary's Medical Society, of which he became joint secretary in 1903. He is said to have played rugby at St Mary's until about that year, but seems never to have been entirely at ease with physical contact. Over-exuberant student backslappers would be stopped in their tracks with a frosty, 'Don't touch me, please.'[4]

Among the corpus of medical students, bright, breezy young men as most of them were, Spilsbury was always a bit of an outsider, aloof, and not especially popular. At St Mary's he worked hard, regularly attending his required course of pharmacology lectures in 1900, in contrast to the cavalier way in which he had cut examinations, lectures and tutorials at Oxford. He had always enjoyed practical work and applied himself eagerly to anatomical dissection. Students were charged an annual fee for their work on a designated corpse, and Spilsbury would have got his money's worth, painstakingly applying a small dissecting knife to his subject, a grey object – barely recognisable as having once been a human being – drawn from a pool of bodies preserved in formalin. The malodorous atmosphere of the dissecting-room could be alleviated, to some extent, by smoking, and Spilsbury may have taken up the habit at this time.

His endeavours eventually produced a modest reward. In September 1901 he was appointed student demonstrator in physiology. The *St Mary's Hospital Gazette*, which recorded the appointment of 'SPILLSBURY [*sic*] B.H., B.A. Oxon', often congratulated appointees, sometimes in affectionately joshing terms. No such congratulations attended this bald announcement.

The following year he became surgical dresser to Mr Pepper. This appointment was honorary and unpaid, but was much more significant in career terms than the student demonstratorship in physiology. Pepper's reputation as a skilled and innovative surgeon was at its zenith in 1902, and Spilsbury was to derive real benefit from the association. Although the *Gazette* would satirise the surgeon's dresser as 'a more or less intelligent being, whose duty is to wipe up the water he had just spilt',[5] there was much to be learnt from the work, which was demanding and involved long hours. One of Spilsbury's predecessors as surgical dresser was William Willcox, seven years older than Spilsbury, who had studied chemistry at Nottingham University, achieving the qualification of Fellow of the Institute of Chemistry (FIC) in 1894, the distinction won eleven years previously by Spilsbury's father. Academically, there was no comparison between Spilsbury and Willcox, who had been one of the brightest entrants to St Mary's, carrying off the Senior Science Scholarship (worth four times Spilsbury's modest Exhibition) in 1895. He gained first-class honours, winning a Gold Medal in each of these three subjects, and several prizes and scholarships. In the six years Spilsbury spent at St Mary's before qualifying in medicine he won no prize, and no Gold Medal would ever come his way. He benefited, however, from association with the cluster of brilliant minds that assembled at the small, underfunded teaching hospital that was St Mary's Paddington in the early years of the twentieth century.

In November 1902 one of the hospital's brightest stars took up the appointment of combined pathologist and bacteriologist. Almroth Wright was prodigiously talented.[6] He read modern languages (in which he obtained first-class honours and a Gold Medal) at Trinity College, Dublin, while at the same time – a remarkable achievement – studying medicine, taking high honours in 1883. Unlike the plodding Spilsbury, Almroth Wright sought further experience abroad, obtaining a travelling scholarship that took him to Leipzig, then a centre of clinical excellence. After experience in pathology at Cambridge, Wright developed a revolutionary immunisation treatment for typhoid fever, which could have saved the lives of thousands of troops during the Boer War, had not the cautious army medical authorities refused to undertake a programme of compulsory vaccination.

On arrival at St Mary's, Wright had to make do with a small room, which shook every time a train passed on the nearby underground railway, making microscopical examination extremely difficult. Similar conditions seemed to afflict the basement pathology department, unflatteringly described as the 'lower regions' of the hospital,[7] where Spilsbury was often to be seen, hard at work on the regular supply of corpses.

Spilsbury was strongly influenced by Wright and is said to have read some of his treatises even before going up to Oxford. He would soon make himself very useful to Wright, filling a significant gap in the glittering professional life of the recently appointed lecturer in pathology. Wright flatly refused to undertake post-mortems (contempt for which was widespread among senior medical and surgical staff at London teaching hospitals). Spilsbury was prepared to do such unpopular and unfashionable work. He was content with his own company and preferred working alone. Unlike the problems faced by colleagues upstairs, the 'patients' would never question his judgement, recover unexpectedly or answer him back.

In the gloomy surroundings of the post-mortem (PM) room, Spilsbury worked at first with John (later Sir John) Broadbent, the last pathologist at St Mary's to combine pathology with private practice as a physician. Consultants at the hospital were unpaid and relied on fees from teaching and private practice for their incomes. Salaried appointments were rare and in fact despised by many high-flyers. Spilsbury's application to his work may have been seen by some at St Mary's as pedestrian, but he impressed such demanding mentors as Wright and Pepper. In 1903 Spilsbury was appointed assistant demonstrator of pathology at the modest salary of £200 per annum.

That year, working with Pepper, he was able to see at first hand a major exercise in forensic pathology. Pepper had been instructed by the DPP to examine human remains found buried in a ditch at Moat Farm, near Clavering in Essex. Pepper's task was not easy. The body was thought to be that of Miss Camille Holland, the owner of the property, who had disappeared four years earlier at the age of 56. It was known that Camille had become infatuated with Samuel Dougal, also 56, a convicted forger, who was ostensibly her farm bailiff. Nobody seems to have missed Camille, but eventually stories of sexual shenanigans at the farm (including lurid accounts of a young woman riding around nude on a bicycle) prompted a police investigation. In the course of digging operations, information about the filling-in of an old drainage ditch, around the time of Camille's disappearance, proved to be the vital clue.

On 27 April 1903 a body in an advanced state of putrefaction was exhumed from the damp, muddy soil of the ditch. Soft tissue had deteriorated into adipocere, 'a greyish-white fatty substance generated in dead bodies buried in moist places',[8] a grisly phenomenon later the subject of a detailed report by Pepper. What had been unearthed was far beyond facial recognition, but a pair of lady's boots, a skirt and 'a frame over which she did her hair' had survived. Camille's bootmaker recognised the boots he had made for her. Better still, a dentist testified that the teeth, which were in a good state of preservation, belonged to Camille Holland.

At post-mortem, Pepper found that the skull had a hole in it, which he ascribed to the entry wound of a bullet that had been found on the left side of the skull. Dougal's cartridges were seized by police, and, after they had been examined by a firearms expert, he was charged with murder. Evidence about ballistics was given by E.J. Churchill, uncle of Robert Churchill, the gunsmith who would later form a double act with Spilsbury – at times controversially – in several murder trials between 1913 and 1947. As in the later Spilsbury–Churchill cases, E.J. Churchill had conducted shooting experiments, although his nephew never used the skinned sheep's heads favoured by his uncle as experimental targets, quickly 'over-ripe' and impossible to produce as exhibits in court. Dougal was convicted and hanged.[9] Pepper retained the victim's skull as a trophy. For a while, students of forensic medicine were confronted with 'Dr Pepper's pride' during examinations, but its origin was widely known, and soon Camille's head was left to rest undisturbed in its glass case.

Spilsbury probably had an allowance from his father, who had been working in the partnership of Blackwell, Hayes & Spilsbury on synthetic rubber, which offered commercial possibilities arising from the early days of motoring. James Spilsbury was also able to support Leonard, now an undergraduate at Emmanuel College, Cambridge, where he was reading mechanical engineering.

Spilsbury pursued a leisurely progress towards his final medical qualifications. He was a 'long-termer', a status abolished after the Second World

War. In the early twentieth century, as long as students were able to pay their fees there was no particular pressure to qualify. It was enough to be present at lectures and obtain the necessary signatures of attendance.[10] Another possible reason for Spilsbury's slow progress at St Mary's may have been a call to the Methodist ministry. Spilsbury, a man of very conservative moral views, even for his time, seems to have been baptised a Methodist. His application to be accepted as a minister of the gospel was, however, rejected.[11]

In 1903 Spilsbury walked the medical and surgical wards for a few weeks, also observing how the physicians and surgeons attended their outpatients, and briefly studied ophthalmology, dentistry and dermatology. The following January, Spilsbury was taught obstetrics. Home births were the norm in those days, and, for just one month in April 1904, he gained his only practical experience of live births, accompanying a midwife on visits to some of the poorer homes in the vicinity of Praed Street. In later years, his lack of experience of hands-on medicine would not prevent him from advancing opinions well beyond his limited clinical experience.

The same year brought classes in medical jurisprudence, 'mental diseases', hygiene and fevers, as well as a striking example of the way in which Spilsbury was starting to make a name for himself, despite his indifferent academic achievement, his unfashionable interest in pathology, and his aloof, rather prickly, personality.

In October 1904 a delegation of leading French medical experts visited London, taking in all the major teaching hospitals.[12] The visit was reported in some detail by *The Times*, which gave a heavyweight account of a demonstration by Almroth Wright involving 'the treatment of tuberculosis and staphylococcal infection by therapeutic injection of the corresponding bacterial vaccine'. The newspaper also noted that the distinguished visitors had been received at St Mary's Hospital by 'Sir William Broadbent, Dr J Broadbent, Dr S Phillips, Mr Juler, and Mr Spillsbury [*sic*]'. At that time, Spilsbury, the holder of a very junior appointment, was still a year away from his final examinations. It was a remarkable feat on his part to have got his name included among the published list of hospital luminaries on the reception committee. The *St Mary's Gazette* sarcastically hoped that 'Mr Spilsbury fully appreciates the honour' given him by the report.

On the same day as *The Times* report, 12 October 1904, the body of a woman was found in a bedroom above a small shop in Commercial Road. Emily Farmer, '64 or 65', kept a newsagent's and tobacconist's shop. A paperboy had found Emily lying dead, face down, on her bed in her ransacked bedroom. She had been gagged, and her hands had been tied behind her back. Emily had suffocated to death. Conrad Donovan, a sailor aged 34, and Charles Wade, a 24-year-old labourer, were charged with Emily's murder. Pepper appears to have been assisted by Spilsbury in the forensic investigation of the case. A police surgeon, in evidence at committal proceedings in Thames Police Court at Arbour Square, gave a curious opinion that suffocation by an accumulation of mucus in the back of the nose was not possible if the person had been gagged, because the effort of breathing would clear the nasal passage. Spilsbury attended the hearing and, although he did not make a formal deposition or give evidence at the subsequent Old Bailey trial, he satisfied the court clerk, Albert Lieck, that this was contrary to common sense. Lieck, an experienced court official, was impressed by the young Spilsbury's 'quiet and convincing' manner.[13] Although no property from the robbery had been found on them, the two defendants were convicted and sentenced to death. 'Cheer up,' shouted a voice from the public gallery as they were led down to the cells and, ultimately, execution.

In December 1904 Spilsbury obtained his second Oxford MB and was already beginning to make his mark in practical work. On 26 October 1904 he made his first demonstration of microscopical specimens to the hospital's medical society. Histology slides were home-made, using a simple technique. Embedding a sample of tissue in paraffin, Spilsbury would cut a fine sliver using a special tool known as a microtome. The specimen, often around ¾in square, would be mounted on a small sheet of glass, about 3in by 1in. Another thin sheet would be laid over the specimen to complete the creation of the slide. Spilsbury made his 'slide drawers' out of strong cardboard folders that could hold up to nine slides. By these means, he showed an impressive exhibition of tetanus bacilli to the St Mary's Medical Society in November 1904 and undertook a series of demonstrations the following year. He returned in good health from a stint at the London Fever Hospital in June 1905. The hospital *Gazette* wryly welcomed his return: 'We are glad to see Spilsbury back in his den, making the paraffin fly', wrote the editor in phraseology suggesting that Spilsbury was still regarded as something of an anorak about the place. He had been lucky not to have picked up any disease at the Fever Hospital. His successor went down with scarlet fever.

Spilsbury's long-drawn-out apprenticeship as medical student ended in July 1905, when he passed his final examinations in medicine, surgery and obstetrics. At long last, he could write 'MB, B.Ch., Oxon.' after his name. The newly qualified doctor was well regarded by Augustus Pepper, now senior pathologist at the hospital. Pepper's recommendation went far in securing Spilsbury the post of resident assistant pathologist, at a salary of £200 per annum.

Spilsbury learnt a great deal from his new boss. One writer has even compared their relationship to that of Conan Doyle and Dr Bell. Spilsbury had the highest regard for Pepper's 'quiet confident manner' in court, noticing that 'he never became flustered or lost his temper'. As Spilsbury would do in so many controversial trials, Pepper displayed 'an absolute certainty in his facts and a quiet competence in the witness-box . . . to the despair of opposing counsel'.[14] Pepper, who must have been aware that Spilsbury was no gold medallist *manqué*, was nevertheless obviously impressed by his junior's capacity for sheer hard work. 'The pupil who did his best was never forgotten and had in Pepper a friend for life,' Spilsbury wrote, with a rare hint of emotion, years after their collaboration had ended.[15]

Despite the occasional glamorous and exciting court case, work in the pathology department was usually mundane, involving routine post-mortems on patients and those who had died within the hospital's catchment area. In March 1906, at a mortuary in Fulham, Spilsbury performed his first autopsy outside the drab confines of the hospital basement. He began to record details of his post-mortems in notebooks and, later, on case cards, useful resources as appearances at inquests became more frequent. Soon he began to earn an appreciable income from fees in the coroners' courts of the London area.

In 1907 Spilsbury was elected a member of the prestigious Medico-Legal Society and was soon appointed one of two honorary auditors. The appointment seems an unusual post for a newcomer, but perhaps Spilsbury had already developed a reputation for being careful with money. He was capable of generosity, wise enough to give generous tips to mortuary assistants, but was fairly economical in his personal life. Clothes were the major extravagance. Spilsbury dressed well, using good tailors, and was always fastidious about his appearance. As a young man, standing 6ft 2in, his good looks made him a striking figure about the hospital and, increasingly, in the law courts. 'Matinée-idol looks' has become a cliché, but it accurately described the young pathologist, who, in his own way, was developing dramatic skills that Owen Nares, Sir John Martin Harvey or Sir Gerald du Maurier might have recognised. The Medico-Legal Society, too, had its link to the theatrical profession. George Bernard Shaw, already an established playwright, author and dramatic critic, was an enthusiastic member, a rare radical spirit among a largely conservative membership. Among the medical men (there were no female members in 1908) were the great names of Littlejohn, Glaister, Pepper and Willcox. Earl Russell, elder brother of the philosopher Bertrand Russell, frequently attended the society's meetings. Cesare Lombroso, the primitive criminologist, was an honorary member.

In April 1908 Spilsbury contributed to a debate about infanticide.[16] Suspicious deaths of the new-born often presented great evidential difficulties in proving a separate existence before death. Until the Infanticide Act of 1929, the mother was charged with murder, but any consequent conviction would usually be for manslaughter or concealment of birth. Sentence would be nominal, such as a discharge or short period of imprisonment. Spilsbury referred loftily to those 'ignorant women' who had difficulty in deciding whether their child was alive or dead after birth. The law, he thought, should require evidence of viability or wilfulness on the part of the accused. A Dr Mercier of Wimpole Street maintained that punishment was inadequate because the accused was usually young and good-looking. Such women were 'not usually of a sensitive nature' and 'got into trouble with their eyes open'. The following month Spilsbury took a firm line on gonorrhoea, telling the society that 'all forms of [this] disease should be notified to the authorities'.[17]

A great believer in family values, Spilsbury married Edith Horton, his remarkably patient fiancée, in August 1908, and set up the matrimonial home at a quintessentially suburban address, The Elms, Hindes Road, Harrow-on-the-Hill.

In October 1908, at a further Medico-Legal Society meeting,[18] he presented an 'exhibit', presumably contained in a glass jar of formalin, described as 'a large persistent thymus gland and a spleen which was enlarged and studded throughout with large white spots consisting of masses of lymphoid tissue'. The specimen came from the body of a young man who had died under a chloroform anaesthetic while being circumcised. An autopsy had revealed 'in a well-developed form, the condition *status lymphaticus*', which Spilsbury described to the society in a short paper. Changes in lymphatic tissue were associated with a fatty degeneration of the heart, which could lead to sudden death from apparently trivial external causes and during anaesthesia.

Pepper retired as senior pathologist at St Mary's in July 1909. His resignation was a surprise, but there seems to have been no reason other than personal choice. He remained Home Office pathologist and carried on work as a surgeon at St Mary's and in private practice. Spilsbury was appointed his successor as hospital pathologist. In March 1909 Spilsbury's growing reputation as a pathologist prompted an invitation to St Bartholomew's, very much a rival teaching hospital, to conduct a post-mortem in a case of 'death on the table', a situation dreaded by every surgeon, where a patient had died under anaesthetic during an operation.

It was, however, a well-publicised death at Harrods in Knightsbridge that set Spilsbury on the road to becoming pathologist of choice to the DPP. On 12 July 1909 a young woman of 21 decided to have her hair done. She had the rather elaborate name of Horn Elphinstone-Dalrymple ('Horn' was an Aberdeenshire placename associated with the family baronetcy). Beatrice Clarke, an experienced hairdresser, began to give Horn a 'dry' shampoo, using a mixture containing the chemicals carbon tetrachloride and carbon bisulphide. The salon had been using this shampoo for six years, although occasionally clients felt faint during the application. An electric fan was employed in an attempt to disperse the pungent fumes. After a few minutes, with her head over the basin, Horn collapsed. Although efforts were immediately made to revive her and a doctor was soon on the scene, she died. At St Mary's Hospital, William Willcox, who had become an acknowledged authority on forensic chemistry, carried out a number of experiments that showed a high toxicity in the mixture, considerably higher even than chloroform.

At the inquest, held at Kensington Coroner's Court, Spilsbury's evidence attracted considerable press interest. At post-mortem, he had found signs of *status lymphaticus*, the morbid condition he had described to the Medico-Legal Society a few months previously. Death was the result of 'syncope', a rather vague term, medically fashionable at the time and a useful pseudonym for cases of otherwise unexplained heart failure. The purport of Spilsbury's evidence was that Horn would not have died if she had not had the shampoo. Although the verdict brought in by the Coroner's jury was 'Accidental Death', the jury added a rider to the effect that Harrods had not been justified in employing an unskilled operator to perform so potentially dangerous a procedure.

The DPP brought proceedings[19] not against Harrods (corporate criminal responsibility was unknown in 1909) but against two unfortunate staff members, William Eardley, the manager of the hairdressing department, and the shampooist, Beatrice Clarke. They both faced the grave charge of manslaughter, which, if the case came to trial, could have resulted in lengthy prison sentences.

The prosecution employed the heavyweight team of William Leycester and Travers Humphreys. Leycester, a small, pinch-faced man, was a quiet and effective prosecutor, whose brother-in-law, Richard Muir, was senior prosecuting counsel at the Central Criminal Court. Humphreys, a veteran of the Oscar Wilde trial, was already a rising star at the Old Bailey. In the Harrods case, these experienced prosecuting lawyers had the chance to see Spilsbury in action as a Crown witness. Leycester and Humphreys would have reported their impressions of Spilsbury to Muir and to the DPP, Sir Charles Mathews.

Committal proceedings took place at Westminster Police Court in Rochester Row and ambled on, at a leisurely pace, from August to October 1909. Pepper had also been instructed by the DPP and, with Willcox and other experts, gave evidence about various experiments and about the procedure employed by the store.

Rather unwisely, Harrods had continued to use the shampoo after the tragedy, and Pepper noticed how one customer's face had become blue with cyanosis as she was being shampooed. He also described how the fumes, heavier than air, could affect people bending forward to receive the mixture. Spilsbury's evidence about the possibility of *status lymphaticus* as a contributory cause of death was already controversial. Another prosecution witness, Lieutenant-Colonel Edward Lawrie, 'late of the Indian Medical Service', had known Horn Elphinstone-Dalrymple personally and was present when Spilsbury performed the autopsy. He agreed that there was a slight thickening of the heart valve – an indication of heart disease – but in his view the sole cause of death was inhalation of toxic vapour. Lawrie did not regard *status lymphaticus* as either a disease or a pathological condition. Spilsbury, called as next witness, moved quickly to defuse a potential threat to his young reputation. There were indications of *status lymphaticus*, he declared, but – in what seems to have been a subtle backtracking exercise – he added that 'it was not a very well marked case'.[20] There was nothing to account for sudden death, including the application of cold liquid. Even a well-ventilated room might not be sufficient to eliminate the threat from the toxic vapours.

Harrods Store was ably represented by Archibald Bodkin, the sonorously named barrister who would succeed Mathews as DPP in 1920. At the end of the evidence, Bodkin invited the DPP to withdraw the prosecution. The DPP's object in bringing proceedings had been to warn Harrods and other establishments of the risks of using carbon tetrachloride shampoo. There was never any intention of arraigning the two Harrods *employés* (as *The Times* genteely described them) in the dock at the Old Bailey, and they were exonerated from blame and discharged. The DPP paid Spilsbury one guinea for his day's work. A year later he would be giving evidence as a lethal witness for the Crown in a murder trial of international fame.

THREE

Dr Crippen

A weedy, goggle-eyed, henpecked, middle-aged little man with thinning ginger hair, pince-nez and a bushy, droopy moustache hardly seems the embodiment of absolute evil. Yet in the popular imagination his name has acquired a notoriety second only to Jack the Ripper.[1] The name 'Crippen' certainly has evocations of 'ripper', 'criminal' and 'creepy', but a major factor in the creation of its enduring fame was the development of mass-circulation journalism over the decade or so before his trial for the murder of his wife Belle Elmore.

Broadsheets such as the *Daily Express* and *Daily Mail* competed with the more downmarket *Daily Mirror*, *Daily Sketch*, *Daily News*, *Daily Graphic* and *Morning Leader*, each jostling for readership with the London 'evening' papers (on sale from around midday), such as the *Evening News*, *Evening Standard*, *Pall Mall Gazette* and the *Star*. Dramatic improvements in photographic reproduction meant that action photographs could be printed in increasingly effective ways. Some cheekier photographers even managed to snap scenes in court with secret cameras hidden in curly bowler hats held on their laps. The old line drawings, universal in Victorian times, were becoming fewer, but artists' impressions were still the norm where judges and magistrates had expressly forbidden the use of cameras.

The background to the Crippen case was crisply, if a little oddly, expressed in a contemporary Home Office minute:

Prisoner (48) is an American 'Dr', who for many years has done business in England selling quack medicines like 'Munyon's remedies', as a 'throat and ear' specialist and as a dentist. About 18 years ago he married, as his second wife, the deceased Cora Crippen (37), known latterly on the music-hall stage as 'Belle Elmore'. Prior to their marriage she had been kept by a man in America. They settled in London and to outward appearance lived on good terms, but according to the prisoner had not cohabited [*sic*] for the last 5 years. During the last 3 years he has been on intimate terms with his typewriter [*sic*] Ethel Le Neve (27).[2]

By 'not cohabited' the prudish Home Office official meant that Dr and Mrs Crippen had not had sexual relations during the time that they lived together at

30 Hilldrop Crescent, a large, gloomy semi-detached Victorian house set in an equally glum street in Camden Town, not far from Archway and Holloway Road.

Apart from Crippen, no one saw his wife alive after 31 January 1910. For the previous three years Crippen had been carrying on a clandestine amour with Ethel Le Neve, his office typist at Albion House, New Oxford Street. They pursued their doomed love affair in seedy hotel rooms. On 19 January 1910 Crippen had bought five grains of hydrobromide of hyoscine, a rarely used – but highly potent – poison, from an Oxford Street chemist. Crippen would later say that he intended to use the hyoscine as a constituent of homeopathic remedies, but produced no evidence to support his claim.

Crippen wrote a letter, ostensibly on Cora's behalf, resigning her position as treasurer of a variety artistes' association because she had to travel to America to attend a sick relative. When pressed on the matter, Crippen said that she had gone to California and could not easily be contacted.

Meanwhile, Ethel had moved into 30 Hilldrop Crescent. On 20 February Crippen took her to a ball given by the 'Music Hall Ladies' Benevolent Fund'. This turned out to be an extremely unwise move, because some of the benevolent ladies recognised items of Cora's jewellery, now being worn by Ethel. Suspicions were increased on 24 March, when Crippen sent a telegram to friends of his wife stating 'Belle died yesterday at six o'clock . . . Shall be away for a week.'[3] He later made out that she had died in Los Angeles.

Cora's friends were now very suspicious. Enquiries made in California found no trace of her death. Scotland Yard was approached. The matter does not seem to have been regarded as particularly urgent, since it was more than a week later when, on 8 July 1910, Crippen was interviewed by Chief Inspector Walter Dew. Crippen told Dew that Cora had left him on 1 February. In a long statement, he readily admitted that he had written the resignation letter and had made up the story of Cora's death to avoid humiliation caused by her leaving him for another man. He believed that she had gone to Chicago to join Bruce Miller. Dew, not the sharpest of minds, made a perfunctory search of 30 Hilldrop Crescent. He did not take in, for example, the significance of Cora's furs and jewellery being left behind there, not something that a wife would normally do when leaving her husband.

Cora's description was circulated as a missing person, and there the matter might have rested but for one dramatic development. On 11 July Dew went to Albion House, only to find that Crippen and Ethel Le Neve had disappeared. Dew made what he later described as a 'careful search' of the house, later claiming that he had examined the coal cellar. He went back again the next day, but it was not until 13 July that he started prodding the brick floor of the cellar with a poker. Some of the bricks came up very easily. They had been laid on clay, which, when dug down to a depth of four spadefuls, revealed what appeared to be human remains, caked in soil, with some lime mixed in. The lime appeared to have been introduced in an attempt to destroy the body parts (there were no bones), but the damp conditions of the subsoil had 'slaked' the lime, a process that acted as a mild preservative.

The story of the pursuit and arrest of Crippen and Le Neve is well known. An international hue and cry was raised. They were eventually identified by Captain Kendall of the SS *Montrose* en route from Antwerp to Montreal. The *Montrose* was equipped with the latest technology: a wireless telegraph. When his ship was 130 miles off the Lizard Point, the captain alerted Scotland Yard by telegram. Someone leaked the story to the press, and the pursuit became a media event.

Dew, with other police officers, boarded a faster ship, the SS *Laurentic*. When the *Montrose* reached the St Lawrence estuary, Kendall suggested that Dew should board the SS *Montrose* disguised as a pilot. Crippen and Ethel Le Neve were arrested on board ship. Crippen did not resist extradition proceedings and was returned to England with Ethel to face trial for murder.

On 14 July the remains, said to have been found wrapped in a pyjama jacket matching a pair of Crippen's pyjama trousers, were examined by Pepper in the cellar. Portions of flesh, which could have been human or animal at first sight, were removed to Islington mortuary. Pepper concluded that these were human remains, including a large piece of a thigh and lower buttock. No bones were found, but most of the internal organs (heart, lung, liver, kidneys, spleen, stomach and pancreas) were recovered, although the lower part of the abdomen, including the genital area, was missing, as were the head and neck. Most significantly, Pepper found two pieces of skin. One measured 11in by 5in, with some attached fat. The other, 7in by 6in, had a mark that attracted Pepper's attention and that would become a central feature of the murder trial. With the remains, Pepper found a Hinde's hair-curler, with a tuft of dark-brown hair on which there was some evidence of bleaching; some fair hair in a handkerchief; and some portions of clothing, apparently female.

Specimens were conveyed, in five glass-stoppered jars, to the pathology laboratory at St Mary's for examination by William Willcox, now a senior scientific analyst to the Home Office.[4] The process of assembling evidence was very leisurely by modern standards. Pepper handed over the second piece of skin to Willcox on 8 August, over three weeks after it had been discovered. At one end of the skin Willcox noticed hairs resembling pubic hair. He made a careful note of its description, 'put the skin in a special fluid designed to prevent further changes of putrefaction',[5] and handed it to Spilsbury for pathological investigation.

By 2 August it was known that Crippen had bought a quantity of hyoscine. Willcox extracted an alkloid from the liver and stomach. On 13 August he put a few drops of the extract on the eyes of a hapless laboratory cat. Gross dilation of the cat's pupils indicated to Willcox that this was a type of mydriatic alkoloid, of which hyoscine was a member. Later analysis suggested that there had been half a grain of hyoscine in the body. In Willcox's view, expressed at the trial, a quarter to half a grain would be a fatal dose of this powerful narcotic poison.

In July 1910 Spilsbury had to abandon a planned holiday in Minehead, spending the summer in London to work on the Crippen case. Despite Pepper's finding on 14 July that the second piece of skin had 'a significant mark', it was not until 9 September that Spilsbury, with Pepper beside him, conducted a microscopic examination of the tissue.[6] It seems unlikely that Spilsbury's preparatory work on the slides could have taken nearly two months, and a remarkably long period elapsed between the find and this crucial investigation.

Both Pepper and Spilsbury were aware that Cora had undergone an operation and, in consequence, had an abdominal scar. One of Cora's women friends would give evidence at the trial that she had seen a long scar on 'the lower part of her stomach'[7] when Cora was undressing, as her house guest in 1909, and had noticed that Cora had a navel. In the remains, however, there was no evidence of an umbilicus.

Sebaceous glands, tiny features of the skin, do not exist in scar tissue. Spilsbury examined sections cut across the suspected scar. The outer skin, the epidermis, had mostly gone. The inner skin, the dermis, consisted of a close network of fibrous tissue resting upon subcutaneous fat. Spilsbury claimed[8] that remains of sebaceous glands were visible, embedded in the dermis on the right margin of the specimen and also in a piece of skin from a fold near the left upper part of the specimen. Signs of sebaceous glands were apparent even in the middle of the fold. In a specimen taken from the suspected scar, however, sebaceous glands were found at each end (but not in the middle) for a distance of an inch and a half, a length of tissue where the dermis was noticeably denser and thinner than elsewhere. Spilsbury concluded that the skin showed 'no putrefactive changes',[9] which does not fit with Willcox's statement that the tissue had been put in fluid on 8 August 'designed to prevent further putrefaction'.[10] Spilsbury's opinion was that the area of altered skin indicated an old, and probably stretched, scar. Stretching was more likely to have occurred in a female subject.

For the Old Bailey trial, which promised to be a media circus, the DPP was carefully preparing his team. Although in poisoning cases the Attorney-General normally led the prosecution, political commitments during the bitter constitutional crisis of 1910 ('*Lords* v. *Commons*') rendered Sir Rufus Isaacs unavailable. Richard (later Sir Richard) Muir, senior Treasury Counsel, headed the prosecution side. When Crippen learnt that Muir was to prosecute him, he said with gloomy foresight, 'I wish it had been anybody else. I fear the worst.'[11] Muir, then 53 and at the peak of his fame, was a portly man of medium height, whose fleshy face was liable to flush with anger when his forensic path was crossed by witness, defendant or even the judge. Like Spilsbury, he came from a middle-class background, and was the son of a Glasgow shipbroker.

Muir helped support himself in his early, penurious days at the Bar by becoming a parliamentary reporter and always kept one eye on the press gallery. Teetotal and a non-smoker, he lived for his work and would often remain in chambers until midnight 'getting together a case that would be absolutely impregnable'.[12] Meticulous preparation, including multi-coloured crayons and a card-index system, was characteristic of this prosecuting monomaniac, who was not popular with easier-going advocate colleagues.[13]

As prosecutor, 'he went out for the triumph of his side', all the more deadly for his fierce application and minute attention to detail. Dour and humourless, he was a Scotsman very much on the make; 'his speeches made infinity intelligible'.[14] He was regarded 'as ponderous beyond belief . . . thorough and dangerous . . . with an unpleasant way of pressing his case a bit too hard against the accused'.[15]

Muir, who wanted the very best team of forensic experts, naturally looked to St Mary's, with its burgeoning reputation in the fields of pathology and toxicology. On his wish-list were Pepper, Willcox and A.P. Luff, a distinguished physician with many years' service as scientific adviser to the Home Office and author of a standard textbook on forensic medicine. Muir, in effect, headhunted Spilsbury. In the Harrods case, William Leycester (Muir's brother-in-law) and Travers Humphreys had observed the young pathologist in action as an impressive witness for the prosecution. His testimony had been simple, direct and low key. Spilsbury had used ordinary language and eschewed technical jargon. This was positive evidence, just the sort that prosecution lawyers and senior policemen wanted to hear.

The choice of judge was also important. Charles Mathews, the DPP, an experienced and successful criminal barrister despite having a high-pitched, rather effeminate, voice, nevertheless wielded an influence that his present-day successor might envy. The selection of a trial judge ought not to be in the gift of the prosecutor, but a letter to Mathews written by a member of his staff on 10 October 1910 reveals the extraordinary extent of the DPP's powers in those days: 'This is one of those criminal trials that . . . the LCJ [Lord Chief Justice] ought always to try – he told me if you thought so too, he would do it – though he is not at all fond of the new Old Bailey, as sitting there usually makes him ill.'[16] Richard Everard Webster, Baron (later Viscount) Alverstone, the LCJ, was not a judge of the highest intellect. Apart from taking an irrational dislike to the new Central Criminal Court, opened in 1907, he comes across as a wordy, interfering and very prosecution-minded fusspot, negative characteristics that emerged clearly in the course of his summing-up in the Crippen case.

For his defence, Crippen secured the dubious services of Arthur Newton, a solicitor with a fashionable West End practice who had represented Oscar Wilde in the famous trials of 1895. Though free representation was available under the Poor Prisoners' Defence Act 1903, there was a risk that, even on a capital charge, an accused might be represented by an inexperienced, white-wigged junior. Newspapers, with the prospect of an 'exclusive', were a source of funds, but only if the case provided opportunities for sensational copy. Newton obtained the instructions of *John Bull*, a populist weekly owned by Horatio Bottomley, a larger-than-life newspaper proprietor and fraudsman. Newton was neither honest nor particularly competent. In the Crippen case, as will be seen, his grubby tactics damaged the medical case for the defence.

Newton faced some difficulty in selecting leading counsel for the defence. Of the great names at the Bar, Rufus Isaacs had always been out of the question, as he was now Attorney-General. A crude attempt failed to brief Muir, Leycester and Travers Humphreys, so that no member of the deadly triumvirate would be available to prosecute Crippen. A.E. Bowker, shrewd clerk to the legendary KC Marshall Hall (see p. 34 below), was alerted by Newton's equivocation on the little matter of fees, aware that Newton was making efforts to secure newspaper funding that might not materialise. F.E. Smith (later Earl of Birkenhead and Lord Chancellor) wisely refused a brief for Crippen, having read the case papers. He formed the view, quite properly, that Ethel should be separately represented and, in Travers Humphreys's waspish recollection, 'not unnaturally chose for himself the much easier task of defending the lady'.[17] In the end, Newton plumped for the little-known Alfred Tobin, 54, who in 1910 had been KC for only two years, achieving that honour tellingly late in his professional life. Tobin never achieved the stature and reputation of a Marshall Hall, a Rufus Isaacs or an F.E. Smith. Like Smith, he had started professional life in Liverpool. Like Smith, he was a Member of Parliament. Like Smith, too, he had tried his luck in London. Unlike Smith, he was a mediocre advocate and, as sometimes happens to second-rank barristers who take silk, found that he had priced himself out of the market. Tobin was in no position to refuse Newton's instructions.

The Coroner's inquest recorded a verdict of wilful murder against Crippen. The Crown's case was set out in detail during committal proceedings at Bow Street in September. While Spilsbury gave his evidence, Sir Melville Macnaghten, Assistant Commissioner CID (a languid Old Etonian who had qualified himself for this important post by spending several years as a tea planter in India), shimmered into the court, bringing with him the Chief of the Berlin Police. W.S. Gilbert was also there to see the show, which promised to be a real trial by jury. In the well of the court, noted the *Daily Mirror*, was 'another whose profession makes him a student of human nature, Mr Gus Elen, the coster comedian'.[18] Gus Elen was a music-hall star famous for his coster-monger act, in which he sang cockney songs. One of these, 'It's a Great Big Shame', contains a line aptly describing the dynamics of the Crippen marriage: 'Isn't it a pity that the likes of her should put upon the likes of him?'

Spilsbury (elegantly clad in tailcoat and silk top hat, and sporting an inverted umbrella) was photographed by the *Daily Mirror* leaving court with his less photogenic companions, William Willcox and Travers Humphreys.[19]

The trial opened on Tuesday 18 October 1910. Press photographers and newsreel cameras recorded the crowds who besieged the Old Bailey for the five days of the hearing. The prosecution's forensic team covered two areas of evidence. Pepper and Spilsbury dealt mainly with the physical state of the remains, including the question of the scar. Willcox and Luff gave evidence about the toxicological analysis and the discovery of hyoscine in the internal organs.

Though Spilsbury was to make his name in the Crippen trial, Pepper was first in the witness-box. He was now 62 and on the verge of retirement as Home Office pathologist; this would be his last appearance in a great criminal trial. Muir, carefully and ponderously, drew from him an account of the finding of the remains. On 9 September 1910 he had been present when a piece of skin was removed for microscopical examination and was present when Spilsbury examined the section. Pepper had 'not the slightest doubt',[20] even before the microscopical examination, that this was a scar. During Pepper's evidence the court was treated to a macabre spectacle: the piece of controversial skin, now safely in preservative, was handed round the jurybox on a china dish bearing a suspicious resemblance to a soup plate.

Tobin had to deal with four questions. First, how long had the remains been in the cellar? Second, what parts of the body were they? Third, what had been the sex of the deceased? Fourth, was there an operation scar on the second piece of skin? His best hope, bearing in mind that there was strong evidence that the pieces of flesh were abdominal and that items of a woman's attire had been found, would have been to concentrate on the first and fourth questions, using them as a smokescreen to diminish the effect of the other evidence. On the first question, he had some ammunition. Pepper had committed himself to what, on modern analysis, seems to have been far too rigid an estimate. Taking into account the place of burial, the lime and earth surrounding them, and the depth of burial, he claimed that the remains had been buried from four to eight months. In a rather loose opinion, Pepper asserted that they had been buried 'very shortly after death'.[21] At committal, Willcox had said that putrefaction would have been delayed by the lime in the grave, but that the formation of adipocere (noted in the Moat Farm case – see Chapter Two) would have been accelerated, a factor that was taken into account in assessing how long the remains had been buried. Another medical witness for the Crown, Dr Marshall, had stated at committal proceedings that some bodies could remain in 'an excellent state of preservation for some years'[22] if buried in lime and in soil such as clay, which practically excludes all air. Tobin did not put Marshall's opinion in terms to Pepper, a particularly unfortunate lapse because, later in the trial, Marshall gave such estimates as 'several months', 'possibly up to seven months', even saying that he 'could say not precisely how long' the body parts had been buried.[23] These were answers that conflicted with his declaration of agreement with Pepper's evidence. The conflict between prosecution experts could also have been exploited when cross-examining Willcox on the hyoscine issue.

As for the scar, Tobin twice put to Pepper questions implying that the section of skin might not have come from the abdomen. This was careless cross-examination, as Tobin must have known that his own defence experts now accepted that it was tissue from that part of the body.

With Pepper, and to some extent with Willcox, Tobin broke one of the cardinal rules of cross-examination: if there is a dangerous expert to cross-examine, counsel should ask few questions, just enough to put the case, and then get the expert out of the witness-box as quickly as possible. Tobin's cross-examination of Pepper lasted for hours. His questions were long and rambling, confusing the judge, and providing Pepper with numerous opportunities for emphasising his findings.

Tobin did pick up one significant discrepancy in Pepper's evidence. In answer to Muir, he stated that he had formed the opinion that there was a scar, visible on the piece of skin, on 15 July. The mark had caught his attention, and he spent several hours examining it. In cross-examination, Pepper said that he had not seen the mark on 15 July 'and therefore the question of the scar did not arise then'.[24]

On Thursday 20 October 1910 Spilsbury – the day's first witness – made his way across the court to the witness-box. After the short, homely, ageing figure of Mr Pepper, Spilsbury presented a complete contrast in style. Youthful, tall and elegant, Spilsbury added to his commanding appearance with a flower in the buttonhole of his tailcoat, a jaunty feature that no one seems to have found out of place in a murder trial. In answer to Muir, he gave a succinct account of his microscopical findings, identifying the scar and using no unnecessary verbiage. Tobin announced, to the judge's evident approval, that he did not propose to repeat his lengthy cross-examination of Pepper. He then put a few further questions. Tobin's short cross-examination would prove to be disastrous.

Spilsbury claimed that, with his naked eye, he considered the mark to be a scar, even before first using the microscope. Tobin put to him that, when Spilsbury first saw the skin, he already knew that Cora had undergone an operation in the lower abdomen. The innuendo behind Tobin's foolish question was that Spilsbury had doctored his evidence in the light of what he had heard. 'Yes,' replied Spilsbury blandly, outwardly unperturbed by the import of the question, 'I believe I had read that in the press.'[25] This was a very unwise tactic, enabling Muir to re-examine Spilsbury with crushing effect. He elicited answers from Spilsbury emphasising his independent evidence ('the fact that I acted with Mr Pepper has absolutely no influence upon the opinion that I have expressed here') and rebutted any suggestion of tailoring his findings in the light of press reports ('the fact that I read in the papers that there had been an operation . . . had no effect at all upon the opinion I have expressed'). Then came a series of knock-out blows to the defence: 'I have no doubt that this is a scar,' declared Spilsbury. 'I have examined microscopically the section . . . to see whether there was any gland or hair follicle in it . . . I have failed to find any hair follicle or sebaceous gland in that area. If there had been any in that area, I certainly would have found them.' In answer to the judge, Spilsbury affirmed: 'I have an independent position of my own . . . I have absolutely no doubt in my own mind as regards the scar.' Spilsbury ended his evidence with a bold theatrical flourish, the first of many in his long career as expert witness: 'I have my microscopic slides here and I shall send for a microscope in case it should be wanted.' Muir 'found in Spilsbury the expert witness so often required in murder trials'[26] and thought that, but for this evidence, Crippen might have been acquitted. Such was the effect of Spilsbury's testimony that he was depicted giving evidence in a popular newspaper, the *Morning Leader*.[27]

When he came to cross-examine Willcox, Tobin had not learnt from his mistake in attacking the probity of the prosecution medical team. He put to Willcox that his findings regarding hyoscine had been made only after he had been told, on 2 August 1910, that Crippen had bought hyoscine. He lost sight of the significant fact that hyoscine had never previously been detected at post-mortem. Tobin threw away the opportunity for a 'defence by confusion', which could have sown doubts about the reliability of the new technique. In the event, in a skilled Muir re-examination, Willcox made reference to the cat's eyes, with their grossly dilated pupils, an evidential vision destined to persist in the minds of the jurymen. Tobin might also have been wiser not to have called the medical witnesses for the defence, Dr Turnbull and Dr Wall, both from the London Hospital. Both experts had previously committed themselves to findings that the controversial skin sections had come, not from the abdomen, but from the thigh. The supposed scar, they found, was merely a fold in the skin. In Turnbull's case, at least, it appears that the unscrupulous Newton had induced Turnbull to make a written statement to that effect after a preliminary examination of the tissue and on the understanding that he would not be called as a witness. In court, both admitted that they had now changed their minds and agreed that the tissue was from the abdominal wall. Muir had a field day with the two unfortunate doctors. Amid all the forensic excitement, however, valuable evidence was 'lost in the wash' (as lawyers say) about the true nature of the supposed scar tissue, whatever part of the body it had come from.

Crippen gave evidence. If he had remained silent, and if his defence counsel had made a better job, he might have walked free from court. Once he was in the witness-box, his evidence about the date on which the pyjama jacket – found wrapped around the remains – had been bought was easily disproved. Crippen was destroyed by Muir's ferocious cross-examination. The judge, prosecution-minded throughout, virtually directed the jury to convict.

On 16 November 1910, shortly before he was due to be hanged, Crippen wrote a bitter epitaph. In the course of a statement that may have been

designed for publication, Crippen repeated Tobin's charge that the experts had
come up with the scar theory only after hearing about the operation. Evidence
about the scar had been based on 'the supposition that the edges of the skin
had been turned under and brought together in sewing up the wound'. In his
view, that was 'most unlikely to have been done by a skilled surgeon . . . the
groove was widest at its lowest point above the pubic bone . . . had [it] been a
stretched scar it [*sic*] widest point would have been much higher up'. He
commented that the absence of signs of a navel, inconsistent with other
evidence, was 'most carefully avoided' at the trial. The operation had been 'a
simple ovariotomy, the incision being from a little above the pubis head to the
navel . . . performed for dysmenorrheoia and prolapsed uterus'.[28]

These late protestations had no effect on the mind of the Home Secretary,
Winston Churchill, and the execution took place at Pentonville on
23 November 1910. Ethel Le Neve, ably defended by F.E. Smith, who
successfully shifted the blame onto her lover, was acquitted at her separate
trial. Newton was convicted of fraud in 1913 and jailed for three years.
Eventually, he became prison librarian at Parkhurst.

Did Spilsbury, supported by Pepper and Willcox, really see the signs of a scar
on that small piece of skin? Dr Turnbull, still smarting from his mauling at the
hands of Richard Muir, always stuck to his view that the microscopical sections
did not confirm Spilsbury's claim. As late as 1917 he made a detailed
'diagrammatic reconstruction of Dr Spilsbury's sections . . . said to contain no
sebaceous glands or hair follicles', in which he set out his reasons for believing
that Spilsbury had been wrong in his conclusions.[29] Spilsbury's slides still exist,
held in the Royal London Hospital archives. In 2002 they were examined by
Professor Bernard Knight. The slides were still in good condition, although the
haemotoxylin, a blue dye used to stain nuclei, had faded. The pink eosin,
however, had a normal appearance. Bearing in mind that the fading caused
some difficulty in interpreting the slides, Professor Knight could not detect
definite indications of scar tissue, as had been so firmly claimed by Spilsbury
when giving his positive evidence in 1910.

FOUR

Moral High Ground

The DPP's gratitude to Spilsbury for 'the excellence of his work' in the conviction of Dr Crippen did not prevent his staff disallowing a fee claim for £72 16s, paying the rising star only £54 6s.[1] Nevertheless, the daily attendance rate of three guineas, although less than the five-guinea rate awarded to Pepper and Willcox, was already three times his fee in the Harrods case. On 28 November 1910 an official hinted that Spilsbury would soon be treated, like his senior colleagues, as a formal expert witness to the DPP. His sterling performance in the Crippen trial was also rewarded with promotion. Pepper retired as Home Office pathologist at the end of 1910. On his recommendation, Spilsbury was appointed his successor, also acting as assistant to Willcox, now Senior Analyst and Pathologist to the Home Office. This was a remarkable feat, since Spilsbury, still only 33, was young for such important public responsibilities and had relatively little experience of court work.

The appointment had a less glamorous dimension. Unlike Spilsbury, Willcox had a large medical practice as physician, which he combined with the increasing demands of laboratory work in toxicology and analytical chemistry. If not quite a dogsbody, Spilsbury, the dedicated pathologist, was available to do the routine and time-consuming work of autopsy in cases of violent crime and unexplained death. Willcox thus 'became gradually relieved of his more sordid duties' by Spilsbury's almost obsessive dedication to the mortuary table.[2] Spilsbury did the rounds of the Coroners' courts, noting down details of his findings at post-mortem in his idiosyncratic, sprawling, left-inclined handwriting, which takes some practice to decipher. Pathology in its various forms was virtually his whole world. Personal relationships were proving a poor second to his professional work, although on 16 December 1910 Spilsbury's marital life was marked by the birth of his first child, Alys Evelyn.

The following year Spilsbury and Willcox teamed up again as expert witnesses in a murder trial that, if not having quite the international profile of the Crippen affair, was widely reported in the British press, not least because the latest forensic techniques were employed to secure a conviction. Frederick Henry Seddon, then 40 years old, was the district superintendent of the London & Manchester Insurance Society.[3] A married man with five children, he was a pillar of the community, a regular chapel-going Christian, an active

Freemason and a figure of impeccable lower-middle-class respectability, when such a background counted for a great deal in life.

Seddon bought a house, 63 Tollington Park, not very far from Dr Crippen's late abode in Hilldrop Crescent. His house was a rather larger version of Mr Pooter's 'nice six-roomed residence, not counting basement, with a front breakfast parlour and a flight of ten steps up to the front door', so pithily described in *The Diary of a Nobody*.[4] Here, Seddon accommodated his immediate family, plus his elderly father and a maid. He used the basement as an office (for which the insurance company helpfully paid him 5s a week) and advertised for a lodger to occupy three top-floor rooms.

From August 1910, his tenant was a Miss Eliza Barrow, aged 49, who moved in with a 10-year-old orphan, Ernie Grant, to whom she had taken a fancy. Elementary hygiene seems to have been alien to Miss Barrow, and little Ernie would sometimes share the lady's unwholesome bed, even during her final insanitary illness. Miss Barrow was also said to have been quarrelsome. She was reputed to have spat at former landlords and others she disliked. 'Her chief characteristics were slovenliness, parsimony, and a love of gold,'[5] which she hoarded in her room, together with a quantity of jewellery. She also had a nest-egg of some £3,000, a small fortune in 1911, invested partly in India stock and partly in the lease of a public house, The Buck's Head, and a next-door barber's shop. Miss Barrow fussed about her money. Lloyd George, then Chancellor of the Exchequer, was putting through measures designed to reduce the number of public houses. She worried that the long-term value of her lease would be eroded.

Seddon, an experienced insurance salesman, was an obvious choice as financial adviser. He expressed the view that she was not a 'good life' to insure but, conversely, would obtain a good annuity income. After some shilly-shallying, she made over the entire proceeds of her stock and lease to Seddon in return for a relatively generous annuity of £153 4s a year, which was paid regularly, in monthly instalments of gold sovereigns, for a short period until her death.

On 1 September 1911, towards the end of the 'Coronation Summer', a gloriously hot season, Miss Barrow fell ill. There was nothing particularly unusual about having abdominal pain, diarrhoea and vomiting that summer, long before the advent of refrigerators. People called this 'the English cholera'. Dr Henry Sworn, a local doctor, attributed the symptoms to gastroenteritis, although he noted on his first visit that she seemed 'very ill'. He prescribed a mixture of bismuth and morphia, but at first she did not respond. After he had changed the treatment to 'an effervescing mixture of citrate of potash and bicarbonate of soda', she appeared to improve. She was still weak, and Dr Sworn ordered her to take 'Valentine's meat juice', with 'some brandy', a curious remedy for an irritable bowel.[6] On 14 September 1911, the day after his last visit, Dr Sworn was surprised to learn from Seddon that Miss Barrow had died in the night. He duly certified her death as due to epidemic diarrhoea and exhaustion.

Seddon moved fast – too fast. He arranged a cut-price funeral for £4 (taking a backhander of 12s 6d for himself), and his late lodger was buried in a common grave. Miss Barrow's closest relatives, cousins named Vonderahe who also lived in Tollington Park, learnt about her death by chance. The cousins were dismayed to find that she had not been buried, as they would have wished, with proper ceremony in the family vault at Highgate cemetery. The cousins were even more disturbed to discover that she had made over her little fortune to Seddon in return for an annuity, which, of course, had ceased to be payable at her death. After a little while, Mr Frank Vonderahe decided to get in touch with Sir Charles Mathews, the DPP.

On 15 November 1911 Mr Vonderahe met Drs Spilsbury and Willcox by appointment at Finchley mortuary, where the exhumed body of Miss Barrow was identified. Spilsbury undertook the business of autopsy, with Willcox in attendance. No disease was found in any of the bodily organs that would account for death, except in the stomach and intestines. At post-mortem, both he and Willcox had been struck by the abnormally good state of preservation, a known characteristic of arsenical poisoning. Reddening in the gut was consistent with either gastroenteritis or an irritant poison. Further investigation was inevitable. At St Mary's, Willcox, assisted by Dr John Webster, an approved Home Office analyst, carried out 'one of the most exhaustive and intricate of scientific investigations hitherto carried out in crime detection'.[7] Their conclusion, which was reported to Sir Charles Mathews on 4 December 1911, was that death was due to arsenical poisoning, and, from analysis of the gut and liver, a toxic dose had been taken in the last two days of Eliza Barrow's life. Seddon was arrested that day.

The trial opened at the Old Bailey on 4 March 1912 before Mr Justice Bucknill, a judge with a reputation for mildness and lenient sentencing, in contrast to the severe and prosecution-minded Alverstone. The Attorney-General, Rufus Isaacs, was now free to follow custom and prosecute this poisoning case in person. Isaacs was a great advocate with a formidable intellect. Born in 1860, he was the son of a Jewish immigrant who had become a successful East End trader; his education at University College School had preceded further study in Brussels and Hanover. By 1904 he was a Liberal MP and, deftly surviving involvement in the 1913 Marconi scandal, he would become successively Lord Chief Justice and special envoy to the USA at a critical period of the First World War. In 1921 the greatest of glittering prizes came his way: ennobled as the Marquess of Reading, Isaacs became Viceroy of India.

The Attorney-General led Muir, S.A.T. Rowlatt (later to become a High Court judge who, in 1930, would try one of Spilsbury's most controversial cases) and the ubiquitous Travers Humphreys (see p. 18 above). For Seddon, the leading defence barrister was the legendary KC, Marshall Hall, popularly known as the 'Great Defender'. At the age of 53, Hall was handsome, comparatively youthful in appearance, and a well-built 6ft 3in tall. As with Spilsbury, such commanding physical attributes went a long way to achieving success in the courtroom. Yet Hall's character, 'childlike, uncontrolled, and mercurial', was a far remove from the popular conception of the lean, ascetic lawyer, coldly and dispassionately expounding his case. The son of a successful Brighton physician, Hall had absorbed some medical knowledge, which he used to great advantage in criminal trials. Something of a misfit at Rugby, where he was known to 'barter revolvers and guns and jewellery',[8] he scraped a pass degree at Cambridge, having taken a two-year sabbatical spent partly bumming round the Latin Quarter of Paris and partly in Australia.

His reputation was secured in 1894, when he defended the unpromising Marie Hermann, a skinny, miserable-looking prostitute aged 43, who had battered one of her few remaining clients over the head with a poker and stuffed his remains into a large trunk. The case is now chiefly memorable as an example of Hall's court histrionics. 'Remember,' he implored the jury, tears running down his face, 'that . . . even this woman was at one time a beautiful and innocent child.' Pointing to his client's shrivelled form, he added the deathless plea, 'Look at her, gentlemen of the jury. Look at her. God never gave her a chance. Won't you?', a finale accompanied by a torrent of applause from spectators in the public gallery, well used to such gushing performances in the theatres and music-halls. Against all the odds, he saved his unprepossessing client's life by securing a verdict of manslaughter.[9]

Time had moved on, and, in any case, tactics like this were not going to be much use in the case of Seddon, who was only too obviously a man of the world. Before the case began, Hall was deeply pessimistic about the outcome and, unusually for him, privately expressed a lack of belief in his client's innocence. That said, Marshall Hall was a fighter and, for all his faults, constituted far greater effective opposition to the Crown's case than anything that the ineffectual Tobin could have offered.

At the trial, Spilsbury played second fiddle to Willcox, who had the difficult task of justifying the new electrolytic 'Marsh-Berzelius' test for arsenic, a refined analytical process designed to obviate the risk of contamination so disastrously apparent fifty years before in the Smethurst fiasco.

Spilsbury entered the witness-box on Thursday 7 March 1912, on the third day of the trial.[10] His evidence was considered sufficiently important for the examination-in-chief to be conducted by the Attorney-General in person. Spilsbury recited his findings at post-mortem. His answers were concise and informed. He did not use twelve words where one would do and avoided equivocation, so often a feature of medical expert testimony. Spilsbury had been present during the complex testing regime carried out by Willcox at St Mary's. His simple précis of the findings provided a firm foundation for the complex detail that the jury would soon hear from Willcox about the methodology and results of the new electrolytic test. 'From what I saw of the results of these tests,' he told the jury, 'my opinion is that the death was the result of acute arsenical poisoning, as distinguished from poisoning by small doses of arsenic over a long period of time.' This opinion lay at the crux of the prosecution case. Spilsbury, in a simply constructed sentence, gave a damning illustration of the poisoner's *modus operandi*, a vision calculated to remain in the minds of the jury: 'I think that two or three doses of two grains upwards within a short period of time would be sufficient to kill an adult person.'

Spilsbury was initially cross-examined by one of Hall's two junior counsel, a Mr Dunstan. This could have been because his leader was in another court at the Old Bailey, perhaps making a short and lucrative plea in mitigation. Dunstan made little headway, and Spilsbury was able to lead the inexperienced defence counsel down a forensic blind alley:

COUNSEL. The reddening [of the gut] would be equally consistent with death from epidemic diarrhoea of ordinary duration?

SPILSBURY. Yes, it would.

COUNSEL. Would it be consistent with death from epidemic diarrhoea extending over some ten or twelve days?

SPILSBURY. Yes, it would.

COUNSEL. The absence of any disease in the other organs would be equally consistent with death from epidemic diarrhoea?

SPILSBURY. Certainly.

COUNSEL. . . . There is nothing inconsistent with Dr Sworn's death certificate in this case from what you saw at post-mortem?

SPILSBURY. That is so, with the one exception of the condition of the preservation of the body.

That last answer, resembling a neat drop-shot at Wimbledon, exemplified a style that would become typical of Spilsbury's performances in court and would prove to be a highly effective forensic technique. Dunstan, undaunted, put it to Spilsbury that 'Styrian peasants' were particularly fond of consuming arsenic, often dying of causes other than arsenical poisoning, but nonetheless leaving well-preserved bodies. Spilsbury smoothly agreed with these propositions, safe in the knowledge that Miss Barrow had no known connection with this obscure corner of the Austro-Hungarian Empire and that no colourfully dressed characters from Mitteleuropa would be called into the witness-box at Number One Court, Old Bailey, to describe their remarkable dietary regime.

Some ill-judged questioning followed about the symptoms of chronic arsenical poisoning. The judge invited Spilsbury to chronicle the last three terrible days of the dead woman, a grim vision of nausea, vomiting, severe pain, violent diarrhoea, great thirst and death, made all the more terrible by Spilsbury's calm, quiet, unemotional delivery. Rufus Isaacs capitalised on Dunstan's incautious questions about chronic poisoning by eliciting evidence of skin rashes, running eyes, thickening of the nails and skin on the soles of the feet and palms of the hands, fatty degeneration of the liver and hair loss – all symptoms typical of chronic poisoning, but none of which had been apparent during the course of Miss Barrow's illness. He ended by asking Spilsbury about his experience.

ATTORNEY-GENERAL. Have you had very much experience in post-mortem examinations?
SPILSBURY. I have.
ATTORNEY-GENERAL. And have you had post-mortem cases of acute arsenical poisoning before this?
SPILSBURY. Yes, I have.
ATTORNEY-GENERAL. And, of course, you are familiar with the works upon this?
SPILSBURY. Oh yes, of course.

Spilsbury was not asked to particularise his experience, which was in truth relatively brief. Throughout his career, Spilsbury seems to have got by largely without being required to produce statistics or detailed background evidence justifying his conclusions.

Marshall Hall, clearly alarmed at the clever way in which the Attorney-General was cementing the prosecution's case, intervened and was allowed a further cross-examination. Circumstances demanded the tactic of defence by confusion. He slyly put to Spilsbury that there was a distinction between chronic arsenical poisoning and chronic arsenical taking. Spilsbury agreed, accepting that small quantities of arsenic could be bought over the counter in proprietary medicines. This was a useful point, but, overall, Hall's cross-examination was not making headway. Desperation is reflected in this short, almost absurdist, exchange, arising from a suggestion that taking small quantities over a long period would not necessarily lead to chronic arsenical poisoning:

MARSHALL HALL. It would not develop any symptoms?
SPILSBURY. It might not develop any symptoms.
MARSHALL HALL. Not unless symptoms of poisoning developed?
SPILSBURY. That is so.

The Great Defender's fruitless attempt to rescue Dunston's feeble cross-examination ended in a typical Marshall Hall riff. Hall put, apparently without any authority, the 'scientific fact' that in the grave arsenic somehow gravitated to the left side of a body. This was obvious nonsense, and Spilsbury's laconic response, 'I was not aware of that', was a sufficient rebuttal.

With Willcox, Marshall Hall had some hope of making progress. The electrolytic test for arsenic, involving the production of hydrogen from platinum electrodes known to be absolutely free from any trace of arsenic, had been developed in 1908.

In Seddon's case – for the first time in a murder trial – Willcox sought to use this analytical process to show how much arsenic had been taken by Eliza Barrow. The process was complex, involving the passage of hundreds of different known quantities of pure arsenic through the apparatus, in each case obtaining a 'standard mirror', which could be compared with a 'mirror' obtained from the unknown extract in the particular organ tested.[11] The body and its constituent organs were carefully weighed and a calculation made of the amounts of arsenic. A potential weakness of the process was that it was sample-based, and the greatest accuracy could have been achieved only by complete destruction of the body, which was neither practicable nor ethically possible. Prudently, Willcox also used the more traditional Reinsch analysis, extracting nearly half a fatal dose of arsenic, 0.8 grains (the equivalent of 32.13mg), from the liver and gut. At the trial, Willcox, who had already had the ground laid for him by Spilsbury's positive evidence supporting his analysis, gave his opinion that Eliza could have taken as much as 5 grains within three days before her death, allowing for about 3 grains to have been eliminated in vomit and by other bodily functions.

Marshall Hall easily established that a minute error in the measurement of a mirror could make a great difference in the final calculation. He also showed that Eliza's body would have lost weight in the grave and that Willcox had not allowed for dehydration in his calculations. Most significantly of all, amounts of arsenic had been found in Eliza's hair that were consistent with chronic poisoning, rather than the administration of a few large doses shortly before death. Yet Marshall Hall made a classic mistake. He pushed his cross-examination too far, making repeated references to arsenic in the hair, which he regarded as a major prop for the defence case. Overnight, Willcox, with Webster's help, experimented with a strand of hair 'borrowed' from an in-patient. In court, Willcox conclusively showed that Eliza's hair had been contaminated by the bloodstained fluids in the coffin.

After this, the defence lost all momentum. Seddon made a poor showing in the witness-box. On the last night of Eliza Barrow's life, when she was dying in agony, he had called the doctor and sat outside her room, calmly smoking a pipe while reading a newspaper. His evidence showed him to be a cold, calculating and callous murderer. A fighting speech by Marshall Hall was to no avail. After an hour's retirement, the jury convicted Seddon of murder, acquitting his wife (although there is now good reason to think that she was his accomplice). Addressing the judge, Seddon indicated that they were both brother Freemasons. Bucknill was 'visibly affected', but had no choice but to pass sentence of death. 'Make your peace with the Great Architect of the Universe,' advised the judge in a tremulous voice.[12]

The case appeared to have some unsatisfactory features. The officer in charge, Chief Inspector Alfred Ward, a tough operator, used heavy-handed methods to extract information from Seddon's teenage daughter, Maggie. Seddon was never proved to have handled arsenic himself. Evidence that he had poisoned Eliza was wholly circumstantial, although the prosecution could show that Mrs Seddon and Maggie had bought fly papers (essential during that hot, fly-blown summer), which contained appreciable quantities of arsenic. By soaking the papers, it was possible to extract the poison with no great difficulty. On the totality of the evidence, the execution of Frederick Seddon at Pentonville prison, on 18 April 1912, cannot be regarded as a miscarriage of justice.

In 1912 Spilsbury, with his wife and young daughter, moved to 31 Marlborough Hill, a large semi-detached Victorian house of three storeys and a basement, in a quiet part of West Hampstead. He was elected President of the St Mary's Medical Society, which, with the Medico-Legal Society, took up much of what would otherwise have been leisure time. He equipped an upstairs room in his house as a laboratory. Even in their own home, Edith Spilsbury and her young daughter were seeing remarkably little of their workaholic husband and father.

Spilsbury was more at home in the conservative atmosphere of the medical school. Just as his own life was marked by paradox, so it was that St Mary's – at the cutting-edge of developments in medicine, surgery, toxicology, immunisation and pathology – was at the same time a vehicle of some deeply reactionary attitudes. In January 1910 Spilsbury had attended a lecture given by Almroth Wright at the hospital medical society entitled 'The Medical Aspects of Women's Suffrage'. Wright held the view that women were physically, biologically and intellectually unfit to be granted the vote. In 1913, provoking threats of violence from militant suffragists (including Ethel Smythe, who threatened to break his windows), Wright published *The Unexpurgated Case against Women's Suffrage*, a best-seller in its day, now regarded by feminists as exemplifying the basest of male chauvinism. 'Woman', he declared, 'belongs to the logical underworld.'[13]

Wright, who made it 'a principle never to write anything that won't give offence to somebody', often clashed with George Bernard Shaw, although their personal relationship was amicable. In his play *The Doctors' Dilemma*, Shaw based the principal character, Sir Colenso Ridgeon, on Almroth Wright, who, unamused by the compliment, walked out of the first night in 1906.

In 1909 Shaw had scandalised the Medico-Legal Society by his paper 'A Socialist Criticism of the Medical Profession', in which he called for 'democratic control' of health, arguing provocatively that doctors had become no more than tradesmen. 'I have always had the very best private medical attendance and advice,' said the windy gadfly, 'and the fact that I hardly ever took it has not created the slightest coolness between the profession and myself.' A socialist system of health provision would give doctors 'the responsible and dignified and independent position of the public servant instead of a private tradesman'.[14]

Such views were anathema to Spilsbury, who also opposed Lloyd George's National Insurance Act, with its additional tax burden, regarding it – correctly – as a step towards the socialised medicine he abhorred. Spilsbury endorsed Wright's views about women, at least to the extent of disliking the idea of female doctors, although he was always courteous, even charming, when encountering women in the course of his work.

Spilsbury vehemently opposed abortion. He maintained that 'the scientific facts could not be doubted' and that a human being was alive from the moment of conception. The fact of birth was a mere incident in life. In his view, 'the only sanction for destroying one life would be that it would endanger another or very seriously prejudice the health of the mother'.[15] From his early days as a pathologist, Spilsbury was zealous in compiling lists of suspected medical abortionists and, as will be seen, had no hesitation in informing the police about his suspicions.

In Spilsbury's opinion, male homosexual behaviour was 'unnatural vice',[16] a widespread view in his day, reflected in the severity of the criminal law, which prescribed a maximum sentence of life imprisonment for 'buggery' and two years, which could be served with hard labour, for those lesser sexual manifestations colourfully termed 'gross indecency'.

Sex raised its head at St Mary's Medical Society in October 1912, under Spilsbury's presidency. Dr Wilfred Harris, a fashionable physician and neurologist, with a larger-than-life personality, gave a talk on nervous diseases. Harris was a forceful man, who promoted a robust school of therapeutics. In his address to the medical society, Harris had no truck with fashionable ideas wafting across Europe from the effete consulting rooms and couches of Vienna. 'He protested against Froid's [*sic*] theories,' reported the *St Mary's Hospital Gazette*, 'and the class of men whom he designated as "prurient sexuo-psychologists", declaring that in all probability their views were evidence of some sexual kink possessed by themselves.'[17]

In July 1920 Spilsbury, now secretary of the Medico-Legal Society, contributed to a discussion on 'The Suicide Idea and Capital Punishment',[18] a rather confused debate on the merits of the death penalty, in which the speaker, Dr Josiah Oldfield, attempted to link a propensity to murder with a propensity to commit suicide. Among a welter of largely meaningless statistics, Oldfield claimed that suicide rates were highest for 'soldiers, doctors, chemists, and innkeepers'. Spilsbury, a doctor, was of course the son of a chemist and grandson of an innkeeper, although this modest family background was not revealed to the members of the Medico-Legal Society. Instead he hoped that Oldfield was not suggesting that doctors were 'more given' to suicide. He had no doubt that suicide figures were high because doctors had 'such ready means of procuring their own death'. As to the morality of capital punishment, Spilsbury was in no doubt that the death penalty should be retained. Citing the case of Seddon, 'a confident prosperous businessman, who . . . thought that he would escape the consequences' of his premeditated murder, Spilsbury stated: 'I quite fail to see that any other method of punishment could be adopted . . . in protecting the community against crimes of this kind.'[19]

FIVE

Brides in the Bath

Alan Spilsbury was born on 5 April 1913. Late in pregnancy, Edith Spilsbury developed appendicitis. Though an operation (risky at the time) was successful, damage had been caused to her unborn child, remembered as being 'always ill'.[1] The expectant father had been kept busy over the months since Seddon's conviction. Not long after Alan's birth, Spilsbury conducted a post-mortem on Julian Hall, airman and alcoholic, who had been shot dead in his Denman Street lodgings by his mistress, Jeannie Baxter.

The autopsy took place on 21 April, a leisurely six days after the shooting. 'Decomposition', reported Spilsbury, 'was just beginning.'[2] Death had been caused by a single bullet through the chest and, in Spilsbury's opinion, would have ensued within five minutes. Another bullet had injured the upper right arm, but would not have been fatal. Hall had been shot while in bed. Jeannie was charged with murder, and committal proceedings produced an early example of Spilsbury's love of advancing theories about the circumstances of a death, often way beyond conclusions justified by the evidence. 'I do not think, if the wound had been inflicted when [Hall] was standing up,' he stated, 'that he could have got into bed, turned towards the room, and pulled the clothes to his middle', nor, if he had shot himself, could he 'have got out of bed, put the revolver on the mantelpiece . . . got back into bed and pulled up the clothes'.[3] Jeannie's story was that Hall, already drunk that morning, started talking about suicide. He had pointed the revolver at his chest, daring her to pull the trigger. When she tried to wrest the gun from his hand there was a struggle, during which the gun went off twice with his finger round the trigger. She fired four more shots herself at the wall to empty the gun.

At the inquest, held three days after the post-mortem, both Spilsbury and Dr Edmunds, the police surgeon, gave their opinion, ominous for Jeannie, that the fatal wound could not have been self-inflicted. The DPP looked for further expert evidence and called in Robert Churchill, gunmaker, of Agar Street, just off the Strand. The case of Jeannie Baxter was the first of a long series of collaborations between Spilsbury and Churchill.[4] They made an odd couple. Spilsbury, tall, aloof, good-looking, cut an elegant courtroom figure. Churchill's appearance – short, squat, very broad-shouldered, and pug-faced – was in complete contrast. Yet, over the years, the pair would perform together like clockwork, a smooth double act. Churchill was the nephew of

E.J. Churchill, who had given evidence in the Moat Farm murder (see Chapter Two). Robert Churchill had developed a passion for guns from boyhood. And, on 17 November 1910, exactly a week before Crippen's execution, E.J. Churchill died. Robert inherited his business, then in a parlous state because of his uncle's business incapacity, and turned it into an internationally known concern.

In the Baxter case, Churchill and Spilsbury also conducted the first of their famous (or, possibly, infamous) experiments, meticulously set out by Spilsbury. The revolver had been fired at material like Hall's pyjama jacket, 'with pieces of leather behind to represent skin'.[5] The revolver was fired at point-black range; then 1 inch; 3 inches; 6 inches; 1 foot; 2 feet; and finally 3 feet away. Spilsbury, who seems to have fired the gun himself, noted that Hall was about his height. On that basis, a self-inflicted wound could not have been sustained more than 1 foot from the muzzle of the gun. The appearance of the exhibited material caused Spilsbury to estimate that the gun had been fired certainly more than 1 foot away and probably about 3 feet, 'and it may have been a little more'.[6] This was damning evidence, even though Spilsbury had to base his conclusion partly on Dr Edmund's description of the holes in the pyjama jacket, because – with a casual attitude unthinkable today – the police had allowed the dead man's pyjamas to be sent to the laundry before Spilsbury made his post-mortem examination.

At her trial, which began at the Old Bailey on 2 June 1913, Jeannie was defended by the old barnstormer Marshall Hall. Jeannie's looks, thought her counsel, might go a long way to gain an acquittal from an all-male jury, who might be persuaded to overlook the strong case for the prosecution, and acquit her of both murder and manslaughter. Marshall Hall seems to have followed the golden rule with expert witnesses when cross-examining Spilsbury and Churchill, preferring to rely on courtroom tactics, such as holding a gun to his own chest in a dramatic reconstruction of the shooting, suggesting that Julian Hall had said 'Here – come and shoot me' and that in the ensuing struggle the gun went off. The scene was set for a great Marshall Hall speech. 'By the fire of his rhetoric,' wrote his biographer, 'he threw a cloak of romance and drama around the sorry figure in the dock, convincing the jury that he believed passionately in every word he said.'[7] In truth, the florid style of Victorian forensic rhetoric, practised by the likes of Edward Clarke and Harry Poland, was beginning to seem a little dated, although Marshall Hall would enjoy later triumphs. Times were changing. The verdict was manslaughter, although the jury recommended mercy. Jeannie was not best pleased to receive three years' imprisonment, a sentence upheld on appeal. To compound her discomfiture, the High Court decided that she could not benefit from Hall's will, as she herself had 'feloniously' caused his death.

England declared war on Germany and the Austro-Hungarian Empire on 4 August 1914. Early in 1915 Spilsbury volunteered his services to the War

Office, but his offer was declined, although, at 37, he would have been young enough for military service. One reason for the official refusal may have been that his post-qualification clinical experience had been limited to examining dead bodies. A Home Office pathologist was no use in the killing fields of Flanders and France. Willcox, on the other hand, with his thriving practice as a physician and an outstanding record as an innovative toxicologist, was summoned by the Director-General of Army Services to help deal with the new phenomenon of gas warfare. Later, Willcox would be sent, as honorary Lieutenant-Colonel, to the eastern Mediterranean and on to Mesopotamia, performing valuable services in the investigation of the toxicology of warfare. Spilsbury remained in England for the duration of the war, during which his reputation blossomed, not least because because his senior colleague from St Mary's was now out of the country. Before Willcox left for Cairo in July 1915, they collaborated in one last murder trial, although this time Spilsbury took the star billing.[8]

Exactly one week before Christmas 1914 a 37-year-old woman was found dead in her bath at an address in Highgate – 14 Bismarck Road (unsurprisingly, the name was changed later in the war to 'Waterloo Road'). Late on the afternoon of the previous day, a Mr and Mrs Lloyd had called at the house, enquiring after a rented room. Mr Lloyd was particularly interested to know whether there was a bath at the premises. There was a bath. The couple took the second-floor room (with use of ground-floor sitting-room) and paid 7s for the first week's rent.

Mrs Lloyd felt unwell. Her husband took her to see Dr Bates, holding his evening surgery at 31 Archway Road, Highgate. She had a headache, a raised pulse of about 100 a minute and a temperature of about 100. She was prescribed a sedative, bromide salycilate and phenazone. Dr Bates thought that she might be coming down with influenza. The following evening, Louise Blatch, the landlady, was in her kitchen. Mrs Lloyd was having a bath upstairs. 'It was a sound of splashing,' Mrs Blatch recalled, 'then there was a noise as of someone putting wet hands or arms on the side of the bath and then a sigh.'[9] A few minutes later, she heard the harmonium playing in the ground-floor sitting-room. Mr Lloyd played a hymn, 'Nearer, my God, to Thee', for some ten n.'nutes before leaving the house, ostensibly to buy some tomatoes for Mrs Lloyd's supper. Shortly after his return, Mr Lloyd raised the alarm. Mrs Blatch, hurrying into the bathroom, found Mrs Lloyd's naked body, held up in the bath by her husband. Dr Bates and a policeman were quickly on the scene, but artificial respiration was in vain. Mrs Lloyd was dead.

Dr Bates conducted a brief post-mortem. Death was recorded as due to 'suffocation from drowning'. Dr Bates used the fashionable catch-all diagnosis 'syncope' to account for Mrs Lloyd's death. He noticed, as would Spilsbury at a second post-mortem, that there was some recent bruising on the outer side of the left elbow.[10] At the inquest, held on 1 January 1915 at Islington, Walter Schröder, an experienced coroner and active member of the Medico-Legal Society, had reservations about the circumstances of death. Schröder tried to persuade his jury to record an open verdict. Mr Lloyd, however, gave a convincing performance as a grieving husband and persuaded a sympathetic jury to record a verdict of accidental death. Before this, Mr Lloyd had already taken the first steps to obtain £700 from Mrs Lloyd's life assurance policy and further benefited from £19 in his wife's will.

Charles Burnham, of Aston Clinton, was a reader of the *News of the World*, a Sunday newspaper that, then as now, relished the reporting of sensational stories. Among the headlines on 3 January 1915 was a report headed FOUND DEAD IN BATH – BRIDE'S TRAGIC FATE ON DAY AFTER WEDDING. Mr Burnham contacted the police. On 19 January Detective-Inspector Neil of Scotland Yard initiated an investigation into Mr Lloyd's history. Watch was kept on the office of Lloyd's solicitor, instructed to proceed with the life assurance payout, and, on 1 February 1915, Lloyd was arrested as he called at the office. That night he was identified by Charles Burnham as George Joseph Smith, who had married Burnham's daughter, Alice, at Portsmouth on 4 November 1913. The couple had moved to Blackpool, where, among other financial manoeuvres, Smith had insured Alice's life. She drowned in her bath on 13 December 1913. Unlike Smith's other victims, she had been a nurse and was sexually experienced. She was also extremely short and fat. In fact, she was so fat and the bath so narrow that, as Spilsbury later stated, she could not have sat in the bath, as her behind would have become wedged about halfway down. When Dr George Billing saw her after the death, she was being held by Smith with her head near the bath taps, roughly in a sitting position, in a scene that appears to have resembled a tragic version of a Donald McGill cartoon. In Spilsbury's view, expressed some time later, she could not have got into that position by herself. No such questions arose at inquest, and the verdict was 'accidental death'. Smith had benefited by £140 cash and £506 from Alice's life assurance.

'Mrs Lloyd' turned out to be Margaret Lofty, whom he had married in Bath the day before he drowned his new bride. Further police enquiries revealed that a third woman had suffered a similar fate. Smith, as 'Henry Williams', had married Bessie Mundy, 33, in Weymouth on 26 August 1910. Her father, a former bank manager, was dead. Bessie owned substantial capital, £2,500, but it was tied up in a trust. Smith managed to persuade her trustees to release about £120 worth of retained income. Once it was paid over in gold, Smith immediately abandoned his new bride.

In Mozart's *Don Giovanni*, Donna Elvira falls not once, but twice, for the wicked seducer. Bessie Mundy did the same in real life. On 14 March 1912 she encountered Smith (Williams) on a promenade at low tide, looking over the vast expanse of mudflats stretching westwards from Weston-super-Mare. Despite sensible advice from a friend, Bessie stood by her man. Smith moved her well away from Somerset to the other side of the country and rented a house at Herne Bay in Kent. An experienced conman, he took counsel's opinion on how to get hold of Bessie's trust money. The formal written advice, dated 1 July 1912, of G.F. Spear, barrister-at-law, of 2 Paper Buildings, Inner Temple, has been aptly described as Bessie's death warrant. The advice was that the couple should execute mutual wills. If Bessie were to die before she had time to alter her will or before her trustees – by the terms of the settlement – had time to exercise their discretion to buy her an annuity (from which Smith, as her husband, would not benefit), then Smith would obtain the £2,500 for himself.

This was a window of opportunity not to be missed. Mutual wills were made within days of Smith receiving Spear's opinion. The local undertaker, by macabre coincidence, also sold bathroom fittings. Smith ordered a cheap, free-standing bath, without fitments or taps, which had to be filled laboriously by hand, taking an estimated 110 minutes. Smith persuaded Bessie to tell her doctor, a recently qualified GP with only two years' experience, that she had suffered two fits, although hitherto her general health had been excellent. On the morning of 13 July 1912 Bessie, probably persuaded by Smith to have a bath, carted innumerable cans upstairs, each full of hot water. At 8 a.m. Dr Frank French received a note from Smith. It read simply: 'Can you come at once? I am afraid my wife is dead.'[11] Dr French found Bessie lying with her head under water, her right hand clutching a piece of soap. Smith, in due course, obtained his inheritance.

Born in 1872, Smith was the son of an insurance salesman, a similar background to the grasping Frederick Seddon. He had numerous convictions for dishonesty. Bessie, Alice and Margaret were three of his seven wives, all bigamous except for the first. He had married Caroline Thornhill in 1898. She was not defrauded, but the marriage quickly broke up and she emigrated to Canada two years later. He did not defraud his second 'wife', Edith Pegler (married in 1908), but the third bride, a Miss Faulkner, defrauded of £300, was left standing in the National Gallery one day in 1909. Between marrying Alice Burnham and Margaret Lofty, Smith married Alice Reavil at Woolwich in September 1914, deserting her a week later, making off with £78 and a piano. He stole money from perhaps as many as twenty other women.

Smith was about 5ft 10in tall, a spare man weighing just under 11 stone, very muscular about the arms and chest. Spilsbury, interested in the 'criminal type', made famous by the early criminologist Cesare Lombroso, would later learn that Smith was regarded – in Lambrosian terms – as having a 'face rather well formed, the features being slightly Grecian. The skull . . . is oxycephalic . . . the situation of the ear may be regarded by physiognomists as rather low.'[12] Various attempts have been made to explain his power over women. Montague Shearman, junior counsel for Smith at his trial, found his client's eyes 'quite terrible . . . he had a horrible way of looking at one'.[13] Hypnotism has been suggested, but the true reason for his extraordinary appeal to women remains a mystery. Whether or not his features could truly be described as 'slightly Grecian', photographs of Smith suggest that he was unprepossessing in appearance. He rarely bathed. He has been accused of being a 'vulgar and all but illiterate ruffian'[14] and was evidently badly educated, frequently making spelling mistakes.

Al Capone, another monster, has been described as 'a man of taste and refinement . . . a great admirer of Shakespeare [who] thoroughly disapproves of the modern miss'.[15] So it was with George Joseph Smith, who also evidenced a great love of Shakespeare, as well as poetry and music. He played the piano quite well and was a reasonably good draughtsman. In 1911 he wrote a bizarre series of letters to the *Bath and Wilts Chronicle*, complaining about the low standard of modern education and the effect of 'objectionable literature' upon the young. 'In my opinion,' he wrote, without the slightest hint of irony, 'the problem of criminal reform is quite as important as the problem of unemployment'.[16]

Spilsbury conducted the three post-mortems in the reverse order of death. On 4 February 1915 he examined the remains of Margaret Lofty, the only one of the corpses to exhibit evidence of bruising. He travelled to Blackpool on 9 February, facing the disagreeable task of autopsy on the putrefied body of Alice Burnham. Smith, true to form, had arranged her burial as cheaply as possible. Amid the damp clay soil, the flimsy coffin had given at the joints. The coffin had tilted in the earth and, when lifted, a great deal of water poured out of the lower end. Soaked in water, the flesh had fallen away from the legs, leaving the bones exposed. Higher up the body, less affected by water, adipocere had formed, more or less preserving the ample proportions of Alice Burnham's trunk. Alice was estimated to have been just under 5ft tall, and the narrow bath, its base only 3ft 9in long, would have been short even for her.

Spilsbury, with a representative of the DPP, inspected the bath at 16 Regent Road, Blackpool. Alice, in Spilsbury's opinion, could have sat comfortably only at the top end, the opposite end to which she was being held by Smith when other people came into the room. In Spilsbury's view, she could not have got into that position by herself. Alice's heart showed some some slight thickening of the mitral valve, which suggests that she was already exhibiting signs of heart disease, though Spilsbury was to state firmly at Smith's trial that this factor would not have caused sudden collapse.

The remains of Bessie Mundy, exhumed at Herne Bay, were examined by Spilsbury on 19 February. Though her body had been buried some eighteen months before Alice Burnham, decomposition, though marked, had not advanced to quite so dramatic an extent. Spilsbury could not find evidence of bruising, but considered, bearing in mind the decomposed state of the body, that it would not have been possible to have detected such marks. Overall, his view was that there was no sign of disease sufficient to account for death in any of the three bodies. Analysis by Willcox and Webster had failed to detect drugs or poison. Case conferences took place between 26 January and 11 May 1915, the last attended by Archibald Bodkin, senior Treasury Counsel (and soon to become DPP), who was to lead for the Crown. Reviewing the evidence, Spilsbury and Willcox told Bodkin of their conclusions: death in each case was homicide. As to the method employed by Smith, which seems to have been the means used to kill the women, Willcox noted: 'We think "Right hand on head of woman. Left forearm of assailant beneath both knees. Left forearm of assailant suddenly raised while right hand is pressed down on head of woman. Then the trunk of the body slides down towards the foot end of the bath, the head being submerged in water."'[17]

Police seized the three baths. On 18 March 1915 Louise Blatch, the landlady of 14 Bismarck Road (the name not yet changed), wrote a despairing letter to Scotland Yard. The owners of the house had given her permission to do as she pleased with the bath. She was a seamstress, with a feeble 85-year-old father to support, and had taken the house to let to boarders, but since Smith's arrest 'people shunned the house'. Louise, who had hoped to 'get a little money' by selling the bath for public exhibition, was now wondering if she would be obliged to pay for 'the removal of the bath from place to place'. There is no record of a reply, and Louise did not get her bath back.[18]

Spilsbury gave evidence about the drowning theory at committal proceedings, held at Bow Street on 13 May 1915 (just two weeks before the birth of his third child, Peter Bernard). The courtroom scene was drawn by an artist for one newspaper.[19] Spilsbury's commanding figure was depicted on the left side of the drawing, and the representation of Willcox, lower down in the drawing, reflects his subordinate role in the proceedings.

George Joseph Smith began his trial at the Old Bailey on Tuesday 22 June 1915, a sweltering hot day. The case was tried by the white-bearded figure of Mr Justice Scrutton. Marshall Hall, leading a future High Court judge, Montague Shearman, appeared for Smith. During the trial, the three baths were produced as exhibits in court, solemnly lifted onto the large, light-oak, solicitors' table that stands in front of the judge's dais. There is a canard that the jury were taken to witness an experiment, in which a nurse – modestly clad in a bathing costume that covered all but the lower arms and legs – stepped into one of the baths, whereupon a police officer grasped her feet and pulled her under the water. The nurse immediately showed signs of distress and had to be revived by artificial respiration. The experiment did take place, but before the trial started. In 1853 Dr Alfred Swaine Taylor had stated that it was impossible to drown an adult without leaving bruises, an opinion still regarded as valid in 1915. With this in mind, Detective Inspector Neil carried out four experiments, but it was the first, in a filled bath, that nearly drowned the female volunteer, although she was a good swimmer, well used to having her head under water. Neil later wrote[20] that the experiments had taken place with the approval of Bodkin and the DPP, but did not state specifically whether Spilsbury was involved. In 1922, at a meeting of the Medico-Legal Society, it was stated that Spilsbury had been aware of the experiments but 'rather discouraged the conducting of them'.[21] In 1942, after Neil's death, Spilsbury gave his own brief account of the episode to the Medico-Legal Society that indicates some personal responsibility for the exercise. 'He [Neil] suggested that he should carry out the experiment,' he said, adding that 'she did not quite lose consciousness, but said . . . that she had a most horrible feeling . . . It was fortunate that the experiment did not prove fatal.'[22]

Smith was indicted for the 1912 murder of Bessie Mundy in 1912, but the decisive feature of the trial was the admission of evidence about the other two deaths. Smith might have been acquitted on the 1912 charge alone, but for a man to have three wives drown in similar circumstances was beyond coincidence. Marshall Hall nevertheless fought hard for Smith. He cross-examined Spilsbury at length,[23] raising the issues of epileptic fit in the case of Bessie and of fainting in respect of the other two victims. Hall exploited the fact that Bessie had been found clutching a piece of soap, a curious feature that was not satisfactorily explained by the prosecution.

> MARSHALL HALL. The clutching of the soap does lend some probability to the theory of epilepsy?
> SPILSBURY. It is not impossible; it is not very likely.

Hall had some mileage with the bruising. Spilsbury gave two very odd answers to defence counsel's probing questions:

> MARSHALL HALL. If you had to hold the head under the water, you would get marks on the head?
> SPILSBURY. Oh, no, not necessarily. Pressure would not produce marks.
> MARSHALL HALL. You really think it is impossible?
> SPILSBURY. Oh, I am sure it is.

Though Spilsbury later wrote that he had meant to say that such pressure would not necessarily produce bruises on the head, the transcript shows otherwise, an early example of a dogmatic style of delivery, calculated to impress the jury, and not always strictly accurate.

Spilsbury pointed out that the victim might not have been alarmed by Smith approaching the bath. A good illustration of Spilsbury's conservative, even prudish, character emerges from his contribution to the 1922 Medico-Legal Society discussion. 'It is difficult to understand', he told the meeting, 'how decent women . . . would allow even their husband to enter the room when in the bath.'[24] Spilsbury's evidence at the trial about the consequences of fit and/or fainting would probably not find favour with modern medical opinion:

MARSHALL HALL. . . . . even supposing you accept the theory that she [Alice Burnham] had a faint in the bath . . . in all probability she would have recovered consciousness at the moment of submersion?
SPILSBURY. Yes.

Despite Marshall Hall's best efforts, the case was hopeless once the jurymen knew about the other two deaths. Smith ranted and raved in court ('I'm not a murderer, though I may be a bit peculiar'),[25] but the jury was out for only twenty-two minutes. Smith was hanged at Maidstone Prison, at 8 a.m. on 13 August 1915, a gloriously sunny morning, by John Ellis and Tom Pierrepoint. He is said to have died 'a sincere and penitent Christian'.[26]

SIX

Night of the Gothas

Spilsbury's workload increased dramatically through 1916, partly because of his increasing fame and partly because other colleagues, not least William Willcox, were away from England engaged in war service. The following year, he became run down and developed an infection in one arm, caused by contact with a post-mortem subject, an occupational hazard for every pathologist.

Early in 1917 Spilsbury worked with Dr John Webster, Pathological Chemist at St Mary's Hospital, Paddington, in the analysis of four glass phials and a small green bottle. Two of the phials (corked and covered with gum paper and paraffin wax) and the bottle were found to contain 'Curari' (curare), about which little was known at the time, beyond its use 'as an arrow poison by the South American Indians', in Spilsbury's words. 'I do not know what would be a fatal dose in man,' he declared. 'No fatal cases of death [*sic*] from Curari poisoning have been recorded in scientific literature.' Although 'a very dangerous and subtle poison', curare was procurable 'from certain firms of wholesale druggists by recognized scientific men'.[1]

At the Old Bailey on 27 February 1917 four people stood in the dock on an indictment alleging that they 'conspired and agreed together to murder the Rt Hon David Lloyd George MP and the Rt Hon Arthur Henderson MP'. They were Alice and Hetty Wheeldon, who lived in Derby, and Alfred and Winnie Mason. Alfred Mason, a lecturer in pharmacy and dispenser at Harley University College, Southampton, had obtained the curare, which was to be used to kill Lloyd George, the Prime Minister, and his Labour Party supporter, Arthur Henderson, a future Foreign Secretary. The Wheeldons and the Masons were revolutionary pacifists, members of the 'Independent Workers of the World Movement', but, with members such as 'Comrade Bert', the group more closely resembled the Tooting Liberation Front than Lenin's Bolsheviks. Alice Wheeldon had a particularly fierce line in socialist rhetoric. She hoped that 'buggers' like Lloyd George and Henderson 'will soon be dead'. Alice also had her sights on the head of state. 'Another bugger that ought to be done is George at Buckingham Palace. He has always ponced on the people.'[2] Hetty, Alice's daughter, was acquitted of involvement in the plot, but died shortly after her release. The others were convicted. Alice was sentenced to ten years' penal servitude, Alfred Mason to seven years and Winnie Mason to five years.

That summer of 1917 Spilsbury's reputation was boosted by professional involvement in a melodrama very much the stuff of contemporary popular fiction, a story that could have been penned by such pulp writers as William Le Queux or 'Sapper'.[3] Lieutenant Douglas Malcolm, the hero of this bizarre episode in English criminal law, certainly shared Bulldog Drummond's murderous sense of honour. The victim was of an altogether different stamp.

Aged 32, Anton Baumberg, originally from Russia, was half-Jewish, and cut a handsome, dark, lazy-eyed, *émigré* figure. In 1917, while Malcolm was serving in France, Baumberg, calling himself the 'Count de Borch', began a passionate affair with Malcolm's wife, Dorothy. She called him 'Wolfheart'. He called her 'Squee'. Home on leave in July 1917 Lieutenant Malcolm, now smitten with a violent jealousy compounded by his *Boy's Own Paper* attitude to life, tracked the lovers to a country house in Hampshire. 'Has this man dishonoured my wife?', he shouted and then lay into Baumberg, who, offering no resistance, was severely beaten, punched and horsewhipped, suffering such a severe facial disfigurement that he was unable to return to London for several days.[4]

After making his exit, Douglas twice challenged his love rival to a duel in terms archaic even in 1917, threatening to 'hunt you out and give you such a thrashing that even your own mother will not know you'.[5] As John Buchan might have written in one of his 'shilling shockers', Malcolm had picked up Baumberg's *spoor* (track). Early on the morning of 14 August 1917, armed with a pistol and a hunting crop, Douglas set off from his house, 59 Cadogan Square. In retrospect, his scheme seems to have been a very unsporting way of tracking down his rival, using tactics far removed from the gentlemanly spirit of the Game Book. Pretending to be a detective, he secured entry to Baumberg's lodgings and, once in his room, shot his victim – who was wearing only a pyjama top. Police found Baumberg dead, lying diagonally across the bed. Baumberg's own gun was found in a half-open drawer, or so it was said afterwards. The press were soon on the trail. This was potentially a high-profile case and the DPP looked to Spilsbury for help. At post-mortem, Spilsbury found that five bullets had struck Baumberg in the chest and abdomen. He drew a neat diagram, which looked like a target in a rifle-range, showing the position of each bullet in the outline of a man's body. The DPP also brought in Robert Churchill, in a second collaboration with the Honorary Pathologist to the Home Office, as Spilsbury was now known.

The Malcolm case did not present any particular forensic problems, but it sheds much light on contemporary social and racial prejudices at the height of the First World War. There was an element of hysteria at large in the country. Three years into the war, with dreadful casualties, there was still no end in sight. The Passchendaele offensive had ground to a halt in a sea of mud. France was being bled white at Verdun. Although the USA had declared war on Germany in March 1917, that 'smartest nation in all creation'[6] was not yet making any significant contribution on the Western Front.

Malcolm's defence had a head start. Richard Muir – normally the iron man of prosecution (see pp. 24–5 above) – pulled his punches in this trial. Douglas was defended, with consummate skill, by Sir John Simon, not known as a great criminal advocate, but here a master of defence tactics, cleverly encapsulating the prevailing public contempt for the half-Jewish, Russian-born victim and his bogus title. 'I don't know whether he marked his pyjamas with a coronet,' he observed in a witty comment that provoked loud laughter in court.[7]

Spilsbury was now famous enough to merit a headline in *The Times*: DR SPILSBURY'S EVIDENCE.[8] The basis of that evidence was simple enough, since the very first shot would have been fatal. Later in the trial, when the judge, Mr Justice McCardie, asked whether there were any marks on the body, Muir replied, 'I am afraid that it is accepted on both sides that this was so.' However, when Spilsbury was recalled to deal with the point, he stated that he had found 'no marks' on the body, although it seems unlikely that all traces of the savage beating received by Baumberg a month before would have disappeared. Churchill helpfully agreed with a defence suggestion that Baumberg had the ability to have fired his pistol by a light touch on the outside of its suede leather holster, though there was no evidence that he had made any attempt to take the gun out of the bedside drawer.

Simon wisely advised his client not to submit himself to cross-examination. Seven years previously, Dr Crippen's own evidence had immeasurably strengthened the Crown's case against him. At the end of Simon's closing address for the defence, the public gallery burst into loud applause. The judge vainly counselled against lynch law, reminding the jury that a man was not entitled to murder his wife's lover, whether or not the latter was English, a blackmailer, a white-slave trafficker or a spy. As to whether Malcolm had honestly shot Baumberg to protect his own life, the matter was pure conjecture, as he had not given evidence. The jury, however, was in no mood for rational deliberation. Malcolm was acquitted of both murder and manslaughter. A woman shouted 'Oh! Thank God!' and the court erupted in cheering, which soon spread to the crowd in the street outside the Old Bailey.[9]

Later that year, under cover of darkness, relays of German Gotha bombers crossed the Channel from occupied Belgium. Between 11.30 p.m. and 3 a.m. on 1 November 1917, in seven groups of three aircraft each, the raiders bombed the centre of London indiscriminately, killing eight civilians and injuring twenty-one more. Anti-aircraft fire from the ground was ineffectual. The planes flew low and the roar of the Gotha engines could be plainly heard by those who had not taken shelter in cellars and underground railway stations.[10] In 1917, unlike in the Second World War, air-raid warnings were not made by sirens. Instead, a primitive warning system was employed. Cyclists would roam the streets, ringing handbells, each with a large placard tied in front bearing the words TAKE COVER. After the raid, the cyclists would return, minus their handbells, with placards reading ALL CLEAR.

In the years before the First World War, Soho, 'Fitzrovia' and adjacent areas had become home to a disparate immigrant community. There were large concentrations of expatriate French and Belgians in the Leicester Square area, and, north of Oxford Street, the population had more raffish elements. A few years later, the writer Patrick Hamilton would recall 'the criminal patches and Belgian penury of Charlotte and Whitfield Streets'.[11]

About 8.30 a.m. on 2 November 1917, after a night of heavy rain, Tom Henry, a male nurse by training, spotted a sodden brown paper parcel in the locked gardens of Regent Square, which was fenced in by metal railings. 'I jumps over,' said Tom, 'takes out my knife, and opens the parcel.'[12] The sheeting inside was quite dry. Investigating further, Tom thought that the parcel contained a sheep, but soon realised that it was 'the body of a woman between the chemise and the combinations', wearing rather smart lingerie, embroidered with lace and blue ribbon. Looking for the woman's head, Tom came across the legs, about a yard away, covered over by a kind of sheet in another parcel. The words BLADIE BELGIAM were scrawled on one of the parcels. There were other important clues among the body parts and wrappings found in Regent Square. One of the sheets had a laundry mark 'II H' stitched in red cotton, which was reproduced and printed in a number of newspapers. The proprietor of a laundry at 57 Charlotte Street recognised the mark and was able to tell police that the sheet had belonged to Mme Émilienne Gérard, a French citizen, who lived in two first-floor rooms, a bed-sitting room and kitchen, at 50 Munster Square. Enquiries of Mrs Rouse, the landlady of 50 Munster Square, revealed that Émilienne had introduced a Mr Louis Voisin of Charlotte Street as her 'brother-in-law' and that Louis had visited her rooms several times in 1916 while Émilienne was in France. Mme Gérard's husband, Paul, who had worked as a chef in a London hotel before the war, was fighting in France, although it subsequently emerged that they had been estranged for some time.

The police investigation was headed by Chief Inspector Fred Wensley, already a seasoned detective and soon to be a founding member of the Flying Squad, becoming one of the Yard's legendary 'Big Four' police chiefs.[13] When he retired, ten years later, journalists dubbed him 'The Most Famous Detective in England'. Although Wensley was nicknamed 'the Weasel', his face had a solemn aspect, causing one writer to compare him to a sorrowful elephant. He had made his reputation as a tough operator in Whitechapel, closely involved in the Houndsditch murders, the subsequent 'Sydney Street Siege' and the associated prosecution of Stinie Morrison for the murder of Leon Beron on Clapham Common. Wensley seems to have had an exceptional memory for detail, although he probably knew less about the ways of London's immigrants than he made out.[14]

Examination of Mme Gérard's rooms at 50 Munster Square revealed marks that appeared to be bloodstains in both rooms, as well as a jug containing a reddish liquid. There was also an IOU for £50 to Émilienne from Louis Voisin. The body parts found in Regent Square were originally examined at St Pancras mortuary by a police surgeon, Dr Gabe, who formed the view – almost a conventional finding in those days – that the dismemberment had been 'very skilfully' done.[15]

Spilsbury began his first post-mortem of Émilienne Gérard at 10.30 on the morning of 3 November 1917. His case card recorded the 'body of a mutilated woman. Head & hands missing, lower limbs amputated at knees . . . Head severed by clean cut across neck.' Émilienne, described as 'well-nourished', had a stomach containing 'a fairly large amount of food, partly digested, including red masses of meat'. Spilsbury's card included a summary of a statement taken by police from Georges Evrart, a Frenchman who had taken Émilienne to dinner at an Italian restaurant in Soho on the night of her death. Spilsbury recorded, in minute detail, that the deceased had 'soup, a small piece of veal, a vegetable, spinach or cauliflower, then half portion of macaroni'. More significantly, Spilsbury found 'numerous minute petechial [*sic*]' on the surface of the heart and noted that the vital organs were pale and bloodless, physical signs from which he would later form his idiosyncratic theory of how she had died. There was some recent bruising, notably on the left thigh and right leg, but Spilsbury had to end his note of this first post-mortem with an inconclusive and frustrating statement: 'No cause of death found so far.'[16]

Police called at 101 Charlotte Street on the evening of 3 November. The basement (a room and kitchen) and part of a stable at the rear of the property, accessed by a side entrance, were occupied by Louis Voisin, who worked as an itinerant slaughterman and ostler at Smithfield. Voisin was later described by his own defence counsel as 'a very ignorant, illiterate French butcher'. A short, thick-set man, with a moustache – Hercule Poirot with a squint – he was at home, sitting in the kitchen with a woman called Berthe Roche. Voisin admitted that he knew Émilienne. She had been his housekeeper at one time and had left for France on the afternoon of 31 October. He had the key of her rooms and had been asked to feed the cat. This story conflicted with information from Mrs Rouse, indicating that, when the air-raid handbells were ringing, she had heard her lodger go down the stairs and into the street. Mrs Rouse was about to take shelter herself in nearby Goodge Street tube station and thought that Mme Gérard had done the same.

Voisin and Berthe Roche were taken to Bow Street police station. Wensley, with the help of a French-speaking officer, invited Voisin, who was not completely illiterate, to write 'Bloody Belgium'. In response, Voisin wrote BLADIE BELGIAM three times, identical misspelling to that found on the brown paper parcel at Regent Square. Voisin and Roche were then both charged with murder. Roche shouted at Voisin, '*Salaud, salaud, tu m'as trompé!*' ('Bastard, bastard, you've deceived me!')[17]

Roche had lost her husband, Martin, on the Somme in November 1916. From around 1910 they had run the Hotel d'Hongrie at 36 Lisle Street, which housed a club popular with French expatriates. In August 1917 she sold the business and a month later moved in with Voisin.[18] Although police had arrested the pair at Charlotte Street, the basement and stable – inexplicably – were not searched until after they had been charged with murder. A key found on Voisin gained access to a cellar extending under Charlotte Street. Here, on the right side of the cellar, adjoining a muddle of wine bottles, crates and stone flasks, was a wooden barrel. In the barrel, lying on sawdust and covered in alum – a butcher's meat preservative – were the missing head and hands of Émilienne Gérard. There were also a number of blood-soaked items, including a towel, to which an ear-ring was attached, which was matched with one remaining on Émilienne's ear. Confronted with this evidence, Voisin changed his story, saying that he had found the head and hands on a visit to 50 Munster Square. He described the grim vision, in translation, as 'a terrible misfortune'. There was blood around, and the rest of the body was missing. In panic, he had not called the police, but rather tried to clean up the blood, later removing the head and hands to Charlotte Street. He had told Mrs Rouse that Émilienne would be away for a week and was expecting 'a sack of potatoes'.[19] These, he claimed, were delaying tactics while he tried to get in touch with Paul Gérard in France.

Spilsbury conducted a second autopsy on 6 November. Examination of the head showed evidence of at least eight blows. There were bruises on both sides of the face, a wound in front of the left ear, and a wound on the right cheek associated with a fracture of the orbit of the eye. Four deep wounds were apparent on the top and back of the head, together with bruising. The skull, however, was not fractured, and there was no injury to the brain. On his case card, Spilsbury endorsed his post-mortem findings: 'Death mainly syncopal but partial asphyxiation preceded or accompanied infliction of injuries. Blows by blunt instrument; at least 4 separate blows in head & 4 on face. Had survived injuries for [half] hour or longer. Body very blanched.'[20]

Spilsbury and Muir, the amateur detectives, visited the Munster Square and Charlotte Street properties. The relatively small amount of bloodstaining at Munster Square, coupled with greater bloodstaining and the other gruesome discoveries at Charlotte Street, convinced Spilsbury that the fatal assault had taken place in the kitchen of Voisin's basement.[21] There were bloodstains on the ceiling and on the back of a door leading out from the kitchen to a yard. Spilsbury took scrapings of blood, which were analysed at St Mary's Hospital. From 1908 it had been possible to distinguish between human and mammalian blood by the precipitin test, but, as will be seen, the science was still inexact, and many of the samples proved too small for definite analysis.

The trial of Voisin and Roche opened at the Old Bailey on 16 January 1918. Whatever the merits of the prosecution case, the trial was a travesty of justice. There was not much sympathy to spare for the French in the last year of a war that seemed to promise endless carnage and misery. Voisin was particularly unlucky in his judge, Charles Darling, whose little, shrunken figure contrasted unfavourably with his massive chair – virtually a throne – behind which was displayed, a shade ostentatiously, the great Sword of Justice. Darling's head, too large for his narrow, sloping shoulders, presented a gargoyle-like appearance, which, when he affected to smile, gave the irresistible impression of a grinning skull. A literary dilettante, Darling fancied his gifts as writer and poet, contributing to a host of long-forgotten periodicals and penning probably some of the worst verse to come out of the nineteenth century. Darling's elevation to the Bench in 1897 was rightly criticised in the press as a political appointment, arising from his close friendship with Halsbury, the Tory Lord Chancellor. *The Times* commented sourly that 'to speak of [Darling] as an eminent lawyer or even a distinguished advocate would be absurd'.[22] His unpleasant habit of making feeble witticisms in murder trials earned him a caricature by Max Beerbohm, depicting a set of bells sewn onto the judge's black cap. Darling did not relish jokes about himself, however, and once jailed an editor who had likened him to the music-hall clown 'Little Tich'.[23] With such a prosecution-minded judge and the appearance of Richard Muir for the Crown, Voisin's case was at a grave disadvantage from the start. His problems were compounded by his defence counsel, provided under the Poor Prisoners' Defence Act. Leonard Morgan May, for Voisin, was a very junior barrister and destined not to shine in his profession.

In preparing his opening speech, Muir had the advantage of conferences with Spilsbury. The two men had formed the view that Émilienne had been killed by a person of no great physical strength. Apart from an injury to the bony orbit of the eye, her skull had not been fractured, despite evidence of several blows to the head. Voisin was a powerfully built butcher, so the argument ran, and could have pole-axed her, or easily killed her with any one of the knives and hatchets on site at Charlotte Street. Spilsbury deduced from the presence in the heart of tiny clots of blood (petechiae), said to be indicative of 'partial strangulation', that the bloodstained towel, with an ear-ring attached, had been wrapped round Émilienne's head while she was being battered by Roche, in order to stifle her screams.[24] On this basis, although Voisin had not rained blows onto the victim, he was just as guilty of murder as was Roche. Although there was no evidence that the two women had ever met, Muir thought that Émilienne had gone to 101 Charlotte Street, threatening to tell the police 'something about Voisin's past' if he would not send Roche away. Roche lost her temper and attacked her rival. Voisin then applied the towel.

This was not how the prosecution's case was presented in court, however. Muir was in some difficulty with Roche. Voisin, although he made three differing statements denying any responsibility for the murder, maintained that Roche had not been involved in Émilienne's death. Roche, for her part, had said nothing. In the event, Muir relied on the finding of incriminating material at 101 Charlotte Street, Voisin's presence there and discrepancies between the statements to support his case against Voisin. It would be easier to convict the man than the woman.

At the Old Bailey, Spilsbury's evidence[25] was confined to descriptions of the bloodstaining at Munster Square and Charlotte Street and an account of the injuries sustained by the victim, including evidence about the petechiae on the heart. The towel theory was not aired before the jury. In respect of the bloodstaining, Spilsbury frequently stated that his samples gave 'the preliminary test' for human blood, although this test was not further described in the context of the precipitin test. Asked about spots of blood found on the oilcloth of a table at 50 Munster Square, Spilsbury said, 'the blood was mammalian blood resembling human blood', and he claimed that there was insufficient staining for the precipitin test. Voisin, of course, had access to animal blood, and the wording of Spilsbury's answers raises doubt as to whether what was found at Munster Square was human blood at all.

Although the kitchen door was set up in court for Spilsbury to point out areas of bloodstaining, Darling decided that the jury should see the basement at 101 Charlotte Street. It appears that the Munster Square rooms had been cleaned up by this time, so there was little point in the jury going there.

> JUDGE. Don't you say a word, Dr Spilsbury, d'you see? I want the jury to see the place. If they ask you to point out what you say is blood, just point out, but don't do more than that.

Later, however, the judge changed his instructions, insisting that 'no evidence will be given and no questions asked'. Accompanied by the High Sheriff of the City of London, the jury went to Charlotte Street 'in a conveyance', where, in dumbshow, Spilsbury pointed out where he thought the murder had occurred. Spilsbury's evidence about the petechiae may explain why his towel theory was not aired in court.

> MUIR. Did you find any indications on the heart of the cause of death?
> SPILSBURY. I found on the heart a number of tiny blood spots, or haemorrhages, such as are seen in cases of death from suffocation.

A later answer seems inconsistent with this opinion:

> MUIR. Had asphyxiation, in your opinion, anything to do with the cause of death?
> SPILSBURY. I do not think so.

Once the jury had returned to court after their visit to Charlotte Street, Spilsbury tightened up his approach to the bloodstaining in a good example of his style of 'positive evidence'. One typical exchange is in relation to Voisin's shirt, which appeared to have been washed (Roche had been seen washing clothing at the unusually early hour of 8.30 a.m. on 1 November). Muir's simple question was matched by an equally simple answer, which gave no indication of the quality of the sample, the quantity of blood available for testing or the nature of the test itself.

> MUIR. Did you test the blood?
> SPILSBURY. I did.
> MUIR. What was the nature of it?
> SPILSBURY. It was human blood.

Spilsbury also maintained that Émilienne had lived 'probably for some time, at least half an hour or it might have been longer', having been killed 'when lying on the ground', answers that have the appearance of pure conjecture.[26] There was no danger, however, that defence counsel would exploit these evidential shortcomings. Morgan May's first words in cross-examination showed Spilsbury that he had little to fear.

> MAY. Dr Spilsbury, you will be patient with me because I am rather out of my depth and am not an expert in these matters . . . ?

May tried to suggest that the blood in Charlotte Street could have been animal blood. He failed to take advantage of the opportunity afforded him by this answer, which made little sense and did not deal with the possibility of bloodstains caused by the dismemberment of an animal:

> SPILSBURY. The blood was so widely distributed on the ceiling, on the walls, and on the articles of furniture around, unless a man is covered with blood I should not expect to see any blood scattered around like that.

Counsel then made a serious error, preceded by a further pointless act of self-deprecation.

> MAY. With regard to your theory, I am very out of my depth, but there was a book called *Tidy on Legal Medicine*. Do you know that book?
> SPILSBURY. Yes.

May's next question enabled Spilsbury to execute another of his neat drop-shots:

> MAY. Is that a well-known book?
> SPILSBURY. It was.

The textbook quoted by May had been published in 1882 and was hopelessly out of date by 1918. Although Spilsbury was able to give only two instances of cases in which he had given evidence about the distinction between human and animal blood, all was lost.

After some perfunctory questioning by counsel for Roche, Muir, in a strong re-examination, elicited from Spilsbury that the precipitin test had been used in the Slough murder case, the Gorse Hall case, and the Stinie Morrison case. No one, not even Darling, who had tried Stinie Morrison, pointed out that Spilsbury had not given evidence in any of those trials.

At the end of the Crown's case Darling ruled that Roche should be tried separately as an accessory to murder, an odd decision in the light of Muir's and Spilsbury's theories and the evidence generally. He directed the jury to find her not guilty of murder. 'There is a good deal of evidence', he told the jury, 'that Voisin committed the murder, but which does not go in any way to show that Roche had anything whatever to do with the actual commission of the murder.' The decision effectively sealed Voisin's fate. He did not go into the witness-box, and his three, conflicting, statements were read to the jury, prompting some squabbling between defence counsel and the judge (who prided himself on his knowledge of French) about the translation, which May boldly described as 'vile'.[27]

In a short, deadly summing-up, Darling made much of the discrepancies between Voisin's statements and his failure, by not giving evidence, to account for the condition of his premises. Endorsing Spilsbury's evidence, Darling observed that it was 'the finding of human blood' that was the crucial point of the case. Voisin was convicted of murder. Ignoring the interpreter, Darling proceeded to pass sentence of death in French, during which Voisin turned deadly pale and clutched the brass rail of the dock before being led down to the cells.[28]

In March 1918 Roche was tried as an accessory to murder before another disagreeable judge, Horace Avory, who would preside in several of Spilsbury's later trials. Spilsbury performed a similar mime at Charlotte Street, where Roche had been on the fatal night. Convicted, she was sentenced to seven years' penal servitude.[29]

The Voisin and Roche cases present a number of curious features, unexplained at their perfunctory trials. Although it is possible that a person of Voisin's strength might not have fractured a skull in the course of a fatal assault, it seems unlikely, on the forensic evidence, that Voisin was the attacker. Edward Robey (son of George Robey, the music-hall comedian), later to be a Stipendiary Magistrate in London, sat through the trial as a youth of 17, heard Spilsbury's evidence and was 'stunned and horrified' by the death sentence.[30]

In the years after the trial, newspapers ran stories, based on a reading of Spilsbury's evidence, to the effect that whoever had killed Émilienne was a person of no great physical strength. 'Innocent Man Hanged' headlined the

Daily Express on 6 July 1923, while Sir Basil Thomson, a former head of the CID, writing in the *Cosmopolitan*, maintained that 'the important testimony in the case was given by the medical expert'.[31] The *Daily Express* had bolstered its argument by stating that Berthe Roche had 'gone mad' in prison and had died in 'St Joseph's Hospital, Highgate' on 22 March 1919. Spilsbury's earlier biographers claimed that 'her rapid descent into insanity suggests that she was always unbalanced . . . In her . . . there was a tigress',[32] and over the years this contention has found its way into innumerable accounts of the trial, most of which posit a manic attack by Roche on her love rival, Voisin desperately trying to smother the victim's screams with a towel. In fact, Berthe Roche developed cervical cancer, which proved terminal. Her release from prison was licensed in September 1919, and she died in St Joseph's Hospice, Hackney, on 22 December 1919. 'No mental cases taken' was the dry comment of Sir Ernley Blackwell, penned neatly in red ink on Voisin's Home Office file.[33]

There is no evidence to establish at what time Émilienne reached 101 Charlotte Street, although it seems that she was murdered there on the night of 31 October–1 November 1917. At the inquest, evidence was given that another man, a Belgian aged about 45, thin, pale, wearing a beard and moustache, was seen with Voisin and Roche at 101 Charlotte Street. He was said to have been their cook and seems to have had access to the premises. Another curious feature was revealed at the trial. Each morning Voisin went to clean out the stables and feed a large number of horses at Smithfield. On the morning of 1 November it appears that he had already fed the horses and cleaned the stables before 6.10 a.m., having crossed London from Charlotte Street in his pony and trap. Allowing for the time taken for the journey and the work, he must have left Charlotte Street around the time of the all-clear – if he had been at Charlotte Street all night – a fact that the Crown's evidence never fully established.

Morgan May, the inadequate defender, wrote to the Home Office giving his 'firm impression' that Voisin was trying to shield someone else. In prison, Voisin claimed that, 'owing to the immoral life of the murdered woman, a paramour was guilty of the crime'. At the trial, Muir claimed that 'there was no evidence that [Émilienne] was an immoral woman', but two letters were exhibited, one from Georges Evrart, her dinner companion on the night of her death, and another from a French soldier. Georges sent her 'a smacking kiss' and the soldier wrote of 'ardent kisses', with a use of the *tu* form suggesting that this friendship was more than platonic.[34]

Another unexplored dimension is the possibility that Émilienne was acting as a British government agent.[35] She was able to travel to France and back during the war without difficulty, and there were German spies among the London *émigré* communities of French and Belgian citizens who might have wanted to kill her.

At the Home Office yet another theory was canvassed. Legal Under-Secretary Blackwell thought that the dismemberment was done at 50 Munster Square, Voisin taking the body there on 2 November, and that, to avoid identification, he had removed the head and hands, taking them back to Charlotte Street. Bearing in mind that 50 Munster Square was in multi-occupation, this scenario seems unlikely. Darling may have been right to conclude that the bloodstains were camouflage and, indeed, the blood may not even have come from a human being. Voisin had butchered a calf at Surbiton on Saturday 2 November 1917 and could have used its blood to splash around the rooms.

According to Home Office information,[36] Voisin had been charged, with others, with the robbery and murder of a farmer at Angers in France during 1903, although there is no record of any trial. On 19 February 1918 Sir Edward Troup, Sir Ernley Blackwell's superior at the Home Office, minuted that, 'even if Roche were to admit that the murder was committed by her hands, I do not think that there can be any doubt that Voisin should be executed'.[37] His appeal was dismissed, and the death sentence was carried out at Pentonville on 2 March 1918. Voisin walked to his death with a stoical calm.

SEVEN

The Button and Badge Murder

On 12 February 1918 Spilsbury travelled to Woolwich Mortuary, at the request of the local coroner, to conduct a post-mortem on the body of Nellie Grace Trew, aged 16, who had worked as a clerk at Woolwich Arsenal. Within a few weeks Spilsbury would become involved in a terrible miscarriage of justice – one of the most blatant of the twentieth century – evidence of which has only recently come to light.[1]

Nellie Trew had lived with her parents at 5 Juno Terrace, Eltham, part of the 'Well Hall Estate'. Juno Terrace was one of a maze of streets lined by single-storey wooden houses – little more than huts – hastily erected at the beginning of the war to provide accommodation for munitions workers at nearby Woolwich Arsenal and at the Vickers Works at Erith. The areas of Woolwich, Plumstead and Erith buzzed with metalworking and engineering of all types, the huge workforce making a vital contribution to the war effort. The area was also crowded with servicemen. A large military hospital stood on the opposite side of Well Hall Road to Eltham Common and the northern fringes of the Well Hall Estate. In a wildly inappropriate gesture, some official mind had named the cheap-looking, regimented streets after the gods and goddesses of Greek and Roman mythology. Juno Terrace, at the east of the estate, adjoined Saturn Road. Mercury Road gave on to Mars Avenue, Venus Road and Hebe Terrace. There was even a 'Uranus Terrace' – though how the local residents managed to cope with its edgy pronunciation is not recorded. Running along the north side of the estate, separated from the Common by a barbed-wire fence, lay Jupiter Terrace, a double row of residential hutments. At no. 13, in the front row facing the street, lived a 21-year-old man, David Greenwood.[2]

The evening of Saturday 9 February 1918 was damp, windy and, towards midnight, very wet and stormy. Nellie, 'a virtuous and highly respectable girl',[3] was last seen by her father at about seven o'clock that night. Mr Trew worked as a principal overseer at Woolwich Arsenal and Nellie's mother had part-time employment as a relief hand at the Carlton Hotel, Eltham. Nellie set off from Juno Terrace on her way to change a library book at Plumstead Library, her usual practice on Saturday nights. If she had walked to Plumstead, the return journey would have taken about two hours, although using a tram would have halved her journey time. She may have visited some shops and, between

8.30 and 9 p.m., Nellie was seen at the library, where she borrowed _The Adventures of Herr Baby_, a sentimental Victorian book by 'Mrs Molesworth' and set in Germany, an odd book to select at that late stage in the war.

By midnight Nellie had not returned home. Mr Trew contacted the police, but it was not until first light that the tragedy was discovered.[4] Well Hall Road was a busy tram route, along which trams ran every three minutes until nearly midnight. At about 8.30 a.m. on Sunday 10 February Charles Hodder, a tram driver, spotted a crowd of men standing around an object on Eltham Common, open ground with no obstruction of view from Well Hall Road. Hodder got down from his tram and investigated. He found the body of a young girl lying near a pond, some 200 yards from the tram stop. Heedless of his passengers' inconvenience, he drove his tram directly to Shooters Hill police station.

PC Willshire went with Hodder to the scene. When the policeman arrived, he saw about eleven men standing about 14 feet away from the body, 'just gazing at it', and immediately ordered them off the Common. The girl lay on her back, the skirt and underskirt raised above the waist, legs wide apart with knees drawn up. A pair of elastic-supported woollen knickers appeared to have been pulled back up, perhaps by her assailant, or by some bystander out of a sense of decency. 'Her bloomers', said Willshire, 'was in the natural position.'[5] The girl's hat was still pinned to her hair. She was wearing gloves and, in her half-clenched left hand and under the glove, were five pennies, possibly change from a tram journey.

Between Well Hall Road and the body, over a distance of some 120 yards, lay a number of articles, including a threepenny piece, an apple, the library book and a hair slide. There was also a cheap reproduction metal badge of a tiger, later identified as the regimental badge of the Leicestershire Regiment. A little nearer the body lay a 'Dorothy' shoulder bag. The soft, muddy soil was noticeably disturbed. The victim had put up a brave fight and was probably dragged by her killer to her last resting-place. The girl's clothes were covered in mud, 'from head to toe'. By 9 a.m. Willshire had made arrangements for the body to be taken to Woolwich Mortuary. Neither the body nor the crime scene was photographed _in situ_, and the area was left completely unattended for an hour.

At the mortuary, Mr Trew identified the body as that of his daughter before Dr Edward Milton, a police surgeon, examined the body. Nellie had been raped and strangled. Rape is always a grave offence, but this assault was particularly savage and perverted, for Nellie had been doubly violated. Dr Milton took samples of semen from the vagina and from the outside of the knickers. The victim had been a virgin and there was evidence of bleeding. Whoever had raped her was likely to have got blood on his trousers. Bearing in mind the evidence of a struggle in that swampy part of the Common, her assailant's outer clothing was also likely to have been covered in mud.

At about 10 a.m. a second police constable, Thomas Fletcher, arrived at the Common. By this time there was yet another small band of morbidly curious onlookers, tramping over the scene of the crime. PC Fletcher started clearing people away, and, after a few moments, a man pointed out a black bone button, with a piece of spring steel wire through two holes, presumably for the purpose of fastening the button to an item of clothing. PC Fletcher did not ask the man his name, and the identity of the bystander remains unknown. The button lay between the shoulder bag and the body, about 75ft from the bag and about 100ft from the body, near some heaped mud and not in a direct line between the bag and the body. The ground about was rough, recalled Fletcher, adding that 'it looked as if there had been a struggle or something',[6] although members of the public had been milling about the area for probably the better part of an hour before the button was found.

The gravity of the crime caused the Coroner to write to the Home Office, asking for the services of a forensic expert. Dr Spilsbury was duly instructed, as it 'was so obviously necessary to have medical evidence of unquestioned authority'. At the inquest, the Coroner was so impressed by Spilsbury's 'precise, skilful, and exact . . . evidence' that he decided to request his assistance in any future important case that came before him.[7] Spilsbury's post-mortem report[8] broadly confirmed Dr Milton's findings. Nellie had been 'well-nourished' and strongly built. Her father would give evidence that she was keen on sport, playing basketball and hockey. Spilsbury noted bruises on the right forehead and cheek, the upper lip and the chin, caused by either blows from a fist or falls. Marks on either side of the neck suggested throttling with the fingers. Petechiae were present on the face, among other signs of strangulation.[9]

On Monday 11 February 1918 David Greenwood travelled to his work as a metal turner at Hewsons, a firm engaged in aeroplane construction, with premises at 6 Newman's Yard, Newman Street, just off Oxford Street. He had started this employment a week before, having previously been employed at the Vickers Works at Erith. Greenwood lived with his widowed mother, a sister and younger brother. Although he would protectively describe her as 'an invalid',[10] his mother seems to have been an alcoholic who, from time to time, took to prostitution to supplement the family's meagre income. Greenwood's sister, Jenny, worked in a tailor's sweatshop, earning a pittance and working long hours, from 8 a.m. to 7 p.m. on weekdays and 8 a.m. to midday on Saturdays. Sam Greenwood, his younger brother, aged 16, was also working at Hewsons.

On 17 August 1914, a few days after the First World War had begun, and apparently under age, David Greenwood had joined the Royal Army Medical Corps, enlisting at High Street, Lewisham. In February 1915 he was sent to France, serving with a field ambulance company until 11 October 1916, when he was attached to the 1st Leicestershire Regiment. During his service, he was buried alive by an exploding shell. At the end of October 1916 he developed influenza. He must have been very ill, as he was repatriated to England, spending over two months in hospital. In June 1917 he was sent back to hospital, the Royal Herbert in Woolwich, suffering from 'disordered action of the heart and neurasthenia'. He was discharged after three weeks, but readmitted to hospital on 14 August 1917. He was eventually discharged on 10 October 1917, the cause of disability being 'Fatigue and Exposure due to Active Service'. His character was assessed as 'Hardworking, intelligent, and honest. Trained in ambulance and first aid duties. An Electrical Engineer by trade.'[11]

On discharge, Greenwood went to a clothing store at Millbank, where he was given a cheap, dark-grey overcoat in return for a chit. In about December 1917 he bought a Leicestershire Regiment badge from Louis Carraloucas, who sold military items at Villiers Street, near the Strand. Carraloucas thought that his customer had paid 2*s* 6*d* [12.5p] for two collar badges, a type then discontinued but of which thousands had been made. Greenwood, who seems to have been a rather fastidious dresser, put the badge on his overcoat lapel. On that Monday morning in February one of his workmates noticed that he was not wearing the badge. Greenwood said that he had got rid of it over the weekend. On Thursday 14 February the *Daily Mirror* published photographs of the badge and the bone button. Prompted by suggestions by his workmates, he went voluntarily to Tottenham Court Road police station 'to clear the matter up'.[12]

Shown the newspaper photo, Greenwood said that it was his badge. He had sold it on a tram, the previous Saturday afternoon, to a man with a bowler hat, who spoke with a Dublin accent (although later he referred to the man as having 'a slight Belfast accent', but the difference does not seem material).[13] While being taken by taxi to Scotland Yard for further questioning, a detective noticed – at this rather late stage – that there were no buttons on the overcoat. Greenwood said that the last button had come off two weeks previously, later varying this to 'four or five' days. He had used the last buttons to 'pack' his lathe.[14] Police soon established that Greenwood had been seen wearing his overcoat fully buttoned up as late as Wednesday 13 February. There was thread around the bottom-but-one buttonhole and a tear, which suggested, according to the police theory, that this button had been torn off in a struggle and that, having seen the *Daily Mirror* photograph, he had removed all the other buttons from his overcoat. That this theory did not accord with evidence of his wearing the coat fully buttoned up earlier that week does not seem to have occurred to the police. Chief Inspector Francis Carlin, the officer in charge of the case (soon to be another of Scotland Yard's 'Big Four' police chiefs – see p. 54 above), later claimed that the button and wire found on Eltham Common fitted the coat buttonhole 'exactly', but there were in fact no holes right through the overcoat, which would have been necessary had the button been attached with wire.[15]

Greenwood made a written statement in which he described his movements on the day of the murder. The statement was broadly consistent with evidence given at the trial. He left work at 1 p.m., had lunch at Lyons Corner House at Charing Cross, then caught a train to Well Hall, had a haircut and went home by tram. Later, he went to Woolwich Public Baths (13 Jupiter Terrace did not have the luxury of a bathroom). He returned home, had tea, went out again, bought some overalls, returning home at about 7 p.m. At about 9.45 he went to the YMCA in Beresford Street, Woolwich, where a great many young men took supper. He correctly described the menu and recalled meeting a young man who had just left Vickers without working out his notice. He was not wearing his overcoat that evening. After making his statement, according to Chief Inspector Carlin and Divisional Inspector Brown, Greenwood said, 'If I say it is my button, what would it mean to me?' Carlin replied, 'I cannot tell you,' at which Greenwood is supposed to have said, 'Well, I won't say anything,' although he later denied saying this.[16]

Greenwood's trial at the Old Bailey for the rape and murder of Nellie Trew in what became known as 'The Button and Badge Murder' opened on 24 April 1918.

He was tried by Mr Justice Atkin, a great civil judge, whose judgments on the law of negligence and on civil liberty are regarded as outstanding. Of Welsh origin, he was devoted to Gray's Inn, his Inn of Court, and was a keen member of the Medico-Legal Society. Atkin would later be responsible for inviting Spilsbury to lecture practising barristers on issues of medical jurisprudence. The ability at an early stage to form a firm view about the merits of a case may be a virtue in civil proceedings, as in the heavy commercial cases in which Atkin specialised before his appointment to the High Court Bench in 1913. In capital cases, where a life could depend on findings of credibility, coming to conclusions about vital issues before hearing the whole of the evidence was to enter dangerous territory. Lord Denning recalled that Atkin 'was inclined to reach a conclusion early . . . if he was against you, you could never get him round', and Lord Dunedin found Atkin 'very obstinate if he has taken a view and quite unpersuadable'.[17] Although said to be 'a criminal judge of high reputation', he had, in fact, little experience in the criminal courts when in practice at the Bar. His conduct of the case and later decisions suggest that he had formed an adverse view of David Greenwood from an early stage in the trial.

Travers Humphreys led for the Crown. Henry Slesser appeared alone for the defence, which appears to have been conducted under the poor prisoners' regulations. Slesser, who would become Solicitor-General in Ramsay MacDonald's 1924 Labour government, was 35 in 1918, a relatively junior counsel, not yet a KC, and 'better known . . . as an authority on Trades Union law and the author of a standard but, for laymen, unintelligible book on the Nature of Being'.[18] His defence of Greenwood, whether or not hampered by lack of funds, was lacklustre and barely competent.

The evidence against David Greenwood was essentially circumstantial. Indeed, this case is regarded as a classic example of where the cumulative effect of various, often disparate, items of evidence was sufficient to bring home the charge without any direct evidence of involvement by the defendant. The trial, of course, took place long before the development of DNA analysis.

Both the medical experts who gave evidence at the trial, Drs Milton and Spilsbury, were witnesses for the prosecution.[19] Dr Milton recounted his preliminary examination of Nellie's body, committing himself to a finding (derived from the appearance of rigor mortis) that she had been dead 'about eight hours' when found on the Common. Such a claim would not be acceptable today. Modern science shows that rigor mortis can last for up to four days in some circumstances.[20] Even Spilsbury's looser contention that the condition 'normally . . . begins at four to six hours after death' is a doubtful proposition. The jury was not given full details of the appalling injuries, which probably mitigated, in some slight way, the anguish of Nellie's parents. A *Daily Mirror* photograph shows this decent, hardworking couple standing together, soberly dressed, the hurt plainly visible in their demeanour.

Spilsbury, who interested himself in the factual background of his cases, is likely to have known the circumstances of Greenwood's discharge from the army in late 1917. Although in many other instances – as will be seen – he was only too ready to give an opinion that strayed beyond the facts of a particular case, or even his own expertise, in this case he was pointedly unhelpful to the defence. Indeed, Spilsbury's answer is a sweeping generalisation, particularly so given the force with which Nellie had so obviously resisted her attacker.

SLESSER. Do you think it likely that a delicate man would be capable of committing these injuries . . . the general injuries on which you based the conclusion that there had been a violent struggle?

SPILSBURY. I think any person assaulting her might have produced the injuries I found.

This was a patently absurd answer, which Slesser should have explored, but failed to do so.

SLESSER. Taking the injuries as found, do they indicate a strong man or a delicate man?

SPILSBURY. I do not think necessarily a strong man by any means . . .

SLESSER. Take the case of a man who had frequently had fainting fits and who had been discharged from the army because of a disordered action of the heart and fainting fits, do you think it likely that that sort of man would overpower a girl of this type in that way?

SPILSBURY. I cannot say that he would not be able to do so, but at that time probably he would be unlikely to do so.

Spilsbury's sly use of the term 'at that time' robbed the defence point of much of its significance, since Greenwood had been discharged six months previously. The defence called no medical evidence about his present condition, although Greenwood complained of fainting and problems with heavy work, and described how his heart would still give trouble if he tried to run upstairs. The fact that he had spent two months in hospital with influenza, which could have adversely affected his health, also seems to have been overlooked by his legal representatives. Whether lack of defence funding precluded the cost of an up-to-date medical examination, or whether the omission was the result of incompetence, remains unknown.

The dramatic effect of Spilsbury's court appearances was aptly described by his later adversary, Dr Robert Brontë. 'A simple report of [Spilsbury's] attendance at a mortuary . . .', he said, 'is enough to condemn an accused . . . to death even before committal proceedings have begun.'[21] Although his evidence in the Greenwood case was in short compass, Spilsbury's very presence in court, giving his testimony on the side of the prosecution, was powerful ammunition for the Crown.

Evidence was given by John Gibson, the manager of Hewsons, that the wire found on the button corresponded with wire used in his workshop. One end of the wire had been sharpened on a grindstone, but this type of wire was widely used in munitions work. Gibson did not accept Greenwood's story of using the last two buttons as 'packing' for his lathe, as, in his opinion, the button would simply fracture and, in any case, it was unusual to require any packing. Asked about Greenwood's work, he replied, 'Yes, he is a turner. And a good turner too.'

In the witness-box, Greenwood emerged as a proud man, deeply ashamed of his poverty and anxious to put the best face on his mother's personal problems (she was, he said, 'very ill . . . an invalid . . . best part of the time . . . in bed'). He had a war pension of 19s 3d a week and had saved between £2 and £3 from Vickers. He had never liked the overcoat, perhaps because it had been given to him. The coat was 'a cheap thing', 'old-fashioned', and the buttons were not secure. When he went home on the afternoon of 9 February he had a grey jacket and waistcoat and blue serge trousers. At first he said that he could not remember where these items of clothing had been before he had started wearing them that day. Atkin's intervention revealed the truth.

JUDGE. What do you mean by saying that you do not remember? Were they pawned?

GREENWOOD. That is it.

JUDGE. You need not be ashamed of it.

To support his alibi, he called his mother, who, not surprisingly, was an unimpressive figure. Mrs Greenwood hobbled into the witness-box. She had probably injured herself when drunk, but claimed that she had 'been kicked by a man' when boarding a tramcar. She was followed by Greenwood's sister Jenny and younger brother Sam. Mrs Greenwood had originally said to the police that Greenwood had arrived home 'very soon' after 10 p.m., which was seized on by the Crown as a significant discrepancy. Sam said that he had been asleep when Greenwood returned, whereas Greenwood said that he had been awake. Both Mrs Greenwood and her daughter, however, had said that Greenwood was not wearing his overcoat that night. Evidence about the conversation in the YMCA at around 10 p.m. on the night of the murder was supported by 19-year-old Frank Hayward, whose statement was subsequently accepted by Home Office officials as probably true.

Atkin, who had clearly taken against Greenwood, directed the jury that they could convict on the circumstantial evidence. The jury, whose foreman was a Special Constable, was out for just under two and a half hours. Their verdict was guilty, but was accompanied by a strange rider, recommending the prisoner to mercy 'in view of his services to the country for three years in the War and his previous good character'. This suggests a disagreement in the jury room, with the doubters eventually satisfied by the recommendation, although the crime of which Greenwood had been convicted was revolting in the extreme. When the Clerk of Arraigns put the *allocutus* to Greenwood (asking if he had anything to say why the Court should not give him judgment of death, according to law), Greenwood, 'pale, but in a firm voice', made a remarkable declaration: 'I am not guilty of this crime. I know nothing about it. I have never seen or spoken to Nellie Trew. I wish your Lordship to take no notice of the recommendation as, rather than face the disgrace, I would pay the full penalty for this crime.'

The Court of Appeal (Lords Justices Darling, Avory and Shearman) declined to hear any appeal, refusing leave on 16 May 1918. In Darling's brutally simple words: 'Although the evidence was circumstantial, it was sufficient to justify the verdict.' Greenwood's fate would be decided at the Home Office. Sir Ernley Blackwell had been Legal Under-Secretary since 1913, responsible for drawing up written advice to the Home Secretary in capital cases, advice that was rarely disregarded. In effect, Blackwell held the power of life and death. A dour Scotsman from a middle-class background, he had thin features that 'were perfectly complemented by the delicate gold frames of his spectacles, behind which lay the cold gleam of his eyes'.[22] In 1916 Blackwell was intimately involved in the decision to execute Sir Roger Casement for treason, bearing prime responsibility for circulating copies of Casement's so-called 'Black Diaries', a stratagem that successfully countered the international campaign for reprieve.[23] Blackwell minuted, as he did so frequently in capital cases, that there were no grounds for interference with the death sentence. Sir Edward

Troup added that he felt 'no doubt' of the prisoner's guilt. Execution was fixed for 31 May 1918.[24]

Greenwood owed his life to a courageous decision by the Home Secretary, George Cave. Educated partly in France, Cave had taken first-class honours in law at Oxford and had pursued a successful, if unspectacular, career at the Bar and in politics. He had represented Kingston-on-Thames as Conservative MP since 1905, had been Solicitor-General, and, with his tall, moustachioed figure, was in every way an Establishment figure. Cave decided to advise a reprieve. It has long been assumed that the jury's recommendation had prompted this course, but the truth is quite different and King George V was not pleased by his Home Secretary's decision. On 30 May 1918 the King's Private Secretary, Lord Cromer, wrote a sloppily phrased letter from the Royal Train, somewhere in England. His Majesty had signed the conditional pardon, but 'wishes Sir George Cave to know that he has done so with great reluctance as HM considers that the opinion of the learned Judge in question should have been upheld [sic].' King George regarded the jury's recommendation to mercy with 'grave apprehensions, as likely to be made use of in future cases which may not improbably arise [sic] by reasons of crimes committed by persons who have served their country'. The great public interest in the case 'would seem to the King all the more reason for firm handling, as a detterent [sic] to any prospective malefactors'.[25] In reply, Cave minuted that, although he 'believed that Greenwood was properly convicted, he could not dismiss from his mind that [he] was a victim of a chain of coincidence and that the murder was committed by another person . . . even if there is a small element of doubt, it is safer not to carry out the irrevocable sentence of death'.[26]

There was wide public concern about the verdict. A well-prepared petition, signed by many local residents, was presented to the Home Office, supported by two MPs, Will Crooks and George Lansbury. More dubiously, Greenwood's cause was taken up by Horatio Bottomley's *John Bull*, much to Blackwell's irritation. In the event, nothing moved the Home Office, and Greenwood began his sentence of penal servitude for life, which meant, in practice, fifteen years' imprisonment in harsh working conditions.

On 2 November 1921 Dr Ernest Peachell, medical superintendent of the Dorset Mental Hospital (later Herrison Hospital) near Dorchester, wrote to the Home Office. Dr Peachell wrote of his 'strong suspicion' that a patient, Albert Lytton, was concerned in the murder of Nellie Trew.[27] Peachell, a contemporary of Spilsbury's at St Mary's, was a tall man whose broken nose reflected a sporting career that embraced rugby and cricket, in which he was said to be 'always cool and collected'.[28] He had been involved in mental health administration since 1905.

Albert Lytton, born on 5 March 1898, had been employed at the Vickers Works, Erith, as an engineer pupil apprentice, between 1916 and 1918.[29] He had already manifested some strange behaviour patterns, but, on 3 April 1918, he 'quite suddenly . . . became garrulous, rushing frantically from room to room – appeared exceedingly worried about some matter, the nature of which . . . he must on no account reveal'. Three days later he was certified insane and was committed to Digby's Asylum in Devon, from which he was discharged briefly in September. After ten days his condition deteriorated again, and he was sent to the Dorset hospital. In March 1919 Dr Peachell put Lytton under the care of a Miss Marguerite Sinclair Kent, a qualified mental nurse, who claimed to have studied psychoanalysis. Peachell did not hold out much hope that Lytton would ever recover from his mental illness, but could see no harm in Miss Kent spending time with his patient.

Miss Kent ultimately wrote two very lengthy reports on Lytton, who, she discovered, had been abused by the headmaster of his boarding school, 'one of a harem of boys'. His sexual history involved a relationship with a much older woman and an Oedipal desire to have sex with his mother. Miss Kent observed that Lytton seemed 'to be attempting to strangle someone with his hands . . . while he pointed distractedly to the region of his generative organs and was . . . terribly distressed'. In November 1920, after attending church, Lytton burst into tears and spoke of 'some terrible thing'. Recalling that Lytton's first breakdown was in April 1918, Miss Kent – like Spilsbury, an amateur detective – trawled through newspaper files around that date, where she found details of the Eltham Common crime.

Not only was Lytton living in Erith at the time of the murder, but he was in the habit of visiting Woolwich in the evenings when he was not working on the night shift at Vickers. A jacket and a pair of stained trousers had been left behind at Lytton's home. The trousers appeared to have been washed and the top button on the trouser fly replaced. Lytton also had an overcoat, but it had been 'given away' by his mother to a tramp. When Miss Kent and Lytton's brother (who worked at the Marconi Station near Dorchester) visited him at Herrison on 25 October 1921, he volunteered the expression, 'I suppose you have cleared up this matter.' Asked what matter, he replied: 'Why, about Nellie Trew and me.' He said that he had 'walked over' Eltham Common with her and 'then we had a cuddle . . . We never knew when we might have to join up and so we got all the love we could . . . I don't remember what happened then, excepting that she screamed . . . the next thing I remember was that there was some blood on my hand . . . [and] on my trousers.' He had washed the trousers, because there was blood and mud on them. The incident happened 'on a Saturday night . . . it was generally a Saturday night that I went to Woolwich'.

At Herrison, Lytton wrote out a short statement: 'I have this afternoon confessed to Miss Kent and my brother Tom that I accidentally [*sic*] murdered Nellie Trew on Eltham Common on Saturday evening in February 1918.' Lytton added that she was wearing 'a white fur', which was wrong, but said that he was with her at 'about quarter to ten', which is consistent with the evidence. The reference to a white fur was made at the end of his interview and may, in the light of his later response to police enquiries, have been a calculated afterthought.

The Home Office initially appeared to take the matter seriously, and the wording of Blackwell's minute is highly significant. 'Lytton was not at work on Saturday 9 February or Sunday 10 February. He was living at Erith . . . and it is *possible* that he may have been in Plumstead or Woolwich . . . and that he followed or accompanied Nellie Trew out to Eltham Common and killed her there.' Blackwell decided that the Home Office 'must have the clothing examined by an expert . . . the assailant would have got blood about his fly-opening'. The police were asked to investigate.[30] Unfortunately for Greenwood, the investigating officer was Chief Inspector Brown, one of the team who had convicted him. Miss Kent, for her part, had a garrulous, even neurotic, personality, although her credibility was never challenged. In his report, Brown questioned her role as amateur detective, noting that she had shown Lytton newspaper accounts of the murder. In effect, Brown accused her of pressuring Lytton to confess. He dismissed the significance of the state of the clothing. He failed to see 'with the naked eye' marks that Miss Kent thought were blood on the trousers. Dr Peachell told Brown that 'microscopical examination would be necessary' to establish bloodstaining, but thought that there was semen on the trousers. This was also dismissed by Brown, on the curious ground that Lytton was 'a moral pervert'.

Brown spoke to Lytton, in the presence of Dr Peachell. Lytton, he reported, 'never remembers making the confession . . . and all that he knew of the murder was what he had been told by Miss Kent and shown by her in the newspapers'. Brown ignored one significant remark made by Lytton during the interview. Lytton said that he had heard about the murder some six weeks after it had happened (that is, at about the time of his first breakdown in April 1918) from Nellie's cousin, 'Frank', who 'worked at Vickers'. Bearing in mind that Vickers employed hundreds of men during the war, this was a remarkable coincidence, but it seems that the police made no attempt to trace 'Frank', or to speak to Lytton's mother, or even his brother, who was living near Herrison at the time of Brown's investigation.

The compelling evidence of Lytton's involvement was effectively rubbished. 'There are no real grounds', Brown wrote blithely, 'to suspect that Lytton was in any way connected with the murder.' A few statements had been taken by the police in their perfunctory enquiry. Mrs Ethel Ewins, of 62 Bexley Road, Erith, remembered that Lytton, her sometime lodger, was 'very excitable' and 'somewhat peculiar in manner', which was also the view of his manager at Vickers, William Hay. One statement, however, was potentially of great significance. Mrs Mary Hampton, of The Homestead, Lesney Park Road, Erith, recalled that Lytton had lodged with her in February 1918. Although she could not remember anything out of the ordinary around the time of the murder (she was being asked about matters occurring three years before), Mrs Hampton remembered that he was 'partial to the opposite sex' and had 'behaved improperly' with her daughter, calling her into his bedroom and pulling her down onto the bed. In a police report, Inspector Albert Grosse – an incompetent detective, whose sloppy investigation of the 1923 Savoy Hotel shooting helped Madame Fahmy secure a wrongful acquittal for the murder of her millionaire husband[31] – claimed that Mrs Hampton had considered this was 'just a fit of passion on the part of the youth', but Grosse's interpretation does not accord with the description given of the incident in Mrs Hampton's statement.

During this period, Blackwell was concerned that Miss Kent had been in touch with *John Bull*, but, in fact, she played by the rules of medical confidentiality. *John Bull* never ran the story. The public knew nothing about Albert Lytton. Hospital records show that he was diagnosed with *dementia praecox*, had hallucinations of sight and hearing, and was 'occasionally violent without provocation'. He was 5ft 9in tall, and, on admission to Herrison, his build was noted as being 'lean and spare'.[32] A senior attendant at Herrison reported that he was 'at times the most violent, the worst patient ever', using threatening behaviour 'of an exceedingly homicidal nature'.[33] Lytton was transferred to the Exe Vale Hospital in 1931, returning to Herrison in 1941, where he died on 6 February 1951.[34]

The Greenwood case could have been referred to the Court of Appeal for reconsideration under section 19(b) of the Criminal Appeal Act 1907. Blackwell sent the papers to Atkin at his private address, 65 Ashley Gardens, Victoria. Atkin, his mind made up long before, seems to have placed too much reliance on the police report. In a short letter to Blackwell dated 9 December 1922 Atkin destroyed any hope of Greenwood's release, writing that it was 'unnecessary to take any further steps'.[35]

In 1924 Dr Margaret Lucy Tyler, who practised from 23 Welbeck Street and was an early promoter of homeopathy, started another, wholly unconnected, campaign for Greenwood's release. This time the attempt was supported by *John Bull*, Blackwell's *bête noire*, but unwittingly based on a bogus confession by an inmate at Parkhurst. Despite the lack of merit in Tyler's repeated submissions to the Home Office, the unsatisfactory background to the Greenwood case attracted the attention of several public figures, including Nancy, Lady Astor, and the crime novelist Edgar Wallace. Blackwell robustly dismissed an article by Wallace in *John Bull* as 'silly . . . as one might expect from the author of *Again the Ringer*'.

In 1927 George Cave, now retired, approached the then Home Secretary, Joynson-Hicks, suggesting a review of the case. Blackwell seems to have kept Cave completely in the dark about the Lytton affair, and his minute regarding Cave's enquiry reveals the depths of a thoroughly cynical approach to his duties as Legal Under-Secretary at the Home Office. There was, he wrote, 'an alleged confession by a semi-lunatic [*sic*] named Lytton . . . we were able to dispose of the alleged confession without reference to the Court of Appeal'.[36] Blackwell was easily able to satisfy Cave that the Parkhurst confession was false. Cave's letter to Joynson-Hicks, dated 11 April 1927, gives a hint of his past reservations about the conviction:

> My Dear Home Secretary
> David Greenwood – so be it. I am sure you have given the fullest consideration to the case . . .[37]

Cave died in 1928, and David Greenwood was released from prison, on licence, on 3 April 1933, having served a fifteen-year sentence for a crime he did not commit. The *Daily Express* noted his 'quiet cultured voice' and reported that he had spent his first day of freedom at the bedside of a sick niece. 'I bear no ill-will to anybody,' he said, describing his imprisonment as 'a dreary nightmare'.[38] In 1929 the *Manchester Guardian* had made a simple, but devastating, point in Greenwood's favour. 'Had a woman been on the jury, she would probably have wanted to know how it was possible for a man whose clothes were covered in mud and blood, not only to wash off the stains, but to dry the cloth again . . . between committing the murder and appearing in the YMCA.'[39]

Preserved in the archives of the Royal London Hospital are two slides made by Spilsbury at St Mary's in respect of the Eltham Common murder, marked 'Pants XIV' and 'Pants XV', and containing samples of semen. These slides may one day reveal the identity of Nellie Trew's murderer. On the evidence as it stands today, there is ample material to justify the posthumous grant of a pardon to the gentle, sad figure of David Greenwood.

EIGHT

Mid-Life Crisis

Early in 1919 Spilsbury gave evidence in another society shooting, with a resemblance to the case of Lieutenant Malcolm (see Chapter Six).[1] Lieutenant-Colonel Norman Cecil Rutherford was a medical doctor and married man with six children. His former pupil at medical school, Miles Seton, then aged 44 and still unmarried, was a frequent visitor to the Rutherford's large house, Carshalton Place, in Surrey, and was godfather to one of the Rutherford children. Rutherford had ill-treated his wife over the years and, although Seton was probably no more to the poor woman than a sympathetic ear, Rutherford made up his mind that they were having an affair. On 13 January 1919 Rutherford, having discovered that Seton was staying with his cousin, Sir Malcolm Seton, at 13 Clarendon Road, Holland Park, left Carshalton armed with a Webley revolver and made his way to the Seton home. There he shot Miles Seton, who fell dying, still in his khaki uniform, near the dining-room door. Rutherford made no attempt to escape and awaited the arrival of the police.

Four days later, Spilsbury conducted a post-mortem on Seton's body, marked by fourteen bullet wounds. Death was, in his opinion, due to that enduringly popular cause, 'syncope', following haemorrhage due to a bullet wound to the heart, the track of which, Spilsbury determined, was 'practically horizontal'.[2] On 18 January, accompanied by Sergeant Hambrook (with whom he was to work again on a major murder enquiry, the Sydney Fox case, eleven years later – see Chapter Fifteen), he examined the dining-room at 13 Clarendon Road. Robert Churchill was soon brought into the frame, and joint detective work resulted in a finding that Seton had been shot from the far side of the dining-room table, directly opposite his assailant, when Seton was facing the door. Rutherford had 'moved to the left, slightly forwards, as he fired',[3] a remarkably detailed conclusion on the available evidence.

Rutherford was tried for the murder of Miles Seton at the Old Bailey in April 1918. There was a temptation for the defence to follow the case of Lieutenant Malcolm, plead the 'Unwritten Law' and hope to sway the jury by emotion. After a lengthy series of consultations in chambers, involving consideration of Rutherford's mental history and current state, the defence team persuaded Rutherford – a desperately difficult client – that to plead insanity was the only way to save his neck. Rutherford was skilfully defended by Rigby Swift KC, who called witnesses to show that there was a family history of insanity.[4] Fellow army officers recalled extraordinary outbursts of temper on the Western Front, and his batman helpfully informed the jury that a horse had once fallen on Rutherford's head. Cogent testimony from 'alienists' (as psychiatrists were then called) helped persuade the jury to return a verdict of 'guilty but insane'. Rutherford was sent to Broadmoor, being released after several years as an in-patient.

Richard ('Dick') Spilsbury, the last of Spilsbury's children, was born on 24 August 1919. During that year Spilsbury's life started to show the first signs of what would now be called a 'mid-life crisis', which would have a dramatic effect on both his marriage and his professional career. All was not well at St Mary's in the pathology department. Dr Kettle, an additional pathologist, and Miss Fox, an assistant pathologist, were appointed. What Spilsbury – who was strongly opposed to the whole idea of women doctors – made of Miss Fox's appointment is not known, but 1919 certainly brought him into sharp conflict with the eminent physician Dr Wilfred Harris, one of the hospital's most senior figures, whose abrasive personality has already been noted. Harris appears to have ordered Spilsbury to conduct a particular form of investigation during a post-mortem held on one of his patients. Spilsbury, angered by being treated as a subordinate, refused to obey, and a major row broke out in which hospital opinion became bitterly divided.[5]

Spilsbury and Kettle wrote letters of resignation, which were put before the hospital's Board of Management on 22 May 1919. The Board, underestimating Spilsbury's temperament and resolve, vainly hoped that 'a little friendly discussion will smooth difficulties'. Spilsbury and Kettle responded, in letters dated 5 June, that they would 'defer action on resignation' until the Board had decided, in effect, to establish a code of conduct and responsibility in relation to consultants' requests for post-mortems. The Board met on 9 October 1919. Harris and Spilsbury seem to have been present for part of the meeting, at which new guidelines for the pathology department were proposed. These read:

1. The essential objects of post-mortem examinations at St Mary's are (1) to ascertain the morbid conditions present and the cause of death; (2) to demonstrate these to all who may be present; (3) to encourage the use of the post-mortem room for the teaching of pathology.
2. The making of any special investigation desired by a member of the staff must depend upon collaboration – and collaboration only – between the member of staff and the pathologist.

Spilsbury, it appears, was happy with the ruling, but Harris actively dissented, and his was a very powerful voice in hospital politics. In Wilfred Harris, Spilsbury had taken on a dangerous adversary. A very senior figure, taking an active part in the life of St Mary's, he was a home-grown hero, considerably more popular than Spilsbury, whose reputation had been earned largely in the law courts, well away from day-to-day life in the hospital. Although the Board's ruling went in his favour, Spilsbury seems to have decided that he could no longer work with Harris and successfully applied for the appointment of lecturer in morbid anatomy, the first ever appointed, at St Bartholomew's Hospital.

On 20 November 1919 the Board accepted Spilsbury's resignation, and, in a resolution moved by William Willcox, his old mentor now back from the war, the Board expressed its 'high appreciation' of Spilsbury's work at St Mary's. The spat at St Mary's and the flight to Bart's accompanied developments in Spilsbury's private life. Among other medical staff at Bart's he worked with Professor Francis Bainbridge FRS, a distinguished researcher in physiology. Bainbridge, a slightly built man in poor health, had married Hilda Smith in 1905. They had a daughter, Joan, born in 1908. After moving to Bart's, Spilsbury met Hilda Bainbridge, forging an association that would ripen as time went by and that was to have profound consequences for both of them.

Although Spilsbury put it about that he disliked being photographed, he allowed press photographers to snap him at Bart's, white-coated, keen-eyed, clean-jawed, sitting at a bench in his lab. Directly in front of him, a microscope and box of slides indicated the vital importance of his work as Honorary Pathologist to the Home Office. Bottles of all shapes and sizes stood on the lab shelves, evidence of the scientific mysteries practised by the great pathologist.

Francis Bainbridge died suddenly of 'heart failure following lung trouble'[6] on 27 October 1921. His widow, Hilda, now a widow with a young daughter to support, applied for a job at Bart's and was sent to the pathology museum. Spilsbury soon had Hilda working as his secretary, taking down post-mortem reports at his dictation, and she was eventually allowed to attend autopsies herself. An intelligent woman, she was unfazed by the blood and smell of the post-mortem room. With her background and Spilsbury's looks, the pathologist and his assistant came to resemble the fictional Harriet Vane and Lord Peter Wimsey, central characters in Dorothy L. Sayer's snobbish crime novels of the period. Their association may have become more than a merely professional relationship. That year Spilsbury began renting a top-floor flat at 1 Verulam Buildings, 3rd Floor South, Gray's Inn, in which he fitted out yet another laboratory. Hilda Bainbridge lived at 21 Chenies Street Chambers, St Pancras, a short walk away from Gray's Inn, where her visits would not attract particular attention.

Spilsbury's family remained at Marlborough Hill. Edith Spilsbury seems to have been rather a distant figure, and the children (Evelyn, Alan, Peter and Dick) were cared for in a large basement nursery by their devoted nanny, Emily Elvy ('Nan'). Nan Elvy perhaps gave the children the love and support they should have had from their parents. Years later Evelyn would pay tribute to her 'loved and loving nan'. From the early 1920s Spilsbury's visits to the family home became progessively rare, and he returned to Marlborough Hill only for Sunday lunch. He did not particularly relish the company of young children and spent much of his time there alone upstairs in his laboratory.[7] Other evidence of increasing remoteness from the family circle arose from his new-found interest in Freemasonry. The Sancta Maria Lodge (No. 2682) at St Mary's had been a prominent feature of hospital life throughout Spilsbury's time there. Several senior medical figures had been initiated into the craft at Sancta Maria, including A.P. Luff and William Willcox, but Spilsbury – for some reason not now known – did not seek to join their ranks. In June 1920, shortly after leaving St Mary's, he was initiated into the Rahere Lodge (No. 2546), based at Bart's, was 'passed', and finally 'raised' into membership on 10 May 1921. Two years later, despite his rift with some former colleagues at St Mary's, he now joined Sancta Maria Lodge and, as will be seen, Masonic interests formed an increasingly significant part of his social and professional life.

In 1921, too, came rumours that Spilsbury was going to retire prematurely, at the early age of 44. People thought that his punishing workload was taking its toll on his health, and he was complaining of back trouble and of losing his sense of smell. He was now smoking fifty cigarettes a day, and this massive habit, which may have contributed to his olfactory problems, also suggests an underlying neurosis. Travelling around the country in all weathers for post-mortems, inquests and other court appearances was undoubtedly tiring and stressful. In the event, Spilsbury did not retire in 1921, but another possible cause of gossip may have lain in the crisis in his marriage arising out of his friendship with Hilda Bainbridge. This would not be the first time that he would talk about retirement. Ever the *prima donna*, Spilsbury maintained the lively attention of his media and professional audience by intermittent hints of a farewell performance.

He continued his quest for non-domestic diversions, and 1921 seems to have been the date of his election to the limited membership of Our Society, otherwise known as The Crimes Club, a dining-club for *aficionados* of crime, founded in 1903 by – among others – H.B. Irving and Ingleby Oddie. Originally limited to forty (and unoriginally dubbed 'The Forty Thieves'), the membership of actors, writers, journalists, lawyers and doctors included Sir Arthur Conan Doyle, Lord Northcliffe, Sir Herbert Beerbohm Tree, Sir Arthur Wing Pinero, P.G. Wodehouse, Sir Henry Curtis-Bennett and Marshall Hall. At each dinner, a speaker would read a paper on a contemporary or historic crime of interest or other crime-related interest. Spilsbury was recalled as 'a quiet and reserved member, whose medical evidence was . . . on occasions rejected'[8] during the discussion that followed the address. On 1 May 1921, at Oddenino's, next to the Café Royal, Sir Ernest Wild KC, the Recorder of London, gave the society his opinion on a burning topic of the day, 'Should Women Serve on Juries?' Wild's strong opposition to the idea was 'vehemently supported by the eminent members of the medical profession present',[9] their stance very much in accord with Spilsbury's known views on the role of women in society.

That long, hot, summer of 1921 brought to prominence other issues concerning women. For some years, certainly since mid-1917, Spilsbury had become increasingly suspicious of Dr Richard Starkie, who practised, ostensibly, as a fashionable and respectable West End physician.[10] Spilsbury suspected that several of Starkie's women patients had died as a result of attempts at criminal abortion. Spilsbury, as has been noted, had very strong anti-abortion sentiments. For many years past he had had no scruples in informing the police if he thought that medical colleagues were performing illegal abortions (and virtually all abortions, at that time, would have been illegal).

The life and career of Richard Starkie are a potent antidote to those who believe that abortionists – backstreet or otherwise – provided a much-needed social service from reasons of altruism. Born in 1873, Starkie was the son of a leather merchant in Rochdale. He began his working life as the manager of Bolton Music Hall, dabbled in property development, then studied medicine at Owen's College, Manchester (where Spilsbury had spent a year in 1893–4). He reached London in 1910, qualifying as a Member of the Royal College of Surgeons (MRCS) and a Fellow of the Royal College of Physicians (FRCP), and worked for a time as a police surgeon before setting up in private practice. The attraction of easy money tempted him to offer abortions to the rich women who attended his plush consulting rooms at 28 Brook Street, Mayfair. Starkie, a small man with a mousey appearance, had a thin face, fair hair and moustache, and a pair of watery, cold, grey-blue eyes. Despite his physical shortcomings and an extremely expensive standard fee of £50 an abortion, he had no shortage of custom.

Although his handiwork probably caused the deaths of some patients, he was fly enough to avoid prosecution until 1921. Even then, he was charged only with administering drugs with intent to procure miscarriage and with administering poison with the same intent, rather than with manslaughter. Arrested in July, on return from a business trip to Serbia with the husband of one his patients, Starkie seems to have tried to use underworld connections to bribe the officer in the case, Inspector John Prothero. 'Cocky' Cohen, an extremely dubious-sounding character, offered Prothero £200 to get Starkie off the charge. Cohen said that he was being paid by a Mr Angell, who was 'a large man of business in the East End'.[11] Mrs Angell had been one of Starkie's patients.

Dr Starkie's trial began on 12 September 1921. The formidable Richard Muir prosecuted, leading Eustace Fulton. Starkie was rich enough from the proceeds of his busy abortion practice to obtain the services of no fewer than three distinguished counsel for his defence. These were Marshall Hall, Roland Oliver and G.D. ('Khaki') Roberts. (Khaki's later court antics, probably inspired by Marshall Hall, sometimes involved deliberately upsetting a pile of law books to distract a jury from noticing crucial evidence.)

Five cases of induced miscarriage were cited. The most striking was that of a Miss Boyle, who miscarried in the ladies' lavatory at the fashionable Frascati's Restaurant in Oxford Street, where she had been having dinner with Starkie's nurse, Miss Hannah Jacobs. Finding that her charge had passed out from pain and loss of blood, Nurse Jacobs, acting promptly, brought Miss Boyle round with a stiff brandy before quickly removing her from the restaurant and taking her back to the Regent Palace Hotel. Several women witnesses did not give evidence in accordance with their original statements. The police thought that they had been pressured by or on behalf of Starkie, but their reluctance to be subjected to a grilling by Marshall Hall and risk further adverse publicity seems wholly understandable.

Nurse Jacobs gave evidence against Starkie, revealing in the course of her evidence that he was in the habit of taking some of his female patients to lunch at the Embassy Club in Bond Street, a fashionable rendezvous for the smart set, including the Prince of Wales and other prominent society figures. Nurse Jacobs was accused by Marshall Hall of misconduct, including having ransacked Starkie's desk for information about his client list. One accusation[12] backfired spectacularly.

MARSHALL HALL. Did you tell Mrs Starkie that her husband was carrying on with other women?
NURSE JACOBS. No, Sir. She knew it. *(Laughter)*

Spilsbury gave evidence the following day. This was a curious forensic exercise on the Crown's part and illustrates how far Spilsbury's reputation had already climbed with the authorities. Although the police believed that Starkie's activities had resulted in the deaths of several women, the present case involved live patients. Spilsbury had not had practical experience of gynaecology and obstetrics since his student days in 1904, and there would have been many more experienced practitioners in London available to give up-to-date clinical evidence to the court. Instruments found in Starkie's possession could, declared Spilsbury, be used for procuring abortion, but he had to agree that they could properly have been in any doctor's possession. A drug mentioned in evidence was 'in his opinion' an abortifacient,[13] although it does not appear that any scientific evidence was called to establish the point.

Starkie claimed that Nurse Jacobs had been told to 'clear out' after she had started to make false allegations and – worse – that she had left 'Bolshevist literature' lying around his consulting room. He denied that his fees were excessive. On the contrary, they were modest, ranging from as little as 2*s* 6*d* to 5 guineas. He had merely 'examined' his women patients. Under Muir's cross-examination, Starkie's story fell apart. He agreed that his records had not been well kept. Changing his account, he then said that his highest fee had been 15 guineas, but he was to receive £50 if an operation 'to procure pregnancy' was successful. Marshall Hall, in his closing address, lambasted Nurse Jacobs in what was little more than a mysogynistic rant, quoting from an old play *The Jealous Lover*: 'The fox, hyaena, crocodile, and all beast of craft have been distilled to make one woman', who was 'the origin of all the ills in the case'.[14]

Although the case was overwhelming, the jury was out a remarkably long two and a quarter hours before convicting Starkie on a single count of the indictment relating to eleven abortifacient pills administered to a Mrs Peterson. Acquittals on the other counts were greeted with loud applause from the public gallery, and Starkie was sentenced to a relatively light nine months' imprisonment without penal servitude. On his release from prison, the rich ladies of Mayfair and Belgravia are said to have hosted a banquet in his honour, although it was not quite 'the last flourish of Dr Starkie's professional career', as claimed by Spilsbury's early biographers.[15] Although Starkie was no longer on the Medical Register, he came to police attention again in the mid-1920s and, in 1932, was convicted of procuring abortions by administering the abortifacient 'elm bark' to women. He was sentenced to eighteen months' imprisonment.[16]

NINE

'Excuse Fingers'

Spilsbury rarely travelled to the north of England. In 1917 he had given evidence at Liverpool Assizes in the murder trial of William Hodgson, and, as in the case of Voisin (see Chapter Six), Spilsbury's evidence about the significance of bloodstains was the subject of controversy. On 2 March 1922, Spilsbury again left the comfort zone of the Home Counties to give evidence at Durham Assizes in a trial that shows him at his best, superbly demolishing the defence of an incompetent doctor.[1] The case also illustrates the abysmal quality of care then available to people in working-class communities. A miner's wife from New Herrington was pregnant. She had developed symptoms of eclampsia, a potentially fatal condition. Dr Edward Willis was a salaried doctor employed by Newbottle Miners' Medical Club, an organisation whose health services had already been condemned by the British Medical Association.

The prosecution case was that Willis had arrived drunk at the miner's house at about 6.30 p.m. The husband told Willis not to proceed with treatment, but it seems that his wife's condition worsened and Willis returned, accompanied by his landlady, acting as a completely unqualified nurse, to carry out a botched operation. The woman suffered severe internal injuries and was in great pain as a result of Willis's drunken incompetence. The landlady said that she had a pad of chloroform over the woman's face 'once or twice', a risky action even when performed by an experienced practitioner. The patient later died from 'shock and loss of blood'.

'Dr Bernard Spilsbury, the Home Office expert', in the words of *The Times*, was called by the Crown. Spilsbury demolished the defence case, bluntly stating that the woman's injuries had not been consistent with reasonable care. With a patient in such a condition, it was the doctor's duty to have placed her in the hands of a competent surgeon. Prosecuting counsel gave his expert witness an excellent feed line, asking Spilsbury to comment on the doctor's failure to seek expert help. The facts of the case fully justified Spilsbury's uncompromising answer:

COUNSEL. If he does not, what do you say about it?
SPILSBURY. That he is condemning the patient to certain death.

Willis, who had 'taken some stout, but was not drunk', claimed to have been trying to induce labour to prevent eclampsia-related fits. Spilsbury's majestic performance in court meant that the jury was out only thirty-five minutes before convicting Willis of manslaughter. The judge imposed what seems today to be the surprisingly lenient sentence of twelve months' imprisonment, poor justice for the miner and his family.[2]

On 2 November 1921 Dr Thomas Hincks, a country GP, had written a fateful letter to the Home Office.[3] One of his patients was a young solicitor in Hay-on-Wye, Oswald Martin, who had recently married the daughter of a local chemist, John Davies. Among the wedding gifts were 'two salt-cellars and some spoons'[4] given by Major Herbert Rowse Armstrong, the only other solicitor practising in Hay-on-Wye. Major Armstrong had recently become a widower. His wife, Katharine, had died on 22 February 1921. Major Armstrong liked to be known in Hay-on-Wye by his military rank. He had joined the Territorial Army in 1900 and had served throughout the First World War, although he never saw action. Armstrong's fussy, bureaucratic tendencies found their outlet in administrative duties, and it seems that the greatest risk to the Major during the war had been getting his fingers caught in a typewriter.

Armstrong's physique ruled him out as an active warrior. He stood 5ft 6in tall, not much below average height in those days, but in 1922 weighed only 8 stone, 'a slim, fragile little man',[5] with a slight build and small facial features. Born in Plymouth in 1869, he took a degree at Cambridge. In 1906 he became managing clerk to Edmund Cheese, Solicitor, of Broad Street, Hay-on-Wye and, three years later, became a partner in the firm, now renamed 'Cheese & Armstrong'. In 1907 he had married Katharine Friend, whom he had met in Devon several years before. From the outset they seem to have been an ill-matched couple. She was a little taller than her husband, which prompted unkind people to call them 'Mutt and Jeff', after two popular cartoon characters. Unlike Armstrong, Katharine was teetotal and a non-smoker. She would boss her little husband around, humiliating him in public and in private. She would not allow him to drink alcohol in the house and confined smoking to one room. Armstrong never showed any public resentment at this treatment. Perhaps, like some men, he took a masochistic pleasure in his wife's abusive behaviour.

Katharine bore him three children, even though her first pregnancy was at the relatively late age of 37. In 1917, apparently in good mental health, she made a will, providing for her children and an annual income for her husband. She had always been a hypochondriac, dosing herself with patent medicines, some containing small amounts of toxic substances such as strychnine, mercury, aconite – and arsenic. She complained to Dr Hincks of pain in the shoulder and numbness in the fingers, which was diagnosed as 'brachial neuritis'. When he visited her in August 1919, Hincks described her physical condition as 'good'.[6]

On 8 July 1920 Katharine executed a new will, making no provision for her children and leaving everything to her husband. Unlike her 1917 will, which she had written out herself, the document was in Major Armstrong's handwriting. Hincks saw her on 1 August. Katharine's manner at that time was quite rational, but later that month he found her to be delusional, manifesting speech problems. She also had a heart murmur. Urine analysis revealed the presence of albumen, indicating a malfunction of the kidney. After Hincks had consulted a colleague, Katharine was certified as 'of unsound mind' and committed to Barnwood, a private asylum near Gloucester. Before she travelled there, Hincks noted that she had developed a rapid pulse, was cyanosed (blue) about the lips and had a sallow complexion. She had been vomiting and complained of pain in the stomach.[7]

Arsenic, it seems, was the drug of choice in the early 1920s. At Herefordshire General Hospital, Armstrong, whose extramarital activities had produced a suspicious sore, was injected with a course of Novarsenobillon (otherwise Neosalvarsan, otherwise Sodium Dioxydiamino-Arsenobenzene-Mono-Methano-Sulphonate),[8] an arsenic-based compound, readily soluble, suitable for intramuscular injection and widely used for the treatment of syphilis before the development of antibiotics after the Second World War.

Ostensibly for domestic purposes, Armstrong had bought his own supply of arsenic: half a pound in June 1919; 5 gallons of weedkiller containing arsenic in May 1920; 3 tins of powdered weedkiller on 4 August 1920; and he would buy a further quarter-pound of arsenic on 11 January 1921, just eleven days before Katharine was due to return home from Barnwood Asylum.

Katharine had canvassed the possibility of suicide by jumping out of an attic window, so a qualified mental nurse, Nurse Allen, was brought in to care for her. She found Katharine very frail. After Sunday 13 February 1921 Katharine was so ill that she could not get out of bed. For the last four days of her life she could not feed herself. She had no strength in her hands and seemed more or less paralysed. Major Armstrong shared a bedroom with his wife, although they slept in separate beds. He would feed her from time to time. Early on the morning of 22 February Katharine told Nurse Allen that she had 'everything to live for – my children and my husband'.[9] At about 8 a.m. she lost consciousness and died at 10 a.m.

Dr Hincks certified the cause of death as gastritis, with heart disease and nephritis (kidney inflammation) as contributory factors. Katharine was buried on 25 February 1921 in the churchyard at Cusop. Major Armstrong went abroad for a holiday, travelling to Malta via Paris and Italy. Probate in Katharine's will was granted to him, as sole beneficiary, on 30 May that year. He inherited £2,278 3s 0d.

Although Armstrong had given wedding presents to Oswald Martin and his wife in June 1921, the two men were becoming bitter rivals for the lion's share of legal work in Hay-on-Wye. Armstrong started to lose clients to Martin. Late in 1921 Martin was acting for two purchasers of land, part of a larger estate broken up – as so many were – in the lean years following the First World War. Deposits had been paid, but Armstrong, solicitor for the vendor, showed persistent reluctance to complete the transaction, so much so that the purchasers threatened to demand rescission of the contracts, plus payment of costs and expenses. Armstrong's behaviour was very odd and unprofessional. In the end, Martin was instructed to proceed with rescission.

Armstrong persistently invited Martin to take tea at his house. After declining several times, Martin at last agreed to come, on Wednesday 26 October. In an episode notorious in the annals of crime, Armstrong offered Martin a buttered scone, saying politely, 'Excuse fingers'.[10] Martin ate the scone and, rather over an hour later, began to feel sick. He ate little at dinner and by 9.15 p.m. was vomiting violently. Later in the night he developed diarrhoea and a fast pulse. Although Hincks put this down to an ordinary bilious attack, John Davies, Martin's chemist father-in-law, was suspicious of the symptoms, which had included foul-smelling, reddish-brown vomit and a raised pulse rate. When he revealed his concern to Martin, it emerged that Martin's wife had become ill on 8 October, with severe gastric symptoms, after eating a chocolate taken from a box of Fuller's Chocolates sent anonymously to Martin. The box had arrived shortly after Martin had written to Armstrong about the completion of the two purchases of land. Dorothy Martin recalled that, in addition to her gastric symptoms, she had had a markedly raised pulse. Examination of the chocolates by Davies showed that two had been tampered with, and later analysis by Dr John Webster – Spilsbury's colleague at St Mary's – revealed that one of them contained 2.12 grains of white arsenic, a potentially fatal dose. Davies also took a sample of Martin's urine, but Martin had been taking a bismuth mixture, containing arsenic, which had been prescribed by Hincks, and Webster's discovery of traces of arsenic in the urine was, to some extent, compromised.

Dr Hincks, left in the dark about the result of the analyses, wrote an elliptically expressed letter to the Home Office, using deliberately unspecific references to 'a patient' (Martin) and to 'the party in question' (Armstrong), who was known to have bought arsenic. At the Home Office Sir Ernley Blackwell took a cynical view of the forces of law and order. 'I rather sympathise with Dr Hincks,' he minuted. 'If the police were to gossip about this, it might ruin his practice.'[11] Gossip was one item in plentiful supply at Hay-on-Wye that winter.

On 23 December 1921 Willcox was telephoned at his Welbeck Street consulting rooms by Archibald Bodkin. The DPP requested a meeting to discuss the Armstrong case, which had a startlingly similar background to the recent murder trial of Harold Greenwood, another Welsh solicitor accused of poisoning his wife with arsenic. After a three-hour meeting on Boxing Day Willcox expressed his view that Katharine Armstrong had died from acute arsenical poisoning and prepared a written opinion, which persuaded Bodkin to authorise the arrest of Major Armstrong on 31 December 1921.[12] At this stage, however, Armstrong was charged only with the attempted murder of Oswald Martin. When searched, Armstrong was found to have two small packets containing arsenical compounds in a jacket pocket, part of a larger number that, he claimed, had been carefully prepared as individual doses to kill dandelions at the roots – weeds that would not appear in his lawn for at least another three months.

In the last week of December 1921 Bodkin wrote to Willcox. 'Will you be good enough', he asked, 'to arrange with Dr Spilsbury and Mr Webster to meet you at some convenient time before Dr S goes to Hereford?'[13] The Home Office had made arrangements for the exhumation of Katharine Armstrong, and, on the morning of 2 January 1922, in bitterly cold winter weather, Spilsbury travelled down from Paddington to a snow-bound Hereford, connecting with a local train to Hay, from where he was driven to the churchyard at Cusop. There he was joined by the Assistant Chief Constable of Hereford and senior police officers. Gravediggers had been working for several hours amid the snow, and, at 6.30 p.m., lit by oil lamps flickering amid the winter darkness, the coffin was raised. Spilsbury noted that the depth of the grave was 4ft 9in, the soil was dry loam and that there was a layer of shrivelled turf under the coffin, which was taken on a bier to the freezing cold Church Cottage, a white-washed building whose lower windows had been boarded up to prevent pressmen and other curious parties from seeing in. After a brief inspection of the coffin, found to be 'clean and dry',[14] Spilsbury and the police officers left the cottage, which was locked up for the night and kept under guard.

The next morning, attended by Dr Hincks, Dr William Ainslie (instructed by Armstrong) and a police officer, Spilsbury began work. The coffin appeared to be airtight, but a strong smell of putrefaction arose when the lid was removed, and some fluid leaked through the base. Katharine's body lay on a bed of sawdust and wood shavings, covered partly by the coffin lining, with a towel over the legs and feet, and a handkerchief over the face. She had been wearing a nightdress and stockings, both of which had rotted away. Spilsbury found that advanced decomposition had taken place on the 'exposed parts', namely the face, lower forearm, the hands and feet, with destruction of the skin. Tendons and some bony joints were exposed. The lower part of her nose was gone and the 'eyeballs [had] collapsed'. With the face so extensively decomposed, the undertaker, Humphrey Webb, and Dr Hincks were able to identify Katharine only by her prominent teeth and long plaits of dark hair, 'black with a few grey strands in it', tied with a ribbon, tresses that 'came away easily' when Spilsbury pulled at them. Another gruesome discovery was a colony of live beetles, with their larvae, present on the exposed areas. On his case card, Spilsbury meticulously recorded the presence of 'larvae Rhizophagus Parallelo-Collis' and the probable presence of 'Phora Aterrhima' larvae, found infesting what remained of Katharine's feet. Samples were taken and later made into slides, Spilsbury noting likely future interest by 'G K Blair, Entomological Dept, British Museum'.

As usual, Spilsbury had brought with him a large number of glass specimen jars. After the post-mortem, he gave sixteen jars to Webster at St Mary's, fourteen of which contained body parts, with samples of sawdust, wood-shavings and soil in the two remaining jars. Spilsbury recorded that the abdomen was largely intact, coloured on the front 'a dark purplish red to dirty brown', with mould growing in some places. The scalp and skull were well preserved. The brain, which smelt offensively, was uniformly green, presumably due to putrefaction, but showed no sign of disease.

Hampered by the extreme cold, which obliged him to break off from time to time to warm his hands, Spilsbury worked his way down the trunk and into the abdomen, all the time taking samples of bodily tissue and contents of the gut. He noticed marked 'fatty degeneration' in the kidneys, which, with the liver, were removed for further investigation. Later microscopical examination revealed that the liver, too, was subject to fatty degeneration. This factor would prove highly significant at Armstrong's trial.

Spilsbury concluded that the body, and particularly the internal organs, were 'unusually well preserved for 10 months after death'. Externally, the body had a shrunken appearance from loss of fluid and developing mummification. The grim effects of insect infestation had not been overlooked. Putrefaction of the exposed areas was 'probably [the] result of action of flies before burial'. Apart from the cold, conditions in Church Cottage were noisome in the extreme. The three detectives who had watched Spilsbury's work took a welcome opportunity to light up cigarettes immediately on leaving the building, to cheers from the waiting crowd. The undertaker was sick.

Spilsbury, loaded down with specimen jars, his dissection equipment and overnight luggage, was driven back to Hay, taking a late train back to London. John Webster was a much faster worker than Spilsbury, and preliminary results were at hand within a day. On 12 January 1922 Spilsbury, Willcox and Webster held a two-hour consultation at Willcox's consulting rooms in Welbeck Street. Tensions between Spilsbury and Willcox were exacerbated when Willcox criticised his younger colleague for 'not getting enough of the gut out', ignoring Spilsbury's complaint about the freezing conditions prevailing during the autopsy.[15]

Webster, assisted by Dr Gerald Roche Lynch, had analysed the stomach and intestines with their contents, tissue samples, bodily organs, sections of bone, skin, muscle, hair, fingernails and toenails. The body was riddled with arsenic, traces of which were found in each item and even in the wood-shavings at the base of the coffin, into which fluid had oozed from Katharine's putrefying body. A total of 208.2mg of arsenic was detected, of which the largest concentrations were in the lower bowel, 37.6mg, and the liver, found to contain 138.0mg, or 2 grains, a fatal dose in itself.

Armstrong was further charged with murdering his wife by poisoning her with arsenic. Spilsbury and Willcox, joined by Webster, travelled down to Hay-on-Wye the following Thursday and, the next day, 16 February, outlined their findings to the magistrates at adjourned committal proceedings in respect of the murder and attempted murder charges.

The prosecution medical case was, in essence, remarkably simple. Nothing had been found at post-mortem to account for death by natural causes. The forensic analysis demonstrated that Katharine must have taken a great deal of arsenic during the last days of her life. There was also evidence to show that she had taken arsenic before going into hospital. Spilsbury, impressive as ever and wearing his customary black morning coat, described his post-mortem findings and said that the fatty degeneration found in the kidneys and liver was consistent with arsenical poisoning. The chairman of the magistrates asked Spilsbury whether an arsenic-based tonic given to Katharine in the asylum over the month of October would have left traces in the body. Spilsbury replied that it would not do so, 'with the possible exception of the hair and nails'.[16]

Spilsbury's evidence, followed by that of Webster, paved the way for the crux of the Crown case to be put by Willcox, who was certain that a fatal dose of arsenic had been taken within twenty-four hours of death because of the high quantities of arsenic found in the gut. Allowing for loss of arsenic due to vomiting and diarrhoea, the amount taken must have been considerably in excess of a fatal dose. In his view, a similar amount of arsenic had been taken before Katharine's admission to Barnwood Asylum, judging by the arsenical residues found in the nails and hair. The defence reserved its case, and, that day, Major Armstrong was committed to stand trial at Hereford Assizes.

Armstrong's trial opened at Hereford Assizes on 3 April 1922. On the first day of the trial, the prosecution medical experts – Spilsbury, Webster and Willcox – travelled down to Hereford by train, putting up at the Green Dragon Hotel in Broad Street. After dinner, the team had a two-hour meeting with young Gerald Paling, the DPP's representative, attending his first murder trial. Although such a conference was not improper, it might have been better if the medical experts and prosecution lawyers had not all stayed at the same hotel. Within the medical group, Spilsbury – at any rate on the surface – deferred to Willcox, who would speak of a 'battle plan', involving detailed discussion of the likely lines of cross-examination by the defence.

Armstrong had secured the services of a formidable defence advocate in the substantial form of Sir Henry Curtis-Bennett KC ('Harry' or 'Curtis' to his many friends). Although Curtis-Bennett had once been lean and fit (he won a

cycling half-Blue at Cambridge), by 1922 his physical appearance amply
justified the description 'the Falstaff of the Bar'.[17] He was an unashamed bon
vivant, an habitué of the Colchester Oyster Feast, and a witty speaker much in
demand at City dinners. Curtis-Bennett was a modern advocate, who eschewed
the blood-and-thunder histrionics of Marshall Hall. Despite his looming
presence (by 1930, he weighed nearly 20 stone), Curtis-Bennett rarely made a
scene in court or mishandled a witness. His polite, quiet but persistent style
made his advocacy all the more effective.

In accordance with traditional practice, the Crown was represented by the
Attorney-General, Sir Ernest Pollock, and the trial judge was the egregious
Gerald Darling (see p. 57 above), whose pro-prosecution sentiments found rein
at the outset of proceedings when, despite an eloquent plea by Curtis-Bennett,
he allowed the Crown to introduce evidence about the alleged poisoning
attempt on Oswald Martin's life. This decision greatly strengthened the
prosecution case, although the story had already emerged in detailed
newspaper reports of the committal proceedings, which were not then subject
to reporting restrictions. The jury, mostly local farmers, were already well
primed.

Spilsbury, again the first of the prosecution team, gave evidence on Saturday
8 April 1922.[18] Darling was impressed by Spilsbury and, in the course of
Pollock's examination-in-chief, posed a sycophantic question. Spilsbury's self-
congratulatory answer was not supported by any statistics:

DARLING. It is a fact, is it not, that you have very, very large experience of
poison cases?
SPILSBURY. A considerable experience; almost weekly, but certainly of
monthly occurrence.

Thus fortified in his task, Spilsbury produced a diagram, held up for the jury to
see, of the lower digestive system, carefully pointing out where the particular
concentrations of arsenic were found, going on to describe the symptom of
fatty degeneration in the kidneys and liver. A question from the judge
prompted another classic Spilsbury response:

SPILSBURY. I say that certainly this condition of the kidneys and the liver and
the heart was due to arsenical poisoning.

His use of unfussy, simple language led his evidence towards an equally direct
statement of the Crown's case, unfettered by scientific ambiguities. Note the
use of the words 'clear' and 'must':

SPILSBURY. From the amount of arsenic which was present in the small and
large intestines, it is clear that a large dose of arsenic must have been

taken within 24 hours of death and from the amount of arsenic which was found in the liver – over two grains – and from the disease which I found in the liver, it is clear that the poison must have been given in a number of large doses extending over a period, certainly of some days, probably not less than a week.

Curtis-Bennett knew that he faced an uphill struggle to make any headway against this powerful evidential force. There had been evidence that suggested Katharine was so weak and bedridden that she could not have taken the arsenic herself, either accidentally or deliberately, in the last four days of her life. Curtis-Bennett questioned Spilsbury about survival rates after the ingestion of large doses of arsenic. The defence case was that she could have taken the fatal dose up to eight days before her death. Spilsbury agreed that people had survived for seven or eight days after taking large doses of arsenic, and that he would expect to find fatty degeneration in the liver in such cases. Curtis-Bennett followed up this apparent concession by clever questioning about the possibility of arsenic becoming 'encapsulated' or 'encysted' in the stomach. At this point, taking into account that the three medical experts had tried to anticipate questions likely to be posed in cross-examination, Spilsbury became uncharacteristically vague. He said that he remembered such an instance, but he could not remember the name of the case, although he 'could turn it up' in 'a book' on toxicology. The book was not further identified, and Spilsbury thought, 'as far as my recollection goes', that this patient had died 'fairly rapidly' after taking arsenic. Curtis-Bennett, sensing his opportunity, pressed on:

CURTIS-BENNETT. Encysted in . . . the stomach. That would cause a remission of symptoms, would it not, until that arsenic freed itself and became dissolved?
SPILSBURY. Yes it might.

A few questions later, however, Spilsbury modified his answer by another that seems to amount to 'a distinction without a difference', in lawyers' jargon:

SPILSBURY. I think . . . that would tend to delay the onset of symptoms rather than produce a remission of them.

Curtis-Bennett returned to the issue of survival rates, quoting an American book, by 'a man named Wood', in which a person had lived up to fourteen days. This prompted another vague answer:

SPILSBURY. I think I have referred to it once or twice but I do not know the book well.

Perhaps Spilsbury knew more about Wood's book than he made out, but he neatly sidestepped questions about it by adding the expression 'I dare say . . . under special conditions' when referring to the possibility of arsenic becoming encysted. Spilsbury had to agree that the arsenic-based tonic given to Katharine at Barnwood Hospital would have tended to impede recovery from arsenical neuritis, had she in fact been suffering from this condition, rather than from ordinary rheumatism, when she was admitted.

In re-examination, Spilsbury rowed back from the concessions made to Curtis-Bennett. In particular, he claimed that Webster's finding of over 2 grains of arsenic in the liver was inconsistent with 'encysted' arsenic in the stomach lining, 'because there must have been very considerable absorption . . . and no encysted arsenic was found in the stomach' after death. The encysted arsenic had to be in one place rather than another '. . . either it is encysted in bulk or it is not'.

During Spilsbury's evidence, reporters noticed that the defence medical expert, Dr Frederick Toogood, was whispering advice in Curtis-Bennett's ear. Counsel for the defence was allowed to resume cross-examination, putting to Spilsbury that another American authority, *Witthaus on Toxicology*, had raised the possibility that arsenic could move through the tissues of a putrefying cadaver by a process of 'post-mortem migration', meaning that inferences about the distribution of arsenic at death were potentially unreliable. Spilsbury immediately and firmly disagreed with this contention. Arsenic, he said, could pass 'in a fluid condition' from one part to another if the organs, in decomposition, became fluid or semi-fluid. He then made a curious statement, which looks suspiciously like a diversionary tactic.

> SPILSBURY. If there were fluid in the peritoneal cavity, it is possible that a migration of a certain amount of arsenic might take place from one part to another.

If this was an attempt to draw off the hounds, it worked. In his next answer, to the Attorney-General, he was able to say that no such fluid had been found. There might in some cases be leakage through the wall of the bowel, but, in this case, the lining was intact. Spilsbury's sidestepping of the Witthaus argument was triumphantly endorsed shortly before he left the witness-box.

> ATTORNEY-GENERAL. . . . paying every tribute to Dr Witthaus's writing in 1911, have you during the course of the last ten or eleven years . . . had the opportunity of making examinations of dead bodies, may I say, by the score . . . ?
>
> SPILSBURY. I think I may say almost by the thousand.

The pert answer provoked sympathetic laughter, 'quickly suppressed', and, a little later, the judge helpfully enabled Spilsbury to end his evidence in robust fashion, emphasising his total rejection of the Witthaus theory:

JUDGE. As to this theory of Dr Witthaus . . . ?
SPILSBURY. No, impossible, my lord.

Modern opinion tends to support the Witthaus theory. Spilsbury's conclusions about the distribution of arsenic and the time of the ingestion of the fatal dose were too rigid and were, in effect, dogmatic.[19]

Spilsbury was followed by Webster and Willcox, who ably crystallised the prosecution case. During Willcox's evidence, when Curtis-Bennett referred to Katharine's remark about suicide in the context of insanity, Darling could not resist making a feeble joke:

JUDGE. A suicide who threw himself out of the window and was cured might do it again and again until he killed himself.
CURTIS-BENNETT. He might go to a higher window the second time.
JUDGE. No, that would show sanity.

In respect of the 'encysted' arsenic theory, the tenor of Willcox's answers, although consistent with the Crown case, was not always so rigid as Spilsbury's had been:

CURTIS-BENNETT. . . . it might become encysted in the stomach and then after three days dissolve and pass on? That is a possibility?
WILLCOX. . . . I think it is extremely unlikely. I cannot deny the possibility, but it is extremely unlikely.

After Armstrong had given evidence, the defence called Dr Toogood, who had a varied medical experience, as a Lieutenant-Colonel in the Royal Army Medical Corps, medical superintendent of Lewisham Hospital, a borough medical officer, adviser to insurance companies and pathologist to the London County Council. Unlike Spilsbury, he particularised his experience of arsenical poisoning cases, citing one fatal case, one of acute poisoning, which recovered, and several of sub-acute and chronic poisoning. Toogood doubted that Katharine had been suffering from arsenical poisoning when she was admitted to Barnwood. Her neuritis and other symptoms were explicable from ordinary physical causes. Toogood thought that she had taken a large dose of arsenic on or about 16 February, five days before she died, and probably more than 6 grains. He supported the possibility of arsenic becoming encysted in the stomach. He also doubted whether Martin's gastric symptoms were due to arsenical poisoning. He agreed with the Witthaus theory of post-mortem migration and, on the basis of encysted arsenic in the stomach, had formed the view that Katharine had died after ingesting one big dose on 16 February, the day that Dr Hincks had called, finding her suffering from severe physical symptoms. Dr Ainslie, who had attended the post-mortem, also held the opinion that Katharine's symptoms before 16 February were not due to arsenical poisoning.

Darling's summing-up favoured the prosecution's case. The encomium given to Spilsbury was extraordinary and practically amounted to a direction that the jury should prefer his evidence to that of the defence:

> JUDGE. Do you remember Dr Spilsbury? Do you remember how he stood and the way in which he gave evidence? . . . Did you ever see a witness who more thoroughly satisfied you that he was absolutely impartial, absolutely fair, absolutely indifferent as to whether his evidence told for the one side or the other . . . ? You should recollect and consider the demeanour of every witness . . . and when you consider Dr Spilsbury, when you have to say whether you trust the opinion that he gave, you are entitled then to remember his demeanour . . . and to act accordingly.

The jury, whose foreman was 'a broad-shouldered, John-Bull like figure', acted accordingly, taking only forty-eight minutes to convict Armstrong of murdering his wife. The foreman told *The Times*[20] that Armstrong's worst day was when the Home Office medical experts gave evidence. 'I don't think there was ever any chance of a verdict of "not guilty" after that,' he recalled.

Armstrong, whose appeal failed, was hanged at Gloucester Prison by John Ellis on 31 May 1922. Armstrong may have poisoned his wife. She might, however, have taken the arsenic herself five days before she died, either accidentally (perhaps, in a confused state, mistaking it for a homeopathic remedy) or intending to commit suicide. There is good reason to believe that Armstrong did not have a fair trial, in the sense that the latter two possibilities were outweighed from the start by the vivid picture painted by the prosecution medical team – in particular by Spilsbury – of a fatal dose administered by Armstrong within twenty-four hours of death, while his wife lay helpless as a result of repeated earlier doses of arsenic.

TEN

'Arise, Sir Bernard'

James Spilsbury died at his home, The Nook, Wake Green Road, Moseley, on 18 April 1922. Although he had been fairly well known in the Birmingham area as 'an eminent pharmacist', his obituary in the *Birmingham Post*[1] mostly remembered him as 'the father of Dr Bernard Spilsbury, the toxicologist [*sic*], whose name has figured prominently as an expert witness in several recent poison trials'. James Spilsbury left a substantial estate, over £25,000, which was placed on trust by his will for the benefit of the four children. Bernard, as the eldest, was executor and trustee. No provision was made in James Spilsbury's will for his wife, who may have benefited from a settlement designed to avoid estate duty. Marion lived on quietly in Moseley for some years, cared for by the unmarried sisters, Connie and Gertie Spilsbury.

Spilsbury was now good copy for the media. 'Spilsbury Called In' had become 'the favourite newspaper headline for the prelude to a story of murder . . . to which . . . elements of mystery attached'.[2] There were occasional lighter moments. On 8 June 1922 *The Times* published his photograph in an unusual pose at Bart's Hospital, a far remove from the ordered calm of Spilsbury's path lab. A smiling Spilsbury (rare sight) was depicted, apparently being addressed by a medical student decked out in Tudor costume. The caption read HELD TO RANSOM – DR BERNARD SPILSBURY IN THE STOCKS AT BARTHOLOMEW FAIR, noting that 'the students held him prisoner until ransom had been paid'.

Before the end of the month Spilsbury was again involved in a sensational murder investigation, leading to his appearance in a trial that had profound political significance. At about 2.30 p.m. on 22 June 1922 Field Marshal Sir Henry Wilson alighted from a taxi and walked towards the front of his house, 36 Eaton Place, Belgravia.[3] He was in full military uniform, wearing a sword, and had returned from Liverpool Street Station, where he had unveiled a memorial to employees of the Great Eastern Railway killed in the First World War. Sir Henry Wilson had a political, as well as a military, profile. His roots were in Ulster. His ancestors, supporters of William III, had acquired land in County Antrim. Wilson had opposed Home Rule and, a former Chief of the Imperial General Staff, had recently become Unionist MP for North Down. Since 1918 three years of violence had convulsed the country. In December 1921 a treaty established the Irish Free State in southern Ireland, with six of the nine Ulster counties remaining part of the United Kingdom. The

Republican movement at once split into pro- and anti-Treaty factions, and a vicious civil war was under way in the newly established Free State.

Reginald Dunn and Joseph O'Sullivan, both 24, were members of the IRA bitterly opposed to the new treaty. The two men, who had been given intelligence about Wilson's movements, lay in wait for his return from the official function. As he crossed the road, they emerged from behind the taxi and fired several shots at Wilson, who seems to have made an attempt to draw his sword, before staggering forwards and falling to the ground. The IRA men made off, not at the fastest pace, since O'Sullivan had an artificial leg. Both assailants were of Irish parentage but English-born, and had served in the British Army during the war, in which Dunn had been severely wounded and O'Sullivan had lost his leg.[4] At gunpoint, the assailants hijacked 'a smart Victoria driven by a footman in livery'[5] and fired at the pursuing posse. They got out of the carriage and started walking backwards, firing at the small crowd. One policeman was shot in the stomach, another in the leg. An off-duty colleague, PC Bush, brought O'Sullivan down with his fist, knocking the Webley service revolver out of his hand. A police truncheon thrown at Dunn struck him on the head; when seized, he was found to be wearing a 'Sam Browne' belt and revolver holster.

Wilson had been carried into his house, but died a few moments later without speaking. The Coroner, Ingleby Oddie, contacted Spilsbury, who carried out a post-mortem the following day in Wilson's study, where the body had been laid out. Strangely, the body was not taken to a mortuary, surely a cooler and more suitable environment than a private house at the height of summer, when bodies were likely to 'go off' to some extent. Oddie justified his decision by reference to the feelings of the murdered man's widow and also 'to allow the military funeral procession to start from the house'.[6]

Spilsbury, noting that the dead man, who was 58 and 6ft 1in tall, was 'well nourished'[7] and otherwise healthy, found evidence of nine bullet injuries on the body. He concluded that the injuries were probably all inflicted when Wilson was standing. Either of two bullets that had passed through the chest, respectively from right to left and from left to right, would have been fatal. A bullet had been fired through the right leg, from directly behind the leg, passing forwards and downwards. Another had been fired through the left shoulder, and wounds in both forearms suggested that they had been inflicted from behind, if the Field Marshal's arms had been at the side of his body at the time of firing. With Spilsbury's usual dogmatic approach to timetabling, the case card reads baldly: 'Two mins unconscious. Death in 10 mins.'

The assassination provoked a general security panic, and Spilsbury also seems to have been caught up in the scare. After finishing the post-mortem, he shared a taxi with his 'technician' at Bart's and was soon convinced that they were being followed. 'Look behind,' said Spilsbury in melodramatic vein. 'There's another cab following us. It must be the IRA.'[8] Spilsbury's driver tried to dodge the supposedly pursuing cab, but it followed them along the Mall, over Trafalgar Square and into the Strand. There Spilsbury jumped out and walked through a hotel, telephoned Scotland Yard and picked up another taxi at the hotel's rear entrance. According to the story, the technician was able to take Spilsbury's famous murder bag, containing bullets extracted from Wilson's body, on to safekeeping at Bart's. Spilsbury is said to have been seconded a plain-clothes officer for protection, and a guard was put on his house at Marlborough Hill, although he was by now spending most his time at his flat in Gray's Inn. He received a death threat warning him not to give evidence, but this may have been a hoax.

Spilsbury's story of being chased by the IRA must be taken with a pinch of salt. Less than two weeks after Wilson's murder, Sir Wyndham Childs, Assistant Commissioner of Special Branch, was complaining about pressure from public figures who thought that they were at risk of assassination, including a Catholic Unionist MP, Colonel Archer-Shee (half-brother of the cadet portrayed in Rattigan's *The Winslow Boy*), and Nancy, Lady Astor, who seemed to think that she was at risk because 'she is pro-Pussyfoot' (that is, in favour of the prohibition of alcohol).[9] The resources of Special Branch were exhausted. Unless the Metropolitan Police Commissioner gave express orders, Childs was not prepared to authorise protection except for members of the Royal Family and cabinet ministers. To emphasise his point, Childs gave a vivid illustration of the effects of scare-mongering, which puts the Spilsbury escapade into context: 'Three days ago, I received a letter from a Member of Parliament enclosing a letter he had received from a friend saying that his wife's maid last February saw two men in the street (as usual) of a "suspicious" character & one of them had a distinctly Irish accent.'[10]

Dunn and O'Sullivan (arrested under the aliases James Connelly and James O'Brien) appeared at the Old Bailey on 18 July 1922. The jury took two minutes to convict both men of murder. From the dock, Dunn named British security officers allegedly guilty of murdering Irish republicans – 'Capt Bowen-Colthurst, who murdered Mr Sheehy Skeffington; Captain Hardy of Dublin Castle, who murdered Brig McKee of the Irish Army' – before the judge stopped him. O'Sullivan declared, simply: 'All I have done, My Lord, I have done for Ireland and for Ireland I am proud to die.'[11] Before leaving the dock, the prisoners shook hands. Their appeals were dismissed. Blackwell minuted that 'the government desires that there shall be no unavoidable delay in this case'.[12] The men, who were not allowed to see each other before their deaths, were executed by John Ellis at Pentonville on 8 August 1922.

That month Spilsbury was instructed by the Home Office in possibly the year's most controversial and celebrated trial, which has proved to be of enduring interest to crime historians, playwrights and novelists. Edith Thompson and Frederick Bywaters were charged with the murder of Percy Thompson, Edith's husband, on 3 October 1922. Percy Thompson, who was 32, worked as a shipping clerk in the City. In 1916 he had married Edith Graydon, then 22, who also worked in the City, as a book-keeper for a firm in Aldersgate. The married couple lived respectably in Ilford.

Percy Thompson seems to have been a dull man, small-minded, fussy and thoroughly pedestrian in character. Edith nursed yearnings towards the higher life. Her firm had sent her to Paris shortly before the war, and she developed a taste for romantic literature. She was particularly fond of gushing, exotic novels written by Robert Hichens, who had travelled widely in the Arab world and was a prolific author. *The Garden of Allah*, set in Morocco, ran to forty-three editions and had been made into a film in 1917. *The Fruitful Vine* was also a pulp best-seller. Probably his best-known work was *Bella Donna*, published in 1909, with a racist plot in which a sinister Egyptian persuades an Englishwoman to poison her husband. Her head filled with such third-rate romances, Edith dreamed over illustrated magazines and indulged her exotic fantasies at the pictures.

In 1920 she met Freddie Bywaters, whose family were friendly with the Graydons. Bywaters, although only 18, had already had an eventful life, serving in the Merchant Navy in the hazardous last years of the war. Bywaters had an outgoing, attractive personality, in sharp contrast to the thoroughly pedestrian Percy Thompson. Bywaters and Edith began an affair and, during his long absences as a steward of a P&O liner, she wrote Bywaters a series of love letters that would ultimately lead to her execution. They may have been fantasies, conjured up by the cheap literature and lurid films she had watched, but she claimed in the letters to have put pieces of glass into Percy's food and canvassed the possibility of killing him by using various poisons.

Bywaters returned from the sea in September 1922, and the couple resumed their passionate affair. Edith continued to live with her husband. On the evening of 3 October, while Edith and Percy Thompson were walking together in Endsleigh Gardens, Ilford, Bywaters suddenly emerged from the shadows. Edith was said to have shouted 'Oh don't; oh don't', but Bywaters stabbed Percy in the head, neck and chest with a dagger. One cut severed Percy's carotid artery, causing his death. Bywaters ran off.[13] Superintendent Wensley, a guileful detective, allowed Edith to glimpse Bywaters as he was being interrogated at Ilford Police Station. Edith's immediate reaction ensured that both would face murder charges. 'Oh God, what can I do?' she cried. 'Why did he do it? I did not want him to do it.'[14]

Bywaters and Thompson were tried at the Old Bailey before Mr Justice Shearman, who has been criticised for his priggish approach to the evidence. Curtis-Bennett, who defended Edith Thompson, faced two insurmountable hurdles. The first of these was the love letters. Curtis-Bennett submitted that they were inadmissible as evidence until the prosecution could show that Edith had taken some active part in the murder,[15] but the judge rejected his argument. They were used by the Crown as evidence of both conspiracy and incitement to murder. Taken literally, they chronicled various attempts by Edith to kill her husband. They could be regarded as incitement for Bywaters to do what Edith had failed to achieve and end Percy's life. On the other hand, they may have been no more than an erotic exercise by parties to an intense relationship. Curtis-Bennett's second hurdle was Edith's insistence on giving evidence. Once in the witness-box, she could be – and was – mercilessly cross-examined by the new Attorney-General, Sir Thomas Inskip (Lloyd George's government had fallen in October 1922 and the Conservatives were in office under Andrew Bonar Law).

Spilsbury came into the proceedings at a relatively late stage. The descriptions given by Edith of attempts on her husband's life were sufficiently realistic to cause the exhumation of the murdered man. On 3 November 1922, in the presence of Dr Drought, a police surgeon who had originally examined the body, Spilsbury conducted a post-mortem on Percy Thompson, who had been buried in the City of London cemetery in east London on 10 October 1922. He described the wounds to the neck and throat, stating at the trial that 'they were stabs . . . with the exception of the one on the right arm, which was a cut'.[16] Spilsbury went on give his findings in relation to the issues of broken glass and poisons, in respect of which further analysis had been carried out by Dr Webster. Although decomposition had affected the internal organs, it had been possible to examine the heart, stomach, liver and intestines.

Spilsbury, although a fast worker on the post-mortem table, was often very slow in preparing reports for the authorities. The Thompson case was no exception, and it was not until 1 December 1922 that he supplied the DPP with his conclusions. 'I have found no indications of poisoning,' he wrote, 'and no changes suggestive of previous attempts at poisoning. I detected no glass in the contents of the intestine.'[17] Some commentators have read into Spilsbury's report and his subsequent court evidence that he was regarded by the prosecution as an 'unsatisfactory witness'. According to one writer: 'The Crown produced this tremendous piece of evidence in a shabby, grudging, discreditable way.'[18] Another commentator found in Spilsbury 'a resistance to [Inskip's] imputations regarding the possible inaccuracy of such scientific evidence'.[19] Various pencil marks alongside passages in Spilsbury's edition of *The Trial of Frederick Bywaters and Edith Thompson* have been seen as evidence that he believed in Edith Thompson's innocence.[20]

In a letter to the *Daily Telegraph* published on 26 June 1951, Fryn Tennyson Jesse, author of the play *A Pin to See the Peepshow* and firm supporter of Edith Thompson, claimed 'officials at Holloway and . . . Sir Bernard Spilsbury . . . considered Mrs Thompson guiltless of any attempt to poison her husband or in any other way to try to get rid of him'. Ms Jesse did not particularise the circumstances in which she obtained Spilsbury's alleged views on the case. Examination of the transcript of Spilsbury's evidence does not lend support to her contentions, although his first two answers on the question of attempted murder seem clear enough.

> INSKIP. Did you find any signs of poisoning?
> SPILSBURY. No.
> INSKIP. Did you find any scars in the intestines?
> SPILSBURY. No, Sir.

Then came a qualification:

> INSKIP. . . . would you, if glass were administered, necessarily expect to find indications in the organs?
> SPILSBURY. No.

Spilsbury went on to explain how large fragments of glass might cut the lining of the gullet, stomach or intestines and, even if not fatal, might leave a scar. Powdered glass would immediately produce innumerable minute injuries to the delicate membranes lining the digestive channel. This would probably cause an acute illness, but if not – or if recovery followed – the glass would 'disappear entirely' from the system, with the possible exception of the appendix, in which fragments might lodge for a long time. Spilsbury said that he had found no indication of powdered glass in the abdomen, but this declaration was followed by a very significant question and answer.

> INSKIP. Is the negative result of your examination consistent with glass having been administered?
> SPILSBURY. Some time previously, yes.

Large pieces of glass, said Spilsbury, could have passed through the system without leaving scars. With regard to the poisons mentioned in the love letters, Spilsbury stated that 'there are very few poisons which would leave any indications, except . . . corrosive or markedly irritant poisons'. Inskip took Spilsbury through Edith's catalogue of poisons, starting with hyoscine, which was not 'markedly irritable', as was cocaine, widely available in the West End, linked to several high-profile deaths, and the subject of sensational reportage in the popular press. With regard to potassium cyanide, Spilsbury doubted if it would leave permanent damage: 'if it was recovered from . . . it would either kill quickly or recovery would occur within a short time'. It would be difficult, he said, to detect traces of sodium antimony tartarate after 'ten days or a fortnight'. Chloride of mercury, an intensely irritant poison, 'might shew results for a very long time . . . possibly some months . . . it might clear up in a non-fatal case within 3 or 4 weeks'. Digitalin would have no irritant effect, and morphine would not leave any traces.

Curtis-Bennett, in cross-examination, could only draw attention to the lack of evidence of scarring and of any powdered glass in the appendix. Defence counsel's shadow-boxing with Spilsbury is evident from the wording of his last few questions:

CURTIS-BENNETT. Some of these poisons you might find a trace of afterwards and some you might not; it depends when they were taken?
SPILSBURY. You are speaking now of the analysis or of the post-mortem appearances?
CURTIS-BENNETT. The post-mortem appearances.
SPILSBURY. There are not many of those poisons which have been given to me this morning which would leave any permanent effect at all.
CURTIS-BENNETT. Some would leave, of course, a trace in that analysis?
SPILSBURY. Yes, for a time.

Contrary to the views expressed by the writers noted above, Spilsbury's evidence in this case is an example of how he was able to put a 'spin' in favour of the prosecution on essentially negative findings. At the end of the day, the jury had to decide whether Edith had intended to kill her husband. The background of adultery and illicit passion undoubtedly fogged the issues in the case. Shearman invited the jury to 'try to understand what the letters mean; but you should not forget that you are in a court of justice trying a vulgar and common crime'. With regard to the eloquence of Curtis-Bennett, whose closing speech for the defence was a *tour de force*, Shearman's cold advice had its effect: 'You are not listening to a play from the stalls of the theatre,' he reminded the jury.

Bywaters and Thompson were convicted and sentenced to death. Many years afterwards, a juror, recalling that the jury had contained two women, showed how destructive the letters were to the defence case. 'Mrs Thompson's letters were her own condemnation,' he wrote, '. . . nauseous is hardly strong enough to describe their contents.'[21] At 9 a.m. on 9 January 1923 she was hanged at Holloway. At the same hour, not far away at Pentonville prison, Freddie Bywaters was also executed. At the end, Edith had to be carried – drugged with morphine, her legs pinioned – to the scaffold. Sir Ernley Blackwell at the Home Office, callous as ever, wrote that the execution was 'carried out in the most humane manner possible . . . it was thought to be more humane to spare her the necessity of walking from her cell, but she was not unconscious'. Although Spilsbury and Ms Tennyson Jesse sat round the same dinner table on at least one occasion after the trial,[22] there is no reliable evidence that Spilsbury ever questioned the rightness of the verdict at the time or had any doubts about the imposition of the capital penalty in the case of Edith Thompson.

In an eventful year officialdom was highly satisfied with the work of the Honorary Pathologist to the Home Office. Shortly before the end of 1922 he received a letter from the office of Prime Minister Bonar Law, indicating that the King had been graciously pleased to bestow a knighthood on Dr Bernard Henry Spilsbury. The public notice of Spilsbury's knighthood duly appeared in the list of New Year honours published in the *London Gazette* on 1 January 1923. He was the first dedicated forensic pathologist to receive such an honour. It was a remarkable achievement for a man of only 45, with no academic or clinical record of substance and who had practised only morbid anatomy full-time since 1905. There must be suspicion that his high media profile as prosecution witness in a series of widely publicised murder trials and his contacts with the judiciary, the Bar and the DPP had prompted the government to bestow this unusual honour. On 15 February 1923, at Buckingham Palace, he knelt before the King and arose Sir Bernard Spilsbury.[23]

The high regard felt for him in such influential circles had been illustrated on 15 December 1922, when Spilsbury, joint Honorary Secretary of the Medico-Legal Society since 1919, attended the society's annual dinner at the Holborn Restaurant (a popular venue for such functions, which stood at the south-west corner of Holborn and Kingsway).[24] The great and the good were out in force. The chairman was Lord Justice Atkin – the judge who had condemned David Greenwood four years before (see Chapter Seven) – and the dinner's guest list included Earl Russell, Mr Justice McCardie (trial judge in the Malcolm case), Sir Richard Muir and that *éminence grise* of the Home Office Sir Ernley Blackwell. Muir, introducing Blackwell as 'a man upon whose wise courses . . . successive Home Secretaries have relied', made particular and glowing reference to Spilsbury. With a clumsy attempt at humour, he said that the great pathologist would explain 'to a listening world that while there is some doubt about the colour of your heart, your kidneys and your liver are splendid'. Muir was well aware of the inestimable contribution that Spilsbury's 'positive evidence' had already made towards securing favourable verdicts in notorious murder trials from Crippen onwards.

In 1923 Spilsbury gave pivotal evidence in a bizarre murder case, where – for once – he must be criticised for what he did *not* say. Indeed, Spilsbury's silence on a vital aspect of the evidence led directly to a wrongful conviction. It was only by chance, two days before the scheduled execution and after his grave had been dug, that a young soldier was saved from being undeservedly hanged. The details of this case have remained hidden from public view for over eighty years. Examination of the official record shows why the Establishment was so keen to suppress the facts.[25]

On 22 September 1923, in boggy ground not far from the Rushmore Arena at Aldershot, in a corner of the 'Long Valley', or, more picturesquely, 'Clayton Bottom', a labourer named William Williams was blackberrying. He had an unpleasant surprise when his foot crunched on something hidden in the grass and rushes. 'I stepped right on his chest,' he later said. Williams had found a skeleton, wrapped in an army greatcoat. The bones 'fell out' when he picked up the coat. A broken quart bottle of beer lay near the remains.

From the outset, foul play was suspected. 'The ankles', reported *The Times*,[26] 'were tied together with rope', and Dr Gibson, a local doctor called to examine the remains at Aldershot Mortuary, thought that death had resulted from 'extreme violence'. Two vertebrae and the upper ribs were broken. The breast-bone was missing, although a portion was later found after a search. There was no injury to the skull, but a blow 'could have . . . stunned' the deceased.[27] There was to be no difficulty in identifying the body. Although the clothing had partly rotted and been gnawed at by rats, it was clear that the deceased had been wearing army uniform, including tunic, shirt, boots, cap and puttees.

Drummer James Ellis, aged 20, of the Leicestershire Regiment (by coincidence the regiment to which David Greenwood had been attached during the First World War) had disappeared from the Badajoz Barracks on the night of 25 May 1923. The army had billed him for £1 19s 9d for the missing greatcoat ('public clothing'),[28] but the money would never be recovered.

Although still a young man, Ellis had been wearing false teeth, which had been found in July – at some distance from the body – by a 14-year-old Boy Scout, Jack Court (of the 4th Aldershot Scouts). Jack had tied them to his scout pole as a rather splendid trophy. His mother, unimpressed, had told him to bury the two plates of teeth, dirty and covered in mud, in the back garden, from which they were eventually recovered.

At the inquest, Ellis was identified by Sergeant Drummer Harry John Ormes, 'mainly by the teeth in and missing from the upper and lower jaws'.[29] According to Sergeant Ormes, Ellis had six teeth missing because of an unspecified 'accident'. He had been stationed with Ormes at Athlone in 1922, when he had complained that he could not play a bugle without the teeth, which 'had been removed', so he was made a drummer. In fact, Sergeant Ormes knew a lot more about Ellis than the Coroner would ever be told.

Barrack-room gossip had pointed the finger at Drummer Albert Edward Dearnley, also 20, one of a family of nine children brought up in a working-class area of Hull. Dearnley had known Ellis, whose family lived opposite his home, since childhood. They had joined up together on 4 August 1918 – the fourth anniversary of the outbreak of war – and had become inseparable. Dearnley knew Ellis as 'Tot'; Ellis knew Dearnley as 'Pat'. Early investigation suggested a stormy personal relationship. They were 'constantly quarrelling and fighting, but . . . were quickly friends again'.[30] When Dearnley's possessions were searched, a letter was found containing 'serious allegations'[31] addressed to him by Hilda Storey, dressmaker of Bishop Auckland, who considered herself to be engaged to Dearnley. There was evidence of a fight in late April 1923 between the two soldiers outside a dance-hall in Aldershot, where Hilda, Orme's sister-in-law, was now living. Ellis, said Hilda, had intended to insult her. Later, Dearnley had told her: 'He is dead and only a mile away.'

Dearnley, questioned by police, made a long statement[32] in which he claimed that Ellis had tried to persuade him to go back to Hull, where they could get money, desert from the army and go to the USA. One night Ellis had said: 'I suppose you have been out with . . . the bloody cow.' Revealingly, Dearnley added that Ellis had later apologised 'and started to cry'. They had a few drinks on 23 May 1923. Ellis said, 'Do you like me?' 'Of course I do,' replied Dearnley. 'Well,' said Ellis, 'we'll have a game then. Let's play Cowboys and Indians,' and told Dearnley to tie his hands and feet and gag him. Ellis would wriggle free and catch up with Dearnley before he got back to barracks. He had put a 'top rod' (army slang for greatcoat) around Ellis's head. After tying him up, Dearnley's last words to Ellis were, 'Are you all right, Tot?' He said 'Yes.' When Ellis failed to return Dearnley did nothing, thinking that his friend had gone to Hull.

Dearnley originally told the police that he had not seen Ellis after 5 p.m. on the night of his disappearance. This inconsistency, coupled with the other evidence, was enough to persuade the coroner's jury to bring in a verdict of 'wilful murder' against Dearnley. Back in Hull, his father, a member of the Salvation Army, collapsed in the street on learning about the arrest and was helped to his feet by Ellis's brother.

Some twelve days after the inquest verdict, on 21 October 1923, Spilsbury, accompanied by Superintendent Davis, visited the place where the body had been found. Later he examined some of the clothing and parts of the skeleton. He quickly demolished Dr Gibson's theories as to the circumstances of the death. The broken bones, said the Honorary Pathologist firmly, had been gnawed by rats and fractured long after death, probably by having been stepped on. The *News of the World* of 4 November 1923 headlined DRUMMER SUFFOCATED – FAMOUS EXPERT'S THEORY OF HIS DEATH.

Ellis's height was just over 5ft 7in, about an inch taller than Dearnley. A drum-rope, some 18 inches long, had been wound round the wrists, led to the ankles, and tied round again behind the back, leaving just 15 inches between the limbs. Part of a pair of soldiers' running shorts, measuring about 2 by 3 inches, had been put in the mouth, over which a large handkerchief had been tied tightly and extending around the head. All the buttons of the tunic had been fastened. The greatcoat had been put over the head, with a belt, just over 2 feet long, originally from the back of the coat, going across the crown of the skull. The belt had been drawn tightly and fastened just behind the right ear. Ellis had also been wearing a ring, apparently one given to Dearnley by Gladys Lee, Ellis's cousin, in October 1918.

Dearnley was tried for the murder of Drummer Ellis at Winchester Assizes, in the Great Hall of the Castle, and before Horace Avory, whose ugly face, with its hooded eyelids and turned-down mouth set over a scrawny neck, superbly fitted his reputation as a hanging judge. Rayner Goddard KC (later to be another great hanging judge) appeared for the Crown. Dearnley's defence, probably a Poor Prisoners' Defence Act brief, was conducted by a single junior counsel, Robert Dummett, later to be appointed a London Stipendiary Magistrate.

The prosecution case was straightforward. According to Goddard, in his opening speech, Ellis had resented the engagement between Dearnley and Hilda Storey, 'although he was not a rival' (in the light of what is now known, this was a very inaccurate statement). On the night of 23 May the two young men had a few bottles of beer and quarrelled. According to Corporal George Smith, Dearnley had said, 'We had a drink or two and I got stuck into him. I gave him a damn good hiding and told him to fuck off.'

Sergeant Ormes gave evidence, stating that he had known Ellis since 1919. Hilda Storey had come to stay with Ormes and his wife at Aldershot on 11 January 1923. He had noticed that Dearnley's hands were bandaged on the morning after the Corporals' Dance, given by the Royal Scots Regiment. Hilda recalled, perhaps rather evasively, how Ellis had approached her on the night of the dance. He had not said anything because Dearnley had put his hand over his mouth. Several bandsmen gave evidence about the relationship between the men. They were 'chums', 'the best of pals', although one drummer thought their behaviour 'very strange'. One minute they would fight and straight away they would make it up. On one occasion, Dearnley attacked Ellis with a scrubbing brush, bruising his forehead. Another time they had fought with bayonets.

Spilsbury, as ever, crisply stated his findings to the court. The handkerchief 'would press this gag well into the throat and so form a very effective means of suffocation and with the overcoat drawn over the face . . . it would so almost completely exclude the air [causing] a very rapid death from suffocation . . . I think he would die within ten minutes.' Spilsbury, referring to the drum-rope, considered that the position would have been 'very painful'. The dead man would have been 'completely trussed' and could not have articulated 'more than a very muffled sound'. Spilsbury's evidence reads oddly. He had not examined the skull at all, but had conducted experiments with his own head in relation to the tightness of the belt and the handkerchief. Dummett, for the defence, in a brief cross-examination, made no attempt to explore this curious testimony. At the end of Spilsbury's evidence, the judge – despite a complete lack of evidence on the matter – raised a deadly point. Spilsbury answered with a typically sweeping statement:

JUDGE. Hypothetically, a person might be stunned by a blow on the skull without leaving any mark on the skull?
SPILSBURY. Yes, very easily.

Dearnley made a poor impression in the witness-box. The jealousy felt by Ellis, however, was well shown in this answer, awkwardly phrased in a long and rambling account of the events leading up to the death in Clayton Bottom:

> DEARNLEY. He did not want me to accompany the young lady. He wanted me to be still close friends with him.

Goddard was easily able to expose areas of inconsistency between Dearnley's written statement and his oral evidence in court. The judge, who had formed the view that Dearnley 'was the sort of person who could never be expected to tell the truth',[33] summed up for a conviction. Avory directed the jury in robust terms about the false teeth, which, according to Dearnley, Ellis had removed in order to drink from the quart bottle of beer.

> AVORY. Did you ever hear anything more ridiculous that that? . . . Have you any doubt that . . . they were knocked out and that is the reason they were found in the place where they were found?

The jury, rejecting the defence argument that this was a case of manslaughter as a result of a game that went wrong, took only half an hour to convict Dearnley of murder. Leave to appeal was refused in December 1923, and his execution was fixed for 8 January 1924.

The case had aroused some public interest, particularly in Hull, where glimmers of the truth may have been beginning to circulate. Moreover, Dearnley was young, fresh-faced and rather good-looking A petition for reprieve attracted over 23,000 signatures, and the local MP, Lieutenant-Commander the Hon. J.M. Kenworthy, wrote to the Home Office supporting the campaign. Legal Under-Secretary Blackwell was unmoved, however. Dearnley's story had been 'quite incredible'. It was 'probable that [the] pr[isoner] struck [Ellis] with his fists or with a bottle & rendered him unconscious'.[34] Dearnley's brother had died 'in an asylum', and his mother had become 'strange' before her death, but the jury had not recommended mercy, and Blackwell, as so often, wrote in his official memoranda, 'No possible grounds for interference.'

On 6 January 1924, two days before the execution date, T.J. Harding, the prison governor, was reading a letter that had been written the previous day by Dearnley to Hilda Storey. There was nothing unusual in a prisoner's correspondence being read before being sent out, and the authorities had powers, which were often used, to prevent undesirable letters (such as those criticising the verdict, the judge, lawyers or the system generally) from release, where they might be published in the newspapers. Harding, who evidently had a sharp eye, noticed a curious phrase in the letter. It read: 'Harry knows why I am here.' Dearnley also revealed that his relationship with Hilda may have been merely platonic: 'You always knew me to be of a quiet disposition, always respectable to you.' It was, however, the reference to Harry – Sergeant Ormes – that prompted Harding to speak personally to Dearnley.

Dearnley told him that, after joining up at the age of 16, he was posted to Ireland as Orme's servant. He spent a lot of time in Orme's room, where Orme was 'in the habit of committing sodomy with him', although, at the time, 'he [Dearnley] did not know how wrong it was'. One day Ellis had 'caught them at it' and, according to Dearnley, had threatened to expose him if Dearnley did not allow him 'to do the same'. Although at Aldershot (five years later, in fact) Dearnley had 'realised the evil of the practice', Ellis would not let him break away. The fights and quarrels were all due to this.

Harding thought that the boy's story 'rings true' and immediately contacted Blackwell, who had no choice but to respite the sentence, pending further enquiries. On 7 January 1924 the matter went to the highest level. Blackwell sent a memorandum to the Foreign Secretary, Lord Curzon, a very grand figure, former Viceroy of India, who had, to his immense chagrin, been passed over as Prime Minister in favour of Stanley Baldwin the previous May. The communication with Curzon, rather than with the Home Secretary, W.C. Bridgeman, may have been due to the fact that the Conservative government, defeated in the election of December 1923, was about to fall, a process that awaited a vote in parliament, paving the way for the first (minority) Labour government. Curzon suggested that Ormes should be interviewed, but Blackwell warned that it was 'a very delicate matter to make inquiry in the regiment as to Orme's association with the pr[isoner]'. Blackwell, understandably, first asked for a medical report on 'the condition of his "back parts"', which, in the coy phraseology of the prison medical officer, 'pointed to the prisoner's story being true'. Sefton Cohen, a lawyer in the DPP's department, questioned Ormes 'in private' on the basis that Ormes could not be prosecuted on the word of Dearnley (Ellis, of course, being safely dead). Ormes readily admitted having sex with Dearnley, although he claimed, a little disingenuously, that he was always drunk or 'had beer' when the events occurred.

In fact, the triangular relationship of Ormes, Dearnley and Ellis was the talk of the barracks. Ellis had been seen getting into Dearnley's bunk, and the two had been known to leave their accommodation after 'lights out', taking a blanket and returning in the early hours. One soldier had already asked Deanley some 'awkward questions' regarding Ormes, who had been instrumental in securing the promotion of his favourite to acting lance-corporal. Three other sergeants had been aware of what had been going on.

The episode now had the makings of a major scandal. Sir John Anderson, the senior Home Office civil servant, accepted Dearnley's story, even to the extent of assuming that Ellis had also played 'the active part'. In a guarded memorandum sent to the King on 11 January 1924 the Home Secretary referred to 'unnatural practices' and asserted that Ellis 'had pursued Dearnley to an extent which made his life a misery'. The King, according to his Private Secretary, Lord Stamfordham, approved the reprieve, exhibiting none of the petulance exhibited in the case of David Greenwood five years before (see Chapter Seven).

Dearnley was released on licence on 11 November 1932, having served just over nine years in prison, during which he was disciplined for the occasional fight, but also studied the violin.[35] He was said to have become 'a useful jobbing carpenter'. Hilda, who married another man in 1926, never visited Dearnley in prison. After the announcement of his release, Dearnley received threats of injury and moved to 56 Reswick Gardens, Ilford. His father 'always thought there was something more behind the affair than we were told at the time', telling the *Daily Mail*: 'You would understand it if I could tell you why . . . someone was thinking about the honour of the regiment . . . I absolutely dare not say why.'[36]

In a petition to the Home Office submitted in 1929 Dearnley had stated that he had 'conceived the idea of binding [Ellis] with rope with a threat to leave him until he gave me his promise to leave me entirely alone'. The truth is likely to have been different. Ellis, the soldier who burst into tears after confronting Dearnley about his fiancée, seems to have been the masochist in a long-standing sado-masochistic relationship, complicated by the interest shown in Dearnley by Sergeant Ormes. Ellis's teeth could have been knocked out in an early sado-masochistic adventure. On the night of his death, Ellis had probably been a willing partner in an exercise involving partial asphyxiation, a dangerous practice that, in some subjects, enhances sexual pleasure. The game of Cowboys and Indians went disastrously wrong. This view was certainly held by Spilsbury. In his 1951 biography the authors speculated that Dearnley had been reprieved because there were doubts about the truth of Hilda Storey's account, but stated: 'it is certain that Spilsbury made his own opinion clear – namely that the tying-up was an act of masochism performed at Ellis's wish'.[37]

Official records were kept very firmly closed for many years. Sir Ernley Blackwell minuted: 'The following papers are separately preserved & are to be kept *absolutely* & *strictly confidential. No-one* is to see them.' The Home Office file cover reads 'Closed 2033'.[38] Whatever Spilsbury may have said afterwards about the case to friends and colleagues, there is no indication in official papers that he made any attempt to tell the authorities his opinion either during the trial or at any time before the date of execution. As far as Spilsbury was concerned, it seems that Drummer Dearnley – a sexual pervert – was to be left to his fate.

ELEVEN

1924: Two Vintage Murders

On 18 March 1924, at a meeting of the Medico-Legal Society, Spilsbury read a paper, prepared with the help of Dr Percy Spurgin, a London police surgeon, entitled 'Cases of Sudden Death from Inhibition'.[1] Spilsbury described three cases from his own experience, noting that there were 'several areas . . . [the] stimulation of which may cause sudden death'. Risky areas were 'the back of the nose, the larynx, the pit of the stomach, the lower part of the abdomen, and the genital organs'. Two further examples were quoted by Spilsbury, both taken from the casebook of Sir Astley Cooper. (Cooper was a most eminent surgeon and anatomist in his day, but he had died in 1841.) The use of such old material illustrates how Spilsbury's career straddled the period between the Victorian age and the modern medical world. Among contemporaries Spilsbury's name continued to attract interest and, that year, he was Lettsomian Lecturer to the Medical Society of London, on the subject of wounding by firearms.

The same year, 1924, also saw Spilsbury's appearance in two famous murder trials, whose chronology overlapped in the first half of the year. The first was a strychnine poisoning case in the Home Counties, with elements of black humour verging on farce, in which Jean-Pierre Vaquier, an immensely vain Frenchman, was convicted of poisoning Alfred Jones, the 38-year-old landlord of the Blue Anchor Hotel, in the Surrey village of Byfleet.[2] Vaquier had been having an affair with the landlord's wife, Mabel Jones, commonly known as 'Mabs'. Vaquier, who had been staying at the hotel, was alleged to have put strychnine in a bottle of health salts that Jones had taken on the morning of his death, 29 March 1924.

Two days later, Dr Carle – a local GP who had attended Jones – removed the dead man's stomach and upper small intestine during a short post-mortem, and, odd as it may seem now, the body of Mr Jones was buried, without further detailed forensic examination, in the churchyard of St Mary's, Byfleet. The organs, accompanied by some surviving crystals, a spoon and the bottle, were, however, submitted to Dr John Webster for analysis at St Mary's Hospital. Webster found traces of strychnine on or in all the specimens.

The Vaquier case, in common with so many other murder enquiries of that era, had a distinctly relaxed forensic timetable. Spilsbury's opinion was not sought until nearly a month after this most suspicious death. On Saturday

26 April 1924 Mr George Herbert Bontell, 'builder and undertaker', raised and subsequently opened the coffin, in the presence of Spilsbury, Superintendent Boshier of Surrey Police, Dr Carle and Dr Brewer, who seems to have been instructed on behalf of Vaquier.[3]

The possibility of Dr Brewer's presence had caused some fluttering in the Home Office dovecot. Two days before the exhumation Sir Ernley Blackwell had noted that it had never been the practice to give notice of intended exhumations, which 'must be carried out with the greatest possible secrecy'. With regard to post-mortem examinations, however, there had been a recent occasion when Spilsbury 'as a matter of professional courtesy [had] intimated to the defendant's solicitor that he was at liberty to bring in medical men', but the autopsy itself was performed by Spilsbury alone. 'We do not wish to admit', wrote Blackwell, in full civil service mode, 'that . . . there is an absolute right on the part of the defence to have notice of the examination and to attend it.'[4] As will be seen, there would be at least one later instance[5] in which Spilsbury would not be quite so punctilious in informing a defendant's representatives of an impending post-mortem.

Spilsbury recorded[6] the appearance of the body as 'well nour[ished]', although press photographs suggested that Mr Jones had been a rather weedy individual. There was clear evidence from the victim's half-clenched hands of the final agonising convulsions caused by strychnine poisoning. Spilsbury removed the remaining internal organs left behind after the earlier post-mortem and took a sample of urine from the bladder, as well as a section of spinal cord. These were placed in the customary glass jars for forward dispatch to Webster, who found a total of $^{17}/_{30}$ of a grain of strychnine. In Spilsbury's opinion, this was just over a fatal dose of half a grain. Journalists, who had also doorstepped possible witnesses in Byfleet, even smuggled themselves into St Bartholomew's Hospital, trying to find out the results of Spilsbury's investigation.[7]

Vaquier stood before Horace Avory at Guildford Assizes on 5 July 1924. As this was a poisoning case, the Crown was led by Sir Patrick Hastings KC, Attorney-General in Ramsay MacDonald's minority Labour government. Hastings, who would later play a significant role in the decline of Spilsbury's reputation, was a reluctant prosecutor. He was a superb advocate, cool and calm at all times, a man who avoided pomposity and who was able to communicate with educated and uneducated alike, real gifts in the courtroom. In his early days at the Bar, he had briefly moonlighted as a journalist on the *Daily News*, reporting theatrical gossip, and never lost his love of the theatre. Unlike Marshall Hall, however, his dramatic sense led to understatement rather than to forensic drama. Although he had done some criminal work, Hastings had never prosecuted a murder case. After reading his brief against this most peculiar of defendants, Hastings felt no sympathy for him, but – unlike the judge, his former head of chambers – he was a humanitarian lawyer and found 'the experience of prosecuting a man to his death was one which I never desire to repeat'.[8]

Vaquier's physical appearance and demeanour were unusual, certainly in an English Assize court. The thick curly hair of his head surmounted a 'scraggy beard' (the unflattering opinion of the police officer in charge of the case), both liberally sprinkled with brilliantine scented with *essence de violettes*. From time to time he would run a pocket-comb through his hair and over his beard. He suffered from rheumatism, had a limp and a harelip, and was also rather deaf. Vaquier was defended by Sir Henry Curtis-Bennett, who considered Vaquier his most difficult client of all, 'a real handful'.[9]

Spilsbury, called to the witness-box by the Attorney-General, was once more acting the *prima donna*. His first two answers make strange reading:[10]

HASTINGS. For many years past, have you been pathologist to the Home Office?
SPILSBURY. Yes, not many years, only recently.
HASTINGS. You have now practically retired and only come in for special cases when you are asked?
SPILSBURY. Yes.

In 1924 Spilsbury, still only 47, had been Home Office pathologist for over thirteen years, and, as before in his career, he was playing with the idea of retirement. Unusually in a case where Spilsbury was the principal medical witness, the defence got a ray of hope from his evidence. Although analysis had revealed $\frac{17}{30}$ of a grain of strychnine in the body, Spilsbury considered that a dose 'considerably more than that must have been taken' when allowance was made for vomiting. Spilsbury went further, now starting to speculate – as he so often did – about the amounts ingested: 'Over a grain, I should think, and not much less than two [grains], I should anticipate.' In cross-examination, Curtis-Bennett, who evidently knew his man, drew Spilsbury on.

CURTIS-BENNETT. . . . . the probability is that he took as much as two grains?
SPILSBURY. Yes. I think that is so. Something approaching two grains.
CURTIS-BENNETT. And it might be more?
SPILSBURY. Yes, certainly.

This was potentially a very good point for the defence, because Vaquier was proved to have purchased less than a grain from a chemist in Bloomsbury (Vaquier knew no English and had signed the poisons book in the name 'W. Wanker'). Unfortunately Vaquier insisted on giving evidence, despite a written agreement and counsel's advice to the contrary. Vaquier irreparably damaged his case by denying virtually all the evidence against him. Hastings had no difficulty in mounting a deadly cross-examination. He privately thought that

Vaquier prepared himself for the demonstrative nature of a French trial and had mistaken the icy courtesies of an English courtroom for acceptance of his preposterous evidence. 'He appeared almost debonair in his manner,' Hastings later wrote, 'and, as the questions proceeded, he was apparently the only person in court who did not feel the horror of the rope being drawn . . . around his neck.'[11]

In his summing-up Avory disposed of the earlier defence argument about the quantity of strychnine ingested. He pointed out that Spilsbury had said that, even if there were only half a grain of strychnine in the dose, 'that of itself would be enough to cause death'. In a significant passage, Avory implicitly criticised Spilsbury's essentially speculative evidence about the amount:

> AVORY. . . . the statement of Sir Bernard Spilsbury that, assuming seventeen thirtieths of a grain is found . . . after death and assuming that the deceased had spat out . . . and vomited twice and brought up some of the poison, that probably two grains must have been taken into the body, taken into the mouth and possibly more . . . That, you will observe, is a mere estimate, based on a number of hypotheses . . . You cannot be sure that the man spat out any of the poison and how much he would have brought up in vomiting is . . . a matter of conjecture.

After two hours' deliberation the jury convicted Vaquier of murder. He seems to have been genuinely surprised and completely lost his self-control, swearing on his mother and father's graves that he was innocent. He attacked the jury for their 'iniquitous verdict' and was forcibly removed from the dock by order of the judge. Before his appeal, he claimed that he had seen someone – hotel staff or Mrs Jones – conceal something in the wall of a passage behind the Blue Anchor. Behind a loose brick the police found two bottles, one containing 23 grams of strychnine and another a strychnine solution, discoveries that, far from helping Vaquier, totally destroyed the defence argument on quantity purchased. At the Court of Appeal he shouted 'Je demande la justice', but this Zola-like statement was to no avail. In prison he attempted suicide two days before his execution by throwing himself at a wall. On the morning of 12 August 1924, like Edith Thompson before him, his legs were pinioned in the condemned cell, where, also unusually, a board was put behind the legs and the hood placed over his head. He was 'smartly lifted by the Assistant Executioner and, before he could realise what was happening (a few seconds only), he was on the scaffold'.[12] There was no struggling or shouting and Vaquier's last words, 'not in a loud voice', were 'Vive la France!'

The second major murder trial of 1924 was a brutal crime of a different sort, accompanied by one of the most ghastly dismemberments in forensic history.

Spilsbury's painstaking reconstruction of the victim's body was a remarkable forensic exercise, one of the high points of his professional life.

In the chilly dawn of Saturday 3 May 1924, at the distinctly unsocial hour of 4 a.m., a powerful police motor-car, headlights full on, pulled out of New Scotland Yard, crossed a deserted and still gaslit Westminster Bridge, and began the 62-mile journey to Pevensey Bay, near Eastbourne.[13] After consultation with Fred Wensley, now Chief Constable at Scotland Yard, Detective Chief Inspector Percy Savage (later to be one of the 'Big Four' superintendents of the Flying Squad) had been sent down to Sussex, accompanied by two other senior police officers. Shortly before 8 a.m., in a miserable rain, the car stopped on a shingle-covered approach road. A small collection of seaside buildings adjoined that forlorn stretch of beach known locally as the Crumbles, a vast stretch of shingle. The object of police attention was a single-storey building, with hipped roof and whitewashed walls, officially described as the Officer's House, Langney Bungalows, Pevensey. The structure stood on the seaward side, only some 25 feet from a row of nine other cottages. These together comprised a disused coastguard station, now let out as a mixture of holiday homes and long-term tenancies.

While Savage and his colleagues paced about, awaiting the arrival of local police and the door keys, they noticed a lurcher dog taking a keen interest in the bungalow, sensitive nose sniffing keenly, paws scratching at the gap between the wooden surround and the shiny black paint of the front door. When Savage and his team entered the property, they encountered a vomit-inducing stench of rotting flesh. Even these experienced policemen were shocked by the dreadful discoveries made within the house in circumstances that prompted an immediate call to a local doctor, Dr Le Crere, who arrived at about 9 a.m. on this 'dirty, drizzly, gloomy morning'.[14]

Immediate contact was made with the DPP, Sir Archibald Bodkin. Spilsbury, working his Saturday away in the private laboratory at Verulam Buildings (perhaps writing up his report on the Vaquier case), was disturbed first by a telephone call and then by a visit from the DPP's man.[15] Spilsbury agreed to come down to Pevensey the next day, surprising the Director's representative (who knew that Spilsbury usually preferred to work alone) by insisting that 'in such a case an assistant was necessary to take notes at [the] examination'. At Victoria Station next day, just after 9 a.m., DCI Savage could have been forgiven for thinking that he was about to accompany a pair of middle-aged newly-weds about to honeymoon at a fashionable south coast hotel. Spilsbury was immaculate, as always, in morning dress, black tailcoat, striped trousers, grey spats and black silk top hat. Although a decorous black appears to have been the colour-coding of her ensemble, Hilda Bainbridge's stylish outfit was remarkably ill-suited to the nature of the task in hand. Elegant patent-leather court shoes set off the slight sheen of her silk stockings. She wore a full-length sable coat, with shawl collar. The entire effect was crowned by a smart cloche hat with shiny black ribbon tied in a bow at the back.

At 11.21 a.m., the down train arrived at Polegate Station, where a hired car was waiting to take the party to the Officer's House. The weather had picked up, and larksong could be heard in the bright sunshine of a crisp May morning. Word had got round about the police activity, and a crowd of sightseers, inevitably accompanied by Fleet Street reporters, had already gathered outside the walled compound of the bungalow, where the blinds had been kept firmly drawn.

The lurcher's enquiring snout had not been misinformed. Spilsbury's progressive loss of his sense of smell served him well on this occasion. Spilsbury took off his tailcoat, detached his shirt cuffs, tied a large white apron over his black waistcoat, and put on a pair of rubber gloves. He had noticed that Savage had been handling body parts with his bare hands, risking contamination and infection, and, as a result of the Crumbles case, the use began of a professional 'murder bag' by the police at crime scenes.[16] Despite what Spilsbury knew he would have to do, he did not remove his spats (years later, Dr Keith Simpson remembered how Spilsbury had emerged from a post-mortem room with his grey spats soaked in blood).[17]

By the standards of his time Spilsbury was a thorough worker. He carefully inspected the whole of the house. The front door opened directly into a sitting-room (decorated with hideous black and yellow 'floral' wallpaper and bright-green curtains), which opened directly into a bedroom. A narrow hall at the rear of the house gave on to two further bedrooms, a dining-room, kitchen, scullery and two boxrooms. In view of the dreadful smell inside the house, much of Spilsbury's work was carried on in the yard outside, in full view of the waiting crowd. There he was photographed by the press, the great pathologist in action, standing outside the back door of the charnel house. In theatrical gesture, he was seen pulling a length of bloodstained cloth from a square leather hatbox. (Certain viscera had been laid out on a Pembroke table, but these seem to have been airbrushed from at least one published photograph.[18]) DCI Savage and another detective, calmly smoking in marvellous 1920s insouciance, were shown standing either side of a well-dressed man, probably the Chief Constable, Colonel C.M. Ormerod DSO (at this time chief constables were usually selected from the ranks of retired army officers). Hilda Bainbridge, looking intently at Spilsbury's examination, seemed to be hiding her face from the press cameras. The newspapers tactfully referred to Hilda as his 'woman assistant'.[19] What Edith Spilsbury made of the extensive publicity is not recorded.

Human body parts were distributed randomly throughout the house. Spilsbury considered this to have been the most gruesome case encountered in his entire career. With cool professional detachment he likened the investigation to 'building up a jigsaw puzzle'.[20] Spilsbury started his examination in the third bedroom, where he found a tenon saw, of the sort used by butchers to cut up meat. 'It was rusty and greasy', he later testified, 'and had a piece of flesh adhering to it.'[21] Nearby were 'a number of articles of female clothing and a teacloth, which were bloodstained . . . most of them were greasy and had coal or coal dust on them'. The dining-room was in an even more disgusting state. Close to the fireplace, whose fender was splashed with grease, subsequently identified as human, Spilsbury could see a saucer full of solid fat and a large two-gallon saucepan, which 'was about half-full of a reddish fluid with a thick layer of grease on the top and at the bottom . . . a piece of boiled flesh with some skin'.

Bloodstains were found on the hall carpet outside the dining-room door. Fireplaces in both reception rooms contained ashes of human bone, as did a dustpan and coalbox in the scullery. Here Spilsbury found an even larger, three-gallon, iron saucepan 'with a deposit of [human] grease', a 'galvanised iron bath containing a little greasy fluid' and an enamel bowl smeared with body fat. The smart, brown-leather hat box, bought from Barkers of Kensington, contained a 'silk-knitted yellow jumper', accompanied by thirty-seven pieces of human flesh. Part of a shoulder bone, collarbone and upper arm was mixed in with 'skin, fat and muscle from the region of the navel', on some of which blonde pubic hair could be seen. All these items, concluded Spilsbury, 'had probably been boiled'.

A cabin trunk, liberally sprinkled with Sanitas disinfectant and found in the first bedroom, contained large, uncooked and rotting pieces of human trunk. Two of these portions were wrapped in a nightdress and a muslin frock. Enclosed in a white silk wrapping were left and right sections of spine and chest, as well as two human breasts, each found in a brown paper package tied up with string. This ghastly collection was unlikely to have featured among *My Favourite Things*. Despite (or perhaps because of) the horror, some grim humour attends other finds at the Crumbles: pink cami-knickers and a pair of spats, discovered in a wardrobe;[22] heart, lungs, bowels, liver and kidneys, vital organs popped inside a tin of Huntley & Palmer's biscuits.[23]

The body had been variously burnt, boiled, chopped up and pulverised. The whole sad collection of fragments was painstakingly gathered together by Spilsbury, with Hilda's assistance, and taken to the laboratory at Bart's. That night, it is said, he worked until 6.30 a.m., 'carried out his usual duties during the day', before recommencing work the following evening.[24] A further night's work completed this immense forensic exercise. Between 900 and 1,000 pieces of bone had to be sifted through, identified and compared – in addition to work on the other dismembered remains. It was probably the most detailed pathological exercise carried out to date in England and remains an exceptional feat of forensic endeavour. Spilsbury's findings were, true to his usual form, concisely and clearly expressed: 'All the material, portions of the trunk, the organs, pieces of boiled flesh, and these fragments of bone', he reported, 'correspond with parts of a human body (no duplicates at all) . . . the four pieces of abdominal wall fit accurately to form one trunk . . . The body was that of an adult female of big build and fair hair.'[25] Milk could be squeezed from the breasts, and, after further microscopic examination, Spilsbury concluded that the woman had been pregnant, 'probably between three and four months'.

Exasperatingly, some body parts were found to be missing, including the skull and the bones of the upper neck, one of the ovaries and the whole of the uterus (with the exception of a small part of the vagina, which Spilsbury pedantically referred to as 'the female congenital passage'). Nor was there any trace of the foetus. With all his application and skill Spilsbury was unable to give a precise cause of death. This seems to have caused Spilsbury – a perfectionist under pressure in a high-profile murder enquiry – intense professional frustration. The woman had undoubtedly suffered from pleurisy, a condition common at the time and not significant. More importantly, a bruise was found on the left shoulder, which could have been the result of a blow or a fall occurring before death, but could not be shown to have been the operating cause of death. By the end of 6 May 1924 Spilsbury, for all his application to the task in hand, could take matters no further.[26]

The DPP was concerned to find 'some method of arresting . . . further decay' of the body parts.[27] It was noted that both the local Coroner's Court and the magistrates' court had 'freezing chambers', and Spilsbury was asked to telephone the Director's office to discuss matters 'in case the remains have to be preserved for future inspection'.

Meanwhile, the police investigation had made considerable progress. On the evening before DCI Savage made his first visit to the bungalow the police had detained a man at the left-luggage office at Waterloo Station, where he had attempted to collect a leather Gladstone bag. The young man was Herbert Mahon, aged 34, born in Liverpool to a family of 'respectable and hardworking people'.[28] An elder brother was the Vicar of Holme in Lancashire. Mahon had a deeply disturbed personality, making 'a suicide attempt with chloroform' in his late teens. In 1910, the year of his marriage to a long-suffering wife, he was bound over at Liverpool Assizes for stealing cheques. The police recorded that he was 'teetotal, a non-smoker, and very fond of women'. Six years later, after allegedly suffering a nervous breakdown, he entered a house in Sunningdale and attacked a young maid laying a fire at 6 a.m. (the joys of domestic service). Pulling a pillow over her face, he struck her nine times on the head with a cloth-covered hammer. Mahon appeared before Mr Justice Darling in June 1916 and received five years' penal servitude, a surprisingly lenient sentence from a normally tough judge, escaping the corporal punishment frequently imposed for acts of violence. Imprisonment also had the effect of keeping Mahon out of the front line in the worst years of the First World War.

Released from prison on April Fool's Day 1920, Mahon assumed the additional name of Patrick. Trading on his Irish extraction, he would whimsically term himself a mere 'broth of a bhoy [*sic*], who deserved to have been born at sea'. He secured a job as commercial traveller to his wife's firm and by 1923 was doing well, earning about £700 a year. Sociable and popular, he was a stalwart of the Church of England Men's Society and a Sunday School teacher. Nonetheless, leaving his wife and young daughter in cheap furnished rooms, latterly at 2 Pagoda Road, Richmond, he habitually overspent his earnings in gambling and womanising. Commercial travelling provided easy opportunities for sexual adventures, which ranged from 'a girl in Belfast' to Florence Russell, wife of the literary editor of the *Daily Express*, a woman whose infatuation caused her to 'loan' Mahon over £200. Although his company went into liquidation, Mahon was so successful a salesman that he was kept on by the liquidators. At the beginning of 1923 the receiver took on a new shorthand typist. Her name was Emily Beilby Kaye.

Emily was born into a professional Manchester family in 1885. Her parents and brothers now dead, she had amassed a small portfolio of stocks and shares, whose interest and dividends supplemented her modest working income. She came from a thoroughly respectable background. After several years spent working in Manchester, Emily – by now in her mid-30s – suddenly left for London, finding accommodation in the Green Cross Club, Guilford Street, which catered for both successful business woman and girls of slender means.

Contemporary descriptions of Emily suggest a hearty, rather lumpy person of a sort later so brilliantly caricatured by Joyce Grenfell, with a hint of Angela Brazil's ripping schoolyarns. Fellow residents of the Green Cross were 'dear old pals', among whom she 'chummed' with the slightly neurotic Miss Warren, whom she knew as 'Fizz'. Miss Warren knew Emily as 'Peter', and the pair would often be seen playing tennis in Lincoln's Inn Fields. 'Fizz' was able to list from memory the contents of Emily's extensive (and expensive) wardrobe and also remembered that her friend wore false teeth and a 'pair of mackintosh knickers' bought in December 1923 to wear with evening dress during her period (which Miss Warren referred to briskly as 'the usual thing'), the knickers being worn 'to prevent the possibility of an accident to her clothing'. Musquash fur coat, tailor-made fawn costume, silk kimono, quilted bedroom slippers, white Panama hat trimmed with black ribbon, yellow and purple striped blazer – and more – all these possessions would eventually find their way from the cosy, gossip-ridden security of the Green Cross Club to the wastes of the Crumbles and the grim status of exhibits in a murder enquiry.

Emily was bowled over by nearly 6 feet of spare, muscular man, deep-set blue eyes and a full head of wavy dark hair attractively flecked with grey. Soon, in the words of a contemporary account, she was 'suffering the acute love-sickness which appears in its most virulent form when contracted by single ladies approaching middle age'.[29] Miss Warren convinced herself that her chum had never enjoyed intimate relations with Mahon: 'You see, she told me so much.'[30] Emily had told 'Fizz' about her first outing with Mahon in August 1923, about Kingston, tea at Nuttall's, the Thames and the rowing skiff – but not about the sex on a quiet part of the river bank near Staines.

By the end of the year Emily was meeting Mahon for afternoon liaisons in cheap hotels. At the Green Cross, tongues were beginning to wag. Miss Warren sneaked a look at the handsome Mahon as he waited in the hall on Christmas Eve 1923, waiting to take Emily to dine and dance at Frascati's, the popular Oxford Street restaurant. In February 1924 she drew £404 from her account. The Treasury notes, as was the practice in those days, were endorsed on the back, but with false names and addresses in Mahon's handwriting. Emily sold investments and bought French francs with the proceeds. She had realised that she was pregnant, but was completely unaware that Mahon was seeing other women, paying for entertainment and gifts of jewellery out of Emily's savings. At the end of March 1924 Mahon bought his new 'fiancée' an engagement ring – with her own money. Her interesting condition would soon be obvious to all.

Emily had to go. On 4 April 1924 Mahon read an advertisement in the *Daily Telegraph*, offering the bungalow at the Crumbles for rental at 3½ guineas a week. That day Emily posted a letter to her unsuspecting sister in Manchester. 'Don't worry, old sausage,' she wrote, 'I know I shall be very happy.' Mahon, as 'Mr Waller', took a lease of the bungalow. On 7 April 1924 Emily left the Green Cross Club. At the bungalow, Emily and Mahon talked about their 'love experiment', but – on Saturday 12 April – Mahon bought a butcher's saw at Stainer's shop in Victoria. On either 15 or 16 April Mahon killed Emily Kaye. He stripped her body, laid it on a bed in the second bedroom and covered it with her musquash coat. He posted a letter written by Emily to Miss Warren ('Dear Old Fizz'), in which she wrote of going to 'Gay old Paris' with Mahon. 'Love to all my pals at the club and lots to yourself, old thing,' she wrote, signing herself 'Peter'.[31]

By Good Friday 18 April Mahon had started to dismember the body. After a few days of indecision in the company of Ethel Duncan, a good-time girl who was remarkably unobservant of conditions in the bungalow, Mahon had to grapple with the serious business of disposing of Emily's remains. On Tuesday 22 April he returned to the Crumbles, lit fires in both grates of the two reception rooms, and burned assorted bits of arms and legs. He claimed to have burned the head at this time. 'It was finished in three hours,' he told police, 'the poker went through the head when I poked it. The next day I broke the skull and put the pieces in the dustbin . . . It is surprising what a room fire will burn.'[32]

Edgar Wallace, the thriller writer and creator of *The Four Just Men* and *The Squeaker*, seems to have been responsible for a forensic canard, part of the

Mahon mythology. In 1928, at the height of his fame, he wrote an introduction to an account of the trial.[33] Claiming inside information ('a curious story which did not come out in evidence'), he embroidered the facts with some fine purple prose. 'The day was dark and heavy', wrote Wallace, when Mahon put Emily's head on 'a huge fire in the room'. Simultaneously 'the storm broke with an appalling crash of thunder and a violent flash of lightning . . . the dead eyes opened and Mahon . . . fled blindly out to the rainswept shingle of the deserted shore'. Wallace's story is easily disproved by contemporary weather reports. Conditions on 22–23 April 1924 were described as involving 'wind variable to north-easterly, light or moderate cloudy periods, fair intervals, risk of showers later . . . cooler'; 23 April was recorded as having featured 'rain or drizzle'. There is no mention of thunder and lightning.[34] A month later Sergeant Sheppard was told to burn a ram's head, with 'the wool and ears attached, just as it was cut off the sheep', in the sitting-room fireplace, and watched 'until it was almost reduced to powder', with the exception of a small and very fragile piece, about 3in by 2½in wide.[35]

On the Friday after burning the skull Mahon returned to the bungalow and, the following day, carried on the process of dismemberment and destruction. A stiff northerly breeze carried the smell of burning flesh out to sea and away from his neighbours in Langney Bungalows. He returned to London on Sunday 27 April and threw some body parts out of a train window between Waterloo and Richmond. On the Monday he deposited a Gladstone bag, with some highly incriminating contents, at the Waterloo left-luggage office.

Mahon's wife, meanwhile, worried about her husband's frequent absences from home, had found a card with Ethel Duncan's address. The last straw was finding the railway luggage office ticket, which Mahon had foolishly left in his jacket pocket. Suspecting no more than infidelity, she instructed a private detective, ex-Inspector Beard, and together they travelled to Waterloo. When the Gladstone bag was opened, Jessie caught a glimpse of white silk before Beard ordered her to stand back. What he found caused him to telephone Wensley at Scotland Yard. In the bag, heavily sprinkled with Sanitas powder, were several heavily bloodstained items of clothing (including 'a pair of torn . . . bloomers'), a tennis racket cover marked 'EBK' and a cook's knife, 'clean and new'.[36]

The inquest on Emily Kaye opened in the sitting-room of the bungalow, into which coroner, jurors, witnesses, policemen and reporters had somehow managed to squeeze. One sharp-eyed hack noted a plate of oranges still displayed on a corner cupboard. A huge crowd watched Mahon, brought over from Hailsham police station, emerge from a car, his face hidden by a russet-brown cloak. In the carnival atmosphere, 'like a bank holiday', cars were parked in the adjoining fields, people ate picnic lunches and hawkers sold sweets and drinks.[37] Some MPs were outraged, and their criticism plainly extended to Spilsbury's well-publicised public demonstration in the walled yard of the bungalow. Major Kindersley complained about 'certain photographs of digging operations' and Lieutenant-Commander the Hon. J.M. Kenworthy was shocked by 'ghoulish pictures' and 'unseemly scenes at the exhumation [sic]'.[38]

On 17 July 1924 the trial of Patrick Mahon began at Lewes Assizes before Avory. Sir Henry Curtis-Bennett led for the Crown. Mahon was represented by James ('Jimmy') Cassels, elected a Conservative MP in 1923, the same year that he took silk. Cassels, then 47 – just a month older than Spilsbury – was also a remarkable man, the son of a magistrates' court usher, who had started his working life as a Fleet Street reporter. Called to the Bar in 1908, he had built up a successful common-law practice. Tall and well-built, his down-to-earth manner and homely London accent went down well with juries. He had little time for the legal elite. 'People who go to a public school and then to Oxford or Cambridge never seem to forget it,' he used to say dismissively. 'They talk about it for the rest of their lives.'[39] He twinkled in court, had an impish sense of humour and, although not a great advocate, could be remarkably persuasive.

Avory had directed that no woman should serve on the jury, given the terrible nature of the evidence, and an elderly juryman collapsed during Curtis-Bennett's opening speech. Dragged from the jury-box, he was laid on the floor of the courtroom, where, at the judge's invitation, Spilsbury attended him. The hapless juror underwent the disconcerting experience of recovering consciousness to find Spilsbury standing over him.[40] The trial resumed, but the man soon collapsed again. Another juror complained of lumbago. After whispered conversations between Spilsbury, Curtis-Bennett, the Clerk of Assize and the High Sheriff of East Sussex, Avory discharged the jury and began again with ten original jurors plus two substitute members.

Mahon's defence, in summary, was that an argument had broken out at the bungalow between him and Emily. He had told her: 'I can offer you nothing but palship [sic]. I cannot be anything to you but a platonic friend.'[41] Thereupon, according to Mahon, she became very angry, threw an axe at him, leapt across the room and clutched at his face. There was a struggle, a chair was overturned and she was beginning to get the better of him when he fainted from fear and shock. He came round to find that Emily had struck her head on a coal cauldron by the fireplace and died.

Spilsbury's performance in the Mahon trial was masterly. When Curtis-Bennett appeared to have overlooked a point, Spilsbury gently, but firmly, made sure that it was not forgotten:

SPILSBURY. May I . . . add one small matter? . . . I am now satisfied that the
    skull and the bones of the upper part of the neck were not present in these
    fragments nor . . . the lower left limb beyond the point at which it was
    severed from the trunk.

The defence case was crisply disposed of in three answers, elicited by Curtis-Bennett, who was helped by the judge:

> CURTIS-BENNETT. In your opinion could Miss Kaye have received rapidly fatal injuries from falling upon that coal cauldron?
> SPILSBURY. No, she could not.
> AVORY. Just put it another way. Do I understand in your opinion a fall upon that coal cauldron would not cause her rapid death?
> SPILSBURY. That is so.
> AVORY. That is what you mean?
> SPILSBURY. That is what I mean.

Cassels, for the defence, made no progress. He canvassed the possibility that Emily might have died suddenly as a result of *status lymphaticus*, but Spilsbury maintained firmly that there was no indication that she had been vulnerable to death in this way. Although Spilsbury could not rule out a fracture of the spine, he quickly re-emphasised the Crown case:

> SPILSBURY. Because no fall . . . such as you have described would be capable of inflicting such injuries to the head as to cause rapidly fatal results.

Cassels was getting desperate. 'Compression of the spinal marrow' was raised, but Spilsbury countered by emphasising the flimsy nature of the coal cauldron, which, according to his view, would act to break the effect of a fall and 'reduce the danger of contact with the floor'. He batted away Cassels's attempt to establish that a twist in falling might have killed Emily:

> CASSELS. In a fall . . . where the coal cauldron had taken a part and the chair had taken a part and the body on top might take a part, you might even get a twist, might you not?
> SPILSBURY. . . . . I cannot conceive how it could occur.

Towards the end of Cassels's cross-examination, Spilsbury laid a neat trap for defence counsel:

> SPILSBURY. . . . . I think every case I have had of rapidly fatal compression . . . has been a case in which there has been disease of the spinal column . . .
> CASSELS. I suppose we need not go so far as to say that only diseased persons die from compression of the spinal cord?
> SPILSBURY. Oh, no. It requires extreme violence.

Mahon gave evidence. He had disguised the prison pallor of his face with a tanning lotion and wore a neat grey suit. Mahon seemed to think that his attractive physical appearance and easy manner would carry him through, but, just as Cassels was ending his examination-in-chief by asking, 'Did you desire the death of Emily Kaye?', there was a flash of lightning and a thunderclap. Mahon was visibly shaken.

Spilsbury was recalled briefly to give evidence, after Mahon had claimed that he had used a carving-knife from the bungalow to cut through pieces of boiled flesh, rather than the cook's knife he had bought. This was a bad point, and one that Spilsbury was able to counter by submitting – apparently without much justification – that the carving-knife, though in fairly good condition, 'as a carving-knife . . . would not be good enough to cut through skin'.

Avory's summing-up began with a tribute to Emily as 'a virtuous and respectable woman', in effect seduced by Mahon. 'Can you accept', he asked the jury, 'that from the first this woman, knowing he was a married man, designed to capture his affections, pursued him with her love . . . ?' Spilsbury's testimony was pivotal to the Crown's case. The defence called no medical evidence. 'You will bear in mind', said Avory, 'the evidence of Dr [*sic*] Spilsbury, than whom there is no greater expert in matters of this description . . . he is satisfied that such a fall could not have caused her immediate death.'

The jury was out for only about forty-five minutes before convicting Mahon. Mahon was sentenced to death. His appeal was dismissed by Hewart as 'a waste of time'.[42] Sir Ernley Blackwell thought that Mahon had 'probably struck her on the head with the coal hatchet' (although there had been no forensic evidence on the matter) and had 'therefore taken great reason to destroy the head'. A similar reason would account for the disappearance of the uterus: the fact that Emily was pregnant would afford a motive for the crime, which was, echoing the words of the Lord Chief Justice, 'a most cruel, repulsive and carefully planned murder'.[43]

As described in the Introduction to this book, Mahon was executed at Wandsworth Prison on 3 September 1924. His freshly hanged body was the subject of an elaborate post-mortem by Spilsbury, whose evidence had helped send Mahon to the gallows.

TWELVE

A Martyr to Spilsburyism

Within six months of his appearance in the trial of Patrick Mahon, Spilsbury was back in Sussex to investigate another human dismemberment, which, as bad luck would have it, also posed fundamental problems about the cause of death.[1] Since 1922 Norman Thorne had lived in a wooden hut near Crowborough, at the Wesley Poultry Farm, a small concern of some 2½ acres, not much more than a sea of mud gloomily fenced in with chicken wire, sited only 20 miles from the almost equally dreary Crumbles. Like Herbert Mahon (see Chapter Eleven), John Norman Holmes Thorne came from a respectable family background. His father was an Admiralty Engineer Overseer in Portsmouth, where Thorne was born in 1900. In April 1918 he joined the Royal Naval Air Service as a mechanic and was sent to France that October. Apart from some awkward landings in aircraft and being blown some distance by a bursting shell, he suffered no serious problems in the last month of the war.

A postwar job in electrical engineering fell prey to the economic slump of 1921. For some months Thorne was unemployed until starting his business at the poultry farm. In the early part of his stay at Crowborough he was a Sunday School teacher at the Methodist chapel, but from about spring 1924 he 'took more to pleasure in dances and whist drives'. He was considered to be 'very reserved . . . of sober habits', but had 'a number of lady acquaintances'.[2] Alan Bennett in *Forty Years On* recalled the despair of ex-servicemen who 'sink their savings in barren smallholdings . . . a few hens . . . [a] converted railway carriage . . . had seemed such a nice little going on in 1919'.[3] Thorne, just such a First World War veteran, had struggled vainly to make the doomed venture pay. By the end of 1924 he was neglecting his business and had become heavily in debt to local tradesmen. He certainly could not afford to get married.

If Thorne could not afford to get married, Elsie Cameron, his long-term fiancée, could not afford *not* to get married – or so she thought. Elsie, who lived with her parents in Kensal Rise, not far from the Thorne family, had been engaged to Thorne for two years. By November 1924 she had convinced herself that she was pregnant. Elsie, who at 26 was two years older than Thorne, had been a typist, but by 1924 was out of work. In poor health, she had been receiving treatment for 'neurasthenia'. In February 1923 she had consulted Dr Andrew Elliott of Southview Road, Crowborough. At first she complained of backache, but then admitted that she had 'a habit of self-abuse', which, Dr Elliott decided, somehow contributed to her back problem. At all events, she visited Dr Elliott several times. He took the view that she was suffering a nervous breakdown.[4] To members of her family she had spoken vaguely of suicide.

Sometime in 1924 Thorne lost interest in his neurotic girlfriend and took up with Elizabeth ('Bessie') Coldicott, a Crowborough girl. In November he was writing to Elsie that he was 'between two fires'. Elsie did not take the hint and responded by telling her fiancé that she now felt sick every day. 'Things will soon be noticeable to everybody,' she wrote melodramatically, 'and I want to be married before Christmas.' Thorne wrote back, admitting that he was seeing another girl. Elsie was outraged: 'I never thought you were capable of such deception . . . I expect you to marry me . . . My baby must have a name.'[5] After some inconclusive visits to the farm Elsie decided to act. She would move in with Thorne. Late on the afternoon of 5 December, after dark, she turned up on Thorne's unprepossessing doorstep. Thorne was the last person to see Elsie alive. By midnight she was dead. Five days later Elsie's father sent a telegram to Wesley Farm. 'Not here . . . cannot understand,' came the reply from Thorne.[6] On 11 December 1924 Mr Cameron informed police about his daughter's disappearance. A police constable spoke to Thorne at the farm, but he denied any knowledge of Elsie's whereabouts. Later, having attended Crowborough police station, he claimed that he had not seen Elsie on 5 December, but had expected to meet her at Groombridge railway station the following day. She had not arrived and he had since written to her, asking why she had not met him as arranged.

By now the press was interested in the story. Thorne, quite calmly, showed reporters and police round his bleak poultry farm, posing for photographs, standing on one of the chicken runs. He even joked with the pressmen that he had cut Elsie up. 'That's where I buried her,' he said, pointing to a chicken run.[7] Unfortunately for Thorne, Elsie had been recognised by two local smallholders walking near the farm late in the afternoon of 5 December. Initially the police seem to have decided that the identification or the date might be wrong, but when, in early January, a neighbour also recalled seeing Elsie that afternoon, Scotland Yard was brought into the frame. Thorne was arrested at Wesley Poultry Farm at 3.30 p.m. on 14 January 1925. The police, who had found items of Elsie's property, some of which had apparently been buried, put these finds to Thorne. He then admitted that he knew where her body was to be found, but denied having killed her.

Thorne made a statement to the police that was broadly consistent with the evidence he gave at his trial. Elsie had called, without warning, at the hut at about 5.30 p.m. on 5 December. She had a cup of tea and ate some bread and butter. Elsie made it clear that she was going to move in with him and insisted on marriage. At about 7.30 p.m., he left the hut to see if some neighbours could accommodate Elsie overnight, but they were out. On his return, Elsie continued to complain about his association with Bessie Coldicott. After supper, at about 9.30 p.m., he told her that he had to go out again, in order to meet Bessie and her mother at the station. Elsie, after some further protests, stayed in the hut with Thorne's dog.

At about 11.30 p.m. he got back to the hut. The dog was outside. On going in, Thorne found Elsie hanging from a cross-beam by a cord, rather like a washing-line. He cut her down and laid her body on the bed. She was dead. He thought of calling a doctor but, realising the awkward position he was in, he panicked and got a hacksaw. He stripped the body, burned Elsie's clothes and sawed off her legs and her head. He put the head, with the neck attached, separately into a biscuit box, because – so he claimed – the neck bore marks caused by the hanging. The trunk, the arms and the two legs were wrapped in sacking. Next morning, at dawn, he buried the box and the sacking-wrapped body parts in a chicken run.

Late on the evening of 15 January 1925 the police disinterred the remains, which were taken to Beacon Hill mortuary, Crowborough, where Spilsbury conducted a post-mortem two days later. Thorne was now under arrest, charged with murder, and although his story about the hanging was already known, Spilsbury (unlike in the case of Jean-Pierre Vaquier – see Chapter Eleven) did not inform Thorne's solicitor of the autopsy 'as a matter of professional courtesy', and no representative of the defence was present.[8] Spilsbury was the sole medically qualified person at the examination of the body, which had been buried 2 feet down in clay soil at the bottom of the sloping chicken run. The four pieces 'fitted together accurately to form [the] complete body of a woman', who had been about 5ft 2¾in tall. He found eight areas of bruising but no injuries to the skin over the bruises. With regard to the possibility of hanging Spilsbury noted: 'No groove in neck other than fold in skin. No indications of asphyxia.'[9]

Although Thorne had maintained that the couple had never had full sexual intercourse (apparently practising a form of *coitus interruptus*), Spilsbury found that Elsie was not a virgin. 'Healthy woman. No natural disease,' he wrote. 'Bruises all shortly before death – in two there immed:[iately] followed by death . . . Cause of death. Shock. Blows by blunt instrument.'[10] These findings were to be refined at Thorne's trial. With regard to death by shock, Spilsbury – years later – made a revealing observation. 'Shock,' he told the Medico-Legal Society, 'I regard as one of the most overworked terms in the medico-legal vocabulary.'[11]

There appears to have been some form of refrigeration at Crowborough mortuary, but the body was not retained in storage pending the outcome of legal proceedings, as would be the case today. Instead, the body parts were reburied, this time properly interred in a coffin, at Willesden cemetery. Thorne was evidently taken aback by Spilsbury's findings, which were revealed during the committal proceedings, particularly in relation to the absence of signs of hanging. In late February the defence brought in two medical experts, Dr Robert Brontë and Dr Gibson. The Home Office agreed to a further exhumation, which Spilsbury also attended. As Spilsbury noted on his case card, with apparent relish, four weeks had elapsed since the second burial and the coffin contained 'large quantities of water . . . reddish brown and foul [which] almost completely covered [the] remains . . . much changed by action of water'.[12]

Brontë drew Spilsbury's attention to two grooves in the neck, where tiny brown spots were visible in the skin. Brontë, according to Spilsbury, suggested that these were petechiae, but microscopic examination revealed, in Spilsbury's opinion, 'adipocere in sebaceous glands'. The stomach was examined and found to contain 'about three ounces of finely divided fat & starchy food . . . no meat'.[13] Both Spilsbury and Brontë took sections of tissue from the body. Spilsbury's specimens were made up into slides by Mrs Bainbridge (who was, of course, not medically qualified), and Brontë sent four tissue samples, in preservative solution, to Dr Woods of the London Hospital, who made up a number of slides. Two of these were taken from the 'grooves' (Brontë's word) on the neck.

Spilsbury and Brontë were temperamental opposites, their sparky interaction exhibiting a fierce clash of cultures. Spilsbury was the stereotypical Englishman, tall, reserved, economical with language. Brontë, almost a stage Irishman, a small compact figure, was gregarious (fond of a rude story) and wordy in the best Shavian traditions. Spilsbury considered his mercurial opponent to be slapdash and speculative in his methods. Brontë, who disliked the Englishman's *hauteur*, would tell a wickedly apocryphal tale of how Spilsbury – with his usual air of certainty – had identified a small body, found in an East End dustbin, as 'a well-nourished child who had undoubtedly been murdered', although the remains were later proved to have been those of a pet monkey.[14]

The trial began at Lewes Assizes on Wednesday 11 March 1925 before Mr Justice Finlay. The shade of Patrick Mahon, condemned in the same courtroom nine months earlier, seemed to haunt the proceedings (see Chapter Eleven). As in that case, Curtis-Bennett led for the Crown, while Mahon's counsel, Jimmy Cassels, led Thorne's defence. Curtis-Bennett, who had booked himself into the sybaritic surroundings of the Hotel Metropole at Brighton, had been briefed at relatively short notice. Two days before the trial, Crown counsel had a lengthy conference at the hotel with the officer in the case, Chief Inspector Gillan. 'Curtis', suffering from a heavy cold and cough, was very glad of the throat lozenges helpfully supplied by Spilsbury throughout the trial.[15]

Spilsbury's evidence lay at the heart of the prosecution case.[16] In answer to Curtis-Bennett, he described the state of the remains at the first post-mortem. He then detailed eight areas of bruising on Elsie's body. The first and second, both large areas (one was 2in by 1½in, the other 4in by 2in), were respectively on the back of the head, rather above the right ear, and on the right temple, extending down over the right cheek. In detailing the second bruise, Spilsbury's answer was in deadly form:

> CURTIS-BENNETT. Was it a severe blow . . . ?
> SPILSBURY. Yes, it was a crushing blow. It was not only the bruise, but the tissue underneath the cheek that had been pulped and a cavity was produced underneath the skin.

The use of the words 'blow' (as opposed to a more neutral expression such as 'injury') and 'pulped' gave the impression of an extremely violent physical attack by Thorne on his small, defenceless female victim. Spilsbury's description of associated bruising and haemorrhage in the right eye reinforced the vision. A third bruise was near the left eye, with some blood in the left eyeball. A fourth, small bruise was apparent on the left elbow, and a fifth, extensive area of bruising was found on the front of the right leg, down to the ankle, on the back of which a separate, sixth bruise was found. A seventh bruise was seen on the left shin, and the eighth was a small bruise on the inner side of the left ankle.

While Spilsbury was correct in stating that all the bruising was inflicted before death, his evidence regarding both the timing and the order in which bruising occurred was seriously flawed, giving the court a misleading picture of events on that fatal night.

> CURTIS-BENNETT. Can you tell from your examination as to which of those bruises were probably caused last?
> SPILSBURY. Yes. In the case of the two bruises on the face, the large one on the right side and the small one on the left side, the amount of bleeding . . . was much less than . . . in the other bruises . . . Those two on the face were, in my opinion, caused later than the others.

Although, in Spilsbury's view, all bruises were caused shortly before death, the two on the face were caused 'immediately before death'. Spilsbury was not asked how he had come to so firm a conclusion. Modern medical opinion holds that it is not possible to tell the sequence of bruises other than by examining their colour over a long period.[17]

Curtis-Bennett then introduced a devastating point against Thorne, apparently taking the defence by surprise, although Cassels raised no objection at the time. The construction of the first question shows that 'Curtis' was well aware that he was treading on delicate ground.

> CURTIS-BENNETT. Could the bruising that you found on the face – just look at those Indian clubs – could the bruising on the face have been caused –

I am not asking you to say it was – but could it have been caused by these Indian clubs?

SPILSBURY. I have not examined them.

CURTIS-BENNETT. Look at them now.

SPILSBURY. Oh, yes, they could. The two on the face certainly could have been.

The Indian clubs, a popular fitness accessory in the 1920s, had been found in Thorne's hut. There was no forensic evidence, such as blood or skin, to connect them with an assault on Elsie. Thorne had not mentioned using them in his statement to the police. Curtis-Bennett's sly fishing expedition with his prize witness had worked brilliantly. Spilsbury declared that the bruise on the back of the head, the bruise on the left elbow and the bruising to the right leg could have been caused by falling against a table in the hut, a fall that could also have caused the heavy trestle top to crash down onto her as she hit the floor. With regard to Thorne's claim to have found Elsie hanging from a beam in the hut, Spilsbury had 'particularly examined the neck' during the first post-mortem with this in mind.

CURTIS-BENNETT. Was the neck in such a condition that you were able to make that examination?

SPILSBURY. Yes, perfectly.

This answer conflicted with Spilsbury's later evidence of severe decomposition, a state of affairs that was not surprising in view of the length and circumstances of the burial in the chicken run. Spilsbury found 'natural creases' corresponding to 'creases commonly found on the front of the neck, especially in women', although Elsie, at 26, was still a young woman and unlikely to have had visible skin creases. Spilsbury claimed that the crease marks were more distinct because of the decapitation, which 'let the skin go up'. In the normal process of laying out a body, the creases would 'disappear'. This assertion is now considered doubtful, leading one present-day medical expert to conclude that Spilsbury would sometimes make up the evidence as he went along.[18]

Spilsbury also asserted that rigor mortis was complete when the dismemberment took place, a situation that would – taken at face value – conflict with Thorne's evidence of cutting up the body around 1 a.m., an hour and a half after finding Elsie dead, and before the body-stiffening process had begun. Spilsbury's evidence on this point seems to have been purely speculative:

SPILSBURY. . . . I think probably not less than six hours when dismemberment took place.

CURTIS-BENNETT. What is the least you would put it at?

SPILSBURY. Possibly five, more probably six or seven; or it might have been twelve or twenty-four hours . . . She died at ten o'clock.

Spilsbury based his timing, again powerful support for the Crown, by reference to the food residues found in Elsie's stomach at the second post-mortem. Curtis-Bennett, ignoring Thorne's statement that the couple had some supper around 9 p.m., referred only to tea at about 5.30 p.m.

SPILSBURY. . . . from the amount of food and its character . . . and from the fact that the same meal extended along the small intestines for a distance of several feet, I came to the conclusion that the period between having food and death was at the most not more than two hours, more probably about an hour and a half.

As with so many other *ex cathedra* pronouncements by Spilsbury, he never explained the methodology that led him to so dogmatic a conclusion. Furthermore, his own chronology was changing:

CURTIS-BENNETT. Supposing she arrives at 5.15 to 5.30, or up to 6 o'clock, in your opinion, by the condition of the stomach, she was dead by 8 o'clock?
SPILSBURY. Yes, 8 o'clock at the outside.
JUDGE. That is, if the meal was over by six, she would be dead by eight?
SPILSBURY. That is so, My Lord.

Modern medical opinion suggests that digestive tract contents are a most unreliable method of estimating the time of death.[19] Spilsbury's stated cause of death is similarly suspect. 'Shock due to bruises on the face, to the head, legs, and feet,' was the opinion of the Honorary Pathologist, but a person cannot die from bruising *per se*,[20] and, as will be seen, there was no evidence of brain damage from the head injuries.

Cassels, for the second time in a year, faced the virtually impossible task of undermining this mighty evidential phenomenon. Spilsbury, who often used cross-examination as a means of elaborating his conclusions, was able to put a gloss on his earlier evidence in a passage that contains propositions now considered invalid:

SPILSBURY. If . . . the woman was first of all thrown back and struck her head in falling, then the table fell on her . . . the effect of the fall would be to produce unconsciousness and blood pressure would fall rapidly and then haemorrhage on the face would be far less than before. If she died from the effect of these blows [with the Indian club] there would be very little blood.

Spilsbury was now 'satisfied' that the blows had taken place almost immediately at the point of death. In a speculative exercise, he had created a picture of Thorne smashing the Indian club onto the fallen body of Elsie Cameron. Cassels put to Spilsbury that Elsie could have died as a result of an attempted hanging. Spilsbury did not accept that death could occur instantly from an attempt at hanging, but it is a known fact that many hangings do cause virtually instantaneous death because of the effect of the rope on the nerves of the neck, which can cause cardiac arrest. Quite wrongly, Spilsbury dismissed the neck nerves as an operative factor in the case. Cassels, however, managed to elicit some significant information about the state of the body as found by the police. The brain was very decomposed, in 'an advanced state of putrefaction', though Spilsbury claimed to have got a view of the base of the brain 'before it crumbled up'. This evidence seems inconsistent with Spilsbury's earlier assertion that the neck was in 'perfect' condition at post-mortem. Cassels also made a little progress in exposing Spilsbury's failure to conduct a microscopical examination of the neck tissue:

CASSELS. . . . did you examine microscopically?
SPILSBURY. No, I examined externally and deeply probed the tissues of the neck.
CASSELS. By the naked eye?
SPILSBURY. Yes, but there was not a sign of abnormality . . . in any part.

Later Spilsbury said that he had made incisions, but found no single area that suggested haemorrhages or crushing of the tissues, or thickening or reddening of the skin from pressure made by a rope. Some of the sections taken by Brontë at the second post-mortem were said by the defence to show 'extravasation' of blood – that is to say, signs of subcutaneous haemorrhage consistent with hanging. Spilsbury dismissed the findings of the defence medical team, arguing – inaccurately, as it now appears – that all that could be found was evidence of 'disintegrated skin glands'.

The scene was set for a grudge match between Spilsbury and Brontë. During Curtis-Bennett's re-examination, Spilsbury made a pre-emptive strike on his opponent:

SPILSBURY. As soon as Dr Brontë saw the two marks on the right side of the neck . . . he made the remark, which I took down at the time, that they were the normal creases of the skin.

If Spilsbury did make such a note, it was never produced in court, and no such record appears on two surviving case cards made up in respect of the Thorne trial.

Dr Robert Matthew Brontë, then 44, said to be related to the literary Brontës, began his medical career in Enniskillen. After becoming assistant to the professor of pathology at Trinity College, Dublin, he held various hospital appointments before becoming Crown analyst in Ireland. More recently he had become pathologist at Harrow Hospital and the Samaritan Hospital for Women. Popular with London coroners, he had considerable experience of post-mortem work. In court, however, he seemed unable to summarise his experience. As opposed to Spilsbury's brief account of his professional appointments, Brontë rambled on from 'Meath Hospital' to 'Dublin Infirmary', from 'The National Children's Home' to 'Hume Street Hospital', not forgetting 'Drumcondree Hospital' on the way. Crushingly, and showing his anglocentricity, the judge halted Brontë's flow by abruptly inquiring, 'These are all in Ireland?'

Brontë stated, quite correctly, that it was impossible on the pathological evidence in this case to say that some bruises had been made later than others. He maintained that, had a deliberate blow been aimed at Elsie's head with an Indian club, this 'would . . . smash that skull like an eggshell'. There was an absence of laceration deep in the skin, and the skull had not been fractured. The extent of bruising gave no indication of the force of any injury: some women, as Spilsbury had himself written, bruise more easily than others. Brontë agreed that the naked eye would not give an indication of hanging. When he came to describe the significance of extravasation, however, he gave a long-winded answer, likening the flow of blood to mountain rivers, flowing into a vast lake, and flowing out again. 'If I may take a homely illustration – ', he started, but Cassels cut him short, directing his witness to the defence case that the cause of death was 'shock following an unsuccessful attempt at self-strangulation'. Brontë would not be diverted from the relentless flow of verbiage. 'I have brought with me, My Lord,' he told the judge, 'records of some four hundred or five hundred investigations, if you so desire to read them.' The judge responded wearily, 'There are limits.'

Curtis-Bennett, having got Brontë to agree that he had been instructed a comparatively short time before the trial, then played his trump card, trying to get Brontë to disparage the Crown's star medical witness with such questions as these:

CURTIS-BENNETT. I am sure you would be the first to agree that Sir Bernard is a very expert and distinguished pathologist? . . . I might say the greatest living pathologist? . . . Sir Bernard would not give evidence unless he had made a very careful examination?

Brontë did not rise to the bait, even when 'Curtis' put a preposterously worded question to him:

CURTIS-BENNETT. [It is] quite possible for an expert to tell the difference between a bruise caused fifteen seconds before death and at the moment of death?
BRONTË. I do not agree.

Brontë denied that he had said to Spilsbury, at the second post-mortem, that the marks on the neck were 'natural' creases (in fact, Spilsbury had said 'normal' creases). Curtis-Bennett also framed a disparaging question about Brontë's slides, noting that Dr Woods was the brother of one of the defence medical witnesses. ('Curtis' doubted the genuineness of the slides and, during March, had a long conference with Spilsbury, Sir Ernley Blackwell, the DPP's representative, and Chief Inspector Gillan at Curtis-Bennett's flat in Piccadilly. Spilsbury accepted that the slides were from Elsie's remains, but everyone at the conference was 'of opinion . . . that the evidence of Dr Brontë was unreliable'.[21])

Brontë, however, was not the sole defence medical witness. In total, seven doctors were called, of whom two stand out. The first was Dr David Nunes Nabarro, a Harley Street physician, who – unlike Spilsbury – had won a Gold Medal in medicine from London University. He was Consultant Pathologist to Great Ormond Street Children's Hospital and had been Assistant Professor of Pathology and Bacteriology at University College Hospital. (In later life Dr Nabarro became an authority on the transmission and prevention of syphilis.) The transcript of Nabarro's evidence in the Thorne case is impressive. Like Spilsbury, he stated his opinions simply and with precision. Unlike Spilsbury, Nabarro attended the trial voluntarily and charged no fee. He had examined the four slides prepared by Brontë. Although there was marked putrefactive change evident in the slide of tissue from the right cheek, rendering the specimen 'almost structureless', the two slides from the neck showed 'very definite extravasation . . . indicating a certain amount of trauma – injuries – either from pressure or from some form of injury'. He agreed that Spilsbury's own slides 'showed very little'. Curtis-Bennett seems to have been impressed by Nabarro and, as a result, kept cross-examination brief. Nevertheless, Nabarro was able to make a significant adverse comment on Spilsbury's emotive reference to 'pulping' of facial tissue:

> NABARRO. I think that a blow of sufficient force to cause pulping of the tissues as Sir Bernard Spilsbury describes would either have torn the skin or broken this bone or done both . . . [The 'pulping' appearance] must have been post-mortem putrefaction, with the growth of organisms and so on.

Dr Hugh Miller Galt, former professor at Glagow University and medico-legal examiner for the Crown in Scotland, gave similar evidence, calling the bruises 'trifling, as one might see in Rugby football every Saturday'. Galt correctly stated that, in themselves, '[bruises] do not cause shock or sudden death'. The prosecution had conceded that Elsie's skull was exceptionally thin. Galt robustly declared: 'I can guarantee . . . that it [the Indian club] would not only make a bruise . . . but smash the skull at one blow.'

The defence evidence was sufficiently cogent to prompt Spilsbury, probably after consultation with Curtis-Bennett, to meet Nabarro and Galt, on Sunday 15 March, so that both sides could examine each other's slides. Spilsbury was later recalled and amended his evidence about a 'cavity' in the facial tissue, downgrading this to 'a small pocket full of fluid', which now had little evidential significance. Spilsbury added that he, Nabarro and Galt 'had a frank and free discussion', probably a euphemism for a very strained atmosphere and an answer that suggests that the gulf between the expert witnesses was as wide as ever.

In the absence of any defence representative police officers had examined the beams of the hut, said to have been covered with undisturbed dust and cobwebs. It was submitted by the Crown that, had Elsie hanged herself, there would have been marks, even indentations, on the beams, but – as Cassels later submitted to the jury – it all depended on how Elsie had attempted suicide. Four years after the trial Helena Normanton, pioneer woman barrister and feminist author, drew attention to a factor that was never considered by the all-male court:[22] Elsie had been on the verge of starting her period. 'The onset of menstruation', wrote Normanton, 'often takes the form of an intense and severe melancholy', a situation that would now be termed pre-menstrual tension or PMT. Normanton noted that it had not occurred to the defence to call medical evidence on the point, which could have corroborated Thorne's evidence of a suicide attempt. If Elsie had suddenly realised that she was not pregnant, she would have realised that her chance of marriage to Thorne had vanished. Her death could have resulted from suicide or from a sham suicide, set up as Thorne came back to the hut late on the fatal night.

Thorne, a stocky young man with a slightly puffy face and jet-black hair, appeared too clever, almost cocky, in the witness-box. His quiet habit of making notes of the evidence had already been observed. He would not admit having had a physical struggle with Elsie, which would have accounted for the bruising, and he was badly tripped up by Curtis-Bennett. Thorne had given evidence that suggested he had agreed, albeit reluctantly, to marry Elsie if she were pregnant:

CURTIS-BENNETT. When you went out at 9.30, did Miss Cameron still believe that you would carry out your promise?
THORNE. Yes.
CURTIS-BENNETT. *(Pausing between each word)* Then – why – did – she – commit – suicide?
THORNE. Why? She left no message behind and I don't think it is safe for me to say.

Reviewing the medical evidence in his summing-up, the judge referred to Spilsbury's evidence, in a eulogistic passage, as 'really the very best opinion that can be obtained'. Although Brontë's less-than-impressive performance had been redeemed to some extent by the cogent testimony of Drs Nabarro and Galt, the Spilsbury effect had triumphed. The jury was out for only half an hour before convicting Thorne of murdering Elsie Cameron. Mr Justice Finlay's voice faltered as he passed his first death sentence. Bessie Coldicott was booed by a large crowd, made up 'almost exclusively of women', as she walked away from court down to Lewes railway station.[23]

Thorne took the verdict with composure and believed that he would succeed on appeal. Before the Court of Appeal he was represented by William Jowitt KC, who would later figure in Spilsbury's most notorious murder trial, that of Sydney Fox (see Chapter Fifteen). Jowitt argued that the bitter dispute between the medical witnesses should be referred to special commissioners under Section 19 of the Criminal Appeal Act 1907. 'Your lordships will never find a stronger case than this,' he submitted, but Hewart, the Lord Chief Justice, blandly declined to disturb the verdict of the jury. With conflicting views in front of them, he declared, they had reached a unanimous conclusion. 'There is no ground whatever for the suggestion that the jury . . . would not be likely to have the capacity to discriminate between the conflicting views.'[24] The appeal was dismissed. Thorne at last broke down, shouting, 'It isn't fair. I didn't do it', as he was taken down to the cells.[25]

The trial aroused widespread public controversy. The influential *Law Journal* expressed 'profound disquiet' at a verdict 'arrived at by a lay jury in so remarkably short a time after a grave conflict of medical evidence', finding it 'something of a shock that twelve men in half-an-hour had "no reasonable doubt" that Sir Bernard Spilsbury's unsupported view was right'.[26] The *Law Journal* castigated the Court of Appeal for following 'the man with the biggest name', noting 'the more than Papal infallibility with which Sir Bernard Spilsbury is rapidly being invested by juries'. Among the newspapers even the ultra-Conservative *Morning Post* considered that 'the doubts of laymen are shared by many members of the Bar', finding that 'a sense of uneasiness prevails' after the Court of Appeal's decision.[27] The *Sunday Express* published a well-written article by 'A Criminal Lawyer', who argued that Thorne could have lied 'out of fear' and that Elsie's injuries were consistent with a struggle in the hut. Thorne's denial that anything of the sort had taken place meant that a verdict of manslaughter had not been open to the jury.[28] The *Daily Mail*, on the other hand, entirely agreed with the jury's verdict.[29] The *Daily Herald* printed a letter from a juror, J.W. Hill, of Moscow Road, Hastings. Mr Hill claimed that the jury had given its verdict 'on a very careful consideration of the evidence', which was 'weighed and sifted'. It was absurd to suggest, wrote Mr Hill, that they had 'invested Sir Bernard Spilsbury with papal infallibility and blindly accepted his evidence on his reputation'. The defence case contained too many 'inconsistencies, inaccuracies and falsehoods' for the jury to have been influenced by 'minor pathological details'.[30] Mr Hill's claim would have carried more weight if the jury had spent rather longer than half an hour to come to their verdict in a capital case, with so complex an evidential background.

Sir Arthur Conan Doyle, who lived near Crowborough, was 'not quite easy' about the case and hoped for a reprieve. Doyle, who at that time was devoting his energies to secure the release of Oscar Slater (wrongly convicted of a robbery and murder in 1908), thought that there might be 'a faint doubt' existing in the Thorne case.[31]

Meanwhile Thorne's father was waging a surprisingly effective campaign for his son's reprieve. Much to the annoyance of the Home Office, letters written by Thorne began to appear 'exclusively' in the mass-circulation *News of the World* soon after the trial, even though he had been forbidden to write such 'autobiographical stuff' (Blackwell's words) while on remand in February.[32]

Thorne's letters were regularly suppressed. In a letter dated 25 March Thorne had written of his belief 'that Spilsbury was called in, not to give *medical* evidence, but to give evidence *for* the prosecution'. In another letter he wrote that people were 'forming their own opinions about Spilsbury . . . the whole case is developing into a medical problem of Spilsbury's theory against my facts'. In yet another, dated 27 March 1924, addressed to his father at 115 Holland Road, Willesden, Thorne complained of 'the verdict of a sleepy jury', adding 'what do they know about sebaceous glands, subcutaneous capillaries, rigor mortis, extravasation etc. They imagine the bruises as being something terrible, instead of being so slight that the great Sir Bernard Spilsbury had to put them under a microscope to make sure that it [sic] was not post mortem signs.'

In another suppressed letter, dated 28 March, Thorne wondered whether his father had received his last two communications, admitting that 'I have put my foot in it by passing some remarks about Spilsbury'. At the Home Office Sir Ernley Blackwell, evidently irritated, noted in Thorne's file that 'pr[isoner] again criticises Spilsbury . . . [the letters] are evidently meant for publication. They are stopped . . . Pr[isoner] should be told that he cannot . . . write disrespectfully of persons in any way connected with the case.'

Just below Blackwell's initials is a short endorsement: 'I quite agree WJH.' The initials 'WJH' stand for William Joynson-Hicks, the puritanical Home Secretary of Stanley Baldwin's Conservative government. 'Jix' began life as plain Mr Hicks, but the adoption of a double-barrelled name attended his rise to political office. A keen low churchman, who today might be termed a fundamentalist Christian, Joynson-Hicks exhibited strongly authoritarian tendencies. He tried to turn the postwar clock back to Victorian values, using such weapons as the licensing acts to persecute or even close down nightclubs of which he disapproved. A populist politician of no great intellect, Joynson-Hicks seems to have been particularly anxious to prevent the Thorne affair from becoming a problematic 'verdict in dispute'. In his secret minute to Joynson-Hicks, Blackwell noted the trial judge's reservations about the murder conviction. Finlay had spoken privately to Blackwell about the matter.

'If Thorne had told the truth', said the judge, '. . . that there had been a struggle and that the girl had died as a result of injuries received, the Jury might have brought in the verdict of manslaughter.' Blackwell swept aside such judicial bleatings. 'I see no reason to doubt', he wrote, 'that the jury were right in accepting Sir Bernard's view that there had been no constriction of the neck.' Joynson-Hicks, spending his Easter break in the Palladian elegance of Kingston Maurward House in Dorset, wholeheartedly agreed with the view of his Legal Under-Secretary. 'I disregard the curious and unnecessary remarks of the judge,' he wrote, later making disparaging reference to the 'stupid *obiter dicta* of Finlay'. The Home Secretary's own reasoning does not exactly win prizes for use of English: 'If he was right, Thorne was not guilty of murder even though he might be a liar. But I disregard it.'[33]

Probably on the advice of Blackwell, the Home Secretary held a 'personal conference' with Hewart, the Lord Chief Justice, on the afternoon of 21 April 1925, the eve of Thorne's execution.[34] 'I regret to say', announced Joynson-Hicks in a letter addressed to Thorne's solicitor, 'that after examining [the case] in detail from every point of view, I can see no reason at all to advise his Majesty to interfere with the sentence.' The following day, the story, which was clearly designed to show how carefully and dispassionately the matter had been considered by the Home Secretary, duly appeared in the national daily press and in the subsequent Sunday papers.

What the public did not know was that the well-publicised meeting was probably unique in English penal history. A neatly penned minute, tucked away in a Home Office file nominally closed until 2026, shows that the Home Secretary's published letter was thoroughly misleading. The practice of being economical with the truth did not begin in the 1980s with Mrs Thatcher and Lord Armstrong. In addition to Blackwell, who minuted the occasion, two other men took their seats at this extraordinary conference, unknown to the public at large. One was Sir Archibald Bodkin, the DPP and therefore Thorne's prosecutor. That was bad enough, but that the other man should have been Spilsbury – a central and highly contentious witness for the Crown – was outrageous and wholly inexcusable. While there is no record that Spilsbury said anything, his mere presence at such a meeting, whose outcome cannot have been in doubt, makes it hard to see how justice was manifestly done in the case of Thorne.

Thorne was executed by Tom Pierrepoint and his assistant, Phillips, at Wandsworth on 22 April 1925. The execution took place at 8 a.m., an hour earlier than expected, with a view to avoiding a demonstration by the 'Christian Mission of Intercession' outside the prison.[35]

In his last letter Thorne wrote to his father: 'A flash & all is finished, *no*, not finished but just starting & I shall wait for you, just as others are waiting for me. With all my love, Your loving son, Norman xxxxx.'[36]

The Home Office was unmoved by Mr Thorne's request to see the suppressed letters from his son. Officials were instructed to lie about the matter. 'The father can be told, if he makes further enquiry about the letters & papers, that they have been destroyed.'[37] Two days before the execution the *Star* had published Thorne's epitaph, words written to his father from the condemned cell: 'Never mind, dad, don't worry. I am a martyr to Spilsburyism.'[38]

THIRTEEN

Not Proven

Spilsbury's public reputation had survived the controversy generated by the Thorne case (see Chapter Twelve), although, in private, doubts about his dogmatic approach to evidence were beginning to surface among legal and medical circles. For the press, however, Spilsbury remained excellent copy, the very mention of his name a boost to circulation. On 11 December 1925, in his role as secretary of the Medico-Legal Society, he had proposed the toast of 'Our Guests' at the annual dinner. One of those guests was Legal Under-Secretary Sir Ernley Blackwell, on whose recommendation hundreds of people had been executed since 1907, who gave the society the benefit of his crabbed opinion that no other country 'could show so a large a number of guilty persons who had left the court without being subjected to any punishment'.[1]

In his own speech Spilsbury referred to a series of addresses, given at Lord Justice Atkin's request, to law students of London University. Keen on the enterprise, Spilsbury had even shown the students round his small laboratory at Bart's. He took the opportunity to argue the need for 'a central institute of medico-legal jurisprudence',[2] noting how far London was behind Edinburgh in this respect. Edinburgh had established the world's first Chair of Medical Jurisprudence in 1807, but nothing comparable existed in London. As in the case of so many of his proposals, Spilsbury seems to have made no serious effort to put his ideas into practice. In fairness, it is possible that he failed to follow through because of the sheer size and diversity of his daily workload. For many years he had coped with heavy post-mortem lists and frequent court appearances in criminal and civil cases, and at inquests. By the mid-1920s he was an active council member of the pathological section of the Royal Society of Medicine (of which he was a fellow); he lectured on morbid anatomy and histology at Bart's and on forensic medicine and toxicology at the London School of Medicine for Women; he was examiner in forensic medicine at Oxford, Manchester and Birmingham universities; and was assistant examiner in pathology at the University of London. Furthermore, in addition to his work at the Medico-Legal Society, he was a member of other medical societies, including the famous Sydenham Club at Bart's. In 1924, at the relatively late age of 47, he had sat and passed an examination to become a member of the Royal College of Physicians (MRCP).

Notwithstanding his superb skills as a witness and his commanding presence in court, Spilsbury was regarded by students as a dull lecturer, who spoke in a dry monotone and showed real animation only when doing practical demonstration work with specimens. Despite a personal antipathy to women doctors, Spilsbury is remembered as having been kindly and courteous to his female students. In general, he seemed genuinely interested in the welfare and careers of those in his tutelary care.

On 2 May 1926 he may have taken time from this relentless schedule to attend a dinner of Our Society at the New Adelaide Gallery, King William Street. A paper on the Vaquier case (see Chapter Eleven), two years on, was given by a crime writer, W. Teignmouth Shore, and by Robert Blundell, who had 'devilled' (which probably meant, in that context, taking a longhand note) for Curtis-Bennett. There would have been no question of Hilda Bainbridge attending such gatherings. The public face of respectability had to be maintained (in any case Our Society did not admit women guests until 1980). Although their lives had largely diverged, Spilsbury was still married to Edith, and their relationship remained politely cordial, if no longer intimate.

At the end of 1926 Spilsbury suffered a cruel personal blow, the effect of which must have been to reinforce his feelings of isolation, introspection and depression. On 20 November Hilda Bainbridge fell ill with pneumonia. Whether she suffered from virus pneumonia or from some other bacterial infection is not known, but in 1926 active treatment for pneumonia was practically non-existent. A vaccine had been developed to combat the *pneumococcus* bacterium, but, according to a contemporary textbook, 'in acute pneumonia the benefit . . . is at present doubtful'.[3] Rest in bed, plenty of fluid and traditional nursing methods formed the basis of care. Hilda's fight for life lasted 'six days, ten hours' until 27 November 1926. Her brother, H.E. Stanley Smith, a solicitor, was present at her death, which took place at her flat in Chenies Street Chambers. Under the heading of occupation, the death certificate gives 'a pathologist's assistant', a simple and moving description of her work with Spilsbury. In the 1920s the professional classes attached great value to reticence. Hearts were, by and large, not worn on sleeves. Discretion and respectability together formed the keystone of many lives.

Spilsbury's 'mid-life crisis', already noted, seems to have started around the time that he forsook St Mary's for Bart's, where Hilda's husband was Professor. The flat at Gray's Inn, with its own laboratory, not far from Chenies Street Chambers, was taken in 1921 – the year of Professor Bainbridge's death. Spilsbury's insistence that Hilda should accompany him to the terrible murder scene at the Crumbles was itself a remarkable request in an era when women mortuary assistants were rare. Hilda kept a large framed photograph of Spilsbury in her home. Although the truth may never be known, circumstances suggest the existence of a close – if intensely private – love affair between the Honorary Pathologist and his assistant.

Just over a month after Hilda's death Spilsbury – in a rare foray as defence witness – was instructed in a Scottish murder case whose 'Not Proven' verdict had ramifications extending well beyond Spilsbury's lifetime. In the words of William Roughead, the great Scots crime writer, the case 'bristles with interest, social and scientific . . . [and] abounds in psychological, evidential and medico-legal problems'.[4] Donald Merrett was born, an only child, in North Island, New Zealand, on 17 August 1908. His parents, who soon moved successively to Russia and Switzerland, were ill-suited, and the marriage was effectively over before the First World War started. Mrs Merrett and her son spent part of the war in Switzerland, where she looked after wounded British officers, later managing to get back to England. Here she worked for the Ministry of Food, even inventing a 'fireless cooker', named after her. After a few years spent in New Zealand, mother and son returned to England in 1924. Donald, now 16, was sent to Malvern College for a year. (By coincidence, Spilsbury's tomboy daughter Evelyn, two years younger than Merrett, was then a pupil at the Abbey School, Malvern.)

As he entered his later teens Merrett seems to have been precociously intelligent and physically developed. He looked older than his years and had quickly developed some alarmingly adult habits. Despite no lack of material comforts, his upbringing had been deeply disturbed. The break-up of his parents' marriage and the frequent long-distance moves probably contributed to a serious personality disorder. Mrs Merrett originally destined her son for Oxford, but his wayward behaviour caused her to move to Edinburgh, where Merrett could attend a non-resident university under her eye. Eventually she took a furnished flat, a conversion on the first floor of a solid Edinburgh terrace house, 31 Buckingham Place, off Queensferry Road, north-east of the New Town.

As a mother Bertha Merrett seems to have been both possessive and over-protective. Her son, possibly in reaction to this stifling attitude, was sly and wayward. Although he enrolled at the university, unknown to his mother he soon stopped attending classes, preferring to visit dance-halls such as the Dunedin Palais de Danse in Picardy Place, at the east end of the New Town, not far from the Calton Hill. By early 1926 Merrett, though still only 17, had become involved with 'a dance instructress'[5] named Betty Christie, buying expensive items and jewellery for her and an 'AJ' motorcycle for himself. On 13 February he bought, for £1 15s, a Spanish .25 automatic pistol and fifty rounds of ammunition from Hardy Brothers at 101 Princes Street. Somehow, despite his youth, Merrett also managed to obtain a firearms certificate. His mother's allowance to him of 10s a week was hopelessly inadequate for life in the fast lane. Merrett became deeply in debt. On 2 February he started acquiring money by forging cheques drawn on his mother's account.

On 17 March 1926, sometime after 9 a.m., Bertha Merrett was sitting at a table in the middle of her sitting-room, writing a letter. Her open writing-desk, a large Edwardian secretaire, stood behind where she was sitting, somewhat to her right. The desk contained pens and paper. Mrs Merrett may have chosen to use a table for writing, rather than her bureau, because the latter's desk-flap was slightly too high for her to write in comfort. Merrett, according to the evidence of the maid, was reading a book, sitting in an alcove on the other side of the room. As the maid was making up a fire in the kitchen she heard a single shot, followed by a scream and the thud of a falling body. Merrett, who seemed upset, came into the kitchen, saying, 'Rita, my mother has shot herself.'[6] He added that they had quarrelled about money. The maid (not a very reliable witness, as it turned out) claimed to have found Mrs Merrett lying on the floor, alive but unconscious, and bleeding from a bullet wound in the right ear. Her chair had fallen over and the gun was lying on the front right-hand corner of the bureau.

The police were called, and Mrs Merrett, on her son's evidence of self-injury, was treated as a person attempting suicide – a crime in 1926 – and incarcerated in a secure ward (Ward 3) at Edinburgh Infirmary. Here she was examined by Dr Richard Bell, who found no sign of blackening or singeing around the wound, although there was a good deal of blood around the ear. The blood was subsequently washed away by Dr Roy Holcombe, who dressed the small wound, described as 'about the size of a slate pencil'.[7] Dr Holcombe did not notice any 'blackening or tattooing', but his account suggests that he did not examine the injury with such possibilities in mind.

The bullet had entered the skull, and from the outset the doctors were aware that the outcome would most probably be fatal. X-rays, taken on glass plates, revealed that the bullet, which had lodged itself at the base of the skull behind the nose, was inoperable. Mrs Merrett, though partly paralysed, regained consciousness at about 12.30 p.m. on the day of the shooting and, that evening, complained of great pain in her ear and asked how it had been caused. Dr Holcombe, thinking that this had been a suicide attempt, said simply, 'You have had a little accident, Mrs Merrett.' She later said that she had been sitting down, writing letters, 'and my son . . . was standing beside me. I said "Go away, Donald, and don't annoy me", and the next I heard was a kind of explosion.'[8] (Merrett agreed that his mother had used these words, but told Dr Holcombe that he had walked towards a corner of the room, heard a shot, and then saw his mother falling to the ground with the gun in her hand.) Mrs Merrett remained conscious and ostensibly rational for several days, even signing a cheque as late as Thursday 25 March, but she developed an infection as a result of the injury and the lodging of the bullet. The next day her temperature rose to 103 degrees, and she became delirious. She lost consciousness on the Saturday and, in the early hours of 1 April 1926, she died from 'basal meningitis, following a bullet wound in cranium'.[9]

Mrs Merrett at no time accused her son of shooting her, but for the whole of her hospital stay she was treated effectively as a mental patient, with few attempts to obtain a more detailed recollection of events. A further complication was that, from the day of admission, she had been injected with morphine periodically to ease the severe pain of her wound, a circumstance that must affect the reliability of her statements. In any event, the police – who seem not to have considered the possibility of a murder attempt – failed to take a dying deposition. They also failed to test the pistol for fingerprints. Meanwhile Merrett, back at the Palais de Danse, took Betty for a spin on his new motor-bike and treated her to the 'flickers' at the Caley Picture House. He compounded this callous behaviour by failing to tell his maternal aunts about the shooting and virtually ignoring an old friend of his mother's who had come to Edinburgh at her request. Shortly before Mrs Merrett died her son ordered a new and more expensive motor-bike. Questioned by police during his mother's stay in hospital, Merrett said that he had left the pistol loaded because he was going to shoot rabbits. His mother had taken the pistol from him and put it in the bureau. He had warned her to be careful.

Mrs Merrett left the bulk of her money to her son, but – no doubt for good reason – the estate was to be held on trust until he attained the age of 25. His trustees sent him to a former vicarage in Buckinghamshire, where – it was vainly hoped – he would apply himself to study. Back in Edinburgh evidence of forged cheques had been accumulating, to a total value of over £450, the last cheque being dated four days before his mother's death. On 29 November a warrant was issued for Merrett's arrest, and he was taken to Edinburgh charged with murder and for 'uttering' (legal language for 'issuing') the forged cheques.

The prosecution, headed by the Lord Advocate, William Watson KC, called in two eminent medical witnesses, Professor Harvey Littlejohn, Regius Professor of Forensic Medicine at Edinburgh University, and Professor John Glaister, who held a similar appointment at the university of Glasgow. Littlejohn came from a distinguished medical background. His father, Sir Henry Littlejohn, had worked as chief surgeon to the Edinburgh police with Dr Joseph Bell, teacher of Conan Doyle and regarded as the inspiration for Sherlock Holmes. Harvey Littlejohn had succeeded his father as Professor of Medical Jurisprudence in 1906. 'Witty and caustic, with a tongue like a needle', Littlejohn was as different from Spilsbury as it is possible to imagine. Unmarried, he was very sociable, 'a born raconteur', with a dramatic style of lecturing that made a lasting impression on his students, and cutting a distinguished figure set off by his prominent, military-looking blonde moustache.[10]

Littlejohn had examined Mrs Merrett's body on the day of her death. Unlike Spilsbury, who could take over a month to write up his findings, Littlejohn produced a report dated 5 April, just four days after the autopsy. After removing the top of the skull he found evidence of infection, with the infiltration of 'purulent matter' in the brain membranes. The brain itself was uninjured, but the nickel-plated bullet was found embedded in the base of the skull. 'There was nothing to indicate the distance at which the discharge of the weapon took place', he wrote, 'the case is consistent with suicide. There is some difficulty in attributing it to accident, although such a view cannot be wholly excluded.'[11]

During the summer of 1926 Littlejohn met a younger colleague, Sydney Smith. Smith, a New Zealander of English extraction, was born in 1883, the son of a municipal contractor. After an elementary school education he found work as an apothecary's apprentice and later as an assistant chemist, eventually qualifying in pharmacy. With none of Spilsbury's financial advantages, Sydney Smith studied scientific subjects in Wellington, New Zealand, as a stepping-stone to Edinburgh. Here – again unlike Spilsbury – he won a scholarship worth £100 a year, graduating MD in 1914, taking first-class honours, a Gold Medal, and the Alison prize. After working in Edinburgh with Littlejohn, Smith became 'principal medico-legal expert' to the Egyptian government, at that time dominated by the British. Here, for some twelve years, he gained considerable expertise in firearms injuries, culminating in his investigation of the murder of Sir Lee Stack, the *sirdar* (commander-in-chief) of the Egyptian army, in November 1924. Smith's *Forensic Medicine and Toxicology*, published in 1925, was an immediate success. He had kept up his medical contacts in Scotland, and there, on vacation the following year, Littlejohn consulted him about the Merrett case. Littlejohn, perhaps a little late in the day, was now concerned about the lack of evidence of suicide. Smith, having reviewed the evidence, told Littlejohn that the shooting looked more like murder. He suggested that Littlejohn should experiment with Merrett's pistol. Anyone attempting suicide by shooting would, thought Smith, put the barrel close to the head and probably no more than 3 inches away.

The Procurator-Fiscal released the gun to Littlejohn and, on 6 August 1926, he obtained from Hardy's, the gunsmiths, similar cartridges to those used in the shooting of Mrs Merrett. The pistol was fired at white cardboard at nine measured distances, ranging from half an inch to 12 inches. At up to 2 inches' distance there was evidence of blackening and tattooing and, at 3 inches, although no blackening was visible, numerous particles of ingrained powder were visible over an area 1½ inches in diameter. Littlejohn, assisted by Glaister, carried out a similar series of experiments on 8 December 1926, using as a target a sheet of skin taken from the recently amputated leg of an accident victim.

Littlejohn, in a second report dated 13 January 1927, concluded that, if the gun had been fired at a distance of 3 inches or less, there would have been 'definite evidence' of the discharge visible to doctors at the time of Mrs Merrett's admission to the notorious Ward 3 of Edinburgh Infirmary. In Littlejohn's revised opinion, the discharge was 'not a near one' and suicide was 'in the highest degree improbable'. Glaister, 'unable to exclude absolutely the possibility of . . . self-infliction', having weighed the possibilities against the improbabilities, also concluded that the injury was not self-inflicted.[12]

The joint opinion of such eminent experts called for an appropriate response from the defence. Merrett, although only 18 and without the possibility of accessing funds in his mother's estate for another seven years, nevertheless assembled a formidable team of defence lawyers and experts. Merrett's defence was led by Craigie Aitchison KC, a fine advocate at the Scottish Bar, father of the distinguished artist of the same name. The defence instructed Professor George Robertson, President of the Royal College of Physicians of Edinburgh, to give evidence about Mrs Merrett's state of consciousness during her stay in hospital, but the star medical witness – appearing, it seems, for the first time as a defence witness in a criminal case – was Spilsbury, once more accompanied by the burly figure of Robert Churchill, reprising the double act that had so impressed observers in the cases of Baxter (see Chapter Five), Malcolm (see Chapter Six) and Rutherford (see Chapter Eight).

Macdonald Hastings, in his entertaining and informative biography of Robert Churchill, describes the defence as 'formidable, expensive and determined'.[13] Spilsbury and Churchill were at the heart of the attempt to save Donald Merrett's young neck. In Sydney Smith's view, Spilsbury was 'very brilliant and very famous, but fallible . . . and very, very obstinate'. Churchill, too, was 'stubborn and dogmatic', and Smith considered the pair to be 'a formidable team – terrifying when they made a mistake, as they did here'.[14]

There is no doubt that both men worked exceptionally hard, even on their own terms, in the preparation of their evidence. Churchill recalled how, during the trial – which lasted for seven days – there were defence conferences 'every evening after dinner, in which we went right through the transcript of the shorthand notes of the day's proceedings and prepared the next day's trial work as well'.[15] Spilsbury would have been aware that the effect of Littlejohn's evidence had already been blunted by his first report on Mrs Merrett's death, in which he had stated that the death was consistent with suicide. Spilsbury also had the advantage of knowing his man personally. Littlejohn was a fellow member of the Medico-Legal Society, and, as early as June 1923, Spilsbury had assisted him in the setting of examination questions in pathology at Edinburgh.[16] On 8 November 1926, shortly before Hilda Bainbridge fell ill, he had written to Littlejohn discussing arrangements for his attendance in Edinburgh as an examiner the following week.[17]

According to Churchill, Spilsbury insisted that the defence should conduct its own experiments. On Thursday 27 January 1927 Spilsbury wrote to Littlejohn from St Bartholomew's Hospital. 'Mr Churchill the gunsmith and I are making shooting experiments,' he told the Crown expert, '& we should like an opportunity of seeing the weapon . . . &, if necessary, of experimenting with it & of seeing the results of experiments which Professor Glaister & yourself have made.'[18]

As to Spilsbury's 'shooting experiments', Churchill was of the opinion that the absence of scorching or blackening around the wound was not material. 'Smokeless powder', he said later, 'will mark paper or cardboard, but it will not indelibly mark skin . . . Superficial powder blackening . . . may be washed away by the flow of blood.'[19] He also doubted whether animal tissue would respond like live human flesh. Churchill claimed to have told Spilsbury that shooting at an inanimate target would prove nothing, but, undaunted, the pathologist obtained the amputated leg of an elderly woman hospital patient. The two experts took the leg, wrapped in brown paper, by train to Churchill's shooting grounds in Kent. A series of shots was fired first at cardboard, then into the leg. On any reading, the experiment began on a false note. The pistol was not the Merrett weapon, although of the same calibre. Ammunition, as in the original Littlejohn experiments, was bought from Hardy's in Edinburgh, and, when they fired at measured distances, there was some blackening on the skin, but less marked than on the cardboard, most of which could be removed without much difficulty. The pitting produced by the powder grains was very similar in either case. Churchill later maintained that the evidence was valueless, not least because 'dead flesh is different from living flesh'.[20] The nature of the ammunition was, as will be seen, another factor that robbed these experiments of any worth.

Littlejohn seems to have acceded to Spilsbury's request for a meeting on Sunday 30 January, when the defence experts were permitted to fire Merrett's gun at cardboard, with similar results to those obtained from Littlejohn's earlier trials. Although Churchill had bought the ammunition used in the Kent experiments at Hardy's, it was ammunition, in his own words at the trial, 'supposedly of similar but of later make'[21] and seems to have come from a later batch. In essence, the whole defence exercise was a waste of time and effort, but, in the time-honoured tradition of 'defence by confusion', it may have justified the expense.

The trial of Donald Merrett opened before Lord Alness, the Lord Justice-Clerk, Scotland's senior criminal court judge of first instance, on 1 February 1927. The indictment, which in Scotland is a précis of the case against the pannel (defendant), was read out to Merrett, who pleaded not guilty. In accordance with Scots legal practice, a jury of fifteen was balloted (empanelled), consisting of nine men and six women. There was no opening statement by the Lord-Advocate, who immediately proceeded to call evidence.

The figure of Donald Merrett, now 18, must have loomed over the dock when standing before the judge. Over 6ft tall and well built, he had an ugly, long face and nose, with full, rather truculent-looking lips. Littlejohn, describing his experiments, declared that at 3 inches the pistol 'left very definite powder and burning marks round the wound in the skin area', discolouration that could not easily be washed away.[22] William Roughead, the crime writer, examined the specimen himself some two years after the trial and found 'the blackening as plain as ever'.[23] In Littlejohn's view, the results of the Kent experiments differed essentially from those conducted in Edinburgh. 'The main difference', he said, 'was that it was not so much blackening, but more yellowness, and evidently a different kind of powder had been used.' Glaister relied not only on the blackening, as revealed in the experiments, but on the direction of the wound. If blackening had been present originally, it could not have been completely removed by a swab at the hospital. Aitchison, a canny advocate, kept Merrett away from the witness-box and so avoided the risk of a highly damaging cross-examination by the Lord-Advocate. Churchill in evidence maintained that any blackening caused by the flake powder in the bullet would have been superficial and 'easily removed'.

AITCHISON. Would the application of a wet swab and the pressure required to remove it remove any blackening . . . ?
CHURCHILL. Yes.
AITCHISON. Have you any doubt about it?
CHURCHILL. Not a bit. . . .[24]

He canvassed the possibility of an accident, assuming that Mrs Merrett had picked the pistol up from the bureau while seated at her writing table. She might have overbalanced and, raising her hand to protect herself, accidentally discharged the pistol in falling. During cross-examination, this speculative theory, which had probably emerged after lengthy discussions with Spilsbury, was damaged by Churchill's admission that he was unaware that there were some 20 inches between the pigeon-hole in which the gun had been left and the edge of the writing-shelf of the bureau.

Spilsbury was described by Roughead – apparently without irony – as a pathologist 'of European fame, of the highest eminence in his profession, and of . . . unfailing fairness'.[25] At one point in evidence, Craigie Aitchison, in his good Scots voice, referred to Spilsbury as 'Saint Berr-nard'; whether this mystic elevation was by accident or design remains a mystery.[26] Spilsbury reiterated Churchill's claims regarding the ease with which any blackening or other markings could have been removed from the area of the injury. Haemorrhage from the ear could have made it easy to fail to observe blackening. Dealing with differences between the Edinburgh and Kent experiments, Spilsbury accepted that 'the depth and blackening in the Edinburgh experiments was much greater at shorter ranges than in the London [Kent] experiments', but maintained that there was no difference between the two series in respect of the ease with which the blackening could be removed. Flying against the facts, Spilsbury gave an answer typical of his style of positive evidence:

AITCHISON. Would you . . . say that your Edinburgh experiments were confirmative of the conclusions which you drew from your London ones?
SPILSBURY. They did not modify my conclusions.

In relation to the reliability of Mrs Merrett's statements in hospital, Spilsbury – not for the first or the last time in his forty-year professional career – stepped well beyond his particular field of expertise:

> AITCHISON. With a brain condition such as must have existed here, in your view would it be safe to place reliance upon statements made by the patient within a comparatively short period – say twenty-four hours – of an acute delirium developing?
>
> SPILSBURY. I think any such statements must be accepted with great caution.

Spilsbury pointed out that the gun was light in weight and had a very short barrel, 'thus rendering it much easier to hold in a position against the side of the head'. The gun could have been held by Mrs Merrett even at 3 or 4 inches away without much strain, said Spilsbury, observing that 'in the case of a woman you often find very considerable range of movement of the shoulder joint owing to the habit of putting up the hair'. In an unusually long answer to the Lord-Advocate, in cross-examination, Spilsbury indulged in a particularly loose speculative exercise:

> SPILSBURY. The mere fact of moving the woman . . . to the Infirmary would almost certainly lead to the escape of some of the blood . . . on the surface of the ear, and it is almost certain that some blood would be wiped off in the removal, and probably there would be bare patches on the skin even although the blood had flowed over the whole of the ear at some time or other.

Spilsbury accepted that the muzzle could not have been pressed against the skin. When asked about the possibility of accidental discharge, a theory canvassed already by Churchill, Spilsbury theorised that Mrs Merrett could have fallen backwards in her chair and, with the pistol in her hand, caught her elbow on the projecting edge of the bureau, causing the pistol to fire. In the witness-box, he demonstrated what he meant. 'I was rather picturing her as falling backwards in her chair when she was originally in the sitting position,' he said, but, when it was pointed out that her elbow would be too low to come in contact with the edge of bureau, Spilsbury put a gloss on his theory:

> SPILSBURY. No, I do not think so. If she had stretched over the bureau to get something out, the arm would presumably be over that part.

Roughead made some calculations from the dimensions of the bureau and the chair in which Mrs Merrett had been sitting. He concluded that, given the position of Mrs Merrett in the room, 'to anyone sitting in a chair of that height, the difficulty of reaching up and over to the drawers or pigeon holes without coming into contact with, and being prevented by, the edge of the flap . . . would seem . . . insuperable', unless Mrs Merrett had 'an extraordinary reach of arm'.[27] Spilsbury's theory simply did not meet the facts.

The jury, sent out at 4.35 p.m. on 8 February 1927, took just under an hour to find the charge of murder 'Not Proven', but found Merrett guilty of the cheque frauds, for which he was sentenced, despite his youth, to a year's imprisonment. A report from the Prison Commissioners had found Merrett 'unsuitable for Borstal treatment'. Roughead afterwards learnt that the jury arrived at the murder verdict by a majority decision, with a vote of ten for not proven and five for guilty.[28]

Sydney Smith had no doubt about Merrett's guilt at the time. He had secured an unjust verdict, Smith felt, because of the sloppiness of the Edinburgh police and the 'misleading evidence of Spilsbury and Churchill, who had made a mistake and were too stubborn to admit it'.[29] After his release Merrett eventually inherited his mother's estate of £50,000, which was quickly dissipated. He later changed his name to 'Ronald Chesney'.

Spilsbury would never know that, in 1954, Merrett would drown his wife and batter his mother-in-law to death. He fled to Germany after the killings and shot himself in the head to avoid capture. His arms were cut off by the German police and presented to the Crime Museum at New Scotland Yard.[30]

FOURTEEN

'Do you think I've come up here for fun?'

On 6 May 1927 a taxi-driver took two young men from the Royal Automobile Club in Pall Mall to Rochester Row police station, next door to Westminster Police Court, where Spilsbury had often given evidence in committal proceedings. The young men, it seems, had been summonsed for motoring offences and were booked in at 1.35 p.m. A man, standing in a doorway on the other side of Rochester Row, hailed the cab, whose driver was slightly discomfited by having to help the man carry a large black trunk, with a curved top, whose wicker frame was covered in oilcloth. Trunks such as this were common enough in those days, but this one was exceptionally heavy. 'It's full of books,' said the man. At Charing Cross station a porter wheeled the trunk on a barrow to the left-luggage office, which bore a large sign, helpfully written in French and English, 'CONSIGNE. CLOAK ROOM'. The office, which was open-fronted, was divided in two, one side with a notice indicating that the public could 'BOOK & CLAIM SINGLE ARTICLES HERE'.

As Sir Ernley Blackwell later wrote, in his customary no-nonsense style: 'On the 10th May the trunk aroused suspicion by the smell . . .'.[1] A police constable opened the malodorous trunk to find, wrapped up in brown paper and string, five portions of a body. The divisional police surgeon, Dr Rose, conducted a brief examination of the remains with Dr Henry Weir, pathologist to the National Hospital for Diseases of the Heart. Rose removed the liver and stomach, which were sent for analysis to Dr Roche Lynch, the Home Office analyst, who found no poison 'or other noxious substances'[2] and, it seems, no traces of alcohol. Rose carefully sewed up the incisions that he had made, and the body parts, taken to the mortuary at Westminster Coroners' Court in Horseferry Road, awaited the arrival of a more senior medical figure, the Honorary Pathologist to the Home Office. Spilsbury, in the presence of Drs Rose and Weir (and the future Scotland Yard Commander Leonard Burt, then a junior officer),[3] quickly confirmed that the trunk had contained the dismembered body of a woman who had been 5ft tall and 'rather stout'. The body had been divided into five parts by amputation, 'sweeping cuts', at each shoulder and hip joint. Putrefaction was well advanced: the head and body were green, gas had accumulated beneath the skin and there was putrefactive change evident in the limbs.[4]

Spilsbury initially thought that the clean dismemberment suggested the work of 'an experienced slaughterman'. Later, possibly after learning that the principal suspect had been a mere butcher's assistant, he modified his view.[5] The presence of two attempted cuts and the way in which one of the hips had been severed suggested that the dismemberer had not been skilled in his art. The woman had a bruise, 2 inches in diameter, on the right temple, and bruising on the outer side of the left eye. A slightly larger bruise was found on the front and right side of the abdomen, over the hip bone. Another bruise was noted over the right lower ribs and three small bruises in the region of the right shoulder blade. Small bruises were also evident on the back of the right arm, on both thighs and on the left knee. The most severe bruising was to the right temple and over the hip bone.

Spilsbury thought that the bruising had been caused by a series of blows, although 'one or 2 may have been caused by falling'. All were inflicted during life and 'very shortly before death'. His case card records findings similar to the doubtful chronology of bruising given in the Thorne case (see Chapter Twelve), concluding that 'the two [bruises] with swelling prob: a little earlier'. The finger-nails were bluish in colour and there were 'petechial haemorrhages on the lungs and heart'.[6] This led Spilsbury to conclude that death was caused by asphyxia, following violence and suffocation, 'that is to say, pressure over the mouth and nostrils . . . probably applied when the woman was unconscious because of an almost complete absence of bruising' in that area of the face.[7]

The 'Charing Cross Trunk Murder', as it became known, was the subject of a classic detective exercise by the Metropolitan Police. The trunk contained a handbag, a pair of smart patent-leather black shoes, as well as a pair of women's knickers, a tweed jacket, other female clothing, a towel and a check duster, which, when washed by the police several days later, revealed the name-tag 'Greyhound'. The knickers bore the name 'P HOLT'. Two laundry marks were found on another item of clothing. By tracing the laundry marks, the police were soon able to trace Mrs Holt, who was probably horrified to find that intimate articles from her wardrobe had been discovered in such disgusting circumstances. Mrs Holt, who also had the disagreeable task of viewing the human remains, identified them as those of a Mrs Rolls, whom she had employed briefly as a cook. Seemingly not 'a good cook, as cooks go',[8] Mrs Rolls had quietly helped herself to items of her employer's clothing.

Fred Rolls also recognised the body. He had lived with the woman, whose real name was Mrs Minnie Alice Bonati (*née* Budd), aged 36 at the time of her death. Their four-year relationship had been stormy. Minnie, bad-tempered and often drunk, would belabour Fred with 'cooking utensils, frying pans, saucepans, anything that came to hand'. Fred considered that Minnie, in such moods, was 'about as strong as two men'.[9] Armed with this information, the police traced her husband, Bianco Bonati, an Italian immigrant who had worked as a waiter in a Soho restaurant for many years. Minnie and Bianco had married in 1913, but had been apart for some years, the break-up being attributed in part to Minnie's fondness for drink. Bonati was able to identify his dead wife from a slightly deformed index finger on her right hand, a congenital malformation, which Spilsbury seems not to have noticed. Bonati also recognised Minnie's 'very small ears'.[10] Although Blackwell later recorded simply that she had been 'living with various men',[11] it seems that, by the spring of 1927, Minnie had taken to prostitution and was almost destitute. She was last seen alive by a Poor Law officer on 4 May that year.

After several days, police were contacted by the taxi-driver who had ferried the trunk and a male passenger to Charing Cross. His information led police to 86 Rochester Row, an office building, the two lower floors of which were occupied by a firm of solicitors. On the floor above were the empty offices of a Mr John Robinson, who had operated – unsuccessfully – as an estate agent for a couple of months from two dingy rooms, trading as 'Edwards & Co, Business Transfer Agents'. On 9 May 1927 Robinson had written to his landlord, informing him that he was leaving because he was 'broke'.[12] There was a cracked window-pane in one room, and a hearth with a broken fireplace fender and loose iron strut. Robinson had employed a clerk, a Miss Moore, who said that, on 4 May, her employer, who appeared drunk, had come back to his office at about 3 p.m. with a guardsman. Miss Moore – perhaps prudently – decided to leave the men together, leaving both the office and her employment that afternoon.

Robinson had left his lodgings, but the police found a telegram addressed to 'Robinson' at the 'Greyhound Hotel'. The telegram had been returned to the lodgings marked 'address unknown'. After checking public houses of that name in the metropolis, they found a Mrs Robinson at the Greyhound Hotel, Hammersmith. She was Robinson's bigamously married second wife. The telegram had been sent back to the Post Office by a new maid at the hotel, unaware that 'Mrs Robinson' was working there. Robinson had wired with a view to meeting 'Mrs Robinson' at the Elephant and Castle pub in Walworth on 19 May 1927. The police had told her about Robinson's previous marriage, and so, not unnaturally, she was now willing to assist in his entrapment. Both she and Robinson kept the appointment – and so did Chief Inspector George Cornish.

Robinson, then aged 37, was born in Leigh, Lancashire, and left school at 12. He had at one time worked as a butcher's assistant, married in 1911, and had three children. After war service he bigamously married the second Mrs Robinson. He had worked variously as bookmaker and barman, though often sacked for drunkenness, dishonesty or both. In about March 1927 he had started to rent the rooms at Rochester Row. Robinson also had a criminal record. As 'Jack Robinson' (a variant of his name that seems entirely appropriate) he was convicted at Ramsgate on 18 August 1924 of stealing £19 in cash from Mrs Cook, a widow, with whom, in Blackwell's descriptive expression, 'he had been carrying on for some time'.[13] More recently Robinson had also been 'carrying on' with a married woman, Mrs Law, who had paid a visit to the office on 6 May, the day that Robinson had deposited the trunk at Charing Cross station.

Taken to Scotland Yard, Robinson, who denied any knowledge of Minnie or the trunk, was put up for identification, but was not picked out by either the taxi-driver, or the Charing Cross porter, or the man who had sold the trunk on or around 4 May to 'a military sort of man, who looked as if he might have served in India'.[14] Robinson was released. In keeping with the lackadaisical police methods prevailing in 1927, it was only after a more thorough search of the offices at Rochester Row that a bloodstained match was found, caught in the wicker frame of an old-fashioned waste-paper basket. In consequence, the police detained Robinson a second time.

According to Robinson, a police sergeant cajoled him into making a lengthy statement by saying, 'come on . . . you're not the kind of man to do a thing like that – that's why I want you to make a statement to justify yourself'.[15] The sergeant later denied making the inducement and, according to the police, Robinson said: 'I want to tell you about it. I done it and cut her up.' Around 4.30 p.m., some time after his tryst with the guardsman, Robinson had gone out 'to buy stamps' and was accosted by Minnie in Victoria Street. She said, in the usual way of streetwalkers, that she could 'take him somewhere'. Robinson suggested his office as a suitable venue, aware that his secretary had just walked out for good. They took a cab to Rochester Row, but, once they were upstairs, an argument broke out about payment. Robinson's evidence in court slightly resembles dialogue from a play by Harold Pinter:

> MINNIE. Well, what about it?
> ROBINSON. What about what?
> MINNIE. Money.
> ROBINSON. Well, you are not going to get any money.
> MINNIE. Well, do you think I've come up here for fun?
> ROBINSON. Well, you are not going to have it.

After this frank exchange of views, Minnie became very angry indeed and bent down, as though to pick up something from the fireplace. He struck her a blow on the side of the head that knocked her down. She hit a chair in falling. 'As she fell, she sort of lay down and rolled over with her head in the fireplace.' Robinson then 'picked up his hat', saying, 'Now then, you can get out of it as quickly as you like. I am off', and returned to his lodgings. He visited his offices the following morning, expecting to find Minnie gone, but discovered her still lying there, dead on the floor. Robinson's evidence on this point is significant. He claimed that he found Minnie lying on a rug, face down, in front of the fireplace.

Presented with the same difficulty that had faced Pat Mahon and Norman Thorne, Robinson decided that he had to dispose of the body. 'I was in a blue funk', he told the trial jury, 'and did not know what to do.' By remarkable coincidence he bought a knife at Stainer's, the same shop visited by Patrick Mahon to purchase the carving-knife and tenon-saw used to cut up Emily Kaye (see Chapter Eleven). Robinson, having dismembered the body, left the parts, wrapped in brown paper, in his office. He realised that disposing of the parcels separately could cause problems and so, next day, he managed to get the trunk – bought in a shop in Brixton Road – onto the top deck of a bus, a considerable feat in itself. Alighting in Vauxhall Bridge Road, he dragged the trunk along Rochester Row, presumably in full view of the police station. By lunchtime Minnie was safely stowed away. Over a drink in a local public house he got talking to a Mr Judd, who was interested in leasing a furnished flat. After a brief business discussion in his office, Mr Judd obligingly helped Robinson downstairs with his monstrous burden. 'Are you travelling in lead?' enquired his perspiring helper. After depositing the trunk, Robinson buried the knife under a hawthorn bush on Clapham Common.

On 11 July 1927 Robinson stood trial for murder at the Old Bailey. His judge was the irascible, red-faced, Rigby Swift. The prosecution was headed by Percival Clarke – Senior Treasury Counsel – assisted by 'Khaki' Roberts and the young Christmas Humphreys (familiarly known as 'Toby'), son of the famous judge Travers Humphreys (see p. 18). Robinson was privately represented. A newspaper or magazine may have met the costs of his representation, but funds evidently did not run to securing the best possible lawyers. Although three barristers were retained for the defence, the most senior, Laurence Vine, not yet King's Counsel, was relatively inexperienced, defending in his first murder trial. His two juniors, M.D. Lyon and A.E. McCloskey, were both 'unknowns' at the Bar.

The Crown called a string of witnesses, broadly representing the progress of the police enquiry, starting with a young shoeblack at Charing Cross station, who had picked up the cloakroom ticket discarded by Robinson on 6 May. Bianco Bonati, in cross-examination, remembered that Minnie had once had 'a little fit', thought to be drink-related, about six years before when in their home at 86 Balcombe Street, Pimlico. A doctor was called, but Minnie recovered after a few minutes. She had been 'practically conscious', but he remembered her 'grabbing with her hands'. Fred Rolls recalled her having a fit in Bonati's house. She was then unconscious, grinding her teeth and grabbing at the bedclothes. She did not come round in his presence. She also had a fit at an address in Cricklewood, falling to the floor and lying there for twenty minutes. Prosecution medical evidence began with Dr Rose, followed by Dr Weir. Both doctors gave the cause of death as suffocation following violence. It was mooted that Robinson had caused the bruising over the right hip by pressure when kneeling on her. Dr Weir expressed the view that she could have been suffocated 'by some soft substance'. A cushion, found in the rooms at Rochester Row, had been produced by the prosecution, for the first time, earlier in the trial.

The Crown saved its trump card for last. Spilsbury, in answer to Percival Clarke, said that he had found 'considerable difficulty in ascertaining the cause of death', but, rarely at a loss for positive evidence, he maintained his opinion that death had been occasioned by covering the mouth and nostrils after the woman had been violently assaulted. He had noticed a smell of gas in the office when he had made an inspection on 25 May 1927, but Minnie 'would have had to have had her mouth over [the gas tap] to have been seriously affected'. There was, in any event, no evidence of carbon monoxide poisoning in the blood.

Laurence Vine, in cross-examination, elicited from Spilsbury that no mention had been made of the cushion in committal proceedings. Spilsbury gave a very curious response to a question about bruising:

VINE. Do you agree that women do bruise more easily than men as a general rule?
SPILSBURY. Not as a general rule, but there are some women who do bruise easily; there are fewer now than there used to be, I think.

With regard to the possibility that Minnie had suffered an epileptic fit, Spilsbury's replies to Vine illustrate how he would sometimes play games, particularly with inexperienced defence counsel. Blandly worded answers led counsel on until Spilsbury's last response, which quietly crushed a potentially valuable defence point on the effects of epilepsy:

VINE. I suppose it would be impossible . . . for a woman, say of 36 . . . to have had a sudden epileptic seizure?
SPILSBURY. Oh, no. Some epileptics start very early in life.
VINE. But she might have some seizure without even displaying, some years before . . . that she had anything of the kind wrong with her?
SPILSBURY. Of course, there must always be a first seizure.
VINE. I mean it would come on quite suddenly without any symptoms being disclosed, say to her husband or anyone else?
SPILSBURY. Oh, yes, until the fit itself showed itself.
VINE. And if death did result from such a seizure, you agree . . . that some similar post-mortem signs would be shown as in death from suffocation or asphyxiation?
SPILSBURY. It depends, of course, upon the circumstances of the death. An ordinary death from epilepsy rarely occurs apart from some complication.

Spilsbury's evidence about bruising is questionable.[16] Referring to the 2in-diameter bruise on the right temple, Spilsbury had been asked by Clarke whether, if the bruise had been caused, as Robinson claimed, by her hitting her head against the fender, 'would you have expected to find it as you found it?'

'No,' replied Spilsbury. 'It would have been a smaller bruise, and almost certainly against a hard projection there would have been some injury to the skin over it.' This answer, which looks like pure invention, was followed by a wholly incorrect analysis of the circumstances and chronology of the bruising, which, as Spilsbury would have it, occurred 'very shortly before death'. His explanation is barely intelligible and would now be regarded as medical nonsense:

SPILSBURY. Because most of the bruises did not show on the surface of the body at all. They were only discovered when the body was cut in different places to search for bruises, and only two of the bruises had any appreciable swelling of the skin at their situation, indicating that the amount of haemorrhage for the size of the bruise was comparatively slight.

It later emerged, in cross-examination, that Spilsbury had not made any microscopical examination of the bruises, a curious lapse given the importance attached to bruising in relation to chronology and the cause of death. Spilsbury again made a dogmatic assertion, similar to the one he made in Thorne, that the bruising had occurred, not just hours before death, but 'minutes' before death. He also made another unwarranted claim that the 'appearance of the bruises pointed to a very rapid death, death within minutes'. Again, as in the case of Thorne, the prosecution brandished an object, inviting Spilsbury to make a comment. In Thorne, the object had been an Indian club. Here, it was a cushion, produced for the first time at the trial.

CLARKE. Could the suffocation be caused effectively by that [the cushion]?
SPILSBURY. Yes, it could, if pressed over the mouth and nostrils.
CLARKE. And without leaving marks of bruising on the face?
SPILSBURY. Oh yes, it would leave no marks except, of course, the tongue might be caught between the teeth by the pressure.

Spilsbury was here trying to link 'slight bruising' found on the tip of the tongue with his theory of suffocation, but this 'bruising' could have been post-mortem change, given the state of putrefaction at the time he had examined the body.[17] Cross-examined by Vine, who put the defence case that Minnie could have suffocated on a rug, Spilsbury gave a thoroughly misleading answer, bearing in mind there had been no evidence establishing that the tongue had been bitten:

VINE. Supposing the mouth and nostrils had rested on some soft substance after being rendered unconscious, would that be equally likely to cause suffocation?
SPILSBURY. It might do so if she was lying face downwards, but I would not expect the tongue to be bitten under those conditions.

The crucial part of Spilsbury's evidence, and the element that effectively 'tipped' a possible manslaughter verdict into one of murder, was his refusal to accept that Minnie had met her death face downwards, as Robinson had claimed. Had this been so, according to Spilsbury, the front of the lungs would have been congested with blood, whereas congestion had been found, on each side, at the back of the lungs.

> SPILSBURY. . . . this woman died and lay for some considerable time after death upon her back and . . . the blood therefore sank into the back of the lungs as a part of the post-mortem changes.
> CLARKE. If she had met her death as my friend suggests with her mouth in the rucked carpet or on her bent arm, would you expect the lungs to be congested at the back or the top or where?
> SPILSBURY. Congestion would . . . appear in the lowest part of the lungs; in the position of the body that would be in the front.

These conclusions, a vital part of the Crown's case against Robinson, were deeply flawed. According to Robinson, the body had lain on its front only between late on the afternoon of 4 May until midday – at the latest – on 5 May, when he dismembered it. The body parts would then have been in various positions in their wrappings, and, once deposited in the trunk, the chest section lay on its back for the next five days. Spilsbury's arguments on this point are inherently unreliable, but, given Spilsbury's vaunted reputation, they probably contributed to the eventual verdict.

The defence relied on Spilsbury's *bête noire*, Dr Brontë (see p. 128), who quickly exhibited his failings as a witness. When dealing with the defence case that Minnie could have suffocated lying face down on the carpet, unconscious – perhaps for two or three hours – with her mouth and nose pressed against the fabric, Brontë's windy answer to a question put by Vine was catastrophic:

> BRONTË. Speaking as a layman . . . not a considered answer or a medical answer, but speaking as a layman and not as a medical man – yes.
> JUDGE. Wait one moment. You are not entitled to come here and speak as a layman or we shall have some thousands of people being brought here.

Eventually Brontë was persuaded to give his opinion not as a layman but as a medical man. He agreed that such a state of affairs could cause suffocation. A later, excellent point, namely that protrusion of the tongue was almost always found in cases of putrefaction, seems to have been lost in the welter of verbiage, as were his arguments about bruising, disputing Spilsbury's doubtful evidence about chronology and causation.

Robinson, plainly a shifty character (although the jury would not have been told about his conviction for theft), was an unimpressive witness. The judge had, like so many of his colleagues, fallen victim to Spilsbury's magic. In his summing-up, charitably including Dr Weir in his encomium, the judge gave the jury the broadest hint about which medical evidence to accept. Directing the jury, Rigby Swift, ever the soapbox moralist, made full use of such pejorative expressions – oblique to the real issues in the case – as 'immoral purpose' and 'gratification'. 'If you accept', said the judge, 'the testimony of these experienced pathologists, can you come . . . to any other conclusion than that . . . this man, having taken the woman to his rooms for an immoral purpose, having failed to acquire the gratification which he desired, first of all knocked her down and then suffocated her?' The jury, sent out at 3.50 p.m. on Wednesday 13 July 1927, asked to have the cushion, a tweed jacket found in the trunk and copies of both Robinson's statements to the police. After twenty-five minutes they returned and found the prisoner guilty of murder. His appeal was dismissed, but while Robinson awaited execution at Wandsworth, Sir Ernley Blackwell at the Home Office received a remarkable communication from Scotland, dated 1 August 1927.[18]

Dr Sydney Smith, who had seen Spilsbury in action earlier that year in the Merrett case, submitted a memorandum 'written after consultation with Professor Littlejohn and a number of confreres with experience in such matters'. In a blistering attack on Spilsbury's evidence, Smith considered that 'the conclusions arrived at were not justified by the facts'. He drew attention to the advanced state of decomposition in which the body had been found, which had a direct bearing on Spilsbury's finding of death by asphyxiation. It was extremely difficult, argued Smith, to diagnose death by asphyxia after putrefaction had occurred. As there was no trace of violence on the mouth or throat, to assume that suffocation must have occurred by placing a soft article over the mouth and nostrils 'is neither more nor less than a guess; it has no justification on the facts'. Assuming that signs of asphyxia were present, it was impossible to prove the cause of the asphyxia in the absence of signs of the asphyxiating agent. Smith concluded his report by stating firmly – and, without doubt, correctly – that 'it is beyond the power of any person to distinguish within a range of a few minutes to half an hour when a bruise was caused', in direct repudiation of Spilsbury's contentions.

Spilsbury replied in a long letter dated 5 August. As evidence of asphyxiation he had found 'small haemorrhages – known as Tardieu's spots – on the surfaces of the heart and lungs and a line of bruising along the margin of the tongue in front'. These spots, very common and non-specific, are found at almost every autopsy and, unless profuse, would be of no diagnostic significance, especially a week after death.[19] In evidence Spilsbury had referred to finding just two such spots on the heart, with 'indistinct' haemorrhages in the lungs, a situation that did not justify a conclusion of 'asphyxiation'. Spilsbury's conclusions about the state of the tongue were rendered questionable by the state of decomposition.

Spilsbury repeated his argument, noted above, about the alleged significance of the tongue's protrusion. He claimed that the bruise on the right temple 'was evidence of such violence as would have rendered her unconscious', but this must also have been an assumption. Even severe bruising does not necessarily cause unconsciousness. Spilsbury's contention that 'it would have been easy to suffocate her by pressure of a soft substance' reads as sheer hypothesis. As to the bruises, these were 'all recent and appeared about the same age', but modern research has shown that, on naked-eye inspection, bruises cannot be dated from infliction to a minimum of eighteen hours, when the first colour change – a greenish hue – starts to appear.[20] With regard to the larger bruises, Spilsbury relied on 'slight swelling' on two of the bruises and 'none at all' on a third to found an erroneous conclusion that these must have been inflicted 'a few minutes' before death, otherwise there would have been 'evident swelling'. Bearing in mind particularly the length of time between death and autopsy, swelling is an unreliable tool in any assessment of the time of infliction.

Modern science holds that 'asphyxia' is an outdated concept, if taken as meaning absence of oxygen (or 'hypoxia'). Most deaths formerly attributed to asphyxia are due to mechanical causes, such as manual or ligature strangulation, where the major factor in death is pressure on the neck, with reduction of blood flow to the brain and reflex neurological stimulation to the carotid sinus and arteries, which may cause rapid cardiac arrest. Pure suffocation, as by smothering a head in a plastic bag, usually has none of the classic signs of asphyxia, including petechial haemorrhage in the skin, eyes or lungs.[21]

Spilsbury must not be judged with the wisdom of hindsight, but no fewer than three contemporary pathologists, Dr Smith, Professor Littlejohn and the garrulous Dr Brontë, were, broadly speaking, correct in their findings, and Spilsbury was manifestly wrong in several important aspects of his evidence. Robinson's actions may have caused the death of Minnie Bonati, but there is good reason to believe that he was guilty, if at all, of manslaughter and not of the capital crime of murder.[22]

On 29 July Blackwell, in a form of words he had so often used before, minuted to the Home Secretary that 'there is no reason whatever in this case for interference with the sentence'.[23] Smith's memorandum was dismissed. The document remained, hidden away, in closed Home Office records until 2005.

John Robinson was hanged at Wandsworth Prison on 12 August 1927.

FIFTEEN

A Disappearing Bruise

In 1927 the Medico-Legal Society elected a woman member. It was a controversial step. Dr Marie Stopes, pioneer advocate of birth control and author of the best-selling *Married Love*, was a formidable character, not afraid to advance her views robustly, without fear or favour. Shortly after her election, Dr Stopes chided the society for not grappling with the ethics of abortion. In a reference to 'back street' terminations she pointed out that 'abortion was attempted and going on to a staggering extent throughout the country'. She herself had received over 10,000 letters asking her to perform abortions. 'The open, bare-faced trade in abortifacients', she claimed, 'was enormous and scandalous and there was no legal redress.' The medical profession refused to perform abortions, and, as a result 'women went to these sharks'. Spilsbury, no doubt mindful of the battle to convict Dr Starkie (see Chapter Eight), and reiterating his personal opposition to abortion, except where not to do so would endanger life or 'very seriously' prejudice the mother's health, agreed that abortion was 'exceedingly rife'. According to Spilsbury, cases brought to court were only a small proportion of those occurring, and, since the war, the practice of abortion had increased considerably.[1]

In the spring of 1928 Spilsbury received an accolade that was almost the equal of the knighthood bestowed five years earlier. The humorous magazine *Punch* – staple fare of railway bookstalls, doctors' surgeries and dentists' waiting-rooms – published a full-page caricature of Spilsbury, drawn by the cartoonist George Belcher. Spilsbury was depicted wearing the famous white rubber apron over a pair of his trademark spats and wielding a large dissecting knife in his left, gloved hand. The picture was accompanied by some excruciatingly bad verse:

> When arsenic has closed your eyes,
> This certain hope your corpse may rest in: –
> Sir B. will kindly analyse
> The contents of your large intestine.[2]

Spilsbury had also become an inspiration for crime fiction. In a short story, *The Pathologist to the Rescue*, R. Austin Freeman had invested his medical detective, Dr Thorndyke, with extraordinary abilities resembling those attributed to Spilsbury. 'I attended the post-mortem and examined the wound thoroughly,' said this fictional *alter ego*. 'The pistol was held in the right hand not more than two inches from the head; probably quite close, for the skin is scorched and heavily tattooed with black powder grains.'[3] Major Cecil Street, writing as 'John Rhode', published over 100 detective novels, including *The Paddington Mystery* (1925) and *The Murders in Praed Street*, which featured 'Sir Alured Faversham . . . the world renowned pathologist', a character apparently created from an amalgam of Spilsbury and Sir Almroth Wright.[4]

In 1971, long after his death, Spilsbury was the subject of *The Medical Witness*, a fictionalised biography by Richard Gordon. 'John Rumbelow', a forensic pathologist of international fame, is tall, elegantly dressed and boyish-looking, a man 'fastidious, rather than dandified', whose 'vanity was of a more cerebral . . . sort'.[5] Rumbelow, who has no interest in teaching, lives in Sydenham (presumably a reference to the Sydenham Society at Bart's, of which Spilsbury was an active member). The 'brilliance and explosiveness of his fame' are set against marital difficulties and a botched abortion, causing Rumbelow to commit suicide by gassing himself.

Throughout 1928 and 1929 Spilsbury continued his gruelling professional schedule, regularly making the headlines during his appearances in capital trials. He also gave widely reported evidence in three sensational inquests arising from the deaths of three members of the same family in Croydon, each poisoned by arsenic. A skilful young barrister, William Fearnley-Whittingstall, blunted the effect of Spilsbury's testimony and ensured that his client, Grace Duff, would never be charged with murder.[6]

The conviction of Sydney Fox for the murder of his mother is the most graphic example of Spilsbury's power as expert witness for the Crown to persuade both judge and jury towards a verdict which was – quite simply – wrong. On Saturday 9 November 1929, Sir Bernard Spilsbury, accompanied by Detective Superintendent Walter Hambrook CID, was driven from London to a remote churchyard in north-west Norfolk. They were to carry out an exhumation order, granted by the Home Office in respect of a Mrs Rosaline Fox, who had died some two weeks previously in mysterious circumstances. Hambrook, during the four-hour journey, briefed Spilsbury about her – and about her wayward youngest son, Sydney Harry Fox, already under arrest on unrelated charges.[7]

Walter Hambrook, another member of the 'Big Four' who had founded the Flying Squad, was a policeman of eccentric opinion. He regarded Fox as 'a devil incarnate', not least because he had blue eyes. 'It is a singular fact', he later wrote, 'that most murderers have blue eyes.' Hambrook had arrested Fox for fraud as long ago as 1916 and knew that mother and son had been successfully bilking a number of expensive south-coast hotels for some months. There were suspicions, but it was still unclear how Mrs Fox had died. In a curious analogy, Hambrook felt 'as excited as a schoolboy on a birds-nesting expedition'. This senior police officer, attending the country's most famous pathologist in an already sensational enquiry, was childishly agog with excitement: 'What would Sir Bernard find?' he wondered.[8]

Adjoining the graveyard was the old village schoolroom, where Fox had received a meagre education some twenty years before. The windows had been fitted with dark curtains to keep out prying eyes. Three trestles were in place to support the coffin and a post-mortem table installed, illuminated by a shiny new lamp. Old school desks were untidily piled up at one end of the dusty room. The Spilsbury party drew up at midday, a miserable afternoon in prospect, with high winds and heavy rain. Waiting for them was a reception committee consisting of the Chief Constable of Norfolk, Captain van Neck, senior local police officers, and the Rector, the Revd H. de Vere Welchman, suitably robed for an exhumation.[9]

Mrs Fox had been buried near the grave of her parents, under a row of leafless elm, chestnut and oak trees. The grave, already opened, had been surrounded by high posts covered with sackcloth. A derrick and pulley protruded above the screen. Mr Welchman said a prayer as the coffin was uncovered, raised (to a mournful grinding sound) and taken to the schoolroom on an ancient wooden bier, with wheels gaudily painted orange and black. Spilsbury took a sample of soil from around the coffin. Good Norfolk clay and loam, it was quite dry, well fertilised from generations of rude forefathers at Great Fransham. Recent interment meant that the coffin was still smart and expensive looking, with polished oak and shiny brass fittings. Fox, who had no intention of paying the undertaker with his own money, had ensured that his mother had the very best of departures from this weary vale of tears. The funeral expenses had come to no less than £47 10s.

Mrs Fox had died in Margate, at the Hotel Metropole, ostensibly as a result of a fire in her room (no. 66). Rather too eagerly, Fox had claimed a total of £3,000 on two short-term travel insurance policies, one of a long series taken out on his mother's life since May 1929. 'Extremely muddy water in this business', telegraphed a suspicious claims investigator.[10] The police were alerted and Fox was arrested in Norwich. Unsurprisingly, the hotel bill had not been paid, and there was enough other evidence of hotel fraud to keep the young man in detention while more serious matters were being investigated.

The coffin had been sealed by a layer of putty below the lid. When the lid was prised off, the body of Mrs Fox was revealed, wearing a short white vest. No doubt to the relief of the watching police officers, used to less wholesome exhumations, the only smell was that of dry sawdust, packed around the body. The undertaker, Mr Gore, stepped forward to identify his late client. The sexton, Arthur Cross, who probably knew far more about Rosie Rallison (as was) than anyone else present, also identified the body. The scar on the bridge of her nose was familiar to him – and possibly much else besides. He remembered her local reputation as 'a flighty one' and knew that the youngest of her four sons, Cecil and Sydney, were not the product of her marriage to William Fox, porter at Great Fransham station. He had walked out on his wife one day in 1896 – though in her grave, for better or worse, she still wore her wedding ring of thin gold. Rosie Fox was a short, dumpy woman, slightly over 5ft tall and weighing some 12 stone. Spilsbury could see no obvious signs of poisoning. There was no medically qualified witness or laboratory assistant present as Spilsbury, with his famed ambidexterity, swiftly carried out the cutting, extracting and preserving processes of the post-mortem, using equipment contained in his large black case, brought in from the car. No doubt the Chief Constable and attendant senior police personnel were duly impressed, but the only professional record of the autopsy lies in Spilsbury's handwritten case cards, running to seven sides.

It is impossible to know when Spilsbury wrote up his findings, but his report was not compiled until 7 December 1929, a full month after the exhumation. Spilsbury was habitually slow in submitting reports, but this seems an excessive delay given the high public profile of the investigation. According to his 1951 biography, Spilsbury sometimes delayed writing up his findings for several days,[11] methodology slack by modern standards. Dr Roche Lynch, the Home Office analyst, did not receive the two jars of stomach contents from Spilsbury until 7 December, a further three jars being sent over the next day. Lynch found no evidence of poisoning, but noted that Rosie had taken some alcohol on the night she died.

As in the Mahon and Thorne cases, nagging problems quickly surfaced in determining the cause of death. Hambrook was already keen to put a case together against Fox for matricide, one of the gravest crimes in the criminal calendar. Spilsbury, at the apogee of his fame, was under severe pressure to deliver forensically credible results. An immediate problem for him was that the body had the appearance of an elderly woman who had died a natural death. Nevertheless, the circumstances of the death, which had been recorded as 'accidental' at a perfunctory inquest held in Margate on 24 October 1929, would provide the seed from which positive evidence might grow.

Before beginning the autopsy Spilsbury would already have been aware of the background to the mysterious fire in Room 66. On that long car journey down to Great Fransham, Spilsbury would also have learnt much about the life and queer times of Sydney Harry Fox, the prime suspect. Fox was a type of young man whom many – including the likes of Spilsbury, Hambrook and, as will be seen, Sir William Jowitt, Attorney-General of the day – thought best removed from decent society.

Sydney Harry Fox (*alias* Lieutenant Sydney Fox Royal Flying Corps (RFC) *alias* Sydney Herbert Fox *alias* Sydney H. Granville Fox *alias* Sydney Harry Lane Fox *alias* the Hon. Sydney Henry Fox) was born on 2 January 1899 in Great Fransham, an isolated and introverted little community, connected by a spur of railway to Norwich and the bright lights beyond. Fox's father was probably the station porter, Tom Newall, but Rosie put it about that her lover had been a gentleman. Fox always nursed the hope of noble lineage, but Rosie did not enter the father's name on the birth certificate.

Fox's first criminal escapade took place late in 1911, when an angelic-looking boy had visited houses in the area, saying that he was collecting money for the local hospital. Donations were entered in a notebook, but the little angel had then gummed pages together, so that some of the forty-five donations could be pocketed. On 16 December 1911 PC Wright administered six strokes of the birch to this precocious conman, just two weeks short of his thirteenth birthday.

A year or so later Fox and his mother moved well away from Norfolk, settling in Thornton Heath, near Croydon, where Rosie worked for a time as a cook. Sydney's aspirations to the Higher Life were rewarded with the post of pageboy to Sir John and Lady Leslie at their London town house, 22 Manchester Square, opposite the Wallace Collection. Lady Leslie found him charming, and old Sir John dubbed him his 'pocket cherub'.[12] His grandson, the Irish nationalist and littérateur Shane Leslie, suspected that Fox had begun to receive money from 'homo-amorous men'. Fox was promoted to the post of junior footman, but in 1916 he stole some of the family silver and was discharged. During his period of service he had waited on Lady Randolph Churchill (Sir Shane Leslie's aunt), Winston Churchill and many other political and social grandees of the Liberal government, such as Lloyd George and Prime Minister Asquith. Fox, a good mimic, quickly began to ape the manners and affectations of the upper class.

Fox soon resurfaced as a clerk at Cox's Bank in the Strand, but was dismissed in late 1916 for forging cheques. Despite his poor schooling he had developed an educated hand, as well as a taste for dining in the best hotels 'correctly garbed and with a correctly critical appetite'.[13] Such expensive tastes required funding. Although still underage, he was ordered to enlist or face prosecution. Fox was rescued from service in the ranks by an admirer and emerged briefly in the more glamorous role as a cadet in the RFC. His benefactor was Brigadier-General Percy Holland CB, then aged 55, formerly of the Indian Army, who was involved at that time in secret war work in the Home Counties.

In the smart uniform of a Second Lieutenant in the RFC, Fox cruised the homosexual underworld of London, using a mixture of compromising address books, indiscreet correspondence and – very probably – a polite form of blackmail. In one police report he was described as obtaining 'such money as he could make out of sexual perversion'.[14] His circle ranged from army officers to 'certain young men who mixed in theatrical circles'.[15]

A 'hectic and glorious' period, in Fox's phrase,[16] came to an abrupt end in December 1917. He had failed his medical for the RFC and been recommended for an infantry commission, but continued posing as an officer cadet. That autumn Fox passed a fraudulent cheque in Brighton, pretending to be a grandson of Sir John Leslie. He was traced to the Royal Automobile Club, Pall Mall, which he was using as a convenient poste restante for private correspondence. The club was watched. One evening, shortly after Christmas 1917, Fox arrived at the club, opened a letter, said to have been 'of the most compromising nature', from Brigadier Holland, and was promptly arrested by an officer of the military police, assisted by Police Sergeant Walter Hambrook. A search of Fox's pockets revealed 'packets of [intimate] correspondence, rouge, and a scented booklet of *papier poudré*'.[17] The Brigadier's incautious love letter sparked off a major purge of senior army personnel, which coincided with the run-up to the notorious 'Black Book' trial at the Old Bailey, a prosecution for criminal libel during which a right-wing MP, Noel Pemberton Billing, peddled wild allegations of a pro-German fifth column and sodomy in high places. This was a period of extreme sensitivity for a government possibly facing defeat on the Western Front. Other senior officers were implicated in the Brigadier Holland scandal, which involved at least one other RFC cadet.

At the end of April 1918 Holland was cashiered and stripped of both his CB (Companion of the Bath) and his entry in *Who's Who*. Fox was jailed for three months and returned to the ranks. He convinced a medical officer that he had epilepsy, neatly avoiding active service in that last terrible year of the war. After his release Fox had a brief affair with Gerald Hamilton, inspiration for the eponymous non-hero of *Mr Norris Changes Trains* by Christopher Isherwood and described as a 'notorious Sodomite' by the aptly named Inspector Goodwillie.[18]

Throughout the 1920s Fox continued to live with his mother, who always took him back after periods in jail. Rosie was his sole partner in crime. She benefited from his personations, his chequebook frauds and the proceeds of his relationships with army officers and the like. She would even write dishonest letters supporting her son's pretence to be a young aristocrat, a member of Society. Generally speaking, Fox's dishonesty was directed at those who could afford to bear the loss.

In 1928 Fox lost a rare honest job, as a clerk with an insurance company, when he broke his leg in a motorcycle accident in Portsmouth. Out of work, at a time of rising unemployment on the eve of the interwar depression, Fox was made bankrupt while he served a further sentence of imprisonment for stealing items of low value from his landlady in Southsea. Rosie was consigned to Portsmouth Workhouse for the duration of Fox's sentence. On Fox's release from prison in April 1929 mother and son were reunited. Rosie quit the workhouse, and, after a spell in lodgings in Norwich, the pair began the strange odyssey that, within a year, would end in both their deaths.

Rosie was in poor shape. She had advanced Parkinson's disease, with severe shaking and restricted movement. People described her as being 'very weak and tottering', with a 'vacant far-away expression'.[19] In April 1929 she was examined by a Dr Leahy, with a view to reinstating a small life assurance policy for £10, originally taken out in 1913. Dr Leahy thought that Rosie looked 'about 70', several years older than her true age of 62. Nevertheless, he certified her fit to have her life policy renewed.[20] On 21 April she made a will in favour of Fox, subject to two small legacies and just one farthing to her eldest son. Fox, of course, wrote out the document. Nine days later he took out the first of a series of travel insurance accident policies, some in his own name. These were all short-term arrangements, valid for a few days at a time. Out of the 176 days before Rosie's death, the policies covered 167. Almost half their joint pension income was being spent on insurance premiums, although Fox was able to supplement funds by claiming money for allegedly lost overcoats and luggage during their travels over south-east England.

As summer slipped into autumn 1929 Fox's *faux* aristocratic manner secured the couple free and very comfortable accommodation at the Red Lion Hotel, Colchester ('wire the amount of the bill'); the Royal Pavilion Hotel, Folkestone; and the County Hotel, Canterbury. In September Fox took his mother to visit the Duisans Military Cemetery, near Arras, where his brother Cecil was buried. From Ostend, signing himself 'Syd', he sent a postcard of the Brussels *mannequin pis*, accompanied by a camp comment, to a gay friend in London.

On 16 October the disabled lady and her dutiful son arrived at the Hotel Metropole on Margate seafront. The hotel, though commodious, had known better days and, as winter approached, was largely the haunt of commercial travellers. Vera Hopper, receptionist at the Metropole, worried that the rooms originally offered were rather cold, suggested communicating rooms side by side, even though Fox had not asked for this – quite an important point in the light of what was to happen.

Two days later, on 18 October, Fox took out two further travel policies, totalling £3,000, in the event of his mother's death from 'violent, accidental, external, visible means'. Both policies expired at midnight on Wednesday 23 October 1929. On Sunday 20 October Rosie complained of pains in her body, saying that she was feeling cold. Fox told hotel staff that his mother had fainted. Dr Cecil Austin, whose surgery was situated in Hawley Street, Margate, was called to the Hotel Metropole. Dr Austin had been drinking, and his physical examination was perfunctory. He prescribed a tonic and then, putting his thumbs to his ears, waggled his hands, declaring, 'You're all right, old lady. Bogey-Bogey!', before staggering out of the bedroom.[21] At his trial for murder, Fox's claim that the doctor had been drunk was challenged by the prosecution. A contemporary police report, however, confirms not only that Austin's alcoholism was common knowledge in Margate, but that he was so drunk when first interviewed by police that no statement could be taken from him.[22] At committal proceedings he had to grab hold of the rail of the witness-box to steady himself.[23] Weeks later, however, Dr Austin seems to have sobered up for the trial in Lewes on the south coast, miles away from his local reputation in Margate. His evidence that there was nothing very wrong with Rosie that Sunday (and his denial of ever having said 'Bogey-Bogey!') was accepted uncritically by judge and jury. Indeed, it was touted by the prosecution as yet another example of dishonest evidence by the prisoner.

There is corroboration, however, that Rosie had been unwell that Sunday from statements made by the hotel manager and a chambermaid. Both stated that Mrs Fox's limbs were extremely cold, and two hot-water bottles were put close to her feet. Given the state of her arteries, these symptoms seem consistent with the onset of a progressive cardiac failure. The episode is highly significant in view of Spilsbury's assessment of the likelihood of death from heart disease.

On Wednesday night, 23 October 1929, Mrs Fox and her son went down to dine in the hotel restaurant. Mrs Fox ate a mixed grill, washed down with a half pint of bitter. Later Fox went for a walk, bought a half-bottle of port, had a glass of beer in the bar and took an *Evening Standard* up to his room. Roche Lynch's analysis of the stomach contents supports the view that Rosie had taken some of the port later that night. Later on the hotel saloon bar was crowded, a venue popular with commercial travellers and assorted seafarers. Other customers and residents were in the nearby billiard-room. At about 11.40 p.m. Fox, practically naked, dressed only in a vest according to some reports, ran down the main staircase, shouting, 'Where is the Boots [Hall Porter]? I think there's a fire.'[24]

Sam Hopkins, a commercial traveller from Walthamstow, proved to be the hero of the hour. After unsuccessfully trying to persuade a group of ship's pilots, tippling in the saloon bar, to help him, he ran into the billiard-room and alerted some fellow commercial travellers, charging up the stairs and along the corridor to Room 66. The door was closed. Other would-be rescuers seem to have helped him get the door open. Inside, the bedroom, completely dark, was thick with smoke. Mrs Fox was lying half on the bed, her right leg hanging over the side. Her false teeth, which would play a part in Spilsbury's conclusions, were discovered in the washbasin. Almost beaten back by smoke, Sam eventually managed to crawl in on his hands and knees, pull Rosie off the bed and drag her ample form – by now a dead weight – into the corridor. She, too, was practically naked, wearing only a cheap cotton vest. As Sam recalled at the trial, Fox made no attempt to rescue his mother. At Fox's trial, much would be made of the arrangement of items, such as a pillow on a bedside table and the position of a wicker chair, but, bearing in mind that several people, including firemen, had blundered into a bedroom filled with smoke and were attempting to extinguish a fire, these factors do not seem significant.

The bibulous Dr Austin was the first medical man on the scene and, having confirmed that Rosie was dead, simply certified the death as due to 'shock and suffocation'.

1. Spilsbury as matinée idol: a studio portrait from about 1923. *(Bryan Senior)*

2. Spilsbury's birthplace above his father's shop in Leamington Spa. *(David J. Tolley)*

3. Spilsbury, aged about 16, with his sisters and younger brother. *(Bryan Senior)*

4. A lecture at St Mary's Medical School in 1904. Spilsbury is on the extreme right of the front row; William Willcox is to the right of the central gangway and Alexander Fleming, discoverer of penicillin, is to the left. *(St Mary's Hospital Archives)*

5–8. Spilsbury the camera-shy celebrity. (Robin Odell)

9. David Greenwood (centre) under arrest, February 1918. *(Richard Whittington-Egan)*

10. Dr Hawley Harvey Crippen. *(Getty Images)*

11. Sydney Fox in 1919. *(The National Archives)*

SPRING FASHION NUMBER ON MONDAY: 24 PAGES

Daily Mirror

THE DAILY PICTURE PAPER WITH THE LARGEST NET SALE

£1,000 FOR A FORECAST: Coupon To-day.

No. 6,661 — Registered at the G.P.O. as a Newspaper. — SATURDAY, MARCH 14, 1925 — One Penny

THORNE'S DRAMATIC STORY IN THE WITNESS BOX

Sir Bernard Spilsbury, who has given in evidence his opinion that a mark on the dead girl's neck was due to a natural fall.

Dr. Bronte, a pathologist from the London Hospital.

Norman Thorne giving evidence at Lewes Assizes yesterday at his trial on the charge of murdering his fiancée, Elsie Cameron.

FREEDOM OF LEEDS FOR PREMIER AND LORD OXFORD

The Premier (left) and the Earl of Oxford (right) receiving from the Lord Mayor the scrolls recording the conferment on them of the freedom of the city of Leeds yesterday. In a speech afterwards Mr. Baldwin appealed for the removal of class hatred from industrial negotiations.—(Daily Mirror.)

Another picture of Thorne in the witness-box yesterday. With a rope he demonstrated to the Court how the girl, as he alleges, hanged herself from a beam in his hut. Counsel for the defence stated that he would call Dr. Bronte and another pathologist in support of the view of the defence that a mark on the girl's neck was consistent either with a fall or with the pressure of a rope.

12. Spilsbury makes the front page. *(British Library)*

13. Hilda Bainbridge (extreme left) hides her face as Spilsbury pulls bloodsoaked clothing from Emily Kaye's hatbox at the Crumbles in May 1924. *(Robin Odell)*

14. Case card of Spilsbury's post-mortem on Nellie Trew, victim of the 'Button and Badge Murder' in February 1918. *(Robin Odell)*

Trew N. G. B. 16.
12.2. 18.
Strang . Throttling .   1
Rex v David Greenwood Murder
Woolwich
Ext. Well nourgirl. Fairlystrongly high. Ht 5ft 6"
Petechiaeg conj. Lips + This relieved . Sl abrasm bridge
of nose. Small bruise ofthr abrasm on midline of upper lip.
Bruiseleft side g chin. Sl: abrasm +bruise rt side g chin
Bruise over rt jaw in front of angle + another small me a
short distance above it (there has ruille on surface). On rt side
neck. Tiny red mark ½ waydown in front ofstern mastoid. One
red Mark at level of above at front border of sterno mastoid

15. Sir Bernard and Lady Spilsbury at Evelyn's wedding, May 1934. *(Robin Odell)*

16. Peter Spilsbury in 1934. *(The President and Fellows of Magdalen College, Oxford)*

17. Evelyn Spilsbury in 1930, a publicity shot for British Movietone News. *(Getty Images)*

18. Sir Bernard and Dick Spilsbury on a Hellenic cruise in April 1937. *(Robin Odell)*

19. Spilsbury in decline, pictured outside the Old Bailey in April 1937. *(Andrew Rose)*

In contrast, the next doctor to arrive, Dr Robert Nichol, also in practice in Margate, was an exceptionally shrewd observer. He spoke to Fox, whom he remembered as being very upset. Dr Nichol noticed, after the bedroom had been cleared of smoke, that there was a section of unburnt carpet between the gas fire and fender, with no obvious connection between the supposed source of the fire and the fire itself.

There is no doubt that the fire had been started deliberately by Fox after his mother's death. The six-month history of short-term travel insurance, entered into by mother and son as willing partners, was now to bear fruit. Rosie's last gift to her son would be the insurance pay-out. The evidence about her physical condition supports the view that both mother and son knew that time was short. What probably happened is that Fox had found his mother's body. She had died from a heart attack brought on in an attempt to get out of bed and use the chamberpot. In order to recover insurance money, there had to be evidence of accidental death, so Fox set light to some old newspapers under an armchair near a gas fire.

Afterwards his behaviour in claiming the insurance money within two days of his mother's death seemed callous and grasping. Furthermore, both Fox and his mother were practically penniless (Fox would claim, with characteristic dishonesty, that the hotel should repay £24 in banknotes supposedly burnt in the fire) and had little more than the clothes they were wearing when they arrived at the hotel. On the other hand, the police had evidence that was never put before the jury. Official records reveal a determined police trawl through the list of Fox's gay acquaintances. The risk of prosecution and imprisonment for homosexual activity was very real, and, by one means or another, the police induced several men to make lengthy statements. The Crown would suggest that lack of funds was a motive for murder, but this hidden evidence shows that Fox could usually find some way to raise cash if the need arose.

It is against this background that Spilsbury came to record his opinion as to the cause of death. There was no trace of soot in the airpassages, indicating, quite correctly, that Rosie had died some time before the fire had broken out. The blood also did not have the bright colour associated with carbon monoxide poisoning. Spilsbury found evidence of coronary artery disease, including 'brown atrophy' of the heart muscle, slight thickening of the heart valves, an area of fibrosis in the wall of the left ventricle, softening of the heart muscle, a patch of disease in the left coronary artery with slight narrowing and slight disease of the aorta. Such manifestations were, according to his report, 'common in elderly persons and not in themselves serious'.[25]

Crucially, however, Spilsbury claimed to have found 'a large recent bruise at the back of the larynx, in the loose tissue between it and the oesophagus'. He described the bruise in the larynx as being caused by 'some mechanical violence, a breaking or tearing of small blood vessels'. Spilsbury also noted a recent bruise, detectable only by incision, on the left edge of the tongue, midway between the tip and the back of the tongue. The bruise was about ¼in in diameter, extending deeply into the tongue. Spilsbury examined Rosie's false teeth, which were very old, dating from 1915, and in poor repair, the pair of metal springs that joined upper and lower sets being respectively broken and missing. The tongue 'could not have been bruised between the toothless gums'. Speculating that Rosie had been wearing her dentures when she was strangled, Spilsbury concluded that, 'if the larynx was forcibly pressed upwards towards the floor of the mouth in the act of throttling, the tension on the tissues between the larynx and the oesophagus behind it might be sufficient to cause bruising . . . as . . . found in this case. Such upward pressure would forcibly close the jaws and might cause the tongue to be bitten.'[26] (Hambrook would later claim, absurdly, that the teeth 'were expelled in the action of strangulation'.[27])

There was a 'small haemorrhage' in the lining membrane of the epiglottis, and the left side of the thyroid gland was 'very congested', with 'recent bruising' on the left side of the surface. Firm pressure between thumb and fingers applied to the larynx could have produced the bruising to the thyroid gland. If Rosie had offered little resistance and the fingers were kept in position until death, there might be no bruising of the skin on the neck. Spilsbury concluded that the injuries found in the neck and the tongue 'can only be accounted for as the result of manual strangulation and the cause of death . . . was asphyxia due to strangulation by the hand'. As in so many other capital trials in which he gave evidence, Spilsbury's findings were potentially lethal for the defendant.

On Saturday 8 March 1930 Spilsbury received a party of professional visitors to his laboratory at University College Hospital, where he now based himself. One was his past collaborator, Dr Henry Weir. The others were Dr Robert Brontë and Dr Sydney Smith, both instructed to appear for the defence in the trial of Sydney Fox, due to start the following week. Both men had crossed swords with Spilsbury in the past, but, as Smith recalled, the great pathologist 'could not have been more courteous or helpful'.[28] Bearing in mind the importance attached by Spilsbury to the bruise on the back of the larynx, they closely examined the larynx, which had been preserved by formalin in a glass jar since the exhumation. Neither expert could see any sign of a bruise. 'Where's the bruise gone?' asked Smith. 'It became obscure before I put the larynx in formalin,' replied Spilsbury. 'That is why I did not take a section.' Smith could not understand how so large a bruise, as claimed, could have been inflicted without damaging tissues on either side of the larynx or neck.[29]

Spilsbury's failure to make a microscopical examination is significant, since it could have revealed the presence of blood in the tissue, extruded in the act of bruising. Some years later, in a paper on bruising read to the Medico-Legal Society, Spilsbury said: 'whenever you see in a dead subject what might be a bruise, always cut into it freely. Very often it will be found that what appears to be a small bruise is a very much larger one when incised.'[30] In the case of Rosaline Fox it seems that Spilsbury did not put his own theory into practice. Smith and Brontë were of the opinion that what Spilsbury had seen was not a bruise but post-mortem discoloration. They reminded him that it was very difficult to diagnose a bruise with the naked eye after putrefaction had occurred. Spilsbury would not budge. He had already committed himself to this opinion in his written report and in his deposition given at the magistrates' court. 'His belief in himself was so strong', commented Smith, 'that he could not conceive the possibility of error.'[31]

The visiting defence experts also dismissed the other supposed signs of strangulation. The pinhead haemorrhage on the epiglottis could have been found in the majority of natural deaths. The bruise in the tongue could have been caused by Rosie's badly fitting false teeth. As for the congestion and alleged bruise on the thyroid, even Dr Weir, who endorsed most of Spilsbury's other conclusions, did not accept that this was a bruise, and – eventually – Spilsbury appeared to concede the point. Smith hoped for a public admission by Spilsbury that he had been wrong about the thyroid, but, as the defence experts left the building, Brontë observed – with uncanny accuracy – 'Not Spilsbury. You wait till we're in court.'[32]

The stage was set for one of the most extraordinary forensic battles in Spilsbury's long career as Honorary Pathologist to the Home Office. The trial of Sydney Fox opened at Lewes Assizes on Wednesday 12 March 1930. The trial judge was Mr Justice Rowlatt, an experienced judge who had been appointed to the High Court Bench in 1912 and had tried Jeannie Baxter (see Chapter Five). The judge was well liked among lawyers, with a kindly manner in private and a gentle sense of humour. He was remembered as being rather 'a dear'.[33] In court his style was unobtrusive, almost scholarly, with none of the disagreeable judicial characteristics of a Darling or an Avory.

The prosecution team was headed by the Attorney-General, Sir William Jowitt KC, an able and ambitious lawyer–politician. Jowitt, elected as a Liberal MP, had crossed the floor of the House of Commons, attaining office in Ramsay MacDonald's second minority government of May 1929. The Attorney-General prosecuted in person, ostensibly because of the gravity of the charge – this was the first trial for matricide in England since the 1870s – but, as will be seen, Jowitt had other official concerns, kept well hidden from press and public. The Attorney-General had the formidable assistance of Curtis-Bennett, St John Hutchinson KC (a personal friend) and Gerald Thesiger, a future High Court judge.

Before the trial started, Jowitt, with the help of his wife and the ample forms of Curtis-Bennett and Hutchinson, conducted a bizarre experiment, predicated on acceptance of Spilsbury's opinions about the cause and circumstances of the death. Lady Jowitt, pretending to be Rosie Fox, lay on a bed, while the three barristers in turn played the part of Fox. They decided that the 'most likely' method used by Fox for killing Rosie would have been holding the throat with the left hand, 'snatched the pillow from under her head with his right' and then pressed the pillow over her face. Fox would 'not need to grip tightly', merely holding the neck in position so as to 'rely on the pillow to shut out the supply of air'.[34] These conclusions seem to posit smothering, rather than manual strangulation, bearing in mind Spilsbury's theories of 'upward pressure' and consequent bruising. A particular problem was highlighted by the marks of lipstick left on the pillow after the experiment. At the Metropole, however, the pillow found on the pedestal cupboard by the bed had no marks on it and, in particular, no traces of saliva.

For the defence, Fox, who may have been funded by the *News of the World* in return for an 'exclusive', had secured the services of 'Jimmy' Cassels (see Chapter Eleven) and two obscure junior barristers, S.T.T. James and C. Pensotti. From the start, the defenders of Fox were hopelessly outgunned by Crown counsel. Cassels, who had unsuccessfully defended Mahon and Thorne in the same courtroom, was a likeable advocate of some ability, but manifestly the intellectual inferior of the Attorney-General. Cassels was also homophobic, a prejudice that, despite his professionalism as a barrister, sat uneasily with a lay client who 'took pride in the fact that his pleasure lay entirely with his own sex'.[35] Given the background to the case, the likelihood is that Cassels was convinced of Fox's guilt even before accepting the brief.

The courtroom at Lewes was small, even intimate, described in the *Daily Mail* as 'picturesque, with its stained glass windows, polished pitchpine, and a cluster of red and pink carnations on the judge's bench'.[36] The trial began on a farcical note. Fully robed, the judge entered the courtroom, followed, at a respectful distance, by the smaller figure of his marshal, Alan King-Hamilton. It was common practice for a young barrister to be attached to an assize judge, acting as informal secretary and factotum while learning about the principles and practice of the criminal law. The judge's chair at Lewes was surmounted by a canopy, from which depended a fringe of cloth. As Rowlatt, a very tall man, walked towards the seat, his wig caught on the fringe and was knocked off his head. King-Hamilton, a keen cricketer, smartly caught the flying object. There was a moment's awkward silence. King-Hamilton whispered to Rowlatt, 'Should we go out and come back in again?', but the judge would have none of that and crammed the wig back on his head. There it remained, at a crazy angle, bunches of grey hair sticking out at the sides, until the lunchtime adjournment.[37]

Sydney Fox, brought up from the cells into the dock, pleaded not guilty to the indictment. He had managed to acquire a neat outfit, 'the suit of a city man', and was wearing a black jacket and waistcoat and striped trousers, with a soft white shirt and sober black tie. He had 'dark hair, inclining to curl', and his face was thought to have 'small, regular features' (in fact, Fox had a minor facial asymmetry, and his left eyelid appeared slightly lower than the right).[38]

The *Daily Mail* reporter, probably well aware of Fox's sexual orientation, snidely drew attention to a 'well-formed, but effeminate, mouth and chin'. His complexion was said to be 'sallow', with 'heavy shadows under his pale blue eyes, which had an introspective expression'.

During Jowitt's masterly opening speech[39] Fox sat quietly, only once showing any emotion. When the Attorney-General referred to Rosie's 'crippled condition', Fox 'buried his face in his hands'. Nearly a quarter of Jowitt's speech was devoted to a summary of the damning evidence that Spilsbury would give in the witness-box. In his instructions to counsel the DPP had privately conceded that 'the case really rests upon the evidence of Sir Bernard Spilsbury'.[40] 'Sir Bernard will . . . produce a model of the larynx', promised the Attorney-General, succinctly encapsulating the heart of the Crown's case in a few sentences. 'He found at the back of the larynx a clear recent bruise about the size of half a crown. He will tell you that that bruise could only have been caused by . . . manual strangulation – strangulation by the hand.'

Hotel staff, gallant commercial travellers, local medical men, firemen, arson experts and police officers all gave their evidence over the first four days of the trial.[41] Heavyweight medical evidence began late on the afternoon of Monday 17 March 1930. Roche Lynch had found 'about a minim' of alcohol in the dead woman's stomach, from which he extrapolated that this 'was consistent with about a quarter of a bottle having been taken', a fair amount, but considerably less than the 'half-bottle' of port that Jowitt, when opening the case, had suggested was deliberately given to Rosie to make her sleep.

Spilsbury was then called to give evidence. Wearing his customary morning-coat, he mounted the steps to the balustraded witness-box, stage right of the judge. Ever the showman, Spilsbury carried a small box, which he carefully placed on the shelf in front of him, where it competed for space – a little alarmingly – with a carafe of water. Spilsbury, recalled as 'deadly cold' in manner,[42] gave evidence in his usual quietly spoken, non-demonstrative way. In answer to Jowitt he first described the post-mortem findings, quickly moving to the condition of the heart and arteries. Jowitt put a series of leading questions (without any protest from the defence), which seem to have been carefully crafted to play down the likelihood of Rosie's sudden death from heart disease. Using such terms as 'slight disease of the main artery', 'slightly narrowed' and 'slight patch of disease', Jowitt brought home the point in a neat summary:

JOWITT. Does it come to this, that you do not think she can have died from heart failure, pure and simple?
SPILSBURY. No, not through the disease which I found in her heart.

On the contrary, 'the area of fibrosis' (or fibrotic plaque, as this manifestation would now be called) noted by Spilsbury in his examination of Rosie's body is firm evidence that she had already suffered a heart attack around three months previously and was a candidate for sudden death at any time. With this background the narrowing of the left coronary artery was unlikely to have been 'slight', as Spilsbury was contending in court.[43]

Spilsbury then opened the box that he had brought with him and, in the manner of a conjurer, produced a porcelain model of the upper respiratory tract, jaw and tongue. Jowitt's introduction resembled the drumroll that precedes an illusionist's trick:

> JOWITT. Now, Sir Bernard, this is a matter of such importance, to get the position of the bruise, that I want you to indicate on your model where it was.
> SPILSBURY. I will use a pencil point . . . here . . . the back of the lower part of the larynx and the centre part of it would, as nearly as possible, be here . . . The bruise was roughly the size of a half-crown, something more than one inch across and it formed an area corresponding to that circle of which this is the centre. It may have been a shade lower than that.

After Spilsbury had given his opinion that the fire could not have caused the death of Mrs Fox, the court adjourned for the day. On 18 March Jowitt resumed his examination-in-chief. Spilsbury dealt with the bruise on the tongue, making an assumption about the wearing of dentures and speculating as to chronology.

> JOWITT. . . . when the bruise was caused, the teeth were in the mouth?
> SPILSBURY. Yes . . . [at the] very outside, I think, one could allow it to be two hours before death . . . the sharp margin was one indication that it was recent . . . [I am] certain it was caused within that [time] margin.
> JOWITT. Is it consistent with that bruise that it was caused, let us say, a couple of minutes before the heart ceased to beat?
> SPILSBURY. Yes, quite.

Spilsbury claimed that it was impossible to bite the tongue with the back teeth. He made much of this tiny bruise, but his theory (and Weir's supporting evidence) was predicated on Rosie having gone to bed with her old, ill-fitting and uncomfortable teeth in her mouth, an unlikely occurrence and one certainly contrary to her usual practice. Spilsbury gave the court his opinion about the 'upward movement', which would have pushed the larynx towards the mouth, but accepted that there was no outward sign of bruising. As to the disappearing bruise itself, Jowitt shamelessly introduced a public figure, in a purely cosmetic exercise, since Captain van Neck had no medical qualifications:

> JOWITT. When you did your post-mortem . . . you had with you the Chief Constable of Norfolk . . . Did you show it [the bruise] to him?
> SPILSBURY. He was watching me and he saw it . . . This bruise, of course, was cut right through when I turned back the gullet and I only took back

to my lab the larynx and the upper windpipe. I probably left some remains of the bruise on the back of the larynx, but owing to the further changes occurring afterwards, post-mortem discoloration, it was impossible to see anything then.

Cassels did his best in cross-examination and certainly made some good points, not least when Spilsbury admitted that he was 'pretty certain that this is the only exhumation I have done in a case of manual strangulation'. There was also an awkward moment when Spilsbury attempted to fit Rosie's battered false teeth into the porcelain model, but found that they were too large for the purpose. Cassels also elicited a strangely worded admission from Spilsbury, who said, referring to the crucial bruise on the larynx, 'I did not made any effort to keep it'. As Brontë had predicted, however, Spilsbury was not going to let go of the thyroid, despite the contrary opinion of the three other pathologists:

JUDGE. Your opinion is still that the thyroid gland was bruised?
SPILSBURY. That is so.

One of the best defence points was that the hyoid bone, which is found in the larynx, was still intact when Spilsbury began his post-mortem. This bone becomes progressively more fragile with age and is easily fractured.

SPILSBURY. . . . examining the other part of the larynx, I am afraid I rather leaned on it with my hand. I first cracked one side and then the other . . .
CASSELS. Very brittle?
SPILSBURY. Yes.

The fact that the hyoid bone and the cricoid cartilege were undamaged made manual strangulation less likely, and Cassels pressed his advantage by going through the classic signs – petechiae, froth, blackening of the face, marks of a struggle, livid fingernails and so on – none of which was found on Rosie's body. Nevertheless, Cassels could not get round Spilsbury's intransigence on the matter of the bruise on the back of the larynx. 'It was a bruise and nothing else,' declared Spilsbury, taking deadly aim at the two defence experts. 'There are no two opinions about it.'

Unhappily for the defence, the wording of Cassels's last question suggests the possibility of a Freudian slip:

CASSELS. I only want to ask you one final question, Sir Bernard. In your experience of strangulation cases, have you known of a case with fewer signs than this?
SPILSBURY. No, I have not.

In re-examination Jowitt quickly disposed of any force this exchange might have had by reminding the court, through his witness, that the dead woman had been in bed and suffering from *paralysis agitans* (or Parkinson's disease).

Dr Weir adopted most of Spilsbury's arguments, accepting that he had taken the history of the case from him. In relation to heart disease, however, he differed from the great man:

> WEIR. In my opinion, except for the bruising, there was sufficient disease of the heart to have accounted for death.

When the time came for defence medical evidence, Smith was the first to be called. He quickly established that he had a much greater experience of manual strangulation than had Spilsbury, mainly because of Smith's long period as a pathologist in Cairo, where throttling was a common form of murder. He emphasised the lack of any external sign of manual strangulation and made the important point that Spilsbury could have preserved the larynx in formalin at the time he first noticed the alleged bruise. As to Rosie's general condition, Smith's evidence was unambiguous:

> SMITH. The heart was in an advanced state of degeneration, the coronary arteries were dislocated, and the kidneys were cirrhosed . . . any additional strain . . . such as . . . [an] attempt at exertion . . . would tend to precipitate death.

Smith's evidence was based on the premiss that the fire had been accidental. In his view, death could have occurred as Rosie was attempting to get out of bed. Jowitt's cross-examination began on Thursday 20 March. From the outset he adopted an unusually aggressive tone towards an expert witness of Smith's calibre. 'I would rather that you should answer my question,' barked Jowitt at one point, even hinting at bad faith. 'It may be difficult for gentlemen who lecture to answer questions . . . but do you think you are being quite candid with me?'

Primed by Spilsbury in consultation and at the height of his brilliant form as an advocate, Jowitt skilfully undermined Smith's opinion that the bruise was no more than post-mortem discoloration. Quoting from Taylor's *Medical Jurisprudence*, a forensic textbook originally written by Dr Alfred Swaine Taylor in the nineteenth century and now edited by Smith, Jowitt successfully muddied the waters by quoting a passage that seemed to suggest that absence of visible signs of asphyxia was not proof that death had not occurred from suffocation. Smith's attempts to point out the context of the passage, which dealt with cases of smothering rather than of manual strangulation, were dismissed. The superiority of Sir Bernard Spilsbury as a pathologist was repeatedly emphasised by the Attorney-General, but Smith bravely held his corner:

JOWITT. Do you suggest that Sir Bernard Spilsbury would not know the difference between discoloration due to post-mortem changes and a bruise?

SMITH. I say no-one can tell by looking at a stain whether it is a post-mortem change or a bruise. Sir Bernard could not have diagnosed a bruise by looking at it . . . I should cut into it.

Brontë, remembered as appearing 'very nervous',[44] succeeded Smith in the witness-box. Brontë had a rather 'hang-dog' facial appearance, and his health may already have begun to deteriorate (see Chapter Eighteen). Jowitt's approach to him was similarly hectoring and, as with Smith, he tried to trap the witness into denigrating the great Spilsbury. Brontë's reply seems to have been uttered with great feeling:

JOWITT. . . . . are you suggesting that Sir Bernard Spilsbury did not see what he said he saw?

BRONTË. Far be it from me to make such a suggestion.

Brontë unwisely brought up the Thorne case (see Chapter Twelve), in which Spilsbury's opinion had prevailed, and admitted that he did not know the meaning of the term 'thug' when Jowitt put to him that these Indian robbers had 'a specially constructed finger band . . . to enable them to strangle a person without any sign'. Nevertheless, like Smith, Brontë was positive that Spilsbury could not have seen a bruise on the larynx.

Modern opinion unequivocally supports the evidence of Smith and Brontë on the vital point. If dissection of the neck is not carried out in a bloodless field, the escape of blood into the neck can mimic the appearance of bruising. This forensic red-herring is sometimes called the 'Prinsloo-Gordon artefact'.[45] Furthermore, both Smith and Brontë were agreed that, such was the poor state of Mrs Fox's circulatory system, she could have died at any time. Overall, Spilsbury's interpretation was fundamentally flawed in an attempt to make the facts fit his conviction that Rosie had been strangled.[46]

Sydney Smith thought that Jowitt seemed 'determined to hang Fox'.[47] Official papers, originally closed for a hundred years, reveal why the Attorney-General was so keen to put a rope around Fox's neck. In his memoirs Jowitt hinted at the reasons that lay behind his determination to see Fox out of the way: 'he had been acting as a male prostitute. I suspect that Fox never altogether abandoned this trade, but from time to time obtained money by this means.'[48] The police trawl through the long list of Fox's homosexual contacts produced the names of army officers and successful salesmen, city merchants and peers of the realm. Statements made by hotel staff also revealed something that must have rung alarm bells in the Establishment.[49] Fox had casually dropped the name of Earl Beauchamp, Warden of the Cinque Ports.

Beauchamp's official residence, Walmer Castle, was not far from the Folkestone and Canterbury hotels in whose comfortable surroundings mother and son had been freeloading during the late summer and autumn. Beauchamp, a family man with seven children, was promiscuously homosexual. By 1929 the Duke of Westminster, who was Beauchamp's wife's brother and a bully, anti-semite and homophobe, was openly referring to his brother-in-law in society as 'my bugger-in-law'. Walmer Castle had been the scene of some infamous and very *louche* parties.[50] The day after Beauchamp's name had emerged in the statements of hotel staff, the police called at Halkyn House, Beauchamp's splendid town house at 13 Belgrave Square.

They interviewed the caretaker and the cook, who both remembered an incident in July 1929 when the house had been closed up at the end of the London Season. A young man had telephoned the house one Sunday, telling the cook that he was 'Wilson Fox', a friend of the Beauchamp family, and that he had lost his wallet. The cook obligingly offered to give him £1. About an hour later, wearing a light mixture suit and trilby hat, Fox cheekily rang the front doorbell. The cook seems to have made no attempt to check his identity, although she could easily have telephoned Beauchamp's household in Scotland. 'Wilson Fox' asked for another £1 so that 'he could get some dinner', and the cook gave him two gold sovereigns.[51] In 1929, £2 was a considerable sum, the equivalent of perhaps £100 today. The circumstances point to a discreet buying-off operation. Sydney Fox had not pulled the name of Beauchamp at random from the pages of *Burke's Peerage*.

During his period as DPP, Bodkin assiduously read his departmental papers.[52] Beauchamp was leader of the Liberal Party in the House of Lords, and the minority Labour government depended on Liberal support for its survival. Bodkin would be aware that the precarious position of the government could be seriously compromised by scandalous revelations. In the event Fox did not reveal any compromising matters, and Jowitt succeeded in keeping the name of Beauchamp, the King's friend, out of the trial. The relevant witness statements were not served on the defence, and hotel witnesses were not asked about Fox's attempts to telephone Walmer Castle. In 1931 Beauchamp fled the country to avoid arrest for the criminal offence of gross indecency: perhaps this time Beauchamp – the inspiration for Lord Marchmain in Evelyn Waugh's *Brideshead Revisited* – had taken one risk too many with a young man outside his own class.

The time came for Fox to go into the witness-box. Softly spoken, he appeared more presentable than his police mugshot, which made him look distinctly villainous. Dressed in a smart dark overcoat, he had a relaxed manner and, unlike Mahon, was not put out when a thunderclap suddenly interrupted his evidence. The impression he initially gave pressmen in court was 'that he must have been a very agreeable and pleasant man to meet in company'. Jowitt, well briefed, destroyed Fox in a classic cross-examination that should be read by students of the technique:

JOWITT. Were you heartbroken at your mother's death?

FOX. Indeed I was.

JOWITT. Quite stricken down when you knew?

FOX. I don't think it is necessary to ask.

JOWITT. That was the most solemn moment of your life?

FOX. It was.

JOWITT. And then did you tell Dr Nichol your mother had £24 in her bag?

FOX. Some time after I did, which was of course untrue.

JOWITT. Were you still heartbroken when you told that lie? . . .

Fox also damaged his case when asked why he had closed the door instead of flinging it wide open, after he had found his mother, as he claimed, in a smoke-filled room: 'My explanation of that is that the smoke should not spread into the hotel.' Most probably he had already found his mother lying dead on her bed, but, in the context of the evidence at trial, the answer caused an audible gasp in the crowded courtroom and further damaged his case.

Called away from the trial to a Cabinet meeting, Jowitt left Curtis-Bennett to make a 'brilliant' closing speech for the Crown, a task made the more difficult because Jowitt had accidentally taken the notes away with him. Rowlatt's summing-up was low key and all the more deadly for that reason. Dealing with Spilsbury, he was more cautious in his approach than judges such as Hewart, Finlay and Darling had been. 'Sir Bernard Spilsbury . . . is a man, of course, of unchallengeable honesty, but he may make a mistake . . . and there the matter rests.' The unbroken hyoid bone, said Rowlatt, was 'a very strong point in favour of the accused'. As to Fox, the judge noted that 'he has said a lot of silly things, but he is not being tried for being silly', and, in what may have been a reference to his sexuality, probably obvious by this time to everyone in court, 'it may be that he is so perverted that when an honest and innocent attitude could be taken, he takes this dishonest one'. With regard to the length of time during which insurance policies had been taken out, Rowlatt made a telling point. Fox could have been saving the old lady up for a later day, or perhaps 'the nerve might fail' on earlier occasions. Taking into account the defence case that Rosie died after the fire had started, Rowlatt ruled out the one explanation that fits the circumstances, namely death by natural causes: 'I think it is too absurd to suppose that she died at this moment without anything in connection with her surroundings at all.' He made no mention of Smith's and Brontë's evidence about the likelihood of sudden cardiac arrest.

The jury took an hour and a half to find Fox guilty. As the ten men and two women filed past the door of the judge's room, their slow pace and heavy footfall told the judge, visibly agitated, and his young marshal, that Fox was doomed.[53] When the verdict reached the crowds in the street outside the courtroom, where 'there were apparently a number of women sympathisers', a female voice shouted 'Shame! Shame!'[54] Fox seemed genuinely astonished at the verdict. 'My Lord, I never murdered my mother', he said before sentence of death was passed.

After the conviction Hambrook seems to have been responsible for releasing a story designed to nullify any prospect of reprieve. In 1927, when living in Southsea, Rosie had become friendly with a Mrs Charlotte Morse. She wanted to divorce her husband, Captain George Morse (or Moran), a merchant navy officer. Captain Morse claimed that his wife had committed adultery with Fox. There is evidence that, on 26 October 1928, she and Fox spent a night together at the Strand Palace Hotel in London. Fox told Cassels that he had never gone with a woman save for money, but it is possible that no sexual contact ever occurred. For the purposes of divorce law it was enough that a chambermaid should find them together in the same room.

Mrs Morse had made a will in Fox's favour, making reference to a promissory note for £5,000, although the will was later revoked and Fox seems to have fallen out with Mrs Morse and her elder son. After Fox's conviction newspapers claimed that he had tried to kill Mrs Morse one night by turning on a gas tap behind a chest of drawers in her bedroom. The fitment was loose, and there is no corroboration of this feeble story, which has found its way into the narrative of the Fox case, supposedly proof of a propensity to murder. After the story broke, Bodkin's successor as DPP, the colourless Sir Edward Tindal Atkinson, sought the advice of counsel to investigate the allegation. Frank Powell, later to become a Metropolitan Stipendiary Magistrate and author of a number of books about criminal law, reviewed the evidence. His conclusions are revealing. Far from being a victim of a murder attempt, Mrs Morse – who had sailed to Australia in October 1929 – may have been party to a dishonest enterprise aimed at getting money from her husband: 'I suspect an arrangement between Charlotte Morse and Fox to provide Fox with the means of blackmailing [Captain] George Moran . . . the promissory note for £5,000 may be entirely fictitious.'[55]

Every convicted murderer since 1907 had lodged an appeal against conviction, even in hopeless cases. Fox did not appeal. Some observers took this as a sign of guilt, but the fight seems to have gone out of him. His mother had been, quite literally, his *raison d'être*, as well as his partner in crime. On 2 April 1930 Sir Ernley Blackwell wrote his customary pre-execution advice to the Home Secretary. In a perfunctory minute, he observed that 'the murder is one of the worst class and, in my opinion, there are no possible grounds for interference with the sentence . . . There is no element of doubt in this case.'[56]

That day S.T.T. James, junior barrister for the defence, wrote a letter to Fox. James evidently did not share his leader's opinion that Fox was guilty of matricide: 'I want to assure you', wrote James, 'that I most sincerely believe you did not strangle your poor mother.'[57] The Morse allegation had its effect, and there was no organised campaign for reprieve. The *News of the World* got its promised exclusive, which included the headline HOW SIR B SPILSBURY GOT

AT THE TRUTH, a fine tribute from a newspaper owned by Lord Riddell, Spilsbury's friend and fellow member of the Medico-Legal Society.[58]

In prison Fox lost all his cockiness, his camp humour, his conman's blarney. 'I'm ready to go,' he said in the condemned cell. 'I've had enough. I feel dead tired.' Sir Shane Leslie's sister, the formidable Lady Theodosia Bagot, visited Fox in his last days for Bible-reading sessions, which may have contributed to this air of despair.[59] Two other women, rather less grand, kept vigil for him. Adelaide Foster would never read her friend's last words, contained in a letter suppressed by the Home Office and hidden from public view for sixty-five years: 'It is now 7.30 am,' ended the message. 'No news. Goodbye.'[60] Pridie Sinclair had been a defence witness at the trial, testifying to Fox's affection for his mother. She had requested the return of a picture postcard. Blackwell could never be accused of sentimentality: 'I wonder this has not been destroyed,' he wrote, '?destroy it now & let the governor tell her simply that it has been destroyed.' Another hand minuted, bleakly, 'Destroyed.'[61]

Wearing a 'smart, blue tailor-made suit',[62] Fox walked, steadily and unaided, into the execution chamber at 8.15 a.m. on Tuesday 8 April 1930. He made no last-minute confession to the young Anglican clergyman who attended him at the end. The bell of All Saints' Church, Maidstone, tolled for fifteen minutes after the execution. Later that day, at the High Court in London, Fox was cited in Captain Morse's divorce action against Charlotte Morse. Not unnaturally, there was no application for costs against the co-respondent. Fox was buried within the walls of Maidstone Prison. He has the dubious distinction of being the last prisoner ever to be executed there.

Perjury consists of wilfully giving material evidence that a witness knows to be false or does not believe to be true.[63] Spilsbury's evidence in the Fox case enters this dangerous territory. By the time of the trial, Spilsbury must have been aware of the real risk of fundamental error in his testimony. Stubbornly peddling flawed opinions may have been simply the result of professional vanity, but an uncomfortable suspicion arises from the particular circumstances of this trial. Given the widespread perception of Fox as a degenerate and unwanted member of society, Spilsbury may have played a lethal game with the truth, allowing his visceral conservatism to affect clinical judgement.

Professor Sir Sydney Smith, writing nearly thirty years after the trial, maintained his belief that Fox was innocent of murdering his mother. 'Perhaps Spilsbury did not fully realise that fame brings responsibility as well as honour,' he wrote caustically. 'I do not think the jury would have returned the verdict . . . if [the] evidence had been given by anyone else than Spilsbury.'[64]

SIXTEEN

The Blazing Car Murder

The so-called Blazing Car Murder, tried in 1931, was probably the high watermark of Spilsbury's career, but shortly before, in 1929 and 1930, he had been called in to another well-publicised murder mystery connected with motor transport, investigating the case of William Podmore.[1]

On 10 January 1929 the body of a 57-year-old man, Vivian Messiter, was found in a lock-up garage and storeroom at 42 Grove Street, Southampton. He had been the local agent of the Wolf's Head Oil Company, and the body was found on its back, with a trilby hat beside the right leg, lying between stacks of oil drums and wooden boxes. The head, which had been severely battered, lay towards a whitewashed side wall. The dead man's left arm was over his chest and his right arm was slightly upraised. Messiter, a quiet man of regular habits, divorced from his wife and badly injured in the First World War, had last been seen at his lodgings, at 3 Carlton Road, when leaving for work on the morning of 30 October 1928.

The body was not in a very good condition. Rats had gnawed at the face, making the features unrecognisable, and the head and brain were severely decomposed. The floor was bloodstained, and blood had been spattered on the boxes and oildrums to a height of several feet, at some distance from the body. Southampton police called in the local police surgeon. Dr Thomas, thought by one senior Scotland Yard officer to be of 'exceptional qualification and experience', turned out to be the medical equivalent of Inspector Clouseau. His first opinion was that Messiter had died of 'a haemorrhage', but, after the body had been removed to a mortuary, Thomas conducted a post-mortem and concluded, equally wrongly, that the dead man had been shot through the head.

Scotland Yard was called in. With a speed typical of the period, it was not until three days after the discovery of the body that a double-headed hammer was found at the back of some oil drums. Chief Inspector Prothero (known as 'Gentleman John' from his well-spoken manner and who, like Spilsbury, had a fondness for grey spats) entrusted this potentially vital piece of evidence to Thomas, who was allowed to remove what he described as a 'portion of reddish substance' from the head. Thomas, after supposedly analysing this mysterious substance, felt sure there was 'no blood' on the hammer. Prothero, who had wasted valuable police time fruitlessly searching for a bullet in the garage, at last seems to have realised that the opinions of Dr Thomas were worthless. In Prothero's words, it was now 'deemed advisable' to send for Sir Bernard Spilsbury.[2]

Spilsbury examined the body in Southampton on 15 January 1929. Messiter, 'well nourished', had stood 5ft 10in tall.[3] There were no signs of recent injury to the trunk or limbs, but there was bruising on the left cheek and a large bruise on the lower part of the back of the head. Spilsbury also noticed a 'large opening' in the skull in the region of the left eye. This injury, which may have induced Thomas to think that Messiter had been shot, was later attributed by Spilsbury to a blow by the sharp point at one end of the hammer. The dead man's skull, recorded as being 'rather thin', was fractured 'everywhere except on top'. Spilsbury noted three groups of fractures, one corresponding with the bruise on the back of the head; another above the right ear; and a third area in which the bones of the left orbit and cheek had been smashed 'with many pieces' over a considerable area. Spilsbury concluded that there had been at least three blows to the head, any one producing immediate unconsciousness.

Prothero showed Spilsbury the hammer, and his case card duly recorded that 'head of large hammer' could have caused most of the injuries. The fractures at the base of the skull and on the right could have been produced while the head was on a hard surface. Spilsbury decided, from the low position of injuries at the back of the head, that Messiter had probably been bending forward at the time of the assault. Puncture wounds on the top of the head could have been caused by striking the edge of a tin box. The hammer was then sent to a qualified expert, Dr Roche Lynch, working at the department of chemical pathology in St Mary's Hospital. Lynch, unlike the incompetent Thomas, detected human blood on both the head and shaft. In addition there was a single human eyebrow hair on the hammer's head. Given the state of forensic analysis in 1929, all that could be said with confidence was that this hair was 'similar in colour' to Messiter's eyebrow hair.[4]

No fingerprints were found on the hammer, but, from documentation found at the garage and other enquiries, Prothero identified a suspect, and the press began a nationwide hunt for 'The Man with the Scar', a lurid description that was also the title of a well-known short story by Somerset Maugham. William Henry Podmore, who had a small scar on his temple, was arrested in London in January 1929. Fortunately for the slow progress of the murder enquiry, Podmore was sentenced to six months' imprisonment on 29 January 1929, for car theft, which kept him within range of the police.

Meanwhile, at the Home Office, concerns arose about the fate of Messiter's skull, which was still in Spilsbury's lab at University College Hospital. Spilsbury wanted to keep the skull 'to complete the work of reconstruction' and show how many blows had been inflicted.[5] As has been seen already, Sir Ernley Blackwell had refused Spilsbury permission to keep part of Mahon's spine, fearing use for 'anatomical purposes'. Spilsbury made it clear that he did not want to keep the skull permanently, but might make a plaster cast or take photographs. He thought that 'ten days or a fortnight' would suffice for his purposes. Later on, the vexed problem remained of what to do with the skull. In the event Messiter's skull was cremated, along with amputated limbs, dead foetuses and sundry other body parts, in the hospital incinerator at St Mary's, Paddington.

On 14 January 1930 Podmore, dressed in a neat blue suit and, like Spilsbury, a pair of spats, sat in the dock at Southampton Coroners' Court to hear the adjourned inquest on Vivian Messiter. 'There was an awakening of interest as the tall, handsome expert took his place in the witness-box,' reported the *Southern Daily Echo*. 'He gave his evidence in quiet deliberate tones, which held the rapt attention of the crowded court.' The Coroner, Mr Trapnell, asked Spilsbury to identify the eyebrow hair. 'I have some left,' said Spilsbury. 'May I have my case?' In a little performance, he produced a tiny package containing some of Messiter's eyebrow hairs, opened it with extreme care, and later 'smilingly' interrupted a solicitor appearing for Podmore. 'Excuse me a moment', said Spilsbury, 'while I put these away. They are rather fragile.'

The trial of William Podmore, held before Gordon Hewart, the Lord Chief Justice, began at Winchester Assizes in March 1930, two weeks before the start of the Fox trial at Lewes. Sir Thomas Inskip, Jowitt's predecessor as Attorney-General, prosecuted. Podmore, though fairly smartly dressed, was in poor shape, with a dead-white face, twitching continuously, and appeared to have lost a considerable amount of weight. Spilsbury's evidence-in-chief was unusually short, although he was – as ever – ready to make a stab at chronology:[6]

INSKIP. Would the blow you last described on the eye and cheekbone have been struck before or after the blow on the side of the head?

SPILSBURY. I cannot say certainly, but I think more probably it was the last blow of the three. It might have been struck in the position in which he was found.

In earlier proceedings there had been defence suggestions that Podmore, who was 5ft 4in tall, would not easily have been able to hit Messiter, who was 6in taller. Herbert du Parcq, for Podmore, was a shrewd advocate and probably well aware of how easily Spilsbury could underline and expand his lethal evidence in the course of cross-examination. Wisely, du Parcq asked four anodyne questions before sitting down, getting Spilsbury to confirm his opinion that Messiter had been struck, first of all, from behind, on the back of the head.

Podmore, using an alias, had worked as a commission agent for Messiter's business. The prosecution was able to prove – by handwriting and other evidence – that Podmore had been defrauding the company. Though no forensic link was ever established between Podmore and the hammer, the jury seems to have accepted the Crown's case that Messiter was killed after he had found out about the fraud and conftonted Podmore. Newspapers thrived on Spilsbury's sense of theatre, absurdly exaggerating his contribution to the verdict. One particularly purple example read: TWO HAIRS HANGED THIS MAN![7]

Spilsbury claimed £21 for his attendance at the mortuary, £21 for the inquest and two days' travelling expenses at £3 6s. The Home Office, which had to foot the bill, reviewed the claim. An official encapsulated Spilsbury's contribution to the prosecution process. 'Sir B Spilsbury is paid in part for his great ability *as a witness*', he wrote. 'He makes a poor living out of a very difficult & exceptional class of work . . . I favour payment in full.'[8]

Spilsbury was now at the height of his reputation. No forensic pathologist, before or since, has achieved such public recognition and regard. His name was a household word. Judges, prosecuting lawyers, police and journalists – all tended to treat Spilsbury as a form of divine manifestation. For his part Spilsbury would deny that he was infallible, even making a little joke against himself. 'I have never claimed to be God,' he would say, 'but merely His locum on His weekends off.'[9]

Spilsbury's quiet, lofty, undemonstrative manner merely added to his image as the greatest living pathologist. With becoming modesty he would habitually shield his face from press cameras. 'He never abated his dislike of being photographed,' wrote his first biographers,[10] but there is undoubtedly something stagey, even Garbo-like, in the many pictures of Spilsbury covering his face with a hand, with a newspaper, or even with a book. In private, however, he gave full rein to vanity. Numerous portrait photographs, taken in fashionable West End studios, survive from those interwar years.

By the end of 1930 Spilsbury had achieved such status that he was being called in to report on matters far beyond his expertise and experience. One particularly ridiculous example emerged from the R101 airship disaster. In the early hours of 5 October 1930 this government-funded airship, en route to India, crashed into a hillside near Beauvais in northern France. Filled with highly inflammable hydrogen, the giant dirigible exploded. Forty-six men on board, including the Air Minister, Lord Thomson, and the debonair Sir Sefton Brancker, an Air Vice-Marshal, were burnt to death. The wreckage was minutely examined by an air ministry team, whose report, dated 7 October 1930, made grim reading. There had been great difficulty in identifying the victims, all the bodies having been 'terribly incinerated'.[11] Newspapers speculated that a woman had been on board the airship because 'an incinerated female shoe' had been found in the wreckage and 'had been placed in a temporary coffin with a male body'. The official report stated firmly that all the bodies examined had been male. The shoe was to be forwarded to London, in a box informatively marked 'female shoe' for examination by a medical expert.

The Air Ministry sought the opinion of Scotland Yard. Spilsbury was the obvious choice. In retrospect it seems remarkable that he took nearly a month to submit his handwritten report. Spilsbury decided that the shoe should be x-rayed. An ordinary x-ray machine was not adequate, he claimed, and it had been necessary to construct 'special x-ray apparatus', using 'a soft gas tube of low penetrability'. Spilsbury minutely described the fragments, toe and heel portions, and other parts, some of them charred, others blackened and distorted. His conclusions added nothing to what was already obvious. 'The shoe is that of a female,' he wrote, 'it is a patent leather shoe, & it is an old shoe; it may have been of foreign manufacture. The shoe contains no human remains & it was not worn at the time when it was burnt.' The shoe had probably been on the hillside before the accident happened.

Spilsbury submitted an enormous bill of 25 guineas to the Home Office 'for examination of the burnt fragments of shoe'. On 19 January 1931 Spilsbury was at the Home Office in connection with another matter (very possibly the Rouse case – see later in this chapter) and an official took the chance to query the fee. Spilsbury justified the expense by telling the official that he had paid 'his man' 10 guineas in respect of setting up the 'special' x-ray facility. During the x-ray session 'some four or five plates had to be exposed', and, naturally, Spilsbury had to be present for the whole of the time it took to take the radiographs. The balance of the fee represented the cost of his report. Officialdom took Spilsbury's words at face value and duly paid a large sum of public money for this preposterous exercise, accepting that 'the Home Office would in similar circumstances have paid such an amount without hesitation, in view of the explanation'.

A month after the R101 crash another fatal fire occurred. This time Spilsbury was in the more familiar territory of a murder enquiry.[12] About 1.45 a.m. on 6 November 1930, in bright moonlight, when people were returning home after Bonfire Night, a Morris Minor saloon suddenly burst into flames in a lane near Hardingstone, a village not far from Northampton. Would-be rescuers, driven back by the intense heat, could see a human shape in the blazing car. Buckets of water were thrown over the car, and PC Copping, based at Hardingstone, arrived at about 2 a.m., joined an hour later by Inspector Lawrence (described as 'tall, blonde, and imperturbable'[13]) and PC Valentine, also of the Northamptonshire Constabulary. With the body still in the car, the vehicle was moved from the road to a grass verge at about 4.45 a.m., and the remains taken to the garage of the Crown Inn, Hardingstone. From the start the local police showed gross carelessness in assembling evidence. The body was removed from the car before the remains could be seen by a doctor. Copping did not make a note of what he saw when he arrived and, apparently, did not think that the position of the body mattered very much. Lawrence, by the headlamps of a police car parked behind the Morris, examined the wreck, but also made no notes of what he saw. No photographs were taken of the vehicle as originally found. And it also appears that the wreck was left unattended for some hours.

The body, wrapped in sacking, was put on the floor of the garage, where Dr Eric Shaw, the local pathologist, conducted his first examination that evening between seven and eight o'clock and again on 8 November. Two days later Spilsbury travelled by train to Northampton, where he was met by Dr Shaw and two senior police officers, and driven to Hardingstone, where the body was still in the garage at the Crown Inn. Some further investigations were made by Spilsbury at the path lab in Northampton General Hospital.

The body had been terribly burnt and proved male only by the discovery of a fragment of prostate gland.[14] There was some evidence of disease in the prostate, normally found in middle-aged or elderly men, but sometimes in younger men who had suffered from gonorrhoea. The top of the head and the vault of the skull had been completely destroyed, exposing a burnt section of brain. There was no evidence of a skull fracture. There was deep burning on the neck and chest, the whole chest wall being destroyed, exposing the heart and lungs. The abdominal skin had been lost, but the fire had not ruptured the lining.

The forearms, hands and left foot were destroyed. The right foot had fallen off and lay on the runningboard. Most of each leg had been destroyed below the knee. A piece of cloth had survived in the crotch area, with fly buttons, and fragments of a shirt and underpants, all of which smelt strongly of petrol. There was a fragment of leather, probably from a pair of braces.

Although exact estimation was impossible, because of the extent of destruction of the limbs, Spilsbury thought the man might have been 5ft 7in or 5ft 8in in height, with adult bone development, and evidence from the state of his teeth, which had not been well cared for, suggested that 'the age was probably nearer 30 years than 21'.[15] An unusual amount of black pigment in the lung indicated that the man might have been a coal miner. Black deposits within the air passage and haemorrhage in the lung, in Spilsbury's view, showed inhalation of very hot air. The man had been alive and continued to breathe for some time after the fire had started. There was evidence that carbon monoxide had been produced in a considerable amount by the fire, but, as no carbon monoxide could be found in the blood, Spilsbury concluded that the period of survival after exposure to the fire must have been very short. The cause of death, unsurprisingly, was recorded as 'shock, due to burns'.[16]

The first three police officers on the scene gave differing accounts of what they saw. PC Copping said that the body lay face downwards, head in the driving seat, trunk lying across the other seat. The right arm appeared to be as if stretched over the back of the passenger seat. The right leg, which appeared to be extended, had been burnt off at the knee. PC Valentine remembered the right leg protruding about 8 inches from the chassis, with the foot burnt off at about the ankle. Inspector Lawrence recalled the right leg destroyed from about halfway between knee and ankle. He also described the right arm as extending upwards to about the height of the passenger seat. Broadly speaking, there was a consensus that the left leg had been doubled up under the body, while the other extended towards the nearside door, but the body had been subjected to intense heat, estimated at 2,000°C.

The registered owner of the car, registration number MU 1468, was discovered to be one Alfred Arthur Rouse. The press published photographs of the car, his name and description, and reported that the police had visited his wife. Rouse, aged 36, had fled to Wales, where one of his many girlfriends lived. Realising that he might be recognised by her family, he took a motor-coach to London, but, on the way to pick up the coach, he talked too freely to a Welsh taxi-driver. The driver contacted the police and, at 9.20 p.m. on 7 November 1930, the coach was stopped on Hammersmith Bridge by plainclothes police. 'Very well,' said Rouse, one of whose many weaknesses was volubility. 'I am glad it is over. I was going to Scotland Yard about it. I am responsible.'[17]

Rouse told police that he had picked up a man on the Great North Road, south of St Albans. The man said he was going to the Midlands. Rouse said, correctly, that a policeman had stopped the car, pointing out that the lights were not working properly. Later he realised that the car was running out of petrol. He needed to relieve himself, so he stopped the car. In those days, with few filling stations, people often carried a can of petrol in the car, and Rouse asked the man to fill the tank, which was situated above the engine and behind the dashboard. The man asked for a smoke, but Rouse had already given him some cigarettes. He had a cigar, which he threw to the man inside the car. The man said he had a match. He had seen the man's hand suspiciously close to his attaché case during the journey, so he took it away with him. He then walked some distance along the road. The car burst into flames. 'I . . . just got my trousers up quickly and ran towards the car.' The man was inside, but Rouse was unable to open the door because of the flames. He panicked and ran as hard as he could along the road, where he saw two men.

Rouse was easily identified by the young men, who had remembered seeing a hatless man – in 1930, a very unusual sight – climbing out of a ditch in Hardingstone Lane, wearing a light mackintosh and carrying an attaché case. The man walked towards a main road, in the opposite direction from the fire. Rouse had made no attempt to call for help. On Saturday 8 November 1930 Superintendent Brumby, of the county police, charged Rouse with the murder of 'a male person, name unknown'.

Four days later the *Evening News* predicted optimistically that Spilsbury's report was 'expected shortly', but, true to his usual relaxed timetable, the report took nearly a fortnight to emerge. Press interest was intense. By the start of committal proceedings in November the old standbys of prurience and prudery were given full rein by the popular press in attention-grabbing headlines. A typical example, from the *Evening News*, is dated 16 December: 'Mystery Woman in the Box – The Waitress with a Wedding Ring – Helen Campbell's Story of Rouse – Whispered Answers – Another Girl's Father and a 'bogus' Wedding – Pale and Agitated – One Glance at Rouse – "So they are not married?"'

The same newspaper, adding copy about the 'veiled woman' brought to court in 'a saloon car with drawn blinds', also reported the 'rush for seats' at the magistrates' court by 'women . . . and young girls'. The hysteria was fuelled by Inspector Lawrence, who referred salaciously to the 'harem' of women in Rouse's life.[18] Rouse was born in 1894 in Milkwood Road, Herne Hill, south London, the son of a hosier. He enlisted as a private in the 24th London Regiment four days after war broke out in 1914, married a girl named Lily in November that year, and was sent to France in March 1915. Two months later he received severe head wounds and other injuries caused by a shell-burst at Givenchy. Repatriated to England, he underwent an operation on his head. He suffered from pain, memory loss, insomnia and some psychiatric disturbance. In September 1918 a medical report noted that 'he lives over again a bayonet attack and melée through which he went – when he missed his man and awaited [the] enemy bayonet thrust'. He was also found to be 'easily excited and talkative', manifestations that appeared to linger on into later life.[19]

After the war he became a successful commercial traveller. He used his reasonably good looks and peripatetic employment to pursue 'scores of women'.[20] In 1921 he had a child by Helen Campbell, a girl of only 15, not long down from Edinburgh. The baby died, and when Helen became pregnant by him a second time he bigamously married her, in 1924. He had another child by her, a boy, of whom he seems to have been very fond, although his wandering nature led Helen to claim maintenance in 1929. Later, in a surprising move, the boy was brought into the Rouse home and cared for by Rouse and by Lily, his accommodating first wife. Rouse also had two children by Nellie Tucker, a young domestic servant who lived in Hendon. By October 1930 his love life was becoming exceedingly complex. Ivy Jenkins, of Gellygaer, in Monmouth, was now pregnant by him, there was another child living elsewhere in England, and yet another in Paris. His lifestyle choices were proving to be increasingly expensive.

Rouse, in severe financial embarrassment, had to sell his furniture to pay for the early stages of representation. The Home Office refused permission for him to be photographed by a newspaper in Bedford Prison in order to raise money. Sir Ernley Blackwell recorded tersely, 'This is on all fours with Sir J Simon's decision not to allow Smith (brides in bath) to write for press to raise money for defence.'[21] Eventually Rouse was allowed two counsel to represent him at trial, in accordance with the Poor Prisoners' Defence Act 1930, which had replaced earlier, less generous, legislation. Douglas Finnemore, then aged 40, from chambers in Birmingham, and A.P. ('Archie') Marshall took the defence briefs. At that time neither barrister had taken silk, although both subsequently became High Court judges. (In 1962 'Archie' Marshall would try Stephen Ward, in the aftermath of the Profumo scandal.) Although public funds did not run to securing the biggest names at the Bar, Finnemore was an able advocate, and, all in all, Rouse could not complain about the quality of his representation at trial.

On 26 January 1931 he stood before Mr Justice Talbot at the County Hall, Northampton (a handsome building, described, unflatteringly and unfairly, in the *Daily Mail* as a 'small, dingy 16th-century court'[22]). The prosecution was led by Norman Birkett KC. The court was packed. Local magistrates and other bigwigs, 'ticket-holders', sat alongside the judge. Reporters homed in on the 'women and girls' in the throng of people who queued for hours to gain admission. Once inside, onlookers had to stand in the cramped space under the gallery, a human crush in sharp contrast to the 'roomy dock' in which sat Rouse and two prison warders. The long-suffering Lily Rouse, and the prisoner's father, were present to hear Birkett's opening speech.

In outline, the Crown's case was that Rouse had killed his passenger in order to stage his own disappearance.[23] A mallet, which had been found at the roadside, had been used to hit the man over the head. While unconscious, the victim was pushed into the car face downwards on the driver's seat. Rouse then probably poured petrol over the man and deliberately loosened the 'petrol union joint' so that petrol also seeped into the car. The fire could not have been accidental, because the engine had been switched off at the time it started. In fact, evidence that the car's petrol feed had been tampered with was equivocal, although Birkett famously discredited a defence expert witness by asking him to state 'the co-efficient of expansion of brass', a question that the unfortunate engineer, who had volunteered his evidence, was unable to answer.[24] Despite suspicious circumstances, however, the prosecution never succeeded in establishing a motive.

The trial could have resulted in acquittal but for two factors. The first, crisply stated by Sir Patrick Hastings KC (who appeared for Rouse in his unsuccessful appeal), was that, 'if Rouse had only kept his mouth shut, he would never have been hanged'.[25] The second was Spilsbury.

At the committal proceedings in December 1930 Spilsbury had confined his evidence to an account of his post-mortem findings and his opinion on the cause of death, noted earlier in this chapter. In relation to the possibility that the dead man might have been a coal miner Spilsbury added that there were 'no signs on the body of mechanical injuries caused during life'. The body was too badly burnt to show evidence of a blow or strangulation.[26] However, the day after the trial started, 27 January 1931, Spilsbury produced a

'Supplemental Report' of a very different character.[27] Spilsbury had not seen the body as it was found in the car, and, as has been noted already, there were inconsistencies in the evidence of the police officers about what they had seen. Examination of the evidence of Dr Shaw, the local pathologist, suggests that he had not been asked to provide a theory of how the man had been killed. It may be that the prosecution, worried that Rouse's explanation might be just enough to secure acquittal, had brought in their biggest gun to aim at the problem.

Spilsbury did not disappoint. Although he had never seen the body as first found and had examined the remains only some ten days after the blaze, he could confidently assert that 'the position of the body . . . is accounted for if the man pitched or was flung into the car from the near side and fell face downwards across the front seats, his right arm catching upon the back of the driver's seat as he fell, and his legs and feet projecting from the near side of the car, the door on that side being open'. This last phrase, 'the door on that side being open', introduced a completely new element into the evidence. Neither Spilsbury nor Dr Shaw had made any suggestion to this effect during the committal proceedings, and Dr Shaw had not claimed that this was the case in his evidence at the trial.

It is difficult to avoid the conclusion that Spilsbury was embellishing his evidence, putting a spin on the sketchy accounts of the police officers at the scene. In his supplementary report, which formed the basis of much of his evidence in court, he also described the effects of 'heat rigor'. This phenomenon, he wrote, would cause 'the limbs to bend as if they were free to move'. Bearing in mind the circumstances that followed the discovery of the body and the intense heat of the fire, many of his conclusions seem to argue certainties not soundly based on the forensic evidence, such as it was in this case. Use of expressions such as 'only', 'at all' and 'would be' served to reinforce an essentially speculative exercise:

If the man had been trapped in the blazing car with the doors closed, the only posture which he could assume which would at all account for the position of the body would be that of lying face downwards across the front seats with his legs drawn up under the abdomen, and the feet against the near side door, a most difficult position to assume in the confined space, if it could be assumed at all. In that posture he would be unable to use his legs to force the door open and this posture would not explain the projection of the right leg from the near side of the car.

Spilsbury was called to give his evidence on 28 January 1931, the third day of the trial. The *Evening News* reported that 'women made a rush for the doors' as the public gallery opened that morning. Spilsbury entered the witness-box, solemnly placing a pile of documents on the ledge in front of him. He agreed with Dr Shaw's post-mortem findings and briefly gave evidence about the lack of carbon monoxide in the blood, giving another of his precise time estimates:

BIRKETT. When you say 'shortly after the fire started', are you able to say precisely as to the kind of time?
SPILSBURY. I should think within half a minute.

Birkett quickly moved Spilsbury on to the evidence of posture and position, the content of the supplementary report. He then dealt with the mallet, which Rouse had agreed was his, found by the roadside 15 yards in front of the car. Three hairs had been found on this object, one of which, thought Spilsbury, was identifiably human. As to the other two, in a demonstration of fairness, he was 'rather dubious' as to whether one was human at all. The other might have been human. 'That is as far', conceded Spilsbury, 'as I think I can safely go.' No fingerprint evidence was adduced by the prosecution, and, for reasons that emerged after the trial – as will be seen – evidence about the mallet was probably of little value. Finnemore tried bravely to tackle Spilsbury's lethal testimony, but did not – in terms – ask why it was that this evidence had not been given during the committal proceedings, when Spilsbury had made a lengthy deposition in court. Perhaps Finnemore realised that it would be counter-productive to challenge, even gently, the great man's bona fides. Counsel did his best:

FINNEMORE. Would it be right to suggest that from that [the fact that the man was dead] the position in which the body and the limbs were found . . . when the rigor had taken place, may not be necessarily a very safe guide as to the exact position when the fire started?
SPILSBURY. No. In the particular circumstances one has to be guided by the extent to which the different parts of the body moved. Any parts upon which there is any restraint would not become distorted in the same way as the parts which are free to move.

In re-examination Spilsbury seems to have come up with a further refinement to his theory:

SPILSBURY. . . . both legs extended, but the right leg was not able to get the consequences of heat rigor because of the seats. The left leg was free to contract.

He also posed two equally deadly alternatives. Either petrol had been sprayed over the car at the level of the seats (the tank was behind the dashboard and a vital nut was loose) or the clothing had been soaked in petrol before the fire started. Spilsbury crushed a defence suggestion that the victim had been vainly struggling to escape: 'He would have been dead long before that happened.' The effect of Spilsbury's evidence was not lost on Rouse, who, once Spilsbury had left the witness-box, leant over the dock and had a close consultation with Finnemore.[28]

Rouse made a very poor showing in the witness-box. Talkative and excitable, just as he had been as a recovering ex-serviceman in 1918, he was easy prey for Birkett, an extremely able advocate, who quietly, but relentlessly, exploited the weaknesses in his story. The defence called Dr Raymond Benedict Harvey-Wyatt, honorary pathologist to the Bedford county hospital and assistant pathologist to St George's Hospital (which then stood at Hyde Park Corner). Unlike Spilsbury, Harvey-Wyatt practised medicine among the living, with consulting rooms at the prestigious address of 46 Wimpole Street. He gave evidence that rebutted the premiss on which Spilsbury's contentions about the position of the body had been based:

> HARVEY-WYATT. . . . I think that one cannot draw very definite conclusions from the position or posture of the body when it was found. We know that great heat does contort the limbs of a burnt body and I do not think one can assume safely that the position the body was found in afterwards was [the position] in which the body was when death took place.

Harvey-Wyatt considered, from the evidence, that the right leg and foot were in the car during the fire. It was possible that the man had tried to get out momentarily as the fire started, and the position of the body was not inconsistent with this having happened. Birkett, cross-examining at length, slightly rephrased an answer given by Spilsbury and elicited agreement from the defence pathologist. 'Sir Bernard put it', said counsel, 'that [death] might be in about half a minute or something like that.' Birkett put to Harvey-Wyatt the Crown's case that the man was struck on the head with the mallet, adding a dramatic courtroom demonstration by grabbing hold of his junior counsel's right arm, in an attempt to convince the jury that Rouse had flung the unconscious man into the car.

Dr Aubrey Telling of Northampton had the disagreeable task of examining the grass verge of Hardingstone Lane. Rouse had claimed that the explosion had occurred while he was relieving himself and, about 150 yards away from where the car been, Dr Telling found 'excreta', but, although Dr Harvey-Wyatt had examined the matter in his laboratory, the doctors were unable to say whether these remains were human or canine. There was, however, faecal staining on a shirt that Rouse had handed to his solicitors and claimed to have been wearing on the fatal night.

On the last day of the trial, as a snowstorm whirled outside the old County Hall, the jury found Rouse guilty after an hour and a quarter's retirement, during which they had inspected the remains of the car and had lunch. The judge wrote to the Home Office the customary letter after a capital conviction, observing that the case was 'very unusual . . . It is not known who the dead man was; nor was any reasonable account given of the motive for the crime.'[29]

Even the skilful pleading of Sir Patrick Hastings, who led Finnemore before the Court of Criminal Appeal – a formidable tribunal consisting of Hewart, Avory and Travers Humphreys – could not persuade the court to interfere with the jury's verdict. Hastings made no criticism of Spilsbury's conjectures about the position of the body, although, after the appeal had been dismissed, Finnemore and Marshall submitted a lengthy memorandum to the Home Secretary drawing attention to the last-minute contents of Spilsbury's 'Supplemental Report'. Eight bulky files on Rouse, originally closed for 100 years, were opened for public inspection in 2003. They show that Clynes, the Home Secretary, told Blackwell of his worries, writing that 'the case is giving me some anxiety'.[30] On 2 March 1931 a meeting was arranged between Clynes, the judge, and Blackwell. Talbot was satisfied with Rouse's guilt, but had not expected the guilty verdict. Clynes, after further correspondence with Hewart, decided – using that most hackneyed of expressions – 'the law must take its course'.

In the few days left before execution extraordinary developments took place. On 7 March Lily Rouse told the *News of the World* that, before the appeal was heard, Rouse had confessed to the murder, although she gave no detail of how the killing was supposed to have happened. On 9 March the *Daily Express* published her retraction.

Rouse was executed at Bedford Prison on 10 March 1931. The following day's *Daily Sketch* published a lengthy confession by Rouse, who admitted to wanting to 'start afresh' because of his personal problems. He had met a man in the Swan and Pyramid pub in Whetstone High Road, a man looking for work, 'the sort of man no-one would miss'. Rouse agreed to drive him north. The man had some whisky and was 'quite fuzzled'. Rouse said that he had strangled the man before setting fire to the car. He had used the mallet to open the can of petrol – as the prosecution had alleged – and then threw it away. He had not expected to be seen leaving the scene of the crime.

The confession contains two curious features. With regard to the whisky, Spilsbury had found no evidence of alcohol in the victim's stomach. Moreover, the Crown's case had been that the man was knocked unconscious with the mallet, rather than being throttled. A possible explanation for the succession of confession, retraction and confession is that Rouse and his wife were playing a game with the press, provoking a battle of chequebook journalism that would help provide for Lily and for Helen Campbell's son, of whom Rouse seems to have been genuinely fond.

Home Office papers reveal a further twist to the story. Contrary to newspaper reports, Rouse 'strictly maintained his innocence' and, apart from the *Daily Sketch* item, never confessed to the murder while he was in prison.

Three days before his execution Rouse made a statement that might – just – be true.[31] Rouse claimed that his passenger had unjustly accused him of making 'an indecent action' and demanded 'a fiver'. Rouse was then outside the car, the man inside. When Rouse refused the demand, the man made as if to hit him. Rouse struck him twice, knocking the man backwards into the car. The petrol can, with which he was about to fill the tank, fell over, leaked and exploded. The story may have been a last-minute attempt to avoid the rope, as Blackwell thought. Rouse repeats the doubtful reference to whisky and also seemed to confirm Spilsbury's conjecture about the open door, evidence that Rouse would have heard in court. Nevertheless there may have been a germ of truth in the story. Reluctance, until the last minute, to admit the existence of a homosexual proposition – a criminal offence in itself – fits with the temper of the times. Rouse could have felt a real worry about its effect on his reputation as a womaniser and about the reaction of his fellow-prisoners. Blackwell found the story 'incredible'. Rouse 'might easily have dislodged him from the car and driven off', he minuted airily, doubting whether the petrol can could have ignited as claimed. Rouse had also claimed that he could identify the victim from a photograph that had been shown to him of 'a man from Middlesborough', but Blackwell minuted that this would serve 'no useful purpose in the inquiry'. Tom Pierrepoint was not to be deprived of his 10-guinea fee for the execution.

In the churchyard of St Edmund's Church, Hardington, stands a wooden cross with an inscription reading 'In Memory of an Unknown Man. Died Nov 5th 1930'. Each year, on the anniversary of the death, someone lays flowers on the grave.

SEVENTEEN

Murder Parade

On 2 June 1931 Spilsbury travelled the short distance from University College Hospital to the mortuary at Hendon, where he examined another badly burnt corpse.[1] Unlike the victim in the Rouse case (see Chapter Sixteen), who had been dead ten days before Spilsbury conducted his post-mortem, the body had been found that morning, when someone noticed a charred arm sticking out from a smouldering refuse tip at Scratchwood sidings, by the railway line running between Mill Hill and Elstree. It appeared that the body, which was male, had been burned by the action of a slow fire in the rubbish dump. The right arm and both the lower legs and feet were missing. The head had been wrapped in sacking, and most of the skin of the face fell away when the wrapping was removed. There was a large bruise on the back of the left hand. Parts of the body had been protected by clothing, and, from the state of putrefaction, Spilsbury estimated that death had occurred about two or three days earlier. The man had been badly beaten. Both jaws were fractured, and the nose had been broken. There was evidence of a blow to the left temple, causing a rectangular fracture of the skull, which, in Spilsbury's opinion, was the cause of death.

The surviving left arm bore a tattoo, and part of a moustache survived. The man was soon identified as Herbert William Ayres, *alias* 'Pigsticker', aged 45, one of a group of itinerant labourers, little more than vagrants, who lived in wooden shacks at Clay Lane Edge, near the railway line and not far from the tip. Members of this 'queer community' – the words of the *Evening News*[2] – were frequently drunk, getting into fights and indulging in petty crime. Police enquiries among the hut dwellers led to two men being charged with murder. Their lifestyle and nicknames, like those of the dead man, seem uncannily like those of characters in a Samuel Beckett play. Perhaps the author read reports of the trial, for the two men charged with murder were respectively known as 'Tiggy' and 'Moosh', *alias* Oliver Newman, 61, and William Shelley, 56.

A bloodstained axe was found under the floor of Newman's hut. Dr Roche Lynch analysed a sample and found 'human blood' on the weapon. Spilsbury gave evidence that the back of the blade fitted the fracture on the left side of the skull. The blade was said to be the same length as the top edge of the fracture. Both men had previous convictions for 'stealing boots, fowls etc.' and were thought by Sir Ernley Blackwell to be 'very rough characters'. They admitted assaulting Ayres, but only with fists, after he had stolen their tea, in order to teach him a lesson. The attack happened late on the night of 30 May, after both men had drunk 'nine or ten pints' of beer. When they realised Ayres was dead, they put the body in the dump.

Their trial at the Old Bailey began on 24 June 1931, before Rigby Swift.[3] Although this was a hanging matter, the men were represented, presumably under the poor prisoners' scheme, by inexperienced counsel. The Hon. E.A.H. Jessel, who had been called to the Bar in 1926, appeared for Newman. Shelley's counsel was Francis Peregrine, who had qualified as a barrister only a year earlier. More senior counsel might have stood up to the hectoring that was, all too frequently, a feature of Rigby Swift's judicial performances. His natural irritability was fuelled by alcohol. One of his young barrister marshals remembered how the judge would begin the day with a stiff whisky at breakfast-time.[4]

Spilsbury concluded that bruising on the left hand had been caused by Ayres trying to protect himself from the axe (although Blackwell later noted that Ayres had been 'a man of great strength, often violent when in drink' and the bruising might have had other causes). Peregrine, who was also trying to establish that the fracture might have been caused by a heavy object falling onto the skull in the rubbish heap after death, had the temerity to suggest that Spilsbury might have altered or added to evidence given at committal. On behalf of Podmore the previous year (see Chapter Sixteen), Herbert du Parcq had been too fly an advocate to try that tactic with Spilsbury, master of the ready answer, whose inflated reputation made it very dangerous to attack him directly. Here, Peregrine pressed on, putting an awkwardly worded question to the great man, which at once aroused the full fury of the judge:

> RIGBY SWIFT. . . . counsel . . . says, 'This man is saying something different to what he said below.' It happens day after day, and it is painful to see what the art of defending criminals has descended to. I will not tolerate it and it is a perfect outrage to put that to Sir Bernard Spilsbury . . . It is an outrage. It is shocking.

In his outburst, the judge injudiciously revealed his opinion of the case against the prisoners in the dock ('defending criminals'), as well as voicing his horror that so eminent an expert witness as Spilsbury should have been subjected to questioning of this sort at all. In fact, such cross-examination questions were then, as now, a perfectly proper line of defence within counsel's discretion. Spilsbury was firm in his opinion that the fracture could not have been caused by fists. There had been no 'bursting effect' caused by the effect of heat on the skull.

The men were convicted and sentenced to death. Shelley responded, in a resigned way, as if from someone who expected little from life, 'Thank you, sir. They ought to have done that years ago.'

While the men awaited execution, Mrs Hazel Neil, of Hedgerow, Buck Lane, London NW9 – an impeccably suburban address – wrote a surprising testimonial for Shelley, an illiterate man, who had 'lived in a hedge at the boundary of our garden' since Christmas 1929. She had found him 'a good friend, honest, quiet, and helpful', and he had even looked after the house when Mrs Neil and her husband were away. Blackwell – who had held the lives of so many other condemned prisoners in his hands – could find no reason to reprieve the men. In his fastidious, neat hand he once more minuted, 'I can see no grounds for interference in this case.' 'Tiggy' and his friend 'Moosh' were executed on 5 August 1931.

Two days earlier, on August Bank Holiday morning at about 7.45 a.m., George Reynolds, a 'scout' (college servant) at Jesus College, Oxford, accompanied by his young son, put a ladder to an upstairs window at the back of an Edwardian semi-detached house. The Boundary, St Clement's Street, Oxford – the left-hand property of the pair – was exceptionally well maintained, with matching check curtains at every window and a neat front garden, laid out with pretty ornamental shrubs. The boy climbed in, went downstairs and let his father into the house, which had been locked. In the dining-room Reynolds was dismayed to discover the body of his sister, the house-proud widow of an Oxford greengrocer.[5]

Mrs Annie Kempson, aged 58, was a keen church worker, who had a female lodger and a small rental income. There was evidence that she had arranged to visit Mrs Smith, a London friend, on Sunday 2 August 1931, but she did not arrive. She had been seen alive by her lodger, who was about to go away for the Bank Holiday weekend, at about 9.20 on the previous morning. Mrs Smith, worried about her friend's non-arrival, wrote to Mrs Kempson's brother. Postal collections and deliveries were more frequent in 1931 than today, and Reynolds received the letter early on the morning of the Bank Holiday.

When found, the body of Mrs Kempson, wearing her pinafore and covered with a mat and three cushions, was lying on the floor. Her long hair straggled either side of her head, which bore signs of three wounds, including a large gash on her forehead. On the right side of her neck there was a sharp clean-cut wound, and the body was soaked in blood. Within an hour the Chief Constable of Oxford, Mr C.R. Fox, had arrived. A telephone call to Scotland Yard brought Chief Inspector Horwell and DC Rees. Soon afterwards, as the *Evening News* reported, 'Sir Bernard Spilsbury, the pathologist, hurriedly left London this afternoon to assist police'.

Spilsbury went to work with his customary attention to detail. 'As soon as he arrived . . . he would ask everyone to be still and then . . . he would sniff for several minutes to see if he could detect any odour.'[6] During one murder enquiry Spilsbury 'bent down over the corpse and sniffed away as if it was a rose garden'.[7] He told one senior police officer not to smoke during his preliminary work. 'I can't smell the smells I want to smell,' said Spilsbury.[8] He carefully examined the house, spending a considerable time there before making the post-mortem examination on Mrs Kempson at Oxford mortuary that night. She appeared to have been battered about the head with a blunt object, such as a hammer, which made 'strikingly similar fractures', indicating that the striking surface must have had a diameter of about 1¼in. The wound in her throat was made by a sharp instrument, possibly a dagger or chisel. The carotid artery had been severed and death would have followed rapidly.

After examining the stomach and intestines Spilsbury found a partly digested meal in the stomach. Further down the digestive tract were the remains of other food, including identifiable tomato skins. Spilsbury, as in the Thorne trial (see Chapter Twelve), extrapolated from this material a chronology that would not now stand up in court. He decided that death had taken place between one and two hours after Mrs Kempson had eaten a meal of bread and butter, and probably custard, while about twelve hours had passed since eating an earlier meal with tomatoes. These suspect timings would prove to be of considerable significance in the Crown case against Henry Daniel Seymour, aged 37.

Seymour, a man with a bad criminal record, including three convictions for housebreaking, had once sold a vacuum cleaner to Mrs Kempson. Now travelling in ladies underwear, he had been seen close to her house on Saturday 1 August 1931. Police enquiries traced him to Brighton, where he was arrested on 15 August. A witness, who had put Seymour up for the night in Oxford, recalled seeing the round head of a hammer and the blade of a chisel in a parcel that Seymour had brought with him. Seymour left the witness's house at 9.30 a.m. on 1 August. Seymour admitted buying the hammer, which had been recovered by police from an address in Aylesbury. He also admitted buying a screwdriver at the same time, but neither chisel nor screwdriver was ever found.

On 12 August 1931 *The Times* stated that 'the report of Sir Bernard Spilsbury on his post-mortem . . . [had not been] received by a late hour last night'. Spilsbury, rather faster than his usual pace, provided a report dated 13 August. On the following day the police sent their enquiries by post to Spilsbury, holidaying at 'Port View', Looe, in Cornwall. They had to wait a few days for his reply, which proved disappointing. 'The surfaces of the head of the hammer', wrote Spilsbury, 'are all too small to have produced the fractures of the skull . . . I am bound to conclude that this was not the weapon used.'[9] Back at University College Hospital, on 18 August, Spilsbury again examined the hammer, now finding ' a group of fine fibres' of cotton adhering to the head and a similar group at the top of the handle. However, he maintained his earlier opinion. It was impossible, he wrote, 'to have produced depressions of the depth of the fractures of the skull . . . the injuries . . . were not produced by this hammer'.[10]

Chief Inspector Horwell, a determined police officer, was not put off the scent: 'He [Spilsbury] does not say whether he has allowed for the . . . hair and scalp flesh which might have been forced through the holes in the skull.'[11] After consultation with the Oxford Chief Constable, Spilsbury was contacted and promised to return to Oxford the following afternoon, when a further consultation took place at Boundary House.

By the time of the committal proceedings in September Spilsbury had changed his mind. He gave evidence of experiments in which, by putting paper and cloth around the hammer, it was possible to cause a dent similar to the dimensions of the fractures.

Even at this early stage the defence challenged Spilsbury's *modus operandi*. Seymour was represented by a very young, but bold, solicitor, R.P. Cole. 'Are you going to give credence to suppositions like that?', he asked the bench, but the magistrates – no doubt suitably impressed by the great pathologist's performance – committed Seymour for trial at Oxford Assizes.[12] Here, on 19 October 1931, his trial began before Rigby Swift, now out on circuit, away from the Old Bailey. St John Micklethwaite KC led for the Crown, W.G. Earengay for the defence.[13]

In his evidence Spilsbury put a spin on his original written reports regarding the hammer head. 'In my opinion,' he now declared, holding up the bare hammer for the jury to see, 'they [the fractures] could not have been caused by this hammer in this condition.' The significance lies in those last words, 'in this condition'. He described his experiments, and, as in the case of Donald Merrett (see Chapter Thirteen), something of an evidential deficit began to emerge:

MICKLETHWAITE. Have you made experiments with this hammer, covering it over with a piece of cloth?
SPILSBURY. I do not think exactly with this hammer, but with another exactly like it.

Spilsbury had struck the hammer, not on a human skull, but on a wooden board, 'noting the differences in the depression when the board was struck'. He then described what had been done to the head of the hammer, a process that led to an inevitable finding, sooner or later, that the hammer head fitted the injuries to the skull:

SPILSBURY. . . . when the head [of the hammer] was thickly covered with brown paper and cloth, the impressions on the board increased in size until I could make them correspond in diameter with the fractures.

In a surprisingly effective cross-examination, given his relative lack of experience, Earengay posed two excellent questions:

EARENGAY. Have you at any time tried experimenting on a human head with a hammer, one, in its native state and, two, covered in paper or with a cloth?

SPILSBURY. No, I have not.
EARENGAY. Will you agree that there is a vast difference between the human
head and a piece of wood . . . ?

Spilsbury later amplified his doubtful methodology. 'I made a cap for the head
of the hammer and tied the cap, consisting of various thicknesses of dusters . . .
some . . . covered in brown paper . . . so that it fitted close and tied it with
string.' Earengay pointed out that there had been no mention at all of fluff at
the committal proceedings. Unlike in the case of Shelley, who had been
represented by the very junior barrister Francis Peregrine, Rigby Swift did not
interrupt this line of questioning, which suggests a growing willingness by
defence counsel to challenge Spilsbury's assertions:

SPILSBURY. I cannot recall now. I know I had it in my report . . . I know
some part of my report was cut out.
EARENGAY. Then may we take it that the importance of this aspect of the
case has grown in your opinion?
SPILSBURY. I think it probably may. Well, it is nothing more than a theory.

The defence would not have had copies of the earlier medical reports.
Spilsbury's first report, dated 13 August 1931, made no mention of fibre or
fluff. The finding was first noted in his second report, made several days later,
in which he still maintained, unequivocally, that the injuries had not been
caused by the hammer. In that context it seems that the Crown obtained a
considerable dividend from Chief Inspector Horwell's insistence that Spilsbury
should return to Oxford for further discussions on 19 August. Asked if this
was the first time that he had performed the exercise of banging a hammer into
a block of wood, Spilsbury gave an evasive answer:

SPILSBURY. . . . I do not recall it being a question of an experiment with a
hammer on a board, but the general method with weapons has frequently
been employed in courts of law.

When attention shifted to Mrs Kempson's stomach contents, the evidence
began to take a distinctly surreal tone, with a hint of Mr Justice Cocklecarrot
in Swift's interjection:

EARENGAY. There were two distinct meals?
SPILSBURY. Yes.
EARENGAY. The earlier one, which consisted partly of tomatoes?
SPILSBURY. Yes.
EARENGAY. And the later one . . . ?
SPILSBURY. Yes.

EARENGAY. No fish and no greenstuff and so on?
SPILSBURY. No.
JUDGE. What did he say?
EARENGAY. The light meal not containing fish or green stuff.
SPILSBURY. Or potato.

There followed a laboured cross-examination about whether Mrs Kempson had peeled her tomatoes carefully or not or at all. Perhaps Earengay, rather than tackling Spilsbury head on, was trying to practise the well-worn technique of defence by confusion. Pressed about timings, particularly in relation to the tomato skins, Spilsbury carefully set out the limits of his opinion. 'All I can say is that they were taken within a certain period before death,' he stated. 'I cannot say what time they were taken.'

The evidence against Seymour was circumstantial. No bloodstains were found on his clothing. No property stolen from Mrs Kempson's house was traced to him. 'There was evidence of opportunity, of motive, of preparation, of flight, of emblems of guilt',[14] but the chisel that probably killed the victim was never found, and, as has been seen, the hammer did not fit the injuries to the skull.

Now that a broader picture has emerged from official records[15] it is possible to see that Spilsbury's evidence about the hammer was essentially flawed. Likewise his dogmatic evidence about the time occurring between the last meal and the murder ('the minimum time allowed by Sir Bernard between meal and death was one hour, therefore the earliest she was killed was 10.35 [a.m.]') appears to be based on wholly unreliable assumptions. Plainly, Seymour had a case to answer for the murder of Mrs Kempson, but – as in so many other prosecutions in which Spilsbury was a major player – the eventual finding of guilt owed a great deal to his positive evidence. Seymour was hanged at Oxford Prison on 10 December 1931.

Two weeks before Seymour's trial started Superintendent Hambrook was in Dorset, investigating a mysterious shooting at the Coverdale gundog kennels, a single-storey wooden complex constructed from an old army hut and built near the tiny River Tarrant, south of Tarrant Keyneston, at that time a relatively remote village in east Dorset, 5 miles west of Wimborne.[16] The manager of the kennels had been shot dead. Ted Welham, a handsome young man of 25, had been in charge of the kennels for nearly two years. He was paid '£2 15s per weeks and tips', had a smart motor-bike, registration number PC896, and lodged at first with the Hathaway family, who lived in a fairly modern semi-detached cottage on the opposite side of the lane from the kennels. Welham had the handicap of not being local, in this most parochial of counties, having been brought up in Shotley, near Ipswich.

The kennels and 600 acres of shooting land were leased by a businessman, Ethelbert Frampton, of Christchurch, who liked Welham, finding him 'always cheerful and happy'. At first, Welham had assisted William Steer, the then manager, but, on 29 December 1929, Steer had been found shot dead – apparently accidentally – near a badger sett in the nearby Ashley Wood. His 12-bore shotgun, with one barrel discharged, lay beside him. Welham, who was then lodging at the True Lovers' Knot, a public house that still serves the village, found Steer dead, or so he maintained.

Steer and Welham had previously worked for Colonel George Badcock at Winterbourne Steepleton in west Dorset, but Steer had been dismissed after surreptitiously selling off game from the estate for his own purposes. Welham left Colonel Badcock's employment in spring 1929, after the Colonel had tried to prosecute him for giving 'the best ferrets' to former employees of his estate. The case was dismissed, and Welham joined Steer at the kennels, which offered gundog training and dogs at stud, and sold gundog puppies, although it appears that Welham was not above selling sickly pups to unsuspecting customers. By autumn 1931 there seems to have been an ugly atmosphere, a poisoned undercurrent, in the village.

Welham's relationship with the local poaching community (sometimes dignified by the term 'rabbit-catchers') was giving rise to problems, as was his love life. The year before he had broken off his engagement to Hilda Lunn, then the village schoolteacher, taking up with another local girl, Elsy Weeks, and seems to have been involved with several other local women. Before she was jilted Hilda had received an anonymous letter, in a semi-literate hand, 'from one who knows, a local resident'. 'Ted Welham is flirting and fooling about with all the girls in Keynston [*sic*],' it read, 'especially that Louie Sc[h]ofield, the school teacher she is always runing [*sic*] up to the kennels to see him and also . . . taking that Mary Hathaway about on his motor bike he is a rotter I thought you would like to know.'

In September 1931 Steer's widow, who lived at 6 Cornhill, Dorchester, also received an anonymous letter, whose ominous message could have come from an Agatha Christie novel: 'You may be required to attend an inquest on Mr E Welham on Thursday.'

A lad called Fred Deaman, a 'cheerful kind of chap', then aged 18, rode his motor-bike over from his lodgings at High Wood, Witchampton, starting his work at the kennels at 7 a.m. on Thursday 1 October 1931. After helping Fred 'do the puppies', Welham went back to the Hathaway cottage for breakfast, presumably leaving Fred alone in the kennels. By 9 a.m. Welham was 'sat . . . at his desk' in his office, a small room that stood in the centre of the block, with accommodation for the dogs on either side. Welham's back was to the outer door. A large cupboard, in which guns were stored, stood, stage right, about one step inside the room and easily accessible from the door. Sacks of dog food stood nearby. Welham had a 16-bore hammer double-barrelled gun, a 12-bore hammerless gun, usually used by Fred, and a .410. Welham's practice was not to store loaded guns.

After Fred had finished cleaning out the kennels he went to see Welham, who told him – according to Fred – 'Go and fetch Peter [a blind springer spaniel] and we will go shooting'. Fred took his 12-bore and the dog with him into a field of kale on the opposite side of the road from the kennels, not far from Welham's lodgings at the Hathaways' cottage. While there he heard a single shot but 'took no notice', thinking that Welham might have shot a pigeon or a jackdaw, and it was only after another ten minutes that he returned to the kennels. The shot was also heard by Harold Hathaway, working in the garden of the Rectory, where he was the 'odd boy', at about 9.30 a.m. Harold had been out shooting with Welham the previous day. He had never heard of any unpleasantness among the staff.

The door of the office was, in Fred's version of events, still shut when he returned. He opened the door, to find Welham lying on his back on the floor in a pool of blood. His cap, which he had been wearing, was riddled with gunshot, and his head, badly injured, was pointing towards the door as if he had fallen backwards from his chair. His 16-bore shotgun lay under him. The right barrel had been discharged and the other trigger cocked with a cartridge.

Fred ran to the Hathaway's cottage. 'Oh, Mrs Hathaway,' he shouted, 'Ted's shot.' Mrs Hathaway remembered Fred appearing very frightened. One local man, Sidney Dennett, 'showed no sign of assistance', so Mrs Hathaway ran to get her husband, Tom, and her other son, Robert, both labourers at Manor Farm. Robert shared a bedroom with Welham. She usually took them both tea at 6 a.m., before Robert went off to milk the cows. Meanwhile Mary Hathaway, her daughter, then aged 16 and the subject of comment in the anonymous letter written the previous month, hurried down to the kennels with Fred. Mary was employed at the kennels, but did not begin her work until 3.30 p.m. Fred ran back along the road, where Tom Hathaway, hurrying down from Manor Farm, asked him where he was going. 'To ring the doctor,' replied Fred, but Tom told him this had already been done. The police later formed the view that Fred 'did not seen anxious to remain in the office'.

When Tom got to the office he found a piece of string 2ft 9in long attached to a hazel stick, lying against the sacks, by a loose slip knot about 5 inches from one end. The other end was either tied to the trigger of the gun or lying about 3 inches from it. Tom immediately suspected suicide, and, according to his version of events, first given to Mr Frampton on 29 October, four weeks after the shooting, he simply put the string in his pocket and propped up the stick in a corner of the office. He said that he wanted the shooting to seem accidental in order to spare Welham's mother the shameful verdict of suicide.

Mary Hathaway noticed that Welham's jacket, unusually, was unbuttoned, and part of his wallet was protruding from the inside right jacket pocket. Later it appeared that £9 could have been taken, as only one £1 note was found, and Welham was in the habit of carrying about £10. Curiously, although Mary was in the office very soon after the alarm was raised, she did not notice either the stick or the string.

PC Head cycled over from Spetisbury (Dorset had to wait another four years for its first police car). With Tom, he lifted Welham, who was alive but unconscious, and laid his head on a cushion. PC Head, who, on his own account, did not know a lot about guns, decided that this might be a case of suicide. Despite his ignorance of firearms, Head later conducted experiments by firing at a board, which convinced him that Welham could not have been shot from the door, a distance of about 10 feet.

Welham was transported by ambulance to Blandford Hospital, where his head was shaved and x-rays taken by Dr Kenneth Wilson, who could find no singeing on the skin suggestive of close contact with a gun muzzle. The spread of shot appeared to be about 6 inches, striking Welham below the shoulder. Welham never regained consciousness and died at 12.21 p.m. on 2 October 1931.

Later on the day of the shooting Major Peel Yates, the Chief Constable of Dorset, visited the kennels and, having made enquiries, decided to call in Scotland Yard. Superintendent Hambrook came down from London, arriving in Blandford just after noon on 5 October. After a conference at the kennels with Peel Yates, Hambrook liaised with the Coroner, Mr Creech, and probably also with Dr Wilson. Although Creech had already issued a burial order, all were now agreed of the need for the expert medical opinion of Sir Bernard Spilsbury. However, before Spilsbury could be instructed, the Coroner had to persuade Dorset County Council to pay his fee, which was eventually authorised later that day.

On 5 October Spilsbury took the last train to Blandford station, from where he was driven to the hospital. With Dr Wilson in attendance, and watched by Peel Yates, Hambrook and other police officers, Spilsbury conducted his usual detailed post-mortem at Blandford mortuary, an autopsy that did not finish until 3 a.m. Spilsbury then walked the short distance to Dr Wilson's house, an elegant Georgian building in Whitecliff Mill Street, Blandford, where Mrs Wilson served breakfast. Mrs Wilson was much taken with her unexpected visitor, the charming, handsome and very famous Home Office pathologist.[17]

Spilsbury found that Welham, who stood 5ft 9in tall, had five small fractures in the lower part of the skull below gunshot injuries on the left side of the back of the head and upper part of the neck. Another smaller area of gunshot injury was found on the back of the left shoulder. Shot had penetrated the brain, and, in Spilsbury's opinion, Welham had had his back to the weapon and 'must have been bending forward either over the desk or near it, close to where the body was found'. Death was caused by brain injury and meningeal haemorrhage from one gunshot. The injuries to the shoulder were superficial, and the main effect of the shot was to the back of Welham's head. The wounds could not have been self-inflicted owing to the distance and direction of the shot. The two areas of gunshot injury had a considerable spread, the lateral spread at the back of the shoulder being more than 3 inches. 'My impression', Spilsbury later said at inquest, 'was that he saw what was coming and ducked to avoid it.'

Experiments were made by Allan Jeffery, gunsmith of C. Jeffery & Sons, 25 High East Street, Dorchester, the firm with which E.J. Churchill, Robert Churchill's uncle, had served his apprenticeship in the 1870s. In October 1927 Allan Jeffery had sold Welham the gun that killed him. In a more reliable exercise than some of those conducted by Robert Churchill, Jeffery carried out a series of tests, using the right barrel of Welham's gun and the same type of cartridges, with No. 5 shot, at the rear of Red Cow Farm, St George's Road, Fordington, to the east of Dorchester.

Using size 5 shot and firing into a wooden board at various distances, Jeffery concluded that the gun was fired 'from 30° to 40° from the left of the right angle' from a distance of about 12 feet 6 inches, the barrel being pointed slightly downwards, and the gun fired within the office itself. In relation to the angle of shot, Jeffery's finding differed from that of Spilsbury, who theorised, from the horizontal direction of shot holes in the wall of the office, that 'the weapon was in a horizontal position when it was discharged'.

Hambrook interviewed a large number of local witnesses, but never amassed sufficient evidence to charge anyone with murder or any other crime in connection with the death. The missing banknotes suggested robbery. It appeared that someone had taken the gun from the cupboard, loaded it, fired at Welham, and then placed the gun under the body. If Tom Hathaway was right, that person had planted the string and stick to make the death seem like suicide. A remarkable aspect of this mystery is that no one in the vicinity – and several people were in earshot of the kennels – heard barking from the forty or more gundogs at the kennels. If any person unfamiliar to the dogs had approached the kennels, from any quarter, including from across the River Tarrant, there would have been a crescendo of yelps and barks. Whoever shot Ted Welham must have been familiar to the sharp-eared and quick-scented animals.

There the story ends, at least until official papers are fully released. Partly because of the idiosyncratic opinion of PC Head and partly, perhaps, because of local prejudices, many villagers continued to believe in the suicide theory. Hambrook, deeply frustrated, wrote of 'the general failure, on the part of the residents of Tarrant Keyneston, to appreciate that a murder was committed'. In a desperate attempt to break the wall of silence, the Rector of Tarrant Keyneston, the Revd G.E. Mann, preached a sermon on Sunday 10 October 1931 based on the murder of Abel and taking as his text Genesis 4: 10 (a curiously apposite verse, given that a .410 shotgun was among Welham's weaponry at the kennels). The text read: 'And he said, What has thou done? The voice of thy brother's blood crieth unto me from the ground.' The Rector told his flock that it was 'our duty to our country to help the officers of the law ... it is also our duty to God ... for the murder – if it is murder – is a crime committed against God'. Village opinion was not swayed by the appeal from the pulpit. One old inhabitant told police that no one in the village would murder anyone. He wanted suspicion removed from the village. 'The boy was too well liked', he said, 'to be slain by anyone here.'

Fred Deaman had an accident on his motor-bike on 29 October, but after a spell in Wimborne hospital he was again interviewed at length by the police. A letter that came into police hands, dated 3 November 1931, contained a cryptic reference to the young kennelman. Addressed to 'My Dearest Boy' by 'Sunny', it referred to Deaman's accident and subsequent concussion. 'I wonder if he rambled', ended the letter, '& let out anything.' Fred seems to have been the prime suspect. He was the first to report the shooting. No one saw him in the field of kale. The complete absence of barking by the gundogs is consistent with his having been in or near the office at the time of the murder. Fred could have loaded Welham's gun while the manager was having breakfast in the Hathaways' cottage and replaced it in the cupboard, which was easily reached from the door of the office. Fred could also have taken the chance to steal money from the wallet (it was not until some time later, after police had spoken to Frampton, that it was realised that money was missing).

The attempt to make the shooting seem like suicide, however, seems relatively sophisticated. The murderer took time to place the gun under the body and carefully left string and stick alongside the body. It may be that other people, not present at the murder scene, were involved in a murder plot. Motives for the killing could have been mixed. Hambrook ruled out a revenge killing for the death of Steer, but there could have been jealousy of Welham's success with girls (including Mary Hathaway, the kennelmaid), as well as a dispute with local poachers, who may have had a grudge against Welham. The mystery remains unsolved.

EIGHTEEN

Ghastly Speculation

In 1931 Spilsbury had received enormous publicity from the Blazing Car Murder, where his evidence had contributed materially to the conviction of Rouse (see Chapter Sixteen), as well as from several other high-profile murder investigations. This was also the year in which Spilsbury – perhaps a little late in professional life – was awarded a Fellowship of the Royal College of Physicians, which entitled him to put the letters 'FRCP' after his name. On 16 March, at a dinner in Jules Restaurant, Jermyn Street, Spilsbury was proposed for membership of the Organon, a dining club founded in 1868, limited to 'members of the Universities of Oxford and Cambridge, who are interested in the progress of the natural sciences'.[1] Luckily for his reputation, none of Spilsbury's tutors from his own university days as a fractious undergraduate seems to feature in the club's attendance records. Spilsbury's election took place the following October, at the instance of his friend Bentley Purchase, who had been a member since 1920. The club's academic atmosphere, 'small, informal and select',[2] appealed to Spilsbury, who attended fairly regularly until 1940. Spilsbury also enjoyed the masculine conviviality of Our Society and the papers, on all aspects of crime, read to its membership of lawyers, doctors, actors, sportsmen and journalists. On 15 November 1931, at the Café Royal, Spilsbury 'held the company spellbound' with his account of the Blazing Car Murder, speaking 'with the victim's calcined jaw in his hand'.

The beginnings of Spilsbury's long decline can be dated from around the spring of 1932. He had appeared for the defence in a murder trial, again in a Scottish court, in the case of *HM Advocate* v *Peter Queen*. Unusually, too, he was paired with New Zealander Sydney Smith, who remembered Spilsbury as being as 'uncompromising as ever' in the witness-box, refusing to budge from his opinion that this was a case of suicide.[3] When prosecuting counsel asked him whether the fact of confession would radically alter his conclusion, Spilsbury replied, quietly but firmly, that he did not think that any such factor would affect his opinion. Although Spilsbury had Smith's cogent support, Lord Alness, in his summing-up, laid greater stress on the circumstantial, rather than the scientific, evidence in the case. A Scots jury, too, may have resented Spilsbury's anglicised and didactic manner. Queen was found 'Guilty as libelled' by a majority of the jury and sentenced to death. He was later reprieved and sentenced to penal servitude for life.

Although the verdict in this Scottish case went against him, Spilsbury's reputation south of the border was not materially affected. His opinion of suicide had been shared by another eminent practitioner, and, in any event, the trial had taken place in another legal jurisdiction.

Once he was back in England signs of decline can be noticed in his contribution to the murder accusation brought against George Kitchen, in a case that has not received its proper share of attention in the assessment of Spilsbury's career as a forensic pathologist.[4] This story, set amid a close-knit, introverted and very isolated farming community, bore some resemblance to the Welham shooting in Dorset (see Chapter Seventeen), as well as the plot and characterisation of *Cold Comfort Farm*, the bleakly comic novel by Stella Gibbons, published in the same year.

Kitchen, aged 63 at the time of his trial, was a Lincolnshire smallholder charged with shooting dead his son, James. George Kitchen, described charitably as 'a crusty old countryman',[5] had personified a mini-crime wave in the Holbeach area for the past thirty years, clocking up numerous convictions for theft of livestock, poaching, drunkenness and assault. He had twice been found guilty of dishonestly obtaining guns. James Kitchen, also a smallholder, lived with his mother at Brook House Farm, Gedney Dyke, running the farm in partnership with his brother William Kitchen. George and James were on bad terms. George, who still worked at the farm, had not been allowed to sleep in the farmhouse for years and had latterly been banned by James from taking his meals there. Some twelve months before the shooting George was said to have shouted at his son, 'I can see I'm not fucking well wanted. I will do you in. I will cripple you.'[6]

On the morning of 4 December 1931 three labourers, one of whom lived at the farm, were riddling potatoes in a field. They saw George walking near the farm, carrying a shotgun and a rabbit trap. The gun was a cheap 12-bore, double-barrelled, with a hammer action, made by a firm called Dyke, and well used in this wildfowling country. George was seen to walk towards the meal house, a farm outbuilding, and, at about 8.20 a.m., a gunshot was heard. The labourers at first paid no attention, as there was nothing unusual about the sound of a shotgun, but soon George Kitchen appeared, saying, 'Come on, Jim's shot.' James Kitchen was still alive, but unconscious, when he was found lying by the door to the meal house. Badly wounded in the left side, James was carried into a barn, where he died. The gun was on the ground in front of the meal house door, just under a foot from the wall, on an uneven surface, with the butt higher than the barrels.

In a statement to the police George said that, after checking the rabbit traps, he returned to the farm and – with gross negligence – stood the gun upright against the meal house wall, loaded in both barrels, with hammers cocked, 'in case some geese came over'. James came into the yard and started cleaning a shovel. His son's black, curly-coated retriever, Prince, was running about. At some point George heard a shot and saw his son 'reel over', saying 'Oh' very loudly.[7]

Police Sergeant Lown of Holbeach reached the farm shortly after 9 a.m. George said that his dog must have knocked the gun down.[8] Dr Bertram Mayhew Bone, a doctor in practice at Spalding, was called to the scene and had some early suspicions about the shooting. He immediately contacted the Chief Constable, Lieutenant-Colonel G.H.R. Holland, CIE, OBE. The Chief Constable 'took steps without delay to engage the services of Sir Bernard Spilsbury, in order that we might have the best possible expert advice at the outset'.[9]

At about 4.30 p.m. on 4 December, as darkness was falling, Spilsbury arrived at Brook House Farm, where the body was still lying in the barn. Not for the first time in disagreeable winter weather Spilsbury proceeded with an autopsy regardless of the cold, though probably having to break off work from time to time to warm his hands. The chilly weather seems to have prevented any serious decomposition, and rigor mortis was still present some thirty-six hours after death. The right knee could not be bent, with evidence of some old injuries and operations, and the right leg was half an inch shorter than the left. The dead man, who stood 5ft 4in, had been smoking at the time he was shot. A partly smoked cigarette was found in the gullet, suggesting that the man was in a relaxed frame of mind and, in Spilsbury's view, making it unlikely that the fatal wound was self-inflicted. There was a large oval gunshot wound in the lower part of the left chest, which had fractured two ribs and was 6 inches below the armpit. The wound had a downward direction of 55 degrees. Shot had penetrated the internal organs, and the gun had been fired at close range.

As early as 15 December 1931 Spilsbury had told the Chief Constable that he did not consider the death was the result of an accident. 'The character and direction of the wound are easily explained,' wrote Holland to the DPP, 'if the gun was fired by another person standing on ground somewhat higher than that on which the deceased had been standing & at a range of one to three yards.'[10] An official at the DPP's office telephoned the Chief Constable on 11 December 1931 to suggest that Robert Churchill should also be brought into the investigation and a report obtained from him before further consultation with Spilsbury. Churchill, wrote the DPP's official four days later, was 'accustomed to giving evidence' and had 'great experience' of such cases.[11]

On 18 December Churchill went down to the farm and examined the dead man's clothing, the gun and the cartridge that had been fired. The left-hand barrel had been fired, although Churchill thought that most people would fire the right barrel first. In his view a possible explanation for this was that some people got into the habit of doing so having learnt to shoot on guns too long in the stock for them. Even at this early stage a dangerous element of speculation was beginning to enter the case. After taking the gun back to London for tests

Churchill reported that the trigger of the left barrel required an unusually high mean pressure of 7 pounds to discharge it, 2 pounds heavier than normal. According to Churchill, this greater pull made the gun safer to use, as it would be less likely to discharge accidentally. Undaunted by criticism of his cackhanded earlier experiments with Spilsbury in the 1927 Merrett case (see Chapter Thirteen), Churchill fired shots at steel, leather and cloth, coming up with a distance of 3 feet as the 'most likely' distance between the gun barrel and the deceased.[12]

On 1 January 1932 Spilsbury, Churchill and the Chief Constable attended a conference at the DPP's offices. The consensus seems to have been that further evidence was required, and, on 11 January, Spilsbury went to Churchill's business premises at 32 Orange Street, where the eagerness of both men to play the detective was to have full rein. In the attic, stripped to the waist, stood Jim Chewter, a member of Churchill's front-of-house staff. Chewter was half an inch taller than James Kitchen had been, but stood an inch shorter because the dead man had been wearing gumboots at the time of the shooting. Chewter suffered the indignity of having a thin wooden rod, about 6 inches long and with a rubber sucker at the end, attached to his body by Spilsbury, using adhesive tape. Spilsbury claimed that the rod was 'in the exact position and projecting at the same angle as the . . . wound'.[13] The subject, originally standing upright, was told to stand sideways. According to Spilsbury, with the body bent slightly forwards and tilted slightly to the left, and with the weight of the body on the left foot, the rod came into alignment with the gun, now in Churchill's possession and held 3 feet away at the shoulder. With the body bent slightly more forward, the alignment occurred with the gun held in the hands rather than at the shoulder.

The unreliability of findings based on such experiments now seems obvious, but in 1932 Spilsbury could confidently state that 'the injury could not have been self-inflicted . . . [and] it was caused by another person firing either from the shoulder or from the hip'.[14] Churchill formed a similar view, although his account of the shoulder-level alignment seems to differ from Spilsbury's account, with a reference to the body being 'slightly turned away to the right'. Churchill concluded first that the shot was fired from a distance of approximately 3 feet and could not therefore have been self-inflicted, and secondly that, as the gun was 'not liable to accidental discharge, it was in the hands of some other person when it was fired'.[15]

On 12 January 1932 the two experts submitted their report to the DPP, and, on the basis of these opinions, George Kitchen was charged with murder. Committal proceedings began at Holbeach on 26 January, with Spilsbury and Churchill as principal Crown witnesses, and both were recalled to give further evidence on 9 February. Spilsbury denied a defence allegation that there had been 'a great deal of speculation' in the reconstruction. The gun had been fixed in position on a stand that, Spilsbury said, a little vaguely, was 'about the height of a man of average height'. Spilsbury knew of one case where a dog had set off a loaded shotgun left in the back of a car, but this had 'obviously been an accident', and no tests were made. Churchill maintained his stance that the shooting could not have been accidental. 'A large wild retriever dog could not discharge the gun by hitting it with his tail,' he stated firmly. 'The trigger must be pulled.'[16]

At an adjourned hearing, on 2 March, Kitchen's very able solicitor, Mr Pettifar, pointed out that a very long time, some fifty days, had elapsed between the shooting and the charge of murder. 'The Home Office opened its circus,' he observed, with a dry wit not far removed from the truth, 'Sir Bernard Spilsbury, as the ringmaster, trotted into the ring and cracked his whip and in came Mr Churchill, the gun expert.'[17] The Lincolnshire solicitor could have made another, very contemporary, rhetorical analogy. Spilsbury and Churchill, as a courtroom double act, might have been likened to the variety favourites Flanagan and Allen, already topping the bill with their hugely popular sentimental songs 'Underneath the Arches' and 'Wanderer'. Bud Flanagan, like Churchill, was short, stocky and plump, and projected an earthy, rather vulgar, personality. Chesney Allen, the undemonstrative straight man, taller and better-looking than his partner, wore a smartly cut double-breasted suit, spoke quietly and addressed his audience in an eminently respectable voice.

Spilsbury's involvement brought some old adversaries into the picture. The defence sought out Dr Brontë and Dr Sydney Smith. Smith tried some experiments of his own with a gun, and, on his recommendation, Pettifar called four firearms experts at committal to show that the gun, far from being safe, had been a dangerous weapon liable to accidental discharge, as, for example, when knocked over by a large dog. Principal among these experts was Major Gerald Burrard, aged 44, a man of very different background from Churchill. The son of a baronet and a former officer in the Royal Field Artillery, he had earned a DSO in the First World War, and was a fellow of the Royal Geographical Society and the author of several books. Burrard, at first blush, seems to fall within the description of 'a Major Somebody who had shot things in Lapland or somewhere of that sort', so cruelly skewered in *Reginald's Christmas Revel*, the short story by Saki. Certainly some of Burrard's published titles would have fitted the fictional profile: *Big Game Hunting in the Himalayas*, *In the Gun Room* and *Notes on Sporting Rifles* featured in his literary output, along with two raffish-sounding novels, *The Tiger of Tibet* and *The Mystery of the Mekong*. There is no doubt, however, that Burrard had accumulated considerable expertise, later to be distilled in a major work, *The Identification of Firearms and Forensic Ballistics*, published in 1934. The following year Burrard addressed the Medico-Legal Society on the intricacies of the identification of firearms by microscopical examination (Spilsbury appears not to have been present at the meeting).

Burrard and Churchill were old enemies. They had first fallen out in 1925, when Churchill had been promoting the use of shorter-barrelled shotguns, made by his firm. Burrard, then gun correspondent for *The Field*, criticised a claim made by Churchill in his recently published best-seller *How to Shoot*. Burrard, who had originally remained anonymous, repeated his statements under his own name in a magazine called *Game and Gun*. Churchill personally attacked Burrard in a robustly worded pamphlet. 'Does he reply in *The Field*?' he asked, 'No? Then where? Funnily enough in a publication known as *Game and Gun*, which is issued by Messrs Spratts Ltd, a firm of biscuit makers.'[18]

On 30 January 1932 the gun had been examined by Dr R.K. Wilson, captain in the Royal Artillery. Five days later, on the upper balcony of the United Service Club – overlooking Waterloo Place and Pall Mall – Burrard, with Dr Wilson, Dr Brontë and Mr Pettifar, further examined the gun, removing the locks. Police Sergeant Lown stood by, to ensure that everything was above board. In Burrard's view, contrary to Churchill's findings, the gun had a 'dangerously light pull' on both triggers. The gun was further examined for the defence by two distinguished gunsmiths, William Mansfield, a director of Holland & Holland, and H.L. Greener of Birmingham.[19]

Before the trial began Churchill consulted Max Baker, described as 'one of the most eminent ballistic experts of his day', although Baker regarded himself more modestly as 'an intelligent and industrious amateur, rather than an expert'. Baker had himself written for *The Field*, and was shooting editor of *Country Life* and secretary of the Gunsmiths' Association. Churchill, perhaps wisely, did not heed Baker's advice 'to drop the gun, say fifty times when cocked and loaded'.[20]

The Old Bailey trial was fixed to start on 11 April 1932, but in the meantime a significant development had occurred. The gun had been handed to Churchill by the police on 8 March, having previously been kept at Holbeach police station, and it remained at his Orange Street premises until 23 March. That day Burrard and Mansfield, accompanied by Police Sergeant Lown, collected the gun and took it to 8 Bream's Buildings, Chancery Lane, the chambers of a Member of Parliament, Linton Thorp, who had been briefed to defend Kitchen. Burrard and Mansfield examined the gun again. Burrard was shocked by what he saw. 'My God,' he said. 'It has been tampered with.' Mansfield thought the same as Burrard. It appeared that the action had been relatively crudely altered to make the gun seem less likely to accidental discharge.[21]

About two weeks before the trial, Spilsbury lost 'that man', as he called him – one of his greatest adversaries, a thorn in his flesh for almost a decade. Dr Robert Brontë had died of heart disease, at the comparatively early age of 52, at his home in Harrow.

Against a background of a serious allegation of malpractice, the trial opened at the Central Criminal Court before Rigby Swift.[23] J.F. Eales KC led Gerald

Dodson (future Recorder of London) and Garth Moore for the Crown. Thorp appeared with Alban Garden for the defence. On the first afternoon the star of the show was Prince, the curly coated retriever, who was brought into court at the judge's request. Prince was lifted up (a dog of substantial weight, said to be 7 stone) and carefully placed on the solicitors' table in the well of the court, where the animal sat, wagging his thick tail and licking the hand of Police Sergeant Lown. According to a local Lincolnshire newspaper, Prince made 'so many friends during the trial' and was dubbed 'the silent witness of the drama'.

The defence was able to show that the dog had been wearing a collar with a name tab fixed on by a split ring. In an early insight into the judicial mind, Swift placed the ring on the trigger, pointing out how easily it slipped on. On the second day of the trial further cross-examination by Thorp introduced the possibility of the dead man having slipped and fallen in the muddy yard immediately before the fatal shot. He had been wearing rubber gumboots, which, as Swift observed, were made of a 'substance . . . very unstable to walk about in on mud'. Whatever were the judge's thoughts, he warned the jury before the midday adjournment that the case was unlikely to finish that day. When the court reconvened after lunch, 'every eye was turned to the tall figure of Sir Bernard Spilsbury, the famous pathologist'. Spilsbury described his post-mortem findings, using a court usher to point out the position of the fatal wound.

EALES. You have stated that the angle of the wound formed an angle of 55 degrees. Is that taken by you on the assumption that the man was erect?
SPILSBURY. It was an angle 55 degrees to the horizontal, so that would be with the body erect. . . .
EALES. Supposing that a man had slipped and fallen on his back, do you think it possible the wound you speak of to have been caused with the body in that position?
SPILSBURY. Either lying on his back or downwards if the body was in such a position to leave the left part of the chest uncovered, which would mean that the left arm would have to be raised.

At this point, Swift made a dramatic intervention. Spilsbury, for once in his career, appears to have hauled down the flag, unable or unwilling to dispute the thrust of the judge's suggestions:

SWIFT. Is there any material point on which a sound theory can be based?
SPILSBURY. The only material points are the distance of the weapon from the deceased and the direction of the wound . . . the fact that the wad was so far in the body and the absence of scorching indicated that the weapon was close by.
SWIFT. It is ghastly speculation, isn't it?

SPILSBURY. There is nothing exact. It entirely depends on the position of the body at the time the man received the wound.

SWIFT. It is pure speculation how this man died?

SPILSBURY. Put that way, My Lord, it is.

Swift immediately stopped the trial, effectively directing the jury to acquit. 'Sir Bernard Spilsbury, to whom you look for every assistance,' declared the judge, 'says that no one can tell what happened.' The compliment could not disguise the fact that Rigby Swift's use of the expression 'ghastly speculation' had been a stinging rebuke. Spilsbury had declared his confident opinion – in post-mortem findings, in his report to the DPP and during committal proceedings – that the fatal injury had been caused by someone firing the gun at James Kitchen and not by accidental discharge.

As a result of the judge's decision, Churchill, who would have been the next prosecution witness, was not called to give evidence. He was thus spared the ordeal of cross-examination, which would have exposed him to the grave allegation of tampering with the gun. Newshounds, however, were on the trail, the *Empire News* tantalising its readership with hints about 'evidence a jury had no chance to hear'.[24]

On 13 April 1932 E.L. ('Lance') Mallalieu, Liberal MP for Colne Valley, approached the Home Secretary, Sir John Simon, at the House of Commons, raising the grave allegation against Churchill. As a result, Burrard and Mallalieu had an interview with Sir Ernley Blackwell at the Home Office. Burrard argued that Churchill had deliberately filed the tail of the 'sear', part of the gun's action, to support his case that the gun was not liable to fire accidentally. For the Home Office this was an exceptionally delicate matter. If Churchill were found to be responsible, a number of convictions based on his evidence, including some for murder, could be in jeopardy. An internal enquiry panel was set up, consisting of Oliver Stanley (the most senior civil servant), Blackwell and the DPP, Tindal Atkinson. A detailed account of this enquiry is beyond the scope of this book, but the result was a complete exoneration for Churchill.

This finding was partly based on an assumption that Churchill would not have risked his reputation by interfering with the gun's mechanism, but it was not really in dispute that tampering had taken place between 1 March and 23 March, during the latter part of which time the gun was at Churchill's premises in Orange Street. The panel, finding that the allegation was 'entirely without foundation', noted that it had been supported by experts 'of conspicuous fairness', but concluded – in a true Civil Service fudge – that these good men had been 'genuinely mistaken in their recollections'.[25]

Spilsbury's abject surrender to judicial pressure in the George Kitchen case is out of character. As an expert witness he would often sit in court listening to the cross-examination of other prosecution witnesses. By this means he could learn about the nature of the defence case, and, in consequence, embellishments sometimes emerged in his evidence. In the Kitchen trial the defence had already raised the possibility of the dead man, wearing rubber boots, slipping and falling just before the gun went off. Spilsbury must have known what was coming, but his evidence seems lame and uncharacteristically vague. It may be that Spilsbury had realised, at this late stage, that his contentions would not stand up to close scrutiny. A darker possibility is that he was aware that Churchill was at risk of a potentially devastating cross-examination. Spilsbury – knowing that his evidence was pivotal to the Crown's case – may simply have 'gone soft', well aware that Rigby Swift, a forceful and experienced judge, would be likely to stop the case. In shielding Churchill he was indirectly protecting his own reputation, for he had closely collaborated with the gunsmith and had taken a leading part in the experiments at Churchill's London premises.

Spilsbury's deeply entrenched public reputation survived the fiasco of the George Kitchen trial. He continued his bachelor-like social life, and there were consolation prizes to be had. In May 1932 he entertained Our Society with a talk on the recent case of Douglas Potts, an undergraduate at King's College, Cambridge, who had shot dead his tutor, a police sergeant and himself. On 21 June that year Spilsbury became Worshipful Master of the Rahere Masonic Lodge and on 8 November was appointed to a similar post at the Sancta Maria Lodge, which accommodated the many freemasons among the medical staff at his old hospital, St Mary's.

NINETEEN

'Laugh, baby, laugh for the last time!'

In the 1932 Old Bailey murder trial of Mrs Barney, Sir Patrick Hastings put brilliantly into practice lessons learnt from studying the evidence given by Spilsbury in the Rouse trial a year earlier (see Chapter Sixteen).[1] Elvira Dolores Barney, 28, was the rich, spoilt daughter of Sir John Ashley Mullens, the Chief Government Broker, trustee of the stock exchange, and a big name in the City of London. Elvira's parents lived in some style, alternating between 6 Belgrave Square and the Manor House, Haslemere.

In the mid-1920s Elvira had nursed ambitions to become a musical comedy star. As a lumpy and talentless *ingénue*, a true daughter of Mrs Worthington, she played a tiny role in a long-forgotten musical, *The Blue Kitten*, which enjoyed a modest run at the Gaiety Theatre. In 1928 she married John Sterling Barney, an American revue artist. There were rumours that Elvira spent the first night of her honeymoon in bed with another woman, while her husband sought solace in a Turkish bath.[2] Barney was alleged to have ill-treated his young blonde wife, and the couple parted after a few months. Blessed with a substantial private income, Elvira abandoned any idea of a career on the stage and, with the help of drink and cocaine, she lived in a world dramatised so deftly by Evelyn Waugh in his early novels *Decline and Fall* and *Vile Bodies*.

Elvira was part of a smart set of people, artists, actors, socialites and assorted spongers, 'a clique [that] indulged in almost every sexual vice which it is possible to imagine', in the words of one puritanical police officer.[3] By late 1931 she had taken up with Thomas William Scott Stephen, then 24, allegedly a dress designer and certainly bisexual. Stephen, known to Elvira as 'Mickey', was the son of a City banker, but had broken with his family. Mickey's father had cut off his allowance, and his brother Francis, a solicitor with the ultra-respectable Herbert Smith & Co, remembered Mickey's 'roving disposition', wistfully observing that a quiet home life in rural Kent had probably not suited him.[4]

As Mickey was virtually penniless, Elvira paid the bills, and the couple took a converted coach house at 21 Williams Mews, off Sloane Street in west London. Mews living was only beginning to be fashionable in 1931, and the lively new residents lived close to chauffeurs, cabdrivers and their families, people who had to get up early and work for a living. Drink, drugs and late nights had turned Elvira into a fleshy caricature of her former self, looking fully twenty years older than her true age. In the early hours of a May morning in 1932, Elvira, after an argument with a taxi-driver, had locked Mickey out of the house and could be heard screaming at him from a first-floor window. Mickey, as usual, was asking for money, but Elvira told him 'Fish for it!' As he was walking away from the locked door Elvira leant out of the window, shouting 'Laugh, baby, laugh for the last time', and fired a shot in the air, holding a pistol in her left hand. Elvira's physical appearance was succinctly described at her trial:

COUNSEL. How was she dressed?
WITNESS. I don't think she had anything on.[5]

Mickey escaped danger by quickly slipping into a greengrocer's van standing in the mews. In those less regulated days Elvira kept a small handgun, a .32 Smith and Wesson with a 3in barrel. Amazing as it now seems, no one reported the incident to the police.

One of Elvira's monthly cocktail parties was held on the evening of 30 May 1932. Despite lurid press reports to the contrary it seems to have been a relatively decorous affair, running from about 6.30 to 8.30 p.m. Mickey, with the help of a maid, dispensed sherry, dry martinis and a 'grapefruit gin cocktail', while Elvira passed round sandwiches and biscuits. One guest, Mrs Sylvia Coke, of 4 Carlyle Square, Chelsea, recalled that 'the gramophone was playing and we danced to it. It was a very gay party and everybody . . . seemed to be enjoying themselves immensely.'[6]

Among the gay company was Waugh's Oxford contemporary, Brian Howard, whose rackety homosexual lifestyle was source material for the characters of Anthony Blanche in *Brideshead Revisited* and Ambrose Silk in *Put Out More Flags*. Waugh would have known many of the guests, who included Howard's then boyfriend, a young German named Anton Altmann; the Hon. Eddie Gathorne-Hardy (who shared a flat with Howard); Olivia Wyndham, the society photographer, and her American partner, Ruth Baldwin; Arthur Jeffress, a rich American art collector; and the Skeffington Smyth brothers. Denis Skeffington Smyth described himself as an actor, 'at present in a musical play, *Casanova*', while his brother Terence, aged 27 and of 'independent income', did no work at all, dividing his ample leisure time between England and the French Riviera.[7]

After the party broke up, Elvira and Mickey, accompanied by Arthur Jeffress, dined at the Café de Paris in Coventry Street. Elvira, after downing a *fernet branca*, ordered sweetbreads and a Welsh rarebit. The men had quails, followed by ices. Two double whiskies paved the way for a bottle of champagne. With a packet of Khedive cigarettes, the bill, paid – of course – by Elvira, came to £2 18s. More whisky flowed at the Blue Angel, 52 Dean Street, where the trio had kippers and were entertained at the piano by Hugh Wade, another of Elvira's party guests. At 12.40 a.m. Jeffress left the couple to host a late-night party of his own. When the three parted, as far as Jeffress could remember, Elvira and Mickey were on friendly terms. Once back at Williams Mews, however, the drinking began again.

At 4.40 a.m. the telephone rang at the home of Elvira's doctor, Thomas Durrant, who lived at 18 Westbourne Terrace, Paddington. His wife answered, but seems to have put down the handset at once, perhaps because the caller was female, hysterical and incoherent. When, a few moments later, the telephone rang again, Durrant realised that the caller was Elvira, who told him to come at once to the Mews. There Durrant encountered his patient, sobbing and very agitated, clutching at the doctor's clothes as he entered the hallway. Mickey's body was lying at the top of the stairs, his left side against a wall, with his feet down the stairs. A loaded revolver lay near his left hand. 'Is he dead?' she cried. 'He can't be dead. I love him so,' she sobbed, before repeatedly kissing the body.[8] Mickey was fully dressed, his head lying on pillows that Elvira had placed under his head. A heavily bloodstained towel was found pushed down his clothes in an attempt to staunch bleeding from a single wound to the chest. Elvira, distraught, threatened to kill herself, and, indeed, a suicide attempt lay at the heart of her story. She told Durrant that they had quarrelled, allegedly over Mickey's interest in another woman, and he had threatened to leave her. She made mention of suicide. Mickey picked up the gun and said, 'You won't do it with this', but she ran towards him and there was a struggle for the gun, first on the landing and then in a spare room, where the gun went off. Mickey staggered into the bathroom. At first Elvira thought he was unhurt, but then heard him say, 'Send for a doctor.' Mrs Hall, a chauffeur's wife, living at 10 Williams Mews, had heard screaming and rowing, followed by a shot. She then heard a man's voice say, 'Good God, what have you done?'[9]

The doctor's chauffeur was told to fetch a police officer, and, by 6.20 a.m., Dr Arnold Harper, the divisional police surgeon, arrived and made the first detailed examination of the body. An hour later Detective Inspector William Winter spoke to Elvira, who was in the drawing-room of the house, 'wearing a kind of kimono'. Elvira lost her temper when asked about the shooting and, when asked to go to the police station, slapped Winter's colleague, Detective Constable Campion, on the face, screaming, 'I'll teach you to tell me you will put me in a cell, you foul swine.'[10] As the daughter of Lady Mullens, Elvira evidently thought that she should not be treated like a member of the common herd. It is a reflection on contemporary social attitudes that she was not charged with assaulting a police officer and that, after making a statement at the police station, she was released unconditionally and taken home to Belgrave Square, where, heavily sedated, she remained at liberty until her arrest four days later.

Although the facts of the case were reasonably straightforward, Winter conducted an elaborate investigation, interviewing at great length people who had attended the party at 21 Williams Mews and, with less justification, those who had attended the late-night party given by Arthur Jeffress at 30A Orchard Street. With so many obviously homosexual men and lesbian women among the guest-lists, police interest in these parties extended well beyond the remit of the murder investigation.

On the morning of 31 May, a few hours after the shooting, Spilsbury was instructed to conduct a post-mortem on Mickey's body, which remained at 21 Williams Mews.[11] Spilsbury arrived at about 1.30 p.m., joining Detective Inspector Winter, Detective Constable Campion, and Dr Durrant. Mickey was wearing a jacket, with a small hole in the left lapel, over a yellow pullover, which had a smoke mark, corresponding to a mark on the jacket, caused by the discharge of the gun. Spilsbury noticed that there were no scorching, singeing or smoke marks on the dead man's hands and wrists. He then undressed the body. From the appearance of a broad stream of blood on the front of the corpse, Spilsbury formed the opinion that Mickey had been either standing or sitting for some time after receiving the fatal injury.

Mickey stood 5ft 8½in tall and was of muscular build, factors that would help Elvira's defence. On the other hand, Spilsbury's theory as to the circumstances of the shooting was potentially very dangerous. The entry wound was 2¾ inches below the left collar bone and 3 inches to the left of the centre of the breastbone. The track of the bullet ended at the top of the sixth rib. In a typical speculative exercise, based on the assumption that the deceased had been standing when the wound was inflicted, Spilsbury gave his opinion that the shot would have been fired from a height of 4 feet 5 inches above the ground. Experimenting with a skeleton used to teach medical students, Spilsbury somehow 'confirmed' that the course of the bullet had been horizontal. The left lung had been punctured, and loss of blood would produce unconsciousness. He estimated that death would have taken place 'not more than ten minutes' after the shot was fired.[12]

Suicide did not seem to be a reasonable possibility. The shot had not been fired with the gun muzzle touching the body, nor was the shot aimed at the heart, both factors usually present in suicides. As to Elvira's story of a struggle, Spilsbury considered that the heavy pull on the trigger meant that, with a bent wrist, there would have been insufficient power for the dead man to have fired the gun. Spilsbury's conclusions had been based, not only on his own post-mortem findings, but on the opinion of Robert Churchill. The double act was in business again, unabashed by the debacle of the George Kitchen trial (see Chapter Eighteen). Churchill firmly stated that the revolver was 'one of the safest ever made', requiring a pull of 14 pounds to discharge a bullet.[13] The two experts estimated, from the condition of the clothing, that the gun had been fired at a distance of 3 inches from the dead man's chest.

No expense was spared by the Mullens family to secure the best available legal representation. With a brief fee of 1,500 guineas (£1,575) and a 100-

guinea (£110) 'refresher' fee a day, Sir Patrick Hastings was an excellent – if exceedingly expensive – choice as defending KC, although he disliked appearing in criminal cases, particularly in murder trials. In 1924 he had been a reluctant prosecutor in the case of Vaquier (see Chapter Eleven). At first Hastings refused to accept the brief, but his daughters had once had a governess formerly employed by the Mullens family. Lady Hastings, who felt sorry for Elvira's parents, persuaded her husband to change his mind. Hastings was careful not to visit Elvira in prison, keeping at one remove from his highly strung and difficult lay client and leaving the business of day-to-day contact to his two junior counsel and his instructing solicitor.

Hastings was probably the finest advocate of his generation. Born in 1880, the son of a solicitor whose madcap financial ventures led to bankruptcy, Hastings had served in the Boer War. His background and experience of life were broader than most of his legal contemporaries, and an artistic element in his mother's family may have led Hastings to try his luck as a playwright. During the 1920s Hastings saw three of his plays produced in the West End, but only *Scotch Mist*, premiered in January 1926, was a success, and this was largely because the sensational American actress, Tallulah Bankhead, played the leading role.

Elvira Barney's trial began at the Central Criminal Court on Monday 4 July 1932.[14] Travers Humphreys was the judge, and the prosecution was led by Sir Percival Clarke, veteran of many murder prosecutions. Arriving at court, Hastings had great difficulty forcing his way through the enormous crowd to the barristers' entrance in Newgate. He gave his name and occupation to a detective, who simply replied 'I've never heard of you' to the former Attorney-General.[15] Once in court Hastings's puritanical nature was shocked by the assemblage of 'fashionably dressed men and women' and 'eminent authors', paid by the newspapers to write emotional accounts of the trial. Less frivolous spectators included Sir Ernley Blackwell and the DPP, Tyndal Atkinson.

Mrs Barney, whom Hastings had not met before the first day of the trial, struck Hastings as 'slightly depressing' in appearance, cutting 'a melancholy . . . figure in the dock'.[16] Dressed in black and wearing a close-fitting black hat, she showed 'great weariness', with her eyes 'heavy and listless' as she glanced at her supportive parents, sitting in the well of the court.[17] Percival Clarke was adept at low-key, but effective, opening speeches and was able to outline his case in a relatively short address lasting only fifty minutes. Hastings was observed to be twiddling his long silver pencil-case during the speech, possibly to distract the jury's attention from the more awkward aspects of the case, or perhaps because he was wondering how he would handle the really dangerous witnesses, Spilsbury and Churchill.[18]

Just before Clarke began to call evidence, Hastings stood up and requested the judge to exclude all Crown witnesses, except police officers, from court until the time came for them to give their testimony. In other trials,

Spilsbury would sit through the prosecution case, listening to the defence cross-examination. Expert witnesses, as opposed to witnesses of fact, were usually allowed to remain in court. The judge was surprised by the application, which Hastings believed had never been made before in a trial. 'Including Sir Bernard Spilsbury?' asked Humphreys incredulously, but Hastings, who said tactically that he 'did not press that', repeated his request, knowing that the judge had little option but to accede. Spilsbury and Churchill had to leave court and wait outside, along with an assortment of chauffeurs' wives and Elvira's raffish friends.

Hastings later wrote that, 'of all the witnesses . . . the one I feared most was Sir Bernard Spilsbury'. Although he paid lip-service to Spilsbury as 'an absolutely fair witness and a most . . . knowledgeable medical man', Hastings was well aware of 'a practice among some prosecuting counsel to treat him almost as an expert on murder'. Having sat through the evidence, Spilsbury would ordinarily be asked by prosecuting counsel whether the defence was consistent with his findings, 'to which Sir Bernard could only say "No"'. The defence would then be faced with the choice of not cross-examining, which would leave the answer unchallenged, or of tackling him, in which case Spilsbury 'would be entitled . . . to give the reasons for the opinion . . . given with all the weight of his skill and experience . . . [and] most deadly for the defence'.[19] Although Hastings did not say so in terms, he must have feared that Spilsbury, having heard his cross-examination of other witnesses, would add to his original findings, much as he had done in the Rouse case. Excluding the country's most famous pathologist was a bold move on his part.

On the second day of the trial Spilsbury, summoned from outside court, mounted the steps of the witness-box, stage left of the judge, and placed on the ledge in front of him a brown Gladstone bag, containing Mickey's jacket and pullover, worn at the time of the shooting. Spilsbury seldom failed to give evidence unaccompanied by some form of stage property and, in the manner of a conjurer, produced these poignant reminders of the tragedy for the inspection of judge and jury.

Picking up the gun, Spilsbury 'gave a vivid illustration . . . of how he had tried to pull the revolver in the position in which it was suggested it went off'. He illustrated the strength of the pull by clicking the trigger several times and, trespassing on Churchill's ground, added that it was 'a long and heavy pull. The trigger has to be moved right back before it can be let off.' Master of the dramatic gesture, Spilsbury then pointed the revolver towards his heart, arguing that Mickey could not have fired the gun himself. 'I find it impossible', he said, 'to discharge it holding it in this position, about three inches from the body. With the wrist bent . . . I could not get enough power to discharge the pistol.'

When Hastings rose to cross-examine Spilsbury, hopes of a major forensic battle were to be disappointed. He posed just three questions, which gently mocked Spilsbury's experiments with the student medical skeleton. 'Well,' responded Spilsbury, with a touch of petulance, 'I had to confirm it upon the skeleton of someone else.' He agreed with Hastings that there are differences in the formation of bones between different people. Hastings lastly asked a deceptively simple question: 'And the best way to see whether a bullet is fired straight at a body is to look at it?' Spilsbury could only answer in the affirmative.

Hastings easily demolished Churchill's contentions about the safety of the weapon by establishing that it carried no safety device. Playing with his witness, Hastings repeatedly pulled the trigger, which clicked noticeably more easily than it had done when in the hands of Spilsbury. Two questions encapsulated Elvira's defence, destroying both Crown experts' theories in an uncomfortable reminder of Rigby Swift's rebuke to Spilsbury at the sudden end of the Kitchen trial:

HASTINGS. . . . . it is quite impossible for anyone who was not there to know exactly how the revolver in those circumstances would go off?
CHURCHILL. Yes.
HASTINGS. It must be speculation?
CHURCHILL. Unless you have a wound which will give the explanation.

The last answer, and Churchill's subsequent evidence, failed to recover ground lost in cross-examination, and Hastings cemented his victory by handing the revolver to his junior, simulating a struggle for the gun. Bearing in mind the impedimenta of wig, bands and gown, this must have been an extraordinary display of courtroom tactics.

Elvira, with occasional sobbings and recourse to smelling-salts, broadly kept to her account, enabling Hastings to make an eloquent closing speech, which the judge found to be 'certainly one of the finest speeches I myself have heard at the Bar'. There was little doubt that Elvira had fired the gun, Humphreys told the jury, but the question was whether she had fired it intentionally. Aspects of morality crept into the summing-up. Elvira and Mickey were 'two rather useless lives'. The dead man, when he did any work, had been a dress designer. 'I suppose', mused the judge disapprovingly, 'that means a lady's dress designer.' Humphreys seemed particularly shocked by the vulgarity of Elvira's mews house, noting that, despite her private income, 'she chose to . . . live . . . in this converted garage, in the lounge of which there was a service counter with a cocktail bar'.

The jury acquitted Elvira after a retirement of just under two hours. A woman shrieked in the public gallery, and Elvira nearly fainted, before being taken home by her indulgent parents. She never thanked Hastings for his efforts on her behalf. A few weeks later Hastings and his chauffeur were driving along a road near Boulogne. Elvira, acting the part of Agatha Runcible in *Vile Bodies*, suddenly appeared from behind, furiously driving her 'blue and beige' sports coup on the wrong side of the road and narrowly avoided a fatal collision.[20]

Elvira seemed destined never to be happy. By 1936 she had formed a relationship in Paris with 'a tall blonde good-looking boy, well known to most of the Paris night clubs and bars'. She spent Christmas Eve in a tour of 'the gay cafes and restaurants of Montmartre, Montparnasse, and the Latin Quarter', breaking off to listen in a flat to midnight mass on the radio from Notre Dame, a service that moved her to tears.[21] After a few more cocktails early on Christmas morning she felt unwell and returned alone to her hotel room. Later she was found dead, still wearing her evening clothes. Elvira, only 31, had suffered a massive brain haemorrhage, no doubt brought on by years of substance abuse.

Poor little rich girl.

TWENTY

Tony Mancini: The Brighton Trunk Murders

In 1932 Sir Bernard's youngest son, Dick, now 13, left preparatory school in Hampstead, where he had been a day-boy, and was sent as a boarder to Sedbergh, a hearty, games-oriented public school in Cumberland. Dick did not relish his schooldays at Sedbergh, where, much to his father's chagrin, he took no interest in the school's Officer Training Corps. Peter Spilsbury went up to Magdalen College, Oxford, in October 1933, following his father's footsteps by studying physiology, with a view to qualifying in medicine. A more social animal than his father, he had an outgoing personality, was popular with his fellow students, and rowed both for Leander and for his college.

In May that year Spilsbury treated himself to a new car, a Humber, a sedate make of vehicle and very much a doctor's choice. In the autumn his professional ego was boosted by his election as President of the Medico-Legal Society, for which office he commissioned a handsome portrait photograph taken by Elliot and Fry of Baker Street. For his presidential address, delivered at 11 Chandos Street, London, on 26 October 1933, his subject was 'Some Medico-Legal Aspects of Shock'.[1] Although Spilsbury had used the S-word regularly over the years in stating his opinion as to cause of death, he now considered that many deaths attributed to shock should really be ascribed to some distinct condition, such as 'injury to a vital organ, concussion of the brain, and so forth'. Much of the address was taken up with a review of deaths from shock due to abortion, a practice that Spilsbury always detested.

In November 1933 he took a boat to Jersey. Spilsbury was not the only medical expert aboard ship. Professor Sydney Smith and Dr Aleck Bourne were also en route to the island, all three doctors instructed to give their professional opinion in a sensational abortion case.[2] As usual Spilsbury was appearing for the prosecution, pitted against Smith, who had the capable assistance of Bourne, for the defence of a doctor charged with performing 'an illegal operation', namely the procurement of an abortion. Although the three stayed at the same hotel in Jersey, Spilsbury remained aloof, seemingly absorbed in his professional work, manifestly unable to relax.

Dr Claude Avarne, aged 42, came from Blaenavon in south Wales and had served as a naval surgeon during the First World War, after which he specialised in obstetrics. Until early 1932 he had been on the surgical staff at St Helier General Hospital in Jersey and subsequently had a Harley Street practice, although he continued to work on the island. Elsie De La Mare was a 28-year-old domestic servant who had worked at the Minors Hotel in Jersey as a chambermaid for several years, earning 15s a week. In 1926 she had a child, apparently by the hotel proprietor, the unfortunately named Mr T.H. Nobes, who packed her off to a maternity hospital in Southampton for the birth. In March 1933 she was pregnant again. Nobes suggested that she should see Dr Avarne, a close personal friend. Nobes maintained that he had never suggested an abortion and that he had left matters in the hands of Dr Avarne. Elsie maintained that Dr Avarne had never suggested anything illegal. Avarne said that he had been asked to perform an abortion, but had refused. All three agreed that no fee had been paid.

Avarne saw Elsie on 27 May 1933 and prescribed a sedative. There was no evidence of any attempt to procure a miscarriage at this time, but two months later Elsie was admitted to the Margarita Nursing Home at Dr Avarne's request. He told Sister Le Feuvre that Elsie was suffering from haemorrhage and abdominal pain and that he proposed to operate.

Avarne, attended by an anaesthetist, operated on Elsie. Sister Le Feuvre was fully aware that what was being done was an attempt to induce an abortion. No miscarriage occurred and so, three days later, on 25 July, Avarne again tried to remove the foetus, but without success. A third operation was contemplated, but Elsie's temperature rose to 105°F and, on 27 July 1933, the child was born dead. Elsie's condition deteriorated, her temperature now a dangerously high 107°F.

Avarne's behaviour was reprehensible. Sister Le Feuvre made repeated attempts that night to contact him without success, and other doctors brought in by Avarne also made themselves scarce. A fourth doctor, Dr Bentlif, attended Elsie, who began to show early signs of recovery. She told Bentlif that she had gone to Avarne with a view to ending her pregnancy. Bentlif immediately telephoned the Jersey police. The dead child and the placenta were placed in glass jars and the remains examined by Bentlif and two other Jersey doctors, who all agreed that there was no sign of 'maceration', the softening of tissue that can occur if the foetus has died in the womb some time before birth. The Jersey Attorney-General then contacted Spilsbury, who, having viewed the specimens, gave his opinion that an illegal abortion had taken place.

The trial of Dr Averne opened on Monday 6 November 1933 at the Jersey November Assizes before the Bailiff and ten *jurats*. Prayers were read, before the jury of twenty-four was empanelled, after eight challenges by defence counsel. The Bailiff nominated a foreman. Some people called for jury service were excused for various reasons, though 'no excuse was offered by Mr Philippe S Hocquard, who has been dead for several months'. Some of the jury spoke English, others French, and it is unclear whether all those present could understand both languages.

Spilsbury took a seat alongside the Public Prosecutor and remained in court to hear the evidence. Twenty-six witnesses gave evidence, among whom

Dr Mattas, a doctor of medicine at Toulouse University, testified in French. Elsie, who had made a complete recovery, told Advocate Briard, for the defence, that she had received no assistance from anyone after leaving the nursing home, not even from the child's father.

ELSIE. Even those interested in the case have not assisted me.
BRIARD. What do you mean by those interested in the case?
ELSIE. Well you for instance.

Loud laughter, quickly suppressed, followed this pert answer. Jersey is a small island, and the scandal had turned Elsie into a celebrity. Spilsbury gave evidence 'in his usual . . . lucid style, didactic and convincing'.[3] In his opinion the baby had died during the second operation. Elsie had not truly been suffering from haemorrhage before entering the nursing home. When she complained of haemorrhage and pains, Avarne should have given the proper treatment for threatened miscarriage, which was complete rest with light food. In answer to Briard, Spilsbury admitted that he had had no clinical experience of pregnancy for the past twenty years, but 'considered himself competent'. He stated his opinion in typically uncompromising fashion:

BRIARD. I submit, Sir, that the foetus was dead on 25 July.
SPILSBURY. I agree. It died during the operation.
BRIARD. I submit it was dead before that.
SPILSBURY. I say it died while the operation was being performed.

Avarne stated in evidence that he had come to the conclusion on 20 July 1933 that the foetus was dead and operated in consequence. Before the trial started Sydney Smith had examined microscopic sections taken from the foetus and, with the help of another Edinburgh pathologist, concluded that there was evidence of maceration in the tissues. Avarne had been right to assume that the child was dead. Smith gave the court his opinion that the foetus had died when Elsie had first entered the nursing home and was therefore dead before 20 July. Smith was followed by Aleck Bourne, who demolished Spilsbury's contentions in an evidential *tour de force*. The resulting antagonism between the two men would reach its climax five years later, when Bourne himself would stand in the dock, charged with carrying out an illegal abortion (see Chapter Twenty-one).

Aleck Bourne, nine years junior to Spilsbury, had an academic record far superior to that of Sir Bernard. Bourne took a first-class honours degree in the Natural Science Tripos at Cambridge and entered St Mary's Hospital with a senior scholarship. At the age of only 25 Bourne had been elected a Fellow of the Royal College of Surgeons (FRCS). Bourne was a full-time practitioner of obstetrics and gynaecology, working at, among other institutions, Queen Charlotte's Hospital. Unlike Spilsbury, who tended to dabble in medical topics,

Bourne published important original works, such as a study on uterine action in labour and in response to various drugs. In 1929 he became a foundation fellow of the Royal College of Obstetricians and Gynaecologists.

In the witness-box Bourne gave a trenchant rebuttal of Spilsbury's opinion. 'Haemorrhage in pregnancy', he said, 'is the cardinal symptom of premature abortion . . . Had I observed . . . such symptoms and had I made up my mind to operate, the fact that haemorrhages had not occurred whilst at the [Nursing] Home would not alter my opinion. I would proceed on the experience of the previous month's observation.' Bourne 'honestly believed' that Avarne was dealing with a dead foetus on 23 July, the date of the second operation. 'If Dr Avarne had wanted to perform a criminal operation,' observed Bourne drily, to some laughter, 'he would not have gone to a private nursing home, but to the home of the child's father.'

As for Spilsbury's views, Bourne observed sarcastically that Spilsbury's 'long and wide experience' was confined to specimens in bottles and that he had 'no inside knowledge of clinical work'. Towards the end of his evidence Bourne mercilessly attacked the great pathologist's reputation: 'When Sir Bernard Spilsbury begins to talk about the symptoms or diagnosis of living things, I cease to listen.'

The jury, sent out at 6.35 p.m. on Thursday 9 November 1933, took only eighteen minutes to reach a unanimous verdict. Avarne was acquitted, to loud cheers in court. 'He's off', shouted someone among the crowd in Royal Square St Helier, who gave Avarne and his lawyer 'a wonderful ovation' as they walked back to Briard's office. Spilsbury, Smith and Bourne travelled back to England on the same boat. Spilsbury took his defeat badly. During the passage across the Channel the 'wizard medical witness'[4] refused to speak to either of his two fellow medical practitioners.[5]

For most of the 1930s, although his star was beginning to wane, Spilsbury regularly attended meetings of the Medico-Legal Society, frequently contributing at length to discussions on a variety of topics and, from time to time, reading papers of his own. At a meeting in 1932 Spilsbury gave his support to a proposal for a Medico-Legal Institute, based in London, perhaps encouraged by one contributor's sycophantic reference to 'a training ground for future Bernard Spilsburys'. While happy with his laboratory at University College Hospital, which he had been offered after leaving Bart's 'to take up whole-time study, as a pathologist, of medico-legal problems', Spilsbury complained that, 'as matters stand, I have to take my material across London to either St Mary's or Guy's'. He could only do this because he knew the bacteriologists and toxicologists personally. The proposed institute, declared Spilsbury in nationalistic vein, 'should be entirely British; there is no need to seek enlightenment from other countries as to our requirements . . . the study of pathology in this country needs no guidance . . . from other nations'.[6] In the event, as with so many other of his enthusiasms, Spilsbury failed to pursue the idea, but his representations may eventually have had some effect on the official mind. The first police forensic science laboratory in England was established by Lord Trenchard, then Commissioner of Police for the Metropolis, at the Hendon training centre in 1934.

On 3 May of that year, in the New Medical School building at St Mary's, Spilsbury addressed 'a large medical audience' on a grandly titled theme, 'The Application of Physiological Principles to Medico-Legal Problems', giving a broad-brush review of developments in the study of bruising, post-mortem changes in blood, death under anaesthesia, the effects of shock on the digestive system (associated with his theories about chronology derived from the passage of food through the gut), and problems posed by 'asphyxia'.[7]

Later that month, on a fine spring morning at the Chapel of the Savoy, Sir Bernard's eldest child, Evelyn, now 23, married John Allistair Steel, a tall, bald and rather dull-looking man eight years her senior. On that day, Saturday 14 May 1934, Spilsbury had dressed suitably for the occasion. Wearing a shiny black silk top hat and morning dress (accompanied by the inevitable pair of spats), he took the arm of his only daughter and led Evelyn into the chapel, watched by a large crowd of onlookers gathered in the narrow street behind Savoy Hill, former home of the BBC. Evelyn, who raised her veil for the waiting press photographers, carried a bouquet of white lilies and wore a white satin wedding-dress, with a close-fitting cut in the latest style. Despite aspects of her private life that might not have earned Spilsbury's approval, Evelyn seems to have got on fairly well with her father. She was an actress and, as early as 1930, had featured in a short talkie filmed by British Movietone News in Torquay. The fine wedding photographs taken by such agencies as Planet News, the Park Press, Central News Photos and Topical Press show a rare side of Spilsbury, smiling, relaxed and obviously proud of his attractive daughter. After the wedding Spilsbury was again the subject of press photography, but, far from hiding his face from the cameras, left the building wearing a broad smile, accompanied by his wife. There is no indication from the photographs that Sir Bernard and Lady Spilsbury were anything other than a happily married couple.

The following month Spilsbury was called down to Brighton to examine the decapitated and limbless body of a woman found in a box at Brighton Station, marking the start of two sensational murder enquiries. On 17 June 1934 attendants at the station's left-luggage office, increasingly concerned by the smell emanating from a plywood trunk, summoned police assistance.[8] Once the trunk was opened, the decomposing body parts of a young woman were found wrapped in brown paper, tied up with cord. Only a few hours later another macabre discovery went some way to complete this depressing human jigsaw. Late that afternoon a cloakroom attendant at King's Cross Station in London noticed an unpleasant odour emanating from a cheap brown suitcase, which was also leaking fluid. He opened the case, using a spare key he had with him, and inside found a parcel, wrapped in brown paper and newspapers and soaked in putrefying liquid, in which were the missing legs of the Brighton corpse, each divided at the knee. The suitcase had been left at the station at about 1.30 p.m. on 7 June, the day after the box had been left at Brighton.

Spilsbury had already been booked to perform an autopsy on the Brighton remains. Putrefaction was advanced, and the skin was 'moist and peeling off', with putrefactive gas present in the abdomen and elsewhere under the skin. One noticeable feature in the uterus was a foetus, soft and decomposed, weighing about 6 ounces. The following day, 20 June 1934, Spilsbury was back in London, where, at Paddington mortuary, he examined the lower limbs found at King's Cross. In his report (which took two weeks to prepare) sent to Norman Kendal, Assistant Commissioner at Scotland Yard, on 4 July 1934 he concluded that the body parts all came from the same person, a young woman of about 25, 'well developed but not stout' and about 5ft 3in in height. A few head hairs found on the body parts suggested that she had light brown hair, with a permanent wave, and bleaching of hairs on her legs could have been the result of sunbathing. She was between four and five months pregnant. Spilsbury concluded that 'the pregnancy had not been interfered with in any way', which suggests that there was no evidence that she had died as a result of an attempted abortion. Her feet, clean and well cared for, suggested that she had been 'particular' in matters of personal hygiene. No anatomical skill or knowledge was displayed in the dismemberment. The complete absence of blood suggested that dismemberment was carried out some time before the parts had been placed in the boxes. As there was no evidence of natural disease, poisoning or violence, Spilsbury was unable to state the cause of death.[9]

Assistant Commissioner Kendal wrote breezily to Dr Roche Lynch at St Mary's, enclosing 'some things' in 'the latest cut-up case': the trunk, two lengths of cord, cotton wool from the trunks and a towel. 'I am afraid the cotton wool is a tough business,' he wrote. 'The towel smells hopeful.'[10] The head and arms were never found. The investigation of 'Brighton Trunk Murder Number One', as it is sometimes called, made little progress after Spilsbury's report, but the episode had a surprising consequence, leading to the trial of a man known as 'Tony Mancini' for 'Brighton Trunk Murder Number Two'.

Among a number of women who had disappeared in Brighton and the surrounding area at about that time was a 42-year-old prostitute, Violette Kaye, sometimes known as Violet Saunders or Violet Watson. In palmier days Violette had formed part of a 'double patter and dancing act', performing from 1922 onwards at such second-rank venues as the Electric Cinema at Crystal Palace and the Balham Hippodrome. Later, with another male partner, she played as a *soubrette* under the billing 'Kay and Kaye – Pep, Punch &

Personality', but the act broke up in February 1933. After this, Violette was seen working the beat in Shaftesbury Avenue and Piccadilly. She had several convictions for soliciting. During 1933, in Sadie's Café, a cheap Leicester Square restaurant, she met a waiter who went by the name 'Tony Mancini', then aged 25. Mancini's many aliases included Jack Notyre, Hyman Nathan Gold, Luigi Pirelli and Antoni Luigi. His real name was the more prosaic Cecil Lois England, and he was born to a law-abiding family in New Cross, south London. A swarthy, ugly man, under medium height, he had a scar on his mouth, and was described by Doris Savill, an East End acquaintance, as having 'the appearance of a Jew'. Doris had once met Mancini in a Stepney pub. They had walked out to some marshes. 'We laid down,' she later told police. 'He interfered with me. He then went to sleep.'[11]

After school in Broxbourne, Mancini had worked for a short time as a footman to the Conservative MP for St Albans. In 1927 he signed up for eight years' service in the RAF, but deserted in September 1929. He had three convictions for petty dishonesty: theft of silver; 'loitering with intent'; and stealing clothing from a dwelling-house. In October 1933 Mancini persuaded Violette to try her luck as a prostitute in Brighton, with him as her pimp, and – by May 1934 – she was sharing a basement flat with him at 44 Park Crescent. Business was brisk, and Mancini supplemented their income by taking a job as a waiter at the Skylark Café in Brighton.

Violette was last seen alive by witnesses (other than Mancini) on 10 May. The following day her sister received a telegram that read GOING ABROAD. GOOD JOB. SAIL SUNDAY. WILL WRITE. VI. The original form, written in capital letters, was subsequently recovered and examined by Gerald Gurrin, an experienced graphologist. In Gurrin's opinion the form had been written by the person who wrote printed capitals on menus at the Skylark Café – in other words, by Tony Mancini.

On 14 May 1934 Mancini moved out of 44 Park Crescent and into another seedy basement, in Kemp Street, near the station. He said that Violette had gone to Paris. A friend helped him move a large, very heavy trunk, which would remain in his room for over two months. Incautiously, Mancini boasted to acquaintances of having struck Violette, giving her a 'slosh up' with a hammer. Squashed down inside the trunk were the remains of Violette Kaye. Mancini continued to sleep in his room, sometimes joined by visitors who, not unnaturally, remarked on the smell. Even though the trunk eventually began to leak, he gave several different explanations, some involving the use of disinfectant and French polish.

Mancini was interviewed on 14 July, but Violette's age, at least twelve years older than the dismembered woman, initially ruled him out as a suspect. Mancini suspected – quite rightly – that the police were going to make further enquiries. He fled to London on the day Chief Inspector Donaldson and other officers obtained access to his room, where they found the black fibre trunk, inside which was Violette's decomposing body, accompanied by various items of male and female clothing, and a number of moth balls. A hammer was found among rubbish in the cellar of the house. Mancini's description was circulated, and, in the early hours of 17 July 1934, two policemen picked him up in south-east London. Mancini denied murder. 'I would not cut her hand,' he said. 'She has been keeping me for months.'[12]

At post-mortem, held on 15 July 1934, Spilsbury found the body badly decomposed.[13] The surface was moist, except the right hand and fingers, which were partly mummified. The brain was very decomposed, a 'green mass', with no structure. There was evidence of bruising to parts of the head. The skull, of normal thickness, had a large depressed fracture on the right side, underneath a bruise, extending down to the base. There was also a short fissured fracture extending upwards from the upper edge of the principal fracture. Violette showed some evidence of heart disease, common in her age group, but the main injury was the depressed fracture, caused by a violent blow or blows with a blunt instrument, such as a hammer. Two small bruises behind her left ear indicated that she had been lying on a hard surface when the blow was struck. The injuries had been inflicted 'within two or three minutes' of the heart ceasing to beat. The cause of death was 'shock, following a fracture of the skull'.

The hammer, examined by Roche Lynch, showed signs of having been put in a fire and revealed no bloodstains. Spilsbury concluded, not surprisingly, that the fracture could have been caused by this hammer. There were a few blood spots on the clothing, also examined by Dr Lynch, but these were insufficient for blood grouping, a relatively new development, although at this time only four human blood groups could be identified.

Mancini was charged with murder. His story was simple. Violette was visited by many men in the basement flat, and he would make himself scarce while business was being conducted. One day in May he had returned to find Violette dead, lying on her bed with a handkerchief around her neck and blood all about. He was frightened that he would be blamed, so he panicked and put the body in a trunk.

Mr Justice Branson presided at Mancini's trial, which began on 10 December 1934 at Lewes Assize court, familiar ground to Spilsbury.[14] 'Jimmy' Cassels prosecuted, leading a young barrister and aspirant politician, Quintin Hogg, later better known as Lord Hailsham, Lord Chancellor in the Thatcher government. Mancini's solicitor, F.H. Carpenter, 'an astute local practitioner',[15] succeeded in briefing Norman Birkett KC.

Roche Lynch gave evidence on the second day of the trial. Dealing with the spots of blood found on a pair of flannel trousers, he described one that was pear-shaped and 'might possibly have spurted from a small artery', a piece of evidence that would gain greater significance when Spilsbury came to testify. Lynch had found a minute trace of morphine in the bodily organs. The advanced decomposition indicated that the quantity taken was 'distinctly greater' than a medicinal dose, leading to a deep sleep and probable unconsciousness. Birkett homed in on this finding. He put it to Lynch that morphine was commonly used by prostitutes. Although Lynch would not confirm this, Birkett had laid the foundation for a promising line of defence.

On the afternoon of Wednesday 12 December 1934 Spilsbury stepped into the witness-box, carrying – with his customary air of mystery – an attaché case containing a very special object. In answer to Cassels he observed that the trunk was 'remarkably small' for the body. Pressure would have been necessary to get the body in, particularly if rigor mortis had begun. Spilsbury, describing his findings at autopsy, opened the attaché case and, to the astonishment of the court, produced a human skull. Like a Baroque *vanitas*, the skull remained on the ledge in front of the witness-box for the remainder of Spilsbury's evidence. Using this macabre stage property, Spilsbury indicated the area of injury, producing a piece of bone, which, he said, was the exact piece forming the fracture on Violette's head.

Birkett was on his feet at once, pointing out that the defence had no notice of the fragment of bone, which was not on the list of exhibits. Cassels replied, a little lamely, 'It is only recently we have known it is available', which suggests a major failure of communication between Spilsbury and the prosecution team. Spilsbury said that the bone was 'lying slightly inside the skull and against the brain', adding that, 'beneath where the piece of bone was situated, there was an artery. The piece of fractured bone had gone through the groove in which the artery lay and must have torn it across. There must have been a considerable rush of blood as soon as the fracture was inflicted.' Death would have occurred after 'probably no more than a few minutes', said Spilsbury, adding, with his usual certainty, 'and there would be complete unconsciousness during that time'. Either end of the hammer could have produced the injury.

Birkett now had considerable ammunition for a courtroom battle with Spilsbury and, from the outset of cross-examination, he began to rattle his target:

BIRKETT. Your views are rightly described as theory?
SPILSBURY. I am not quite sure that is right, when my opinion is based on experience.
BIRKETT. But, in the result, they are no more and no less than theory?
SPILSBURY. They are the results of my experience and that is as far as I can go.
BIRKETT. They are the results of your experience, but, without question are mere theories?
SPILSBURY. They are, in the sense that they are not facts.

Birkett then asked Spilsbury how long he had been in possession of the piece of bone, produced for the first time on the third day of the trial. 'Since the first examination,' replied Spilsbury. Birkett's next question produced a very strange answer:

> BIRKETT. Did it not occur to you that the defence might have been informed that in your possession was that small piece of bone?
> SPILSBURY. I am afraid it did not occur to me. The bone was not ready to produce at the time I gave evidence at the police court.

As for the 'rush of blood' from the artery, Spilsbury claimed to have referred to 'an effusion' in committal proceedings. (Birkett would not have known that Spilsbury's private case card made no mention of the piece of bone, the artery or the possibility of such a haemorrhage.) After Spilsbury had outlined the piece of bone against the skull, using a pencil, the skull was passed round the jury box. The thrust of Birkett's questioning was to lay the ground for other theories to explain the post-mortem findings. Violette could have fractured her skull after falling down the steps leading to the flat; she could have been killed by a client; or she could have died of morphine poisoning. Spilsbury agreed that there was more than one possible theory to account for the death, but would not admit that a fall down the outside steps, which had a stone ledge or brace at the top, easy to trip over, could have caused such a depressed fracture:

> BIRKETT. Are you really telling . . . the jury that, if someone fell down that flight and came upon the stone ledge, he [sic] could not get a depressed fracture?
> SPILSBURY. He could not get this fracture.

Birkett pointed out that the depressed fracture was 'one-eighth of an inch'. Spilsbury changed his earlier evidence by stating that it was more likely that the fracture was caused by the smaller end of the hammer, rather than the larger end. He agreed that someone might recover consciousness after a fall and do various things, including walking about, before death supervened. The judge intervened during Cassel's re-examination, asking whether Violette, with such a head injury, could have recovered sufficiently to walk to the bed or undress herself. In reply, Spilsbury, for the second time in the trial, introduced a completely new evidential hypothesis:

> SPILSBURY. I have said it is possible to have happened after a depressed fracture, but in this case it is clear that it had not happened. If she had survived any extent of time, she would not have died of shock. She would have died from haemorrhage of the brain.

Birkett was on his feet again. 'This is the very first time that this has been suggested in the whole history of the case,' he protested, at the very end of the court day.

Birkett's opening speech was, in the opinion of his clerk, 'one of the most powerful opening speeches it has been my pleasure to hear'.[16] Spilsbury, that most dangerous of Crown witnesses, was in his sights. 'Take the evidence of Sir Bernard Spilsbury,' he asked the jury. 'A man may go into that box with a great name, with a great reputation, but the most powerful people in this court . . . are the jury.' Repeating the first few questions and answers of his cross-examination of Spilsbury, Birkett drew attention to a major disparity in his evidence. During committal proceedings Spilsbury had said that 'the general size of the fracture corresponds pretty well with the larger end of the hammer', whereas in court, the previous day, he said it was 'more probably' the smaller end that had caused the injury. As for Roche Lynch's evidence suggesting blood spurting from an artery, the defence was able to show that Mancini had acquired the trousers after Violette's death.

As Mancini was taking the oath, the judge noticed that he had put his hand in his pocket and taken out an object, which turned out to be a black rosary. In Graham Greene's *Brighton Rock* the anti-hero is 'Pinky Brown', a young thug and lapsed Catholic. There was much in this trial that resembled aspects of Greene's novel, not least this exchange:

JUDGE. Are you a Roman Catholic?
MANCINI. I was.

Chief Inspector Donaldson was impressed by Mancini's 'remarkable composure' as a witness. 'It was obvious', he later wrote, 'that he had been "schooled" . . . and he was by no means shaken under cross-examination.'

In his closing address Birkett again attacked Spilsbury, whose over-precise chronology was now fair game for defence counsel. 'Sir Bernard said that death came within two or three minutes of the blow,' he reminded the jury, before putting the simple, but devastating, rhetorical question, 'How did he tell?' When emphasising the discrepancy about the use of the hammer, Birkett said that he was not attacking Spilsbury's good faith, but 'high or low, famous and obscure, known and unknown, men are all human and fallible'.

After a summing-up from Mr Justice Branson, 'a humane and sophisticated judge',[17] the jury took two and a half hours to find Mancini not guilty. Detective Inspector Donaldson, who privately thought that the jury had 'their vision distorted by the eloquence of counsel', shook hands with Birkett. Mancini, discharged from the dock, looked dazed. 'Not guilty, Mr Birkett? Not guilty, Mr Birkett?' he repeated.[18]

Spilsbury's reputation suffered a nasty knock in the Mancini case. Birkett had mercilessly exposed the great pathologist as fallible, even incompetent. Spilsbury would never know that, in 1976, Mancini was to confess to a Sunday newspaper that he was the murderer of Violette Kaye.

The identity of the victim of Brighton Trunk Murder Number One has never been ascertained. In the 1970s the writer Jonathan Goodman contacted Chief Inspector Donaldson, then retired and living in New Zealand. *The Railway Murders*, first published in 1984, reveals that, in July 1934, Donaldson had information leading him to suspect that the young woman had died during an abortion attempt carried out by a Dr Edward Massiah, then in practice at 8 Brunswick Square in Hove. Spilsbury's evidence at the post-mortem in Brighton Trunk Murder Number One does not seem to support Donaldson's belief that death occurred as a result of a failed abortion by a qualified doctor. Spilsbury, always on the look-out for evidence of malpractice of this kind, found no sign of interference with the pregnancy and was also of the opinion that the dismemberment showed no particular anatomical skill.

Spilsbury, once described as 'almost an honorary member of the CID',[19] was probably aware of police interest in Dr Massiah. The following year Faith McCawley, a young woman of 24, who had visited Dr Massiah's surgery, was found dead in the bathroom of a flat in Sutherland Avenue, Maida Vale. Spilsbury performed an autopsy, and, outside Paddington Coroners' Court on 17 April 1935, a press photographer snapped two middle-aged men, both wearing bowler hats, apparently engaged in earnest conversation. Dr Massiah stood unsmiling, neatly dressed in a double-breasted suit with a pearl pin in his tie. On the left, in a dark overcoat, carrying books and papers and peering very intently at the other man, was Spilsbury. 'Only a small proportion of cases of alleged abortion go any further than the coroner's court,' Spilsbury had said in 1933, 'hence many guilty persons probably escape trial.'[20] Dr Massiah was never prosecuted. After a year or two he left England and appears to have spent the rest of his days in comfortable circumstances, living near Port of Spain, Trinidad. He remained on the British Medical Register until 1952.

TWENTY-ONE

Spilsbury in Decline

On 1 February 1935 the *Daily Express* – owned by Lord Beaverbrook and a leader in the mass circulation market – published the results of a popularity contest on its front page. People had been invited to write in, naming the people they most liked (or disliked) reading about. A league table was drawn up from a 'random' selection of contributors. George Bernard Shaw easily won the prize for 'Bore No. 1', heading a list, 'in strict order of boredom', that included Amy Johnson, Ramsay MacDonald, Hitler, Lady Astor, Ghandi and de Valera. 'Public Favourite No. 1' was Lloyd George, followed by Winston Churchill, with Beaverbrook winning an improbable third place (perhaps the selection was not so 'random' as claimed) over Gracie Fields, the Lancashire entertainer. The list of popular favourites also included Franklin D. Roosevelt, Greta Garbo, Mussolini – and Spilsbury.

'What is it . . . which attracts this searchlight of interest?' mused the *Daily Express*. The newspaper's answer was that, 'whatever they choose to do well, they do it slightly differently from the others. There is a bit of colour about them and the way they do things.' Spilsbury, the paper admitted, was a surprise choice. 'Nothing would horrify the staid Home Office pathologist more', it wrote, 'than to hear of the public's voracity for reading about him.' By 1935 Spilsbury was indeed looking staid. He had aged visibly, even since Evelyn's wedding the previous May, and his uniform of formal clothes and spats had begun to seem outdated, fashions swept away by the Prince of Wales and other contemporary trend-setters. Social changes, not least the influence of American movies, were also beginning to be reflected in the style of newspaper reportage.

George Orwell, in his essay 'The Decline of the English Murder', argues that the character of murder began to alter in about 1925, but a review of the media coverage afforded to Spilsbury suggests significant changes also took place in the mid-1930s. In 1933, for example, Lord Beaverbrook decided to axe the *Daily Express* gossip column, then largely devoted to the activities of the English upper class, called 'The Talk of London' (the *Daily Mail* put out a similar feature with the odd title 'People and their Doings'). Influenced by *Time*, the successful American magazine, the 'William Hickey' column was launched, with its theme 'These Names Make News', written in a 'sharply flavoured and jagged prose style'. Film stars, millionaires and assorted 'personalities' filled the column inches, and the aristocracy – in the absence of headline-grabbing activities – was relegated to the shires.[1] Spilsbury's starchy, old-fashioned image was starting to seem increasingly out of kilter with the national *Zeitgeist*. Spilsbury was, nonetheless, still a firm favourite with the judiciary. Summing up a murder case in March 1935, Hewart, the Lord Chief Justice, could barely restrain his enthusiasm: 'That wonderful witness,' he declared, 'so fair, so clear.'[2]

In 1936 Spilsbury was once more badly caught out in cross-examination.[3] Nowadays this episode would probably lead to debate in our hugely expanded media, with widespread adverse publicity, but in 1936 informed comment was left to the privacy of clubs, bar messes and hospital common-rooms. There seems little doubt, however, that word was getting round among both legal and medical practitioners about the quality of Spilsbury's judgement as a forensic pathologist.

Linford Derrick was a lawn tennis coach (already rather a smart occupation in 1936), remembered by his counsel as 'a good-looking, clean-limbed type of man', aged 41. He coached boys at Sherborne School, although his home address was in Ealing. Derrick was on very friendly terms with fellow Ealing residents Arthur Wheeler, an insurance clerk, and his wife, Kathleen. The friendship was close enough to be 'almost a *ménage à trois*', although, until August 1936, 'there was never the slightest suggestion of impropriety'.[4] Derrick bore a good character and was widely regarded as an even-tempered, likeable man. Wheeler, however, became jealous of Derrick's perceived interest in his wife, and the two men quarrelled at Wheeler's house, in the absence of Kathleen Wheeler, on the evening of 4 August 1936. Neighbours were aware of raised voices and heard Derrick drive away at about 11.30 p.m.

Just before 11 a.m. on 5 August Derrick walked into Ealing Police Station and announced to the desk sergeant, 'I've just murdered my best friend.'[5] Police officers found Wheeler dead from severe head injuries, lying in his pyjamas on the landing of his house. The dead man's face and shoulder were badly bruised, and there were severe wounds to the head. A shirt was tied round his neck. Some of the landing banisters were broken and Wheeler's feet were covered in blood. Bloody sockprints led down the stairs.

Derrick claimed that he had returned to the house, on foot, to patch up the quarrel. Wheeler, in pyjamas and carrying a truncheon, let him in, but his manner was hostile. Derrick followed him upstairs into a bedroom, trying to find some way of getting through to Wheeler, who suddenly said, 'You would bloody like to see yourself in bed with Kath, I suppose.' Derrick called him 'a swine' for saying this, whereupon Wheeler said, 'I'll settle you, you bloody swine', and came at him with a truncheon. Derrick seized his left arm, but Wheeler grabbed his throat with his right hand, almost causing Derrick to lose consciousness. He remembered grabbing the truncheon and hitting Wheeler blindly as hard as he could. Both men fell to the floor, exhausted, until Derrick

– in a daze – saw Wheeler's hands coming towards him. Seeing a shirt on the banister rail, Derrick picked it up and, scarcely conscious, tied the shirt around Wheeler's neck. Wheeler 'suddenly became still', and Derrick collapsed over the body. Unlike Wheeler, Derrick bore no signs of injury from the alleged struggle. In an attempt to get away he faked a break-in, taking some money and jewellery. He took off his bloodstained trousers and put on a pair of Wheeler's trousers before walking home.[6]

Spilsbury, called in to examine the body, wrote a report for the DPP that formed the basis for a charge of murder. The trial began at the Old Bailey on 22 September 1936, before Mr Justice Greaves-Lord.[7] 'Khaki' Roberts (see p. 82 above) led for the prosecution. Derrick was defended by Cassels, wearing his left arm in a black silk sling after an accident in his garden. His junior was J.D. Casswell, an experienced barrister and veteran of several capital trials.

The case for the Crown was that Derrick was in love with Kathleen Wheeler and had decided to get rid of her husband. He had walked to the house because his car would be recognised. The evidence of stockinged feet indicated that he had taken off his shoes so as not to be heard when he climbed through a downstairs window. As for use of the truncheon, Wheeler had been right-handed, which was inconsistent with Derrick's statement to the police. Basing his opening speech on Spilsbury's findings, 'Khaki' Roberts submitted that Derrick first hit his victim a blow to the left cheek and then, as Wheeler lay on the ground, rained 'six terrible blows on the head', before cold-bloodedly strangling Wheeler with his own shirt.

Spilsbury was the principal prosecution witness. Casswell later recalled 'his customary quiet assurance'.[8] On the right side of the forehead, Spilsbury told the court, there were three wounds. In front of the skull, on the forehead, were three smaller wounds, close together. Spilsbury was adamant that there were 'six separate and distinct wounds', which could have been caused by blows from a truncheon. There were bruises on the right cheek and shoulders, and ten small abrasions on the neck, some of which might have been caused by a hand grasping the throat. The cause of death, said Spilsbury, was 'concussion resulting from head injuries accelerated by strangulation by the ligature round the neck'. The head injuries were 'undoubtedly' inflicted before the ligature was applied. When the judge asked whether the person who had received the head injuries was capable of resistance, Spilsbury's reply was couched in the most definite terms. 'No,' he told the judge, 'he certainly would be unconscious.'

Casswell, a sharp advocate, remembered that at committal proceedings Spilsbury had referred to 'three parallel cuts' on the forehead, caused by 'a rain of blows, any one of which would have rendered Wheeler unconscious'.[9] Casswell had served as a special constable at the start of the First World War and knew about police truncheons. In particular, he recalled that Wheeler's truncheon had three parallel rings, which together formed the grip. This could mean that, instead of three blows to the forehead, as Spilsbury had claimed, the evidence was consistent with only one blow. Cassels at first did not understand his junior's point, but, after a demonstration in chambers involving Casswell, Cassell's clerk and a ruler, it was obvious that, in the struggle for possession of the truncheon in Wheeler's hand, Derrick would have grabbed the wrong end. Furthermore, the fact that there was copious blood on Wheeler's feet suggested that he had fought on for some time.

Cassels was well primed before cross-examination began. Spilsbury agreed that scratches on the throat might have been caused by Derrick holding Wheeler back to prevent him attacking. Cassels, in a dramatic gesture, then whacked the truncheon on counsel's bench, asking whether Spilsbury could guarantee that a rain of blows, delivered as Wheeler lay still, would not cause a fractured skull.[10] Spilsbury replied, quite correctly, that it was quite possible that such blows would not fracture the skull.

Nevertheless, Cassels had cleverly seeded a doubt about Spilsbury's certainties in raising the possibility of fracture. His best point, of course, lay in the physical structure of the truncheon. Cassels was able to demonstrate to the jury that the space between the three rings corresponded with the three wounds on the dead man's forehead. He also pressed Spilsbury about the blood found on Wheeler's feet, and, in Casswell's words, 'the "expert" reluctantly agreed that he had been mistaken'[11] in concluding that Wheeler had been rendered unconscious by blows from the truncheon.

In addressing the jury after Derrick had given evidence, Cassels posed a question that emphasised the destruction of Spilsbury's opinion. 'Who can tell with the particularity of a slow-motion picture the sequence of events?' he asked. 'It is only the opinion of Sir Bernard Spilsbury that Wheeler must have been unconscious when some of these blows were dealt.' Only a few years before it would have been a brave defence counsel who used the expression 'only the opinion of Sir Bernard Spilsbury'. Spilsbury had been humiliated in the witness-box, shown up, not only as dogmatic, but as incompetent.

Although the defence team thought that Derrick stood a good chance of acquittal, he was convicted of manslaughter. The jury seem to have accepted that there had been provocation on Wheeler's part that led to violence, but such factors as Derrick's light injuries and the evidence of strangulation may have led them to their verdict. Greaves-Lord sentenced Derrick to ten years' penal servitude, a harsh penalty, but Derrick, despite counsel's advice, did not appeal. At any rate, Cassels and Casswell between them had undermined the effect of Spilsbury's evidence, which, unchallenged, could have led Derrick to the execution chamber.

In April 1937 Spilsbury had taken his youngest son, Dick, now aged 17, on a Hellenic cruise. Despite the fragmented nature of his education, Spilsbury could read Latin and Greek and had maintained a lively interest in ancient history.

The choice of holiday may have been influenced by Dick's progress in classical studies. He had won a second Greek prose prize at Sedbergh in 1936, as well as two Latin prose prizes. Later that year Dick was awarded a Demyship at Magdalen College, an achievement that, in a very different discipline, had eluded his father forty years earlier. Pursuing historical themes, well away from contemporary murder trials, Spilsbury read a paper to Our Society on 7 November 1937, exploring the role played by Titus Oates in the furore following the killing of Sir Edmund Bury Godfrey in 1678 on the eve of the notorious 'Popish Plot'. Peter Spilsbury had graduated from Magdalen that summer, taking second-class honours, as his father had done, in physiology. Like his father, too, he had become interested in freemasonry, joining the college lodge (St Mary Magdalene). Peter began work as a medical student at St Thomas's Hospital the following October, the same month in which his younger brother went up to Oxford.

In the latter part of 1937 Spilsbury gave evidence in the trial of Frederick Nodder, charged with the murder of 10-year-old Mona Tinsley from Newark.[12] Originally charged simply with abduction, Nodder was convicted at Birmingham Assizes in March and sentenced by Rigby Swift to seven years' penal servitude. On 6 June 1937 Mona's body was found in the River Idle, south of Bawtry, and Nodder – now in prison – was charged with her murder. At this trial, before Mr Justice Macnaghten, Spilsbury and Dr John Webster were able to satisfy the jury that Mona had been strangled. The presence of adipocere in the body indicated immersion for between five and six months. Nodder, who had probably also raped the little girl, was convicted and subsequently executed.

In March 1938 Percy Casserley was shot dead with his own gun at his Wimbledon home by Edward ('Ted') Chaplin, the lover of Casserley's wife, Ena. The lovers unsuccessfully tried to persuade the police that Casserley had been shot by an intruder during a burglary, but, when this line of defence failed, Chaplin claimed that the gun – a light pistol of .25 calibre – had gone off accidentally in the course of a struggle.[13]

Spilsbury twice visited Casserley's house, examining the scene in detail before conducting an autopsy. He was of the opinion that, given the absence of tattooing or scorching, the fatal bullet found in the victim's brain had been fired 'with the muzzle . . . pressed firmly against the skin'.[14] Although the wound could have been self-inflicted if the gun had been held in the left hand, it would have been very difficult for someone else to have inflicted the injury in the course of a struggle. Most of the blood on the floor came from a ruptured artery beneath the skin of the head. A second bullet wound across the back of the neck also had an absence of tattooing, but, paradoxically, this was said to be indicative of a discharge at more than 6 inches.

The case involved another collaboration with Robert Churchill, whose experiments had shown 'appreciable tattooing' at a muzzle distance of

6 inches. Spilsbury made findings inimical to the defence. 'It would have been impossible', he claimed, 'for the deceased . . . to have discharged the weapon at that range.' The oblique downwards direction of the bullet showed that the other person must have been standing close to Casserley, who was at 'a much lower level', in other words, already lying on the ground.[15]

Three head wounds, found at the back of the head, and three bruises on the trunk were all produced by a heavy, blunt object. Spilsbury, shown a 'life-preserver', or cosh, found in Chaplin's flat, said that 'it might be responsible for the injury'. Despite evidence that the weapon had recently been cleaned, a 'spot of blood' was found. Times were changing. Dr J.C. Thomas, a 'serologist' from the newly established Metropolitan Police science laboratory at Hendon, identified the blood as belonging to Group 'A', Casserley's blood group, as opposed to Ted Chaplin, who had blood from Group 'O'.[16]

On 22 and 23 April 1938, Spilsbury gave evidence in committal proceedings at Wimbledon. Ted Chaplin was represented by Derek Curtis-Bennett, barrister son of Sir Henry, who had died in 1935. The DPP's representative could hardly have been more deferential to the great man. 'The cause of death, Sir Bernard?', he asked, followed by, 'Now the head wounds, Sir Bernard?' and finally, 'What about the bleeding, Sir Bernard?' After reciting his findings about the injuries, Spilsbury, referring to the position of bloodstains in the sitting-room, came up with a theory that the head wounds and bruising were inflicted from behind, by 'another person standing close to the bureau with his back to it', because this was 'the only position one could get at that part of the body at all'. The large number of the lines of blood spots on the wall high above the bureau would be caused by blood flung off a bloodstained weapon. As a result of the blows Casserley would have been in a dazed condition when he went to the part of the room were the bullets were fired, 'incapable of offering resistance' or of shooting himself. Splashes of blood on the wall above the deceased were 'probably flung off the bloodstained hand of the assailant'. Curtis-Bennett had already objected to Spilsbury's use of the word 'assailant', but to no avail. Spilsbury, in full flight, would not be deterred from expressing his opinions, although there may be force in Curtis-Bennett's comment that these theories 'advanced in the latter part of Sir Bernard's evidence' were 'a very high flight of imagination'.[17]

Ted Chaplin and Ena Casserley appeared in front of Travers Humphreys at the Old Bailey, where Norman Birkett led Curtis-Bennett for Chaplin. During his evidence Spilsbury, incorrigible as ever, used the word 'attack' in evidence. Birkett's objection found no favour with the judge. 'What phrase do you suggest the witness should use?' he asked counsel grumpily. 'Somebody who hit him?'[18]

Churchill gave evidence that the gun, which had been poorly maintained and needed oiling, had a defect that meant, at the time of the shooting, it had to be cleared manually. This, according to the judge's biographer, 'seemed to disprove the argument that the gun could be fired twice by chance'.[19] On the other hand, as recorded by Churchill's biographer, Birkett secured an admission that the owner of a pistol known to be defective could 'work it more easily' than a stranger.[20]

Although there was no evidence that Casserley, or Ted Chaplin for that matter, knew anything about the gun's mechanism, Birkett made good use of the admission in his closing speech. Chaplin was convicted of manslaughter. The jury's verdict suggests that they did not accept Spilsbury's detailed theories, which were – in effect – consistent only with murder. Spilsbury was losing the dominance that he had once exercised in court. Had this violent death occurred ten years earlier, when Spilsbury was at the height of his powers as a forensic medical witness, the fate of Ted Chaplin could have been very different.

In April 1938, around the time of the Chaplin–Casserley trial, Spilsbury treated himself to a new car, a six-cylinder Armstrong Siddeley, registration number AGN 250. The large, solidly comfortable black saloon retailed at £475. Despite this comparative extravagance, surviving records show that Spilsbury earned far less than some of his professional colleagues. Without a private practice as a physician or surgeon, he derived his income mostly from coroners' cases, evidence given in criminal trials and civil cases, hospital lectureships and fees as an examiner.

In addition to his heavy professional workload, Spilsbury administered the family trust fund, set up by James Spilsbury for the benefit of his four children. He enjoyed a modest income from the investments, and his sisters, Connie and Gertie, who never married, seem to have been largely dependent on the fund for their income. His brother, Leonard, married (for a second time) in 1938 and settled in Stockholm with his new wife, Mary Weismann. Leonard's foreign domicile was an added complication for his brother as principal trustee, and surviving correspondence suggests that the relationship between the two brothers was polite, but not particularly close.

The year 1938 saw Spilsbury's final battle with Aleck Bourne, bitter enemy since Spilsbury's humiliation in the Jersey abortion case five years before (see Chapter Twenty). The case arose from a brutal sexual assault.[21] On 27 April 1938 two teenage girls were walking along Whitehall in central London. As they passed under the archway to Horse Guards Parade, troopers asked the girls if they wanted to see 'a green-tailed mare'. 'Miss A', then aged 14 years and 9 months, went into the stables. Trooper Victor Lloyd Pullin, aged 21, tried to kiss her and, pulling her into a loose box, pushed her against a wall. 'No use hollering,' said Pullin, 'if you let me do what I like, I'll only keep you five minutes.' Although Miss A, sobbing, screamed out for help, no one came to her aid and, as Pullin unsuccessfully tried to rape her, she was aware of someone else looking through a hole in the wall. The girl was prevented from leaving by Troopers Henry Richard Reeves, 23, and David Thomas, 22. Miss A was dragged into the barrack-room, thrown on a bed and raped by Thomas, aided and abetted by Reeves.

The troopers were tried at the Old Bailey in June 1938. Thomas and Reeves, who did not give evidence, were convicted of rape. Pullin, arraigned separately, pleaded guilty to attempted rape. When the police had told him Miss A's true age, Pullin replied, 'I like the 14 years and 9 months. She looked more like 19. One of the men thought she was 23.' At the first trial, the judge, Mr Justice du Parcq (who had defended Podmore in 1930 – see Chapter Sixteen), seemed more concerned about the civilian dress worn by the defendants than the brutal fate of their victim. 'I think it ought to be known', he declared, 'that . . . witnesses who are members of the armed forces should appear here to give evidence in uniform according to their rank.' Lord Sudeley, an officer representing the Royal Horse Guards, attested to the good character of the defendants. Thomas and Reeves received sentences of four years' penal servitude and Pullin a mere two years' imprisonment, the maximum sentence at the time.

Miss A's ordeal was not confined to the horrific circumstances of the assaults. As a result of the rape she became pregnant. On 6 June 1938 she had been admitted to St Mary's Hospital, Paddington, where Bourne was consultant obstetrician. The police surgeon who had originally examined her, the factory doctor at her workplace and her school doctor 'all feel that curettage should be allowed her'. Dr Joan Malleson, of St Mary's, noted that '[her] parents are so respectable that they do not know the address of an abortionist'. Bourne kept Miss A under observation for eight days 'to be sure of the type of girl I was dealing with'. Although at first she seemed composed, on one occasion when Bourne was taking a swab 'she wept beyond control', causing Bourne to reflect, in emotional language for a health professional, that she was 'withal, an innocent child'. He decided to operate.[22]

By section 58 of the Offences against the Person Act 1861 it was a criminal offence to procure an abortion. At 10 a.m. on 14 June 1938 Bourne terminated the pregnancy. By 6 p.m. two police officers entered the hospital and began collating evidence with a view to prosecution. In reply to questions from Chief Inspector Bridges, Bourne made no secret of what he had done. 'This morning, I induced abortion. In my opinion as an obstetric surgeon it may be dangerous for a girl of her age to bear a full-term child.'[23] The case presented serious ethical and legal problems. On 23 June Norman Kendal, Assistant Commissioner at the Yard, wrote to the DPP, expressing his reservations: 'I do not like this abortion case one bit . . . [I am] extremely doubtful whether it would be good policy to start a prosecution.' Kendal, however, had no time for Bourne and his sort: 'The object of these fanatical doctors, male/and female, is to obtain publicity at the expense of this wretched child . . . If there is no prosecution, then these doctors can get no publicity as they dare not publish broadcast [*sic*] what they have done.'[24]

Proceedings were nonetheless initiated, and, on 1 July 1938, Bourne was committed for trial at the Old Bailey. The DPP, now in a quandary about evidence, sought help from a trusted source. On 16 July 1938 Spilsbury wrote from the Institute of Anatomy and Embryology at University College, enclosing 'four copies of my observations in this case', entitled 'Report Respecting the Diagnosis of Early Pregnancy'. It is difficult to read the covering letter and the report without feeling that Spilsbury was motivated by hatred of Bourne, in which his drubbing during the Jersey abortion case was a major factor. Spilsbury, whose practical experience of obstetrics had been confined to one month in 1904, wrote that he had 'searched most of the standard textbooks on Midwifery', which asserted that the only justifiable grounds for termination were either to save the life of the mother or to preserve the mother's health 'if it is likely to be damaged by the continuance of the pregnancy'.

Citing a list of conditions 'which *might* justify the procuring of an abortion' in similar circumstances to those of Miss A, Spilsbury commented, without any real relevance to the matter in hand: 'If any of the above . . . are stated by Dr Bourne to have been the reason for . . . operating . . . it may be asked why he was guilty of a breach of professional conduct in making the fact public.' With regard to the issue of preservation of the mother's health Spilsbury made an astonishing claim. His report reads: 'it is significant that the textbooks on Midwifery do not refer to the child-mother at all, this implying that there are no special problems presented by pregnancy at an early age.' Spilsbury had been 'unable to find any statistics of the mortality rate of the child-mother', and, after quoting some academic figures of stillbirth rates and birth weight, he concluded that 'there is no especial risk to the child-mother during the period of pregnancy or in the course of labour'.

The report ended with a further swipe at Bourne: 'It is interesting to note that the youngest case recorded at Queen Charlotte's Hospital (where Dr Bourne was at one time on the staff) was of a girl of 9 years who . . . was delivered of a healthy full-term child.' Probably realising, after writing his report, that he had not considered the psychological aspects of the case, Spilsbury added a handwritten note to his covering letter: 'P.S. If Dr Bourne gives the mental condition as his reason for operating upon her it might well be asked whether she was examined by a mental expert before the operation was decided upon.'[25]

Two days after the DPP received Spilsbury's report, Aleck Bourne – a gaunt, sparely built man, wearing round glasses and a bow tie – stood in the dock at the Old Bailey. The charge under the 1861 Act was grave, with a maximum penalty of life imprisonment, and the Attorney-General Sir Donald Somervell KC, MP prosecuted in person. Despite the aggressive tone of Spilsbury's advice, Somervell called no medical evidence, whereas Roland Oliver KC, for the defence, summoned distinguished medical figures to the witness-box, including Lord Horder, the royal gynaecologist, in support of Bourne's action. Bourne's case was that abortion was justified because the risk to either physical or moral health was as valid as the certain risk of death. Dr Rees, a psychiatrist, spoke of the 'deep and lasting neurosis' suffered by women after rape. Contrary to Spilsbury's report, Mr (later Sir) William Gilliatt, senior gynaecologist at King's College Hospital, stated that abnormalities in labour occurred in nearly half of girls under the age of 16 in his care.[26]

Mr Justice Macnaghten summed up for a 'purposive' interpretation of the 1861 Act. It was open to the jury to find 'if the doctor is of opinion . . . that the probable consequences of the pregnancy will . . . make the woman a physical or mental wreck', that he had operated for the purpose of preserving the life of the mother. The jury took only forty minutes to acquit. *The Lancet* described Bourne's action as 'an example of disinterested conduct in consonance with the highest traditions of the profession'.[27] Spilsbury's opinion of the verdict is not recorded.

TWENTY-TWO

Wartime

After the outbreak of the Second World War Spilsbury continued to live in his flat at 1 Verulam Buildings in Gray's Inn. Alan, his eldest son, assisted his father in the laboratory, acting as secretary and maintaining records of Spilsbury's work. Alan's poor health (he may have been epileptic) precluded him from military service, but Dick was called up, joining the Royal Artillery.

On 13 March 1940 Sir Michael O'Dwyer, aged 75, a former Governor of the Punjab, was on the platform in the Tudor Room at Caxton Hall, Westminster, a room 'in which distinguished people are married', as the *Daily Express* later noted.[1] The East India Association and the Royal Central Asian Society had been discussing 'Afghanistan: the present position'. O'Dwyer had been sitting alongside several other notable figures from the halcyon days of the British Raj, including Lord Lamington and Sir Louis Dane, both in their eighties, Sir Percy Sykes and the Marquess of Zetland, Governor of Bengal from 1917 to 1922. As the meeting was ending, a heavily built man, medium height, of Asian appearance and wearing western clothing, positioned himself to the side of the stage. He pulled out a .455 Smith & Wesson revolver and fired six shots. O'Dwyer, who had been sitting on the last chair on the right of the front row, was killed instantly from a shot in the back. Zetland, who had risen from his chair, received a glancing wound to his ribs. Lamington and Dane were also slightly injured.[2] The assailant was grabbed by Miss Bertha Herring, a valiant middle-aged lady and dachshund owner, of Wraysbury House, Buckinghamshire. Miss Herring, who bore a distinct resemblance to the comedy actress Cicely Courtneidge, said: 'I got hold of the lapels of his coat . . . and a man sprang on his back and brought him down.'[3] Dr M.R. Lawrence, elder brother of 'Lawrence of Arabia', gave first aid to the survivors.

Uddam Singh (otherwise known as Mohammed Singh Azad) had been in the United Kingdom for many years, working as a carpenter and driver, although – as the Home Office gravely minuted – he had been drawing unemployment benefit at the rate of 17s each week for the previous four months. After his arrest Singh stated that the shooting was in revenge for the 1919 Amritsar massacre, when General Dyer had ordered troops to open fire on a crowd demonstrating against British rule. Some 400 demonstrators were killed and 1,500 people injured. Singh claimed that his brother and sister were among the dead. Spilsbury conducted the post-mortem on O'Dwyer at Westminster mortuary on 14 March 1940, finding two bullet wounds, one entering about 7 inches below the right shoulderblade and the other about 4 inches lower than the first wound.[4]

Before Singh's trial Spilsbury appeared in a civil case that was to have an unexpected personal dimension.[5] In June 1939 a 46-year-old policeman died at the London Hospital. He was suffering from a brain contusion and chronic tuberculosis of the adrenal and lymphatic glands, with other features of Addison's disease. Eighteen months earlier he had been severely injured while riding his bicycle along the North Circular Road after catching his front wheel in a tram track. The London Passenger Transport Board (LPTB) admitted negligence in respect of the condition of the tram track, but disputed liability for the policeman's death, maintaining that death was due to natural causes not attributable to the accident.

The widow sued the LPTB, and the case was heard at the High Court by Mr Justice Hallett on 15 April 1940. Sir William Willcox, Spilsbury's senior colleague from his days at St Mary's, gave evidence supporting the view that the pre-existing disease had been reactivated by the trauma of the accident, which had undermined the body's immune defences. It was probable that, but for the accident, the disease would not have developed as it did. Spilsbury was called to testify on behalf of the LPTB. This was only the second time that he had given evidence against Willcox. In 1927 Spilsbury had been on the losing side in a civil claim involving an allegation of food poisoning at a London restaurant. In the present case he argued that death would have occurred in any event, but the sensitivity of adrenal glands to damage by shock was already the subject of academic study, and his submission was rejected. The judge found for the widow and awarded damages against the LPTB. While giving his evidence Spilsbury looked strained and tired, beads of perspiration being visible on his face. 'Perhaps', as Willcox's biographer later wrote, 'it was the strain of finding himself up against his old friend and colleague and of fighting a cause he feared to be doomed to failure.'[6] Spilsbury did not take failure well, but there may have been a physical explanation for his haggard appearance. In mid-May 1940, a month after the civil case, Spilsbury – now aged 63 – suffered a stroke while conducting an autopsy. Three weeks later Singh's trial began at the Old Bailey. Because of political sensitivities only a few spectators were allowed into court to hear a token defence to the murder charge. Singh claimed that the shooting had been an accident. He had tried to point the gun at the ceiling but 'someone forced his hand down'.[7] Singh was convicted of murder and later hanged.

On 5 June 1940 the *Daily Express* had carried the headline SPILSBURY ILL, ATTENDS O'DWYER MURDER TRIAL. Spilsbury had been in hospital 'under treatment for foot trouble' and was helped into court at the Old Bailey. He could not manage the steps to the witness-box and gave his evidence from a chair in the well of the courtroom. The reality was that Spilsbury had been in hospital receiving treatment for his stroke. Perhaps understandably, he was anxious that press and public should not learn the truth about his declining health. As a result of his illness he gave up his fifty-a-day cigarette habit, but serious damage had already been caused to his circulatory system.

Compounding his ill-health came a terrible loss. His son Peter, who had graduated with an Oxford MB and Ch B that year, had been appointed a house surgeon at St Thomas's Hospital, hoping to obtain a commission in the Royal Army Medical Corps. The hospital, situated in the centre of London and just across the river from the Houses of Parliament, was particularly vulnerable to enemy action in the blitz, which started in September 1940. Early in the morning of Monday 9 September a bomb destroyed three floors in a block on the north side of the hospital, killing two nurses and four masseuses. Patients were moved into basements as bombing continued during the following nights. The noise of the air-raids and anti-aircraft batteries 'made sleep difficult', in the understated words of a contemporary report.[8] Peter Spilsbury, along with other staff, treated air-raid casualties from the surrounding district. Two bombs fell on St Thomas's on the Friday morning, causing severe damage to another part of the hospital, but with light casualties, but two days later, at 8.30 p.m. on Sunday 15 September 1940, there were several direct hits on the main corridor immediately south of the Central Hall, causing the collapse of the medical outpatients' block, wrecking the kitchen, canteen, dispensary and administrative block, and putting all essential services out of action. The bombs penetrated to the hospital basement, and there the explosions killed four staff members and injured three others. The dead comprised a first aid dresser, a nurse and two house surgeons, one of whom was Peter Spilsbury.

Although the fatal air-raid had taken place on a Sunday evening, Sir Bernard – for some reason not now known – was unaware of the tragedy until the following morning. He had travelled through the bomb-damaged streets from his flat in Gray's Inn to Westminster Coroner's Court in Horseferry Road, no great distance across the river from St Thomas's Hospital. After giving evidence in one inquest he opened some letters that had been sent to him at the court. By the cruellest stroke of fate, one was a letter of condolence on the death of his son, but did not give a christian name. As Spilsbury read the words, he seemed 'on the verge of collapse'.[9] He knew that Alan was not the victim, because he had seen him earlier that day. Dick, as he knew, was in the armed forces, but further enquiry confirmed that Peter had been killed. Of all Spilsbury's three sons, Peter had been the most outgoing and sociable. The choice of medicine as a career necessarily brought him closer to his father. Estranged from his wife, Spilsbury – whose personality was recessive and uncommunicative at the best of times – bore his grief alone. His few relatively close friends thought that he 'began to fail' after so terrible a blow.[10]

In his professional world, too, developments were in train that he would find distressing and unwelcome. Younger pathologists were beginning to make their mark. In addition to Sydney Smith, Keith Simpson and Francis Camps, both then in their early thirties, were potential rivals to his pre-eminent position. In due course, as will be seen, the older man gave way to symptoms of jealousy. Spilsbury gave up 31 Marlborough Hill early in 1941. He had not lived in the house in any real sense for twenty years. Edith moved out to St Alban's, a slightly safer area to live in than north London. Evelyn, who during the war lived at 8 Eton Hall, Eton College Road, Chalk Farm, was occupied driving London County Council ambulances during air-raids. Alan seems to have spent the war in lodgings, at one stage living in Willesden Green. Dick, now a lieutenant in the Royal Artillery, was posted to North Africa with the First Army in October 1942, initially serving in Tunisia.

Spilsbury remained in his flat at Verulam Buildings until 'bombed out' in March 1941, after which he joined his ailing sister, Connie, at the Langorf Hotel, 20 Frognal, in Hampstead. The hotel, a Victorian five-storey red-brick terrace house, stood in a quiet street, leading southwards to Finchley Road and northwards, steeply uphill, to Hampstead. Connie died a year later, but Spilsbury stayed on at the hotel until the end of his life, latterly occupying Room No. 5, a small bedroom on the second floor.

In spring 1941 a young journalist. Molly Lefebure, took the post of secretary with Dr Keith Simpson, already a busy Home Office pathologist. Two weeks after starting her work she was introduced to Spilsbury at Hackney Coroner's Court. Despite the legend that attached to his name, Molly Lefebure found him 'reserved, modest, and courteous in manner', appearing to exist for nothing but his work. Very tall, though beginning to stoop, Spilsbury in 1941 'looked . . . like a prosperous gentleman farmer', with 'a ruddy, open, earnest face', carrying his celebrated bag of autopsy instruments. When she later saw him waiting to give evidence at the Old Bailey she remembered him busily writing notes, using green ink, and with handwriting 'like some hieroglyphic which professors despairingly pore over'. When she sat down beside him, Spilsbury would greet her with a charming smile.[11]

After Spilsbury had moved to Hampstead, Molly met him by chance outside a chemist's shop, where both were looking for the weekly soap ration. After raising his hat, he jokingly referred to the 'very difficult choice' that had to be made between the only two brands available, 'French clove' or 'English rose'. After this, Spilsbury and his rival's secretary would often meet to buy their soap ration together.[12]

For about three years from 1941 Dr Hazel Baker – then a medical student at the Royal Free Hospital in Gray's Inn Road – would sometimes walk down with Spilsbury from King's Cross Station to the hospital. From the outset she realised that his 'very smart, dapper figure' masked severe depression, which gradually worsened during their acquaintance. Spilsbury, 'very buttoned-up', spoke of his sense of loss at Peter's death, but never mentioned other family members. He wanted to communicate, but seemed unable to do so. The acquaintance brought no professional advantage for the young student, whose first examination in forensic medicine involved questions about the use of a 'Higginson's syringe' in abortion. Spilsbury failed her.[13]

Spilsbury, in his loneliness, sought company through his contacts in the world of freemasonry. On 5 May 1941 he was chosen as Worshipful Master of the St Mary Magdalen Lodge, which he had joined in 1931. During the war he attended Masonic functions at a large number of lodges, including the Abernethy Lodge, the Grand Lodge, the Grand Steward's Lodge, the Rahere Chapter and the St Luke's Medical Lodge. Although he seems not to have attended dinners of The Organon after 1940 (possibly because his old rival, Professor Sydney Smith, had become an active member in the late 1930s), Spilsbury occasionally contributed to meetings of the Medico-Legal Society. He dined regularly at one or other of his two clubs, the Junior Carlton, then at 30 Pall Mall, and the United University Club in Suffolk Street, just off Trafalgar Square. Although he had a large number of acquaintances, associates of long-standing such as Bentley Purchase, the St Pancras Coroner, they were 'never on terms of the closest friendship' with him.[14] Dr Eric Gardner was probably the closest to Spilsbury, who would sometimes visit him at his Weybridge home, but, as late as 1944, Spilsbury would refer formally to 'Dr Gardner' in his diary entries.

In February 1942 Spilsbury examined the three women victims of Gordon Cummins, a 28-year-old airman who killed for gain, pervertedly inserting objects into his victims after death. 'The evidence of Sir Bernard Spilsbury as to the character and sites of the wounds inflicted', reported the prison doctor, '. . . points to a sadistic basis for the murders.'[15] Cummins had no viable defence and was executed in June 1942. Spilsbury, as in the cases of Patrick Mahon (see Chapter Eleven) and several other convicted murderers, conducted the post-mortem on the body of a man his evidence had helped to hang.

He also examined the bodies of executed spies, charged – as foreign nationals – not with treason, but with 'treachery'. Later in 1942 Spilsbury advised the Admiralty in Operation Mincemeat, involving the case of the 'Man Who Never Was'.[16] With the prospect of an allied invasion of Italy, members of an inter-service committee – which had an intelligence and security remit – canvassed a bold idea of disinformation. The body of a man, dressed as a staff officer, would be dropped in the sea near the coast of Franco's Spain. Papers on the body would be likely to mislead the Germans – who had many agents operating in Spain – that the allied attack would take place in mainland Italy, rather than in Sicily, the true site of the invasion. The body had to have the appearance of someone who had died in an aeroplane crash over the sea. One of the scheme's originators was a naval officer, the Hon. Ewen Montagu, a barrister and King's Counsel, who was sufficiently confident in Spilsbury's ability and discretion to approach him for help. The two men met for a drink at Spilsbury's club, the Junior Carlton. 'That extraordinary man', wrote

Montagu, 'listened to my questions . . . without ever . . . giving vent to the curiosity which he must have felt.'[17] Spilsbury advised him that victims of air accidents over the sea could die from exposure and shock, as well as from injury or drowning. Montagu went away, happy that his task was simplified and, after an anxious period, the body of a young man, in his thirties, was obtained. The cause of death was a combination of pneumonia and exposure.

At a further meeting Spilsbury confirmed that pneumonia would lead to fluid in the lungs. If a man had died at sea, there could be liquid in the lungs. Spilsbury made the observation, which seems a little cavalier, that there was little practical likelihood that the difference between sea water in the lungs and pneumonia-induced fluid would be noticed. 'You have nothing to fear from a Spanish post-mortem,' observed Spilsbury, with a touch of his old arrogance. Discovery that the victim had not died at sea after an air crash 'would need a pathologist of my experience and there aren't any in Spain'.[18] Spilsbury advised that the body should be kept in dry ice to minimise putrefaction, so that the condition would be consistent with a few days' immersion. The body was put in the sea off the south coast of Spain. The audacious ruse worked, probably saving many thousands of allied soldiers' lives. 'Major Martin RM' was buried in a Catholic cemetery at Huelva, where, years later, his false identity proved to be a headache for the Imperial War Graves Commission.[19]

At Easter 1943 Spilsbury had another stroke, a slight one, and his blood pressure was found to be 'very high'.[20] He stopped working for a time before resuming lectures and examining in the summer term. He took a month's holiday, with Alan, staying at the beautiful and ancient Luttrell Arms at Dunster, a favourite destination on Exmoor. Spilsbury was on friendly terms with Colonel Luttrell, the principal local landowner, and, at his suggestion, had opened the municipal swimming baths at nearby Minehead.

That summer saw another collaboration with Robert Churchill in a murder trial whose facts resembled those of the Malcolm case a quarter of a century earlier (see Chapter Six).[21] Lieutenant Ludomir Cienski, of the Polish army, was accused of murdering another Polish citizen, Lieutenant Jan Buchowski, who had been having an affair with Cienski's wife. The defence, predictably, was that the gun – a .32 Colt automatic – had gone off in the course of a struggle. The weapon had been in perfect working order and required a firm double pressure on the trigger before it would fire. Three shots had been fired.

Spilsbury, who conducted a post-mortem on Buchowski, found that he had died instantly from a shot through the heart. A second bullet had caused a head wound. In Spilsbury's opinion this shot had been fired after the victim was already dead by some person standing in front of him. In support of his view, Spilsbury claimed that Buchowski had collapsed, with his head bent forward, after the first fatal shot. No blood had flowed from the second wound. The absence of scorching on the dead man's clothing or around the wounds caused

Churchill to conclude that the shots had not been fired in the course of a close physical encounter, as claimed by Cienski. The position of the empty cases, ejected from the gun, convinced Spilsbury and Churchill that the two men had been standing apart at the time the gun was fired.

The trial opened at the Old Bailey on 1 June 1943 in front of Travers Humphreys. L.A. Byrne prosecuted, and Cienski was defended by Patrick Hastings. True to form, Hastings did not meet his lay client until the morning of the hearing. Byrne, in opening his case, canvassed the possibility that what had happened was the result of a duel, a form of Russian roulette, but no defence to a charge of murder under English law. As in the Barney trial (see Chapter Nineteen), Hastings avoided lengthy cross-examination of either Spilsbury or Churchill. In careful diversionary tactics, not unlike those adopted by Marshall Hall, he persistently referred to the gun as a 'revolver', which it was not, and – without any real basis – broached the possibility of suicide, simply ignoring Spilsbury's opinion that the wounds could not have been self-inflicted. Hastings also secured an unexpected admission from Robert Fabian, the police officer in charge of the case, that he did not know whether Buchowski's fingerprints were on the gun.

Cienski, an upright man, proudly wearing his medals, gave evidence that was broadly consistent with the statements made to the police. In his closing address Hastings played on the negligence of the police in not examining the gun for fingerprints, strategically overlooking the fact that there had been no dispute that both men had handled the gun. After a short retirement the jury returned a verdict of not guilty.

On 18 September 1943 Spilsbury wrote a rare letter to his brother Leonard in neutral Sweden, where he and his wife, Mary, were effectively trapped for the duration of the war. Family news was variable. Spilsbury's sister, Gertie, had become mentally ill. Settling into 'a chronic delusional condition', she had been certified, with Spilsbury appointed as her receiver. He was worried about the value of shares in the family trust set up by James Spilsbury. The industrial companies were doing well, but – no doubt with memories of the slump that followed the end of the First World War – Spilsbury thought that 'we ought to sell most of them whilst the going is good' and invest the proceeds in gilt-edged securities.

After his stroke Spilsbury halved his coroners' court appearances. The Exmoor holiday had helped lower his blood pressure, but his hand still tired easily. Nevertheless, Spilsbury hoped 'to write a book giving the fruits of my experience'. He also contemplated setting up a flat at his Hampstead hotel, so that he could move in his furniture and books. He needed his library.

Dick Spilsbury fought in Sicily and Italy, where he was wounded by shrapnel in November 1943. An incompetent surgeon left a needle in his thigh, which prevented him returning to active service. He was flown back to England in January 1944 and, promoted Captain, was sent to Glasgow University, where he instructed army cadets in gunnery.

Spilsbury had given up his title of Honorary Pathologist to the Home Office in 1934. Theoretically he could have given evidence for the defence in English criminal prosecutions at any time thereafter, but appears not to have done so until his appearance in the retrial, in late March 1944, of a celebrated wartime murder case.[22]

Mrs Rose Robinson was the landlady of the John Barleycorn public house in Commercial Road, Portsmouth. By November 1943 she was a widow, probably set in her ways, as she and her late husband had kept the house for some forty years. Although she had the external appearance of a well-preserved woman of 63, she had a heart condition. On the night of 28 November 1943, after closing time, Mrs Robinson cashed up and, as was her unwise custom, put the money – perhaps £400 – in handbags that she took up to her bedroom. She slept alone above the house, a fact that an ill-disposed person could have easily discovered.

The next morning Mrs Robinson's body was found lying on the floor of her bedroom. The room had been ransacked and the wartime blackout blind torn down. An intruder had gained entry through a window at the back of the house. A small black button, like a cuff button, was found nearby, with some thread attached. It was apparent to the police surgeon that Mrs Robinson had been strangled. On 30 November 1943 Dr Keith Simpson, then lecturer in forensic medicine at Guy's Hospital, examined the bedroom and later conducted an autopsy at Portsmouth City Mortuary. Despite her heart condition, Mrs Robinson seemed to have put up some resistance, with evidence of bruising consistent with a stumbling fall and of struggling to free herself from being throttled.

In a report prepared for committal proceedings, Simpson described the signs of manual strangulation, which he regarded having happened 'as from the strong and maintained grip of a R. hand applied from in front'. Simpson noted: 'A single deep bruise as from the application of a thumb . . . a curved scratch characteristic of a finger nail impression. . . . Three rather lighter bruises, as from the opposing pressure of the fingers . . . Two finger nail type scratches . . .'. He concluded that Mrs Robinson had been 'strangled (as part of an attempt to stifle her cries) by a grip from a R. hand by a person sitting or kneeling astride her'. She had died 'some time early in the morning of . . . 29th November . . .'.[23]

Nearly a month later police officers arrested a man for being in 'unlawful possession' (an offence now abolished) of a pair of shoes in Waterloo Road, London. According to the policemen, the man – Harold Loughans, a 47-year-old criminal with an appalling record – began confessing to all sorts of crimes, including a robbery in St Albans and, most surprisingly of all, a murder in Hampshire 'about fourteen days ago'. Loughans was also supposed to have said: 'It's the trapdoor for me now.'[24] Loughans made statements in which he admitted strangling a woman in the course of a robbery. A boot belonging to Loughans carried fibres resembling those in a mat lying beside Mrs Robinson's bed; a feather, similar to feathers in her eiderdown, was found on his coat; and there was evidence that the thread found on the black button was similar to thread on the cuff of his jacket. During committal proceedings at Portsmouth, however, Loughans changed his story, completely denying the murder and robbery.

He was tried at Winchester Assizes before Mr Justice Atkinson. J.D. Casswell KC led for the Crown, and John Maude KC (a man with a very grand manner and accent to match) appeared for the defendant. At the end of the trial, the jury failed to agree a verdict, no doubt impressed by some extraordinary (but apparently bona fide) alibi evidence from four witnesses, who all claimed to have seen Loughans in Warren Street underground station, used as an air-raid shelter, between about midnight and 5.15 a.m. on 29 November 1943. Three of the witnesses identified Loughans in part because of his deformed right hand. Loughans said that at the age of 15 he had lost most of the fingers of his right hand as a result of an industrial accident in a brickyard.

In March 1944 Spilsbury visited Brixton prison. For once he would not be conducting an examination of a recently hanged corpse. His subject, very much alive, was Harold Loughans. Spilsbury examined the prisoner's right hand and arm. Loughans claimed to have got his hand caught in machinery, an accident that had also damaged the muscles of his arm. Apart from the thumb and one finger, there were three stumps left on the hand. These were useless and could be bent in any direction. In Spilsbury's opinion the injury had rendered Loughans incapable of exerting any pressure and even to leave any scratch on the skin. Spilsbury asked Loughans to put his hand around his throat, but the stumps 'scarcely touched the skin'.[25] Loughans, according to Spilsbury, could not have strangled Mrs Robinson.

After the jury's disagreement Atkinson had ordered a retrial, and Loughans appeared before Mr Justice Cassels at the Old Bailey on 27 March 1944. When the defence case opened, the prosecution was taken completely by surprise when Maude, appearing for Loughans, announced: 'I now call my next witness, Sir Bernard Spilsbury.' Keith Simpson recalled how Maude 'declaimed this most dramatically, sounding like a toastmaster announcing the great man's entry'.[26] Spilsbury (now being privately dubbed 'Sir Oracle' in legal circles[27]) described the limp, flabby handshake he had received from Loughans in prison. Casswell made little progress in cross-examination, other than to obtain an admission that Spilsbury had not known that the injury had taken place more than thirty years previously, during which time Loughans could have improved the use of his damaged hand. Spilsbury did not accept that he had been hoodwinked, but Molly Lefebure, who attended the trial as Simpson's secretary, noticed how Loughans placed his right hand on the edge of the dock and 'flapped it about' as Spilsbury gave evidence.[28]

Earlier in the trial Maude had exploited a weakness in Simpson's original autopsy findings that seemed to suggest that a complete right hand had throttled the victim. Simpson attempted to explain the apparent discrepancy by declaring that nail marks could have been caused by the withdrawal of the dead woman's hands as she vainly tried to prise away the murderer's grip. A further weakness in Simpson's evidence was that he had not examined Loughans's hand, but had seen only a plaster cast and photographs, given to him by Detective Sergeant Taylor on 7 January 1944. According to Simpson, the marks on the neck 'could clearly have been caused by the hand', whose dimensions were 'adequate', stumps of the index, middle and little fingers being 'sufficiently long and capable of the stretch necessary to effect the grip'.[29]

Maude cleverly exploited these evidential shortcomings. The alibi evidence remained unshaken, and Loughans was acquitted. During the trial Spilsbury's attitude to his younger competitor showed – at this late stage in his professional life – the characteristics of a deeply jealous and frustrated inner man. Seeing Simpson in one of the corridors of the Old Bailey, Spilsbury remarked tartly, 'I find it difficult to separate fact and opinion in your report', adding magisterially: 'You should keep the two apart.' The dubious roll-call of Spilsbury's own court performances over the years makes this a fine example of the pot calling the kettle black. Simpson tried to explain his findings, but Spilsbury – waving him away – said brusquely: 'No, don't bother me now. I'm involved.' Such rudeness was not typical of the man, and Simpson could see that Spilsbury was unwell, his powers 'beginning to fail . . . nearing the end of his great career'.[30]

After the trial Loughans was immediately re-arrested and later convicted for the robbery in St Albans, during which he had used his supposedly useless right hand to tie a semi-paralysed elderly woman to a chair with wire, almost killing her. He was jailed for five years and later sentenced to ten years' 'preventive detention', a lengthy sentence option for habitual criminals. Many years after Spilsbury's death Loughans contacted a Sunday newspaper and confessed to the murder.

Questions remain about the Loughans case. Discrepancies existed between the two statements made to different police forces. The account allegedly given to the Portsmouth police, who knew about the circumstances of the death, was factually correct, whereas an earlier statement made to the London police, who were not aware of the details, contained inaccuracies. If Loughans had arranged an alibi, this would appear to have involved him driving down to Portsmouth and back to Warren Street between about midnight and 5 a.m. In the blackout only tiny slits of light shone from covered headlights. It seems improbable that such a journey could have taken place, given wartime conditions and the known chronology.

Spilsbury's diary and address book for 1944 survive, recording the life of a desperately lonely man.[31] In addition to commonplace entries, noting meetings and court appearances, there are passages that seem obsessional in their detail.

Spilsbury took a full page to set out the specifications, including engine capacity, tyre size, engine, body and batch numbers, and price of his much-loved Armstrong Siddeley car. Details of fourteen Masonic lodges appear, as well as the names of over one hundred members of the Junior Carlton and eighteen members of the United University Club, many of whom were little more than slight acquaintances. Although Spilsbury saw Evelyn from time to time and Alan worked with him in the laboratory at University College Hospital, his social engagements – apart from Masonic functions and an attendance at a Medico-Legal Society meeting in October – were rare. Among the handful of entries are a concert at the Wigmore Hall in January, lunch with Lord Alness (judge in the Donald Merrett trial – see Chapter Thirteen) in September, and dinner with his solicitor, Ernest Goddard, at the United University Club in October. 'Books to read' included *English Saga* by Anthony (*sic*) Bryant; *Juan in America* by Eric Linklater; *Peace and War* (*sic*) by Tolstoy; and – perhaps most appositely – *Napoleon: The Last Phase* by Lord Rosebery. Spilsbury also wanted to see the American movie, *Crash Dive*.

In March 1944 he had to cancel a dinner of the Sydenham Society in order to travel by train to Liverpool, where he conducted *viva voce* examinations. He also acted as examiner at London University. The year before, Dr David Foster, then a medical student, faced 'an imposing figure, redfaced . . . rather like a Bateman cartoon'. During the *viva* for Foster's final examinations in forensic medicine Spilsbury courteously posed the alarming question: 'What do you know about seminal stains on female underclothing?'[32]

Examining and lecturing at various London hospitals together brought him in a total of £463 18s that year. Most of Spilsbury's time in 1944 was taken up with routine post-mortem evidence at coroners' courts, which earned £1,279 10s. By this time some London coroners were choosing not to use Spilsbury, and an examination of records set out in his diary shows that, out of nearly 200 inquest attendances, most were at Hackney, closely followed by St Pancras, where Bentley Purchase was coroner. Westminster accounted for only seven appearances, the other two being at Pentonville and Wandsworth prisons, probably inquests arising from post-execution autopsies. He also earned a small fee from evidence at a US court martial, held at the American Embassy in Grosvenor Square on 20 October 1944.

Income from his father's trust and other small investments totalled just under £200. His gross total income for the year seems to have been around £3,000, but wartime taxation was high. Spilsbury, with no private medical practice to sustain him and no pension provision from employment, would have lost nearly half his income in tax. Money worries are all too evident from the entries in the diary.

Just before the end of the war, on 6 April 1945, Spilsbury, holidaying with Alan at the Luttrell Arms, wrote again to his brother Leonard. Evelyn had been released from ambulance driving. 'I do admire these girls who carried on for a very sticky time', wrote Spilsbury, '& were gay and gallant through it all.' Gertie, on the other hand, was 'a confirmed case of delusional insanity', confined to the Mead Home in Hayes, Middlesex.

A further slight stroke, probably during 1944, caused Spilsbury to give up examining students. Although he had reduced his coroners' work by half, the severe winter conditions of 1944–5 were 'very trying' and 'almost put me out'. He suffered from arthritis, and, with the effects of the strokes, autopsies were becoming physically distressing. Although he now tired easily, Spilsbury was determined to complete a card index of 'all my cases of medico-legal interest' – about 20,000 of them – with a view to writing a book. 'I have such wonderful material,' he wrote wistfully to his brother. 'I want it down if possible before I finish.'[33]

TWENTY-THREE

Last Years

Spilsbury's bleak little laboratory in the Department of Pharmacology was accommodated on the second floor of a three-storey block, with a single window overlooking an internal courtyard at University College Hospital. Boxes of slides and drawers filled with case cards stood on grimy tables. A wicker wastepaper basket, microscope, glass flasks and pipettes, a cabinet refrigerator, sink, an aluminium kettle, a battered wooden chair, gas taps and a Bunsen burner – all these constituted a gloomy *mélange* seemingly unrelieved by any personal touches. In the last few months of the war Alan Spilsbury worked at the laboratory five, sometimes six, mornings each week. The entries in his pocket diary, written in a small, neat hand, suggest a deeply introspective, socially inverted, personality, the most damaged of Spilsbury's 'moody and displaced'[1] children.

Alan evidently lived by routine, visiting his mother in St Albans most weekends, occasionally seeing Evelyn and Dick, with whom he once went to a concert at the National Gallery. The bathetic flavour of Alan's diary appears in the entry for 8 May 1945, a great day for the nation: '8 Tues Lab. morn. VE day. Collect trousers Willesden valet (on Friday).' Apart from an enigmatic reference to 'Pte. Cooke, 827, R.A.M.C. (5Th Battalion)' and occasional mention of the much-loved 'Nan', Emily Elvy, who had looked after the Spilsbury children in the 1920s, Alan appears to have had no social life beyond his immediate family circle.[2]

'Like Noël Coward and the Duke of Windsor, Spilsbury did not fit comfortably into the world left by Hitler's war,' wrote Richard Gordon in an amusing and perceptive essay.[3] Spilsbury was now forced, by increasing disability, to reduce his punishing work schedule. In 1945, accompanied by Alan, he took two holidays in Dunster, travelling there and back by train. Spilsbury's driving was becoming increasingly erratic. That year he collided with a pony cart at Odiham, Hampshire, and was fined £10 for dangerous driving.

Dick Spilsbury had been anxious to leave the army and resume his studies at Oxford. 'He has developed into a fine man,' wrote Spilsbury to his brother Leonard; '. . . I am desperately anxious to see Dick through the rest of his Oxford career – he wants another two years up there to get a good degree.'[4] On 10 November 1945 the army made a decision to release Dick Spilsbury 'in order to return to work of national importance as directed by the Ministry of Labour and National Service',[5] which meant, in effect, that he was free to return to Oxford early the following month. The news may have prompted modest celebrations in this rather dysfunctional family unit. Alan's diary records that, on 15 November, he had lunch with Spilsbury ('F') and Dick, followed by dinner with his mother ('M') and Dick.

Delight was shortlived. The last entry in Alan's diary, dated 19 November 1945, is yet another reference to dry cleaning: 'Sketchley (overcoat and pullover)'. Eight days later he died in St Andrew's Hospital, Dollis Hill. Although Spilsbury had described his eldest son as 'fit & well' in early April,[6] Alan had developed a virulent form of tuberculosis, phthisis (sometimes called 'galloping consumption'), virtually incurable at the time. For the second time in five years Edith Spilsbury had to alter her will. In October 1940 her son Peter had been replaced as executor by Dick, and now Alan, the chief beneficiary, had also died. The estate would now be divided between Dick and Evelyn, with 'Nan' receiving a small legacy. There was no provision for her estranged husband.

Towards the end of 1946 Spilsbury advised a medical colleague, Dr Charles Robert Gibson, in relation to a murder charge brought against a Bristol woman, Mrs Rosina Cornock, then aged 34, whose husband, Cecil, also 34, had been found dead in the bath, suffering from multiple injuries and with indications of masochistic bondage.[7] Mr Cornock was also a transvestite, who, among other sexual practices, insisted that his wife should beat him. He took pleasure in being tied up by the wrists and ankles, often while wearing a woman's dress and spreadeagled over the hot water boiler in the kitchen of their home, 142 Wellington Hill West, Henleaze, a detached and unremarkable-looking 1920s house in suburban Bristol.

Mrs Cornock had formed a friendship with a disabled man, Gilbert ('Gil') Bedford, ten years her junior. Bedford, who had been badly affected by osteomyelitis as a child, walked only with the aid of sticks. Although Bedford denied having sexual relations with any woman, Mrs Cornock was two months' pregnant at the time of her husband's death and told the police that she had not lived 'normally' with her husband for some years. The prosecution alleged that Cornock, after being tied up and possibly struck on the head with a heavy toy boat, was pushed under the water and drowned. Police photographs appeared to confirm severe bruising to the head, but sections, microscopically examined, showed little bruising. Gibson thought that the injuries were less serious than the Crown was alleging and that the marks could have been caused when Mrs Cornock and Bedford had dragged Cornock from the bath, pulled his body into a bedroom and attempted to revive him. Gibson, who had been advised by Spilsbury on an earlier occasion, approached the great pathologist for help.

Spilsbury's last contribution to discussion at the Medico-Legal Society, in October 1944, had been on the subject of 'Death in the Bathroom', a paper given by his friend Dr Eric Gardner.[8] On 5 February 1947 Gibson met the ailing pathologist at his laboratory. 'I was rather struck', he recalled, 'with the toll which the past ten years had taken . . . he looked considerably older than his years.' Mentally, however, Spilsbury seemed alert and 'his grasp of a . . . complicated story was completely sure'.[9] After reviewing notes of evidence given at committal proceedings and photographs of the body, and examining slides, Spilsbury endorsed Gibson's opinion, although his conclusion was necessarily second-hand with regard to the physical appearance of the injuries. The photographs, it was claimed, had darkened the areas of injury, which, in Spilsbury's opinion, were 'abrasions' rather than bruising, the appearance of much darker areas.

Spilsbury felt too frail to give evidence in Bristol, but on the last morning of the trial – possibly on information fed by Mrs Cornock's solicitor – the *Daily Mail* headlined 'Spilsbury Advises the Defence', a powerful endorsement that may have helped secure Mrs Cornock's acquittal.[10]

In July 1947 Spilsbury gave evidence at the Old Bailey for the last time. Christopher Geraghty and Charles Jenkins, both in their early twenties, and 17-year-old Terence Rolt had been indicted for the murder of Alec de Antiquis on 28 April 1947.[11] The criminal scenario foreshadowed the plot of *The Blue Lamp*, a film made three years later, in which Dirk Bogarde played the young hoodlum who gunned down 'PC George Dixon' (Jack Warner) to secure his get-away from an armed robbery. Alec de Antiquis was not a policeman, however, but a courageous passer-by. The gang of three robbers, faces masked with handkerchiefs, had burst into Jay's jewellery shop 'next to a bomb site'[12] north-west of the junction of Charlotte Street and Tottenham Street, not far from where Louis Voisin had lived in 1917 (see Chapter Six).

The men were armed, but the raid was amateurishly conducted. Although the manager, Albert Stock, was pistol-whipped and a shot was fired at his 17-year-old assistant, who threw a stool at the intruders, they fled from the shop with no more than a silver cakestand, which was dropped in the street. Pursued by a heavily bleeding Mr Stock, the trio of robbers made for their car, parked nearby. Had the raid been better planned, a wheelman would have been in position, with the engine running. As it was, the car refused to start, a lorry blocked their way and the gang jumped out.

Alec de Antiquis, 36, was a short, handsome man, with a dark moustache, the great-grandson of Italian immigrants. Married with six children, he worked in a motor-cycle repair shop in Collier's Wood and, that afternoon, was riding his motor-bike on a business errand, carrying a spare wheel. Three weeks earlier he had courageously entered a burning house in Croydon where it was believed a child had been trapped. When someone shouted 'Stop them', de

Antiquis responded by pursuing the raiders, one of whom turned and shot him through the left side of his forehead. He died a few minutes later, lying in the street beside his fallen motor-bike.

The case aroused strong public indignation, already inflamed by press reports of a post-war crime wave. Acting Superintendent Robert Fabian ('Fabian of the Yard', inspiration for a popular TV crime series in the 1950s) led the 'biggest police dragnet' for some years.[13] The *Daily Mail* launched an appeal for the de Antiquis dependants, raising nearly £6,000, including the proceeds of a special matinée of the play *Power without Glory* at the Fortune Theatre.

Spilsbury conducted the post-mortem on the body of Alec de Antiquis in the presence of Robert Fabian. The great pathologist, 'whose sureness of hand and decisive perception had become legendary',[14] was seen to be fumbling. Spilsbury was puzzled because he could not find the exit wound of the fatal bullet, which was still in the skull. As Spilsbury lifted the dead man's head, the bullet fell out onto the floor of the mortuary, but – as Fabian could see – he had not noticed that this had happened. Tactfully, Fabian picked up the bullet and made out that Spilsbury had found it himself.

The murder trial was also the last appearance of the well-tried partnership of Spilsbury and Robert Churchill. Spilsbury's performance in court was well below par. In contrast with the confident and detailed evidence given in earlier firearms cases, his answers were vague. According to the judge's note, Spilsbury admitted in cross-examination: 'I don't know what type of powder was used. Couldn't really say from what distance fired.'[15]

All three were found guilty of murder. Rolt, at 17, was too young to be hanged. Geraghty's former teacher petitioned the Home Office for reprieve, describing him improbably as 'a conscientious, quiet lad, a delight to have in the school and never any trouble in any way'.[16] Although Jenkins was officially regarded as 'the leader of this gang of desperadoes', both young men were hanged at Pentonville on 19 September 1947.

Spilsbury was nearing the end. In 1946, Bentley Purchase had been disturbed to find that Spilsbury had accidentally written out duplicate reports on a post-mortem. Arthritis had affected his hands, which in turn made writing painful and slowed his autopsy work. As a result of the strokes he had suffered, his gait was affected, and he walked slowly and with difficulty. At one stage he had fallen off a chair in the mortuary and had to be picked up, almost in a state of collapse. He was unable to keep up the working pace of earlier years, but still relied on coroner's work for most of his diminishing income. Sometimes he would put his head round the door of the office at St Pancras: 'Anything for me?' he would ask.[17]

He had now seen Dick through Oxford, proud that his youngest son had gained first-class honours in PPE and had been appointed lecturer in philosophy at the University College of Wales in Aberystwyth. By December 1947 Spilsbury's stock of post-mortem forms was beginning to run out. He did not order any replacements. Dr Philip Willcox's sister met Spilsbury in the street. 'How are you?' she asked him. 'I'm finished,' he replied wearily.[18] Dr Gardner was on holiday in Switzerland when he received a letter from Spilsbury telling him – in a rare personal confidence – that 'it will all be over' by the time Gardner read the lines.[19]

Two days later, on 17 December 1947, hotel staff at the Langorf noticed nothing unusual as Spilsbury left for work. 'He was his usual cheery self,' said one.[20] Spilsbury collected his Armstrong Siddeley from a garage in Finchley Road, where it was kept, and drove to Hampstead mortuary, where he performed a post-mortem on the wife of a naval commander who had died during an operation. Back at the hotel, the manageress noticed that he had left his front door key on the dressing-table. He returned briefly that afternoon, but did not pick up his key.

Returning his car to the garage, he gave Christmas gratuities to the staff, telling them that he would not be using the car again before the holiday. Late in the afternoon he travelled down to his laboratory in Gower Street. After Alan's death he had allowed no one to touch the room and, although hospital staff knew that Spilsbury frequently visited his laboratory in the evening, it was 'to potter about' and – in contrast with the earlier years of glory – 'nobody knew what he was doing'.[21] Spilsbury tidied up his laboratory and destroyed papers, including a wedding photograph of Evelyn Spilsbury and John Steel on that seemingly happy occasion in 1934. He then had an early dinner at the Junior Carlton Club, returning his locker key to the hall porter.

Spilsbury was back at Gower Street by 7.30 p.m. He carefully hung up his hat and coat; then, sitting on the cheap, battered wooden chair, he turned on the gas tap that fed the Bunsen burner standing on the tiled work surface alongside the laboratory sink. Forty minutes later a hospital technician, passing by the laboratory door, smelt gas and noticed that a light was on inside the room. He knocked, but there was no answer. The door was locked. The technician ran to find the hospital watchman, who opened the door with a pass key. They found Spilsbury lying on the floor, as if he had fallen from his chair. A faint pulse was detectable, and, loosening his collar and tie, the men attempted artificial respiration. Dr Ralph Wilsdon, Resident Medical Officer at the hospital, pronounced Spilsbury dead at 9.10 p.m. Bentley Purchase, summoned urgently to the scene, was too late.

Spilsbury, who had carried out so many autopsies over his forty-year career, was now the subject of his own post-mortem, conducted by Dr R.H.D. Short, pathologist at University College Hospital, supervised by Professor Sir Roy Cameron. Short concluded that Spilsbury had died from 'coal-gas poisoning and severe coronary atheroma'.[22] At the inquest, held at St Pancras Coroner's Court on 20 December 1947, Evelyn and Dick, his surviving children, gave evidence that their father had complained of very poor health. Although Spilsbury had not left a note, Dr Gardner had already been in touch with Bentley Purchase, who was 'close to tears' when he pronounced a verdict of suicide. 'It is my reluctant impression', said Purchase, '. . . that Sir Bernard realized that his professional life, and possibly his other life, was drawing to a close and that he had taken his life. The Sir Bernard who had done that was not the Sir Bernard who had made the reputation which he justly held . . . his mind was not as it used to be.'[23]

Spilsbury's body was cremated at Golder's Green Crematorium on Monday 22 December 1947. Just twenty-two mourners attended, including eight people sitting in the family pew. Robert Churchill at first thought that he had come to the wrong funeral. 'The few of us sitting in the back', he later recalled, 'made a very poor show.'[24] There were no flowers. There was no memorial service.

The full story behind Spilsbury's suicide may never be known. The inquest file has been destroyed,[25] and efforts to trace the letter he wrote to Eric Gardner have been unsuccessful. Plainly, declining health was a significant factor, but – as is clear from his 1944 diary – worries about money also preyed on his mind. His lonely existence in a private hotel, separated from his wife, two sons dead, and no likelihood of grandchildren, must all have contributed to his severe depression. Spilsbury, increasingly forgetful, may also have suspected that he was developing the senile dementia better known nowadays as Alzheimer's disease. Over the years a story has circulated alleging that Spilsbury committed suicide because he had been discovered lying on top of a female corpse in the hospital mortuary.[26] Although the tale has been popular among lawyers and medical students, this scurrilous rumour has never been confirmed.

The way in which Spilsbury chose to end his life was curious, given that he had extensive experience of suicide cases, medical knowledge and access to pharmaceutical supplies. He could have obtained barbiturates, or other toxic substances, or even sat in his Armstrong Siddeley car with the engine running while carbon monoxide was introduced by means of a hose attached to the exhaust pipe. Yet, in what seems to have been a well-planned exercise, he turned on the tap of his Bunsen burner, filling his laboratory with a potentially explosive quantity of coal gas. He would not have known how long it would be before someone raised the alarm. People were used to him staying at his workplace until late into the night, and there was no particular reason for anyone to have visited his laboratory that evening. Spilsbury's suicide can be seen as a nihilistic exercise, which could have caused a major explosion at University College Hospital, with possible loss of life.

Such thoughts seem not to have troubled his obituary writers. *The Lancet* wrote of a man who 'for thirty years stood alone and unchallenged as our outstanding medico-legal expert . . . [with] a flair for simple exposition', providing 'a pillar of security in the medical evidence for Crown prosecutions'.

The obituarist had to concede, however, that Spilsbury was 'aloof . . . retiring and outwardly frigid . . . disliked visits from strangers and seemed somewhat distant to casual professional acquaintances . . . a lonely man'.[27] The *British Medical Journal* commented that Spilsbury 'was a witness after the judge's heart . . . always sure of his case and speaking with unmistakable authority'.[28] The *University College Hospital Magazine* noted that Spilsbury 'had put forensic science in the witness box on its own separate importance and not as being ancillary to anything else'. In his appointment as the 'only Honorary Pathologist (the post was invented for him), the Home Office singled him out rightly from all others'. The writer, who had known Spilsbury for over a quarter of a century, recalled that, 'as a witness, he was incomparable', but was also painfully aware that, 'with the passing of the years, his delivery deteriorated'.[29]

In his simple will, dated 26 June 1922, Spilsbury left all his real and personal estate to his wife, Edith. Probate, granted on 25 March 1948, revealed a relatively modest estate of £9,932 4s 10d. After the war Edith returned to Hampstead, living latterly at 24 Lyndhurst Road. She died on 16 December 1962. Spilsbury's sister Gertie, confined to a home in Middlesex at the time of his death, lived on until the same year. Evelyn, whose unhappy marriage was childless, died in 1967. Leonard Spilsbury, a civil engineer, was awarded the Military Cross in 1918. He died in Stockholm in 1948. His wife, Mary, lived until 2002.

Dick – when asked whether he had any connection with Sir Bernard Spilsbury – would only admit to being 'vaguely related'.[30] Although he retained some photographs of Spilsbury and two letters written by him, and gave some information to the authors of the 1951 biography, he did not have a copy of the book. He seems to have resented Spilsbury's treatment of his mother in relation to the Hilda Bainbridge episode and was unhappy that his father's evidence had helped hang so many people, with the possibility of wrongful convictions.[31] Like his father, Dick suffered from severe depression. On 5 July 1984 he drowned while swimming in the sea off Hastings.

In the assessment of Spilsbury's legacy it must be remembered, above all, that 'he secured a hearing for the forensic pathologist in his difficult speciality',[32] bringing forensic medicine out of its nineteenth-century shadows. As Spilsbury himself acknowledged,[33] 'one of the great difficulties . . . is that of putting . . . evidence into such language that . . . is easily understood by the uneducated layman . . . without a sacrifice of accuracy'. He, most of all his contemporaries, was aware that, 'when medical witnesses use only technical language . . . juries do not appreciate the points sought to be made'.[34]

During his professional lifetime Spilsbury appeared for the Crown in 'nearly two hundred trials for murder', of which 'only a handful ended in an acquittal'.[35] His power as a witness to win over judge and jury to his opinions derived, in his own words, from 'an absolute certainty in his facts and a quiet competence in the witness-box'. Spilsbury's capacity for hard work was legendary. 'Often for weeks on end,' wrote Dr Roche Lynch, 'he would work most of the night, snatching only a few hours' sleep.'[36] Yet, in the light of his modest academic achievements, this hard grind suggests that Spilsbury was perpetually looking over his shoulder, obsessively concerned to keep ahead of possible rivals, concerns that became even more acute from the mid-1930s as he aged visibly and younger pathologists entered the race.

Another corollary of this intensive application was the growth of a belief that, as he had done all that was humanly possible to solve a forensic problem, he must have the right answer. This attitude was a short step from the 'Jehovah complex' noticed by some contemporaries[37] and that notorious obstinacy in defending his opinions. Spilsbury promoted the dangerous fallacy that forensic pathology is 'an absolute science, capable of absolute proof', putting forward 'old beliefs in accurate estimation of time of death, the value of *rigor*, the reliability of chemical changes' and encouraging a belief that 'forensic problems are capable of instant diagnosis at the scene or in the mortuary'.[38]

The desire for simple answers to complex questions still besets scientific evidence. On many occasions in his long career Spilsbury may well have been correct in his diagnoses and opinions. Sometimes he was palpably wrong, advancing flawed conclusions with consequences that could – quite literally – be lethal.

'One might almost hope', wrote his great contemporary, Professor Sir Sydney Smith, 'that there will never be another Bernard Spilsbury.'[39]

Notes

Abbreviations

B&T   D. Browne and E.V. Tullett, *Bernard Spilsbury: His Life and Cases* (Harrap, 1951; published in the USA as *The Scalpel of Scotland Yard*)
CC   Spilsbury's Case Cards (followed by the name of the post-mortem subject)
FT   Famous Trials (followed by the name of the defendant)
MH   M. Hastings, *The Other Mr Churchill* (Harrap, 1963)
M-LS   Medico-Legal Society
NBT   Notable British Trials (followed by the name of the defendant)
PW   P.H.A. Willcox, *The Detective-Physician: The Life and Work of Sir William Willcox* (Heinemann, 1970)
TNA: PRO   The National Archives: Public Records Office
    ADM   Admiralty
    AIR   Air Ministry
    CRIM   Central Criminal Court
    DPP   Director of Public Prosecutions
    HO   Home Office
    MEPO   Metropolitan Police
    PCOM   Prison Commissioners

Introduction

1. TNA: PRO PCOM 8/94.
2. Information from Museum of Net Manufacture, Loders, Dorset.
3. TNA: PRO HO 144/4100.
4. TNA: PRO PCOM 8/94.
5. Information from Curator, Metropolitan Police Crime Museum.
6. *News of the World*, 7 September 1924.
7. TNA: PRO PCOM 9/470.
8. M-LS, 'Cases of Judicial Hanging', *Transactions* (1925).
9. CC Herbert Patrick Mahon.
10. *News of the World*, 7 September 1924.
11. *Manchester Guardian*, 4 September 1924.
12. *News of the World*, 7 September 1924.
13. TNA: PRO HO 144/4100.
14. *Ibid.*
15. 27 December 1947.
16. See M-LS, *Medico-Legal Journal* (1948), p. 14; B&T, p. 29.
17. 'Sir Bernard Spilsbury', *Dictionary of National Biography*.
18. Quoted in B&T, p. 146.
19. Quoted in *ibid.*, p. 362.
20. *Ibid.*, p. 207.
21. R. Gordon, 'Doctor Death', in *Great Medical Disasters* (Hutchinson, 1983), p. 87.
22. Professor Sir Sydney Smith, *Mostly Murder* (Harrap, 1959), p. 144.
23. Keith Simpson, *Forty Years of Murder* (Harrap, 1978), p. 26.

24. See R. and M. Whittington-Egan, *The Death Doctors*, in *The Bedside Book of Murder* (David & Charles, 1988).
25. *The Lancet*, 27 December 1947.
26. B&T, p. 409.
27. Personal information from Lord Hutchinson QC.

Chapter One

1. P.H. Reeney and R.M. Wilson, *Dictionary of British Surnames* (2nd edn, 1976), p. 329.
2. Personal information from Chris King and Andrew Baker, Stafford.
3. See Henry Spilsbury's will, proved 4 April 1888, Probate Registry.
4. Anon., *The Trial of William Palmer* (Ward Lock & Co., 1856), *passim*.
5. R. Graves, *They Hanged My Saintly Billy* (Cassell, 1957), p. 100.
6. *The Lancet*, 17 September 1859.
7. Photograph in Local Collection, Leamington Public Library.
8. Anon., *Leamington Past & Present* (D. Sarney, 1884).
9. Advertisement in *Leamington Spa Courier* (April 1884).
10. *University College School Register* (1937).
11. B&T, p. 20.
12. Manchester Grammar School archives.
13. Magdalen College, Oxford, archives, P2 33/2/C3/1, fo. 31.
14. *Ibid.*, fo. 33.
15. *Ibid.*, fo. 50.
16. *Ibid.*, fo. 95.
17. B&T, p. 22.
18. Magdalen College, Oxford, archives, P2 33/2/C3/1, fo. 111
19. *Ibid.*, fo. 125.
20. *Ibid.*, fo. 142.
21. *Ibid.*, fo. 57.

Chapter Two

1. St Mary's Hospital Archives, MS/AD28/334.
2. *British Medical Journal*, 28 December 1935.
3. *Ibid.*, appreciation by Sir William Willcox.
4. B&T, p. 24.
5. *St Mary's Hospital Gazette* (January 1906).
6. See M. Dunnill, *The Plato of Praed Street* (Royal Society of Medicine Press Ltd, 2000).
7. *St Mary's Hospital Gazette* (October 1901).
8. *Oxford English Dictionary* (Oxford: Clarendon Press, 1977).
9. *The Times*, 19–23 June 1903.
10. Information from Kevin Brown, Archivist, St Mary's Hospital.
11. Information from Mrs Elspeth Griffiths, Archivist, Sedbergh School (Spilsbury applied at the same time as Mr Willan Batty (b. 1884), whose application was also rejected).
12. *The Times*, 12 October 1904.
13. A. Lieck, *Bow Street World* (Robert Hale, 1938), p. 107.
14. *The Lancet*, 28 December 1935.
15. *Ibid.*
16. M-LS, *Transactions* (1908), pp. 81 ff.
17. *Ibid.*
18. M-LS, *Transactions* (1909), pp. 239–41.
19. PW, pp. 16–19; *The Times*, 12 October 1909.
20. *The Times*, 12 October 1909.

Chapter Three

1. NBT Crippen *passim*.
2. TNA: PRO HO 144/1719/195482.
3. NBT Crippen, p. 14.
4. PW, pp. 25–6.
5. *Ibid.*, p. 26.
6. NBT Crippen, p. 62.
7. *Ibid.*, p. 15.
8. TNA: PRO DPP 1/13.
9. *Ibid.*
10. PW, p. 26.
11. S.T. Felstead, *Sir Richard Muir* (Bodley Head, 1927), p. 5.
12. *Ibid.*, p. 15.

13. A. Rose, *Stinie: Murder on the Common* (Bodley Head, 1985), p. 54.
14. Sir C. Biron, *Without Prejudice* (Faber, 1936), p. 118.
15. Lieck, *Bow Street World*, p. 60.
16. TNA: PRO DPP 1/13.
17. T. Humphreys, *A Book of Trials* (Heinemann, 1953), p. 63.
18. *Daily Mirror*, 17 September 1910.
19. *Ibid.*
20. NBT Crippen, p. 54.
21. *Ibid.*, p. 49.
22. *Ibid.*, p. 65.
23. *Ibid.*, p. 67.
24. *Ibid.*, p. 54.
25. Quotations from Spilsbury's trial evidence are from NBT Crippen, pp. 62–4.
26. Felstead, *Sir Richard Muir*, p. 84.
27. Undated extract in Metropolitan Police Crime Museum collection.
28. TNA: PRO HO 144/1719/195492.
29. Royal London Hospital archives.

Chapter Four

1. TNA: PRO DPP 1/13.
2. PW, p. 15.
3. NBT Seddon, *passim*; MEPO 3/215.
4. G. and W. Grossmith, *The Diary of a Nobody* (Penguin Modern Classics, 1965), p. 19.
5. Hon. E. Marjoribanks, *The Life of Sir Edward Marshall Hall* (Gollancz, 1929), p. 292.
6. NBT Seddon, pp. 89–91.
7. PW, p. 44.
8. Marjoribanks, *The Life of Sir Edward Marshall Hall*, p. 22.
9. *Ibid.*, pp. 94–5.
10. Quotations from Spilsbury's trial evidence, NBT Seddon, pp. 101–8.
11. PW, p. 45.
12. NBT Seddon, p. 411.
13. L. Colebrook, *Almroth Wright* (Heinemann, 1954).
14. M-LS, *Transactions* (1909) (paper delivered on 16 February 1909).
15. M-LS, *Transactions* (1927).
16. *The Times*, 25 January 1913.
17. St Mary's Hospital Archives (Medical Society meeting, 9 October 1912).
18. M-LS, *Transactions* (1919), pp. 38–58.
19. *Ibid.*, pp. 54–6.

Chapter Five

1. Information from Mrs Joy Cotton.
2. TNA: PRO CRIM 1/139/6.
3. *Ibid.*; see also *Daily Graphic*, 26 April 1913.
4. MH, pp. 58–62.
5. TNA: PRO CRIM 1/139/6.
6. *Ibid.*
7. Hon. E. Marjoribanks, quoted in A. Rose, *Scandal at the Savoy* (Bloomsbury, 1991), p. 96.
8. NBT Smith, *passim*.
9. *Ibid.*, p. 185.
10. PW, p. 98; NBT Smith, p. 196.
11. NBT Smith, p. 117.
12. M-LS, *Transactions* (1922) (paper read by Eric R. Watson, 30 May 1922).
13. *Ibid.*, contribution of Montague Shearman, junior counsel for Smith.
14. B&T, p. 77.
15. *Daily Express*, 19 March 1930, *The Talk of London* (probably by Tom Driberg).
16. Quoted in PW, pp. 105–7.
17. *Ibid.*, p. 101.
18. TNA: PRO MEPO 3/225B.
19. Unidentified newspaper cutting.
20. A.F. Neil, *Forty Years of Manhunting* (Jarrold, 1932).
21. M-LS, *Transactions* (1922) (paper read by Eric R. Watson, 30 May 1922).
22. M-LS, *Medico-Legal Review* (1942), pp. 130–3.
23. Quotations of Spilsbury's trial evidence are taken from NBT Smith, pp. 204–9, 212–38.
24. M-LS, *Transactions* (1922) (paper read by Eric R. Watson, 30 May 1922).
25. Marjoribanks, *The Life of Sir Edward Marshall Hall*, p. 345.
26. PW, p. 105.

Chapter Six

1. TNA: PRO CRIM 1/166.
2. *Ibid.*
3. D. Malcolm, *Family Secrets* (Hutchinson, 2003), *passim*; TNA: PRO CRIM 1/168/5.
4. *The Times*, 11 September 1917.
5. *Ibid.*
6. *Punch*, vol. 21 (1851), p. 205.
7. *The Times*, 11 September 1917.
8. *Ibid.*, 12 September 1917.
9. *Ibid.*; see also *Daily Graphic*, 12 September 1917.
10. *The Times*, 1 November 1917.
11. P. Hamilton, *Twenty Thousand Streets under the Sky* (Vintage, 2004).
12. TNA: PRO HO 144/2183.
13. F. Wensley, *Detective Days* (Cassell, 1931).
14. Rose, *Stinie*.
15. TNA: PRO HO 144/2183.
16. CC Émilienne Gerard.
17. TNA: PRO HO 144/2183.
18. TNA: PRO DPP 1/49.
19. *Ibid.*
20. CC Émilienne Gerard.
21. Felstead, *Sir Richard Muir*, pp. 330–1; B&T, pp. 102–4.
22. *The Times*, 26 October 1897.
23. Rose, *Stinie*, pp. 68–9.
24. Felstead, *Sir Richard Muir*, p. 331.
25. Quotations from Spilsbury's trial evidence are from TNA: PRO HO 144/2183.
26. Medical information from Professor Bernard Knight.
27. TNA: PRO HO 144/2183.
28. *Ibid.*
29. *The Times*, 2 March 1918.
30. E. Robey, *The Jester and the Court* (William Kimber, 1976).
31. *Cosmopolitan*, undated; see TNA: PRO HO 144/2183.
32. B&T, p. 104.
33. TNA: PRO HO 144/2183.
34. *Ibid.*
35. B&T, p. 99.
36. TNA: PRO HO 144/2183.
37. *Ibid.*

Chapter Seven

1. TNA: PRO HO 144/17537–17539, opened to public inspection on 3 February 2005.
2. TNA: PRO CRIM 1/174/5.
3. TNA: PRO HO 144/17537, report of Sir Ernley Blackwell.
4. TNA: PRO HO 144/17527 [Part Two], transcript of David Greenwood's trial.
5. *Ibid.*
6. *Ibid.*
7. H.R. Oswald, *Memoirs of a London County Coroner* (Stanley Paul, 1936).
8. TNA: PRO HO 144/17537.
9. CC Nellie Grace Trew.
10. *Ibid.* [Part Two], transcript.
11. *Ibid.*, report of CI Francis Carlin, 2 May 1918.
12. Oswald, *Memoirs of a London County Coroner*.
13. TNA: PRO HO 144/17538, Statement of David Greenwood, 14 February 1918.
14. F. Carlin, *Reminiscences of an Ex-Detective* (Hutchinson, 1927), *passim*.
15. TNA: PRO HO 144/17537, petition for reprieve 1918.
16. *Ibid.*, transcript.
17. Quotations from G. Lewis, *Lord Atkin* (Butterworth 1983), which does not make reference to the Greenwood case.
18. *Dictionary of National Biography*.
19. Quotations of trial evidence taken from TNA: PRO HO 144/17537 [Part Two], Transcript.
20. Medical information from Professor Bernard Knight.
21. Quoted by Professor Michael Green, *Is Sir Bernard Spilsbury Dead?*, in A.R. Brownlie, *Crime Investigation* (Scottish Academic Press, 1984).
22. Rose, *Stinie*, p. 139.
23. B. Inglis, *Roger Casement* (Coronet Paperback, 1974).
24. TNA: PRO HO 144/17537.
25. *Ibid.*
26. *Ibid.*
27. *Ibid.*
28. *St Mary's Hospital Gazette* (April 1901).

29. The account of Lytton's history until 1922 derives from TNA: PRO HO 144/17538.
30. TNA: PRO HO 144/17537.
31. A. Rose, *Scandal at the Savoy* (Bloomsbury 1991), pp. 71–2.
32. Letter to author from North Dorset NHS Primary Care Trust, 27 February 2006.
33. TNA: PRO HO 144/17538.
34. Letter to the author from North Dorset NHS Primary Care Trust, 12 April 2006.
35. TNA: PRO HO 144/17537.
36. *Ibid*.
37. *Ibid*.
38. *Daily Express*, 10 April 1933.
39. *Manchester Guardian*, 2 November 1929.

Chapter Eight

1. See MH, pp. 89–90 and *passim*; B&T, pp. 110–12; TNA: PRO DPP 1/54.
2. TNA: PRO DPP 1/54.
3. *Ibid*.; *The Times*, 19 April 1919.
4. E.S. Fay, *The Life of Mr Justice Swift* (Methuen, 1939), pp. 37–46.
5. St Mary's Hospital Archives, Medical Committee Minutes 1919.
6. *The Times*, 29 October 1921.
7. Information from Mrs Joy Cotton.
8. Our Society, Rule Book 2004.
9. *Ibid*.
10. TNA: PRO MEPO 3/1015.
11. *Ibid*.
12. *The Times*, 14 September 1921.
13. *Ibid*., 15 September 1921.
14. *Ibid*.
15. B&T, p. 120.
16. TNA: PRO MEPO 3/1015.

Chapter Nine

1. *The Times*, 3 March 1922.
2. *Ibid*., 4 March 1922.
3. TNA: PRO HO 144/1754/425994.
4. R. Odell, *Exhumation of a Murder* (Harrap, 1975), *passim*; see also NBT

Armstrong, and M. Beales, *Dead not Buried* (Hale, 1995).
5. TNA: PRO HO 144/1754/425994, Report of Dr J.A. Bell.
6. NBT Armstrong, pp. 77–8.
7. *Ibid*., p. 78.
8. J.M. Bruce and W.J. Dilling, *Materia Medica and Therapeutica* (Cassell, 1921), p. 134.
9. NBT Armstrong, p. 49.
10. Odell, *Exhumation of a Murder*, p. 32.
11. TNA: PRO HO 144/1754/425994.
12. PW, p. 175.
13. TNA: PRO DPP 1/63 [Part Two].
14. CC Katharine Armstrong; see generally for details of post-mortem.
15. Information from the late Dr P.H.A. Willcox.
16. Odell, *Exhumation of a Murder*, p. 115.
17. S. Curtis-Bennett, *The Curtis-Bennett Chronicle* (Phillimore, 1998).
18. Quotations from trial proceedings are from TNA: PRO DPP 1/63 [Part One] and NBT Armstrong.
19. Medical information from Professor Bernard Knight.
20. *The Times*, 17 April 1922.

Chapter Ten

1. *Birmingham Post*, 21 April 1922.
2. *British Medical Journal*, 27 December 1947.
3. TNA: PRO HO 144/3689 *passim*; TNA: PRO MEPO 38/125.
4. *Daily Express*, 29 June 1922; *The Times*, 3 July 1922.
5. *Evening News*, 1 July 1922.
6. S. Ingleby Oddie, *Inquest* (Hutchinson, 1941) p. 154.
7. CC Sir Henry Wilson.
8. B&T, pp. 118–19.
9. TNA: PRO MEPO 38/125.
10. *Ibid*.
11. *The Times*, 19 July 1922.
12. TNA: PRO HO 144/3689.

13. R. Weis, *Criminal Justice* (Hamish Hamilton, 1988), *passim*, and NBT Bywaters and Thompson.
14. Wensley, *Detective Days*.
15. E. Grice, *Great Cases of Sir Henry Curtis-Bennett* (Hutchinson, 1937), p. 46.
16. TNA: PRO HO 144/2685, transcript, p. 115.
17. TNA: PRO DPP 1/70.
18. See E. Lustgarten, *The Murder and the Trial* (Odhams, 1960), and *Verdict in Dispute* (Wingate, 1949).
19. Weis, *Criminal Justice*, p. 215.
20. B&T, pp. 267–8.
21. *Daily Telegraph*, 22 June 1951.
22. B&T, p. 196.
23. *The Times*, 16 February 1923.
24. M-LS Transactions (1924).
25. TNA: PRO HO 144/15934–5 *passim*; TNA: PRO PCOM 8/386, and see W.L. Woodland, *Assize Pageant* (Harrap, 1952).
26. *The Times*, 23 September 1923.
27. *Ibid.*, 10 October 1923.
28. TNA: PRO HO 144/15935.
29. *The Times*, 29 September 1923.
30. *Ibid.*, 19 October 1923.
31. *Ibid.*, 10 October 1923.
32. TNA: PRO HO 144/15935, transcript of trial evidence.
33. TNA: PRO HO 144/15934, report of Sir John Anderson, 10 January 1924.
34. *Ibid.*
35. TNA: PRO PCOM 8/386.
36. 9 November 1932.
37. B&T, pp. 366–7.
38. TNA: PRO HO 144/15934.

Chapter Eleven

1. M-LS, *Transactions* (1924).
2. NBT Vaquier, *passim*; TNA: PRO HO 144/4081.
3. TNA: PRO HO 144/4081.
4. *Ibid.*
5. See Chapter Twelve.
6. CC A.P. Jones.
7. TNA: PRO HO 144/4081.
8. P. Hastings, *The Autobiography of Sir Patrick Hastings* (Heinemann, 1948), p. 159.
9. Grice, *Great Cases of Sir Henry Curtis-Bennett*, p. 30.
10. Quotations from Vaquier's trial proceedings are from TNA: PRO HO 144/4081, transcript.
11. Hastings, *Autobiography*, p. 169.
12. TNA: PRO HO 144/4081, report of Deputy Governor, Wandsworth Prison.
13. *Ibid.*, report of CI Savage; see also Wensley, *Detective Days*.
14. *Eastbourne Gazette*, 7 May 1924.
15. TNA: PRO DPP 1/78.
16. G. Honeycombe, *The Complete Murders of the Black Museum* (Leopard Books, 1995), p. 174.
17. Information from Molly Lefebure.
18. *Daily Sketch*, 6 May 1924.
19. e.g. *ibid.*; *Eastbourne Gazette*, 7 May 1924.
20. B&T, p. 156.
21. TNA: PRO HO 144/4100. Quotations from Spilsbury's evidence are taken from the trial transcript.
22. TNA: PRO DPP 1/38.
23. TNA: PRO HO 144/4100.
24. B&T, p. 156.
25. TNA: PRO HO 144/4100.
26. See also CC Emily Beilby Kaye.
27. TNA: PRO DPP 1/38.
28. See *ibid.* and TNA: PRO HO 144/4100 for background information about Mahon and Emily Kaye.
29. K.L. Savage (ed.), *The Trial of Herbert Patrick Mahon* (A. Rogers & Co., 1928), p. 6.
30. TNA: PRO HO 144/4104.
31. *Ibid.*
32. *Ibid.*
33. E. Wallace, Foreword, in FT Mahon.
34. *The Times*, 22 and 23 April 1924.
35. TNA: PRO DPP 1/38.
36. TNA: PRO HO 144/4100.
37. *Daily Mirror*, 8 May 1924.
38. TNA: PRO HO 144/4100.

39. I. Adamson, *A Man of Quality* (Frederick Muller, 1964), p. 22.
40. *Daily Sketch*, 17 July 1924.
41. Trial evidence quotations are taken from TNA: PRO HO 144/4100, transcript.
42. TNA: PRO DPP 1/38; R. Jackson, *The Chief* (Harrap, 1959), p. 164.
43. TNA: PRO HO 144/4100.

Chapter Twelve

1. FT Thorne, *passim*; TNA: PRO HO 144/5193; TNA: PRO PCOM 8/153.
2. TNA: PRO HO 144/5193, report of Chief Constable, East Sussex, 27 March 1925.
3. A. Bennett, *Forty Years On* (Faber and Faber, 1969), p. 64.
4. TNA: PRO HO 144/5193, transcript of trial evidence.
5. FT Thorne; Honeycombe, *Complete Murders of the Black Museum*, pp. 177–8.
6. *Ibid.*
7. I. Adamson, *A Man of Quality* (Frederick Muller, 1964), pp. 91–2.
8. TNA: PRO HO 144/5193, letter from Thorne's solicitor dated 19 February 1925.
9. CC Elsie Cameron.
10. *Ibid.*
11. M-LS, *Medico-Legal and Criminological Review* (1933), p. 1.
12. CC Elsie Cameron.
13. TNA: PRO HO 144/5193, transcript.
14. A.E. Bowker, *A Lifetime within the Law* (W.H. Allen, 1961), pp. 78–9.
15. Grice, *Great Cases of Sir Henry Curtis-Bennett*, p. 18.
16. TNA: PRO HO 144/5193. Quotations from the evidence of Spilsbury, Brontë, Nabarro, and Galt are taken from the transcript of trial evidence.
17. Medical information from Professor Bernard Knight.
18. *Ibid.*
19. *Ibid.*
20. *Ibid.*
21. TNA: PRO MEPO 3/1610.
22. Helena Normanton, Introduction, in FT Thorne, pp. 29–30.
23. *Daily Telegraph*, 17 March 1925.
24. Jackson, *The Chief*, pp. 165–6.
25. Honeycombe, *Complete Murders of the Black Museum*, p. 182.
26. *Law Journal*, 18 April 1925.
27. *Morning Post*, 20 April 1925.
28. *Sunday Express*, 12 April 1925.
29. *Daily Mail*, 21 April 1925.
30. *Daily Herald*, 21 April 1925.
31. *Evening Standard*, 20 April 1925.
32. TNA: PRO PCOM 8/153, which also contains the four other letters quoted.
33. TNA: PRO HO 144/5193.
34. *Ibid.* contains the account of the secret Home Office meeting.
35. *The Times*, 23 April 1925.
36. *News of the World*, 26 April 1925.
37. TNA: PRO PCOM 8/153.
38. *The Star*, 20 April 1925.

Chapter Thirteen

1. M-LS, *Transactions* (1926).
2. *Ibid.*
3. Bruce and Dilling, *Materia Medica and Therapeutica*, p. 627.
4. NBT Merrett, p. 1 and *passim*; see also MH, pp 105–17, and J. Symons, *A Reasonable Doubt* (Cresset Press, 1960), pp 134–44.
5. NBT Merrett, p. 149.
6. *Ibid.*, p. 62.
7. *Ibid.*, p. 103.
8. *Ibid.*, pp. 104–5.
9. *Ibid.*, app. III, p. 315, medical report by Dr John Glaister, 10 December 1926.
10. *British Medical Journal* (August 1927), p. 1058.
11. NBT Merrett, app. I, p. 313, first report of Professor Harvey Littlejohn, 5 April 1926.
12. *Ibid.*, app. II, pp. 313–14, second report of Professor Harvey Littlejohn, 13 January 1927.
13. MH, p. 108.

14. Smith, *Mostly Murder*, p. 144.
15. MH, p. 108.
16. Letter from Spilsbury to Harvey Littlejohn, 17 June 1923, Royal College of Surgeons, Edinburgh.
17. Royal College of Surgeons, Edinburgh.
18. *Ibid.*
19. MH, p. 110.
20. *Ibid.*
21. *Ibid.*, p. 115.
22. *Ibid.*, p. 111.
23. NBT Merrett, p. 39 n. 3.
24. *Ibid.*, p. 222.
25. *Ibid.*, p. 40; quotations from Spilsbury's trial evidence are from *ibid.*, pp. 226–39.
26. B&T, p. 333.
27. NBT Merrett, p. 42 n. 4.
28. *Ibid.*, p. 45 n. 6.
29. Smith, *Mostly Murder*, p. 145.
30. R. Whittington-Egan, *William Roughead's Chronicles of Murder* (Lochar Publishing, 1991), p. 149.

Chapter Fourteen

1. TNA: PRO HO 144/10732 and *passim*; see also Wensley, *Detective Days*, and G.W. Cornish, *Cornish of the 'Yard'* (John Lane, 1935).
2. TNA: PRO HO 144/10732, report of Dr Roche Lynch, 11 June 1927.
3. L. Burt, *Commander Burt of Scotland Yard* (Heinemann, 1959), pp. 158–9.
4. CC Minnie Bonati.
5. NA: PRO HO 144/10732, transcript of trial evidence.
6. CC Minnie Bonati.
7. TNA: PRO CRIM 1/403, deposition of Spilsbury at committal proceedings.
8. Saki, *Reginald on Besetting Sins, in Reginald* (Methuen 1904), pp. 76–7.
9. TNA: PRO HO 144/10732, transcript of trial evidence.
10. *Ibid.*
11. *Ibid.*, advice to Home Secretary, 29 July 1927.
12. Fay, *The Life of Mr Justice Swift*, p. 165.
13. *Ibid.* and TNA: PRO CRIM 1/403.

14. TNA: PRO HO 144/10732.
15. *Ibid.* Quotations from the evidence of Robinson, Spilsbury, Brontë and other witnesses are taken from the trial transcript.
16. Medical information from Professor Bernard Knight.
17. *Ibid.*
18. TNA: PRO HO 144/10732.
19. Medical information from Professor Bernard Knight.
20. *Ibid.*
21. *Ibid.*
22. See also Burt, *Commander Burt of Scotland Yard*, p. 162
23. TNA: PRO HO 144/10732.

Chapter Fifteen

1. M-LS, *Transactions* (1927), pp. 68–9.
2. *Punch*, vol. 164, p. 305.
3. R.A. Freeman, *Dr Thorndyke: His Famous Cases* (Hodder & Stoughton 1929), p. 594.
4. E.A. Heaman, *St Mary's: The History of a London Teaching Hospital* (Liverpool University Press, 2003), p. 189.
5. Gordon, *The Expert Witness*, p. 2.
6. R. Whittington-Egan, *The Riddle of Birdhurst Drive* (Harrap, 1975).
7. NBT Fox, *passim*; TNA: PRO MEPO 3/862; TNA: PRO HO 144/11767–11771; TNA: PRO PCOM 9/280; TNA: PRO DPP 1/90.
8. W. Hambrook, *Hambrook of the Yard* (Robert Hall, 1937), pp. 213–14, 215; see also pp. 206–36 *passim*.
9. *Eastern Daily Press*, 8 and 9 November 1929.
10. NBT Fox, p. 33.
11. B&T, p. 241.
12. Letter from Sir John Leslie Bt to the author, 19 March 1997; and see Sir S. Leslie, *Long Shadows* (John Murray, 1966), p. 83.
13. Saki, 'Adrian', in *The Chronicles of Clovis* (Bodley Head, 1930), p. 156.
14. TNA: PRO MEPO 3/862.

15. NBT Fox, p. 7.
16. *News of the World*, 23 March 1930.
17. NBT Fox, pp. 5–7.
18. TNA: PRO MEPO 3/862.
19. TNA: PRO HO 144/11769.
20. *Ibid.*
21. See e.g. NBT Fox, p. 169.
22. TNA: PRO HO 144/1767, first report of Superindent Hambrook, 27 November 1929.
23. *Isle of Thanet Gazette*, 7 February 1930.
24. TNA: PRO HO 144/11771, transcript of trial evidence.
25. TNA: PRO MEPO 3/682.
26. *Ibid.*
27. Hambrook, *Hambrook of the Yard*, p. 225.
28. Professor S. Smith, *Mostly Murder*, pp. 156–8.
29. *Ibid.*, p. 156.
30. M-LS, *Medico-Legal Review* (1938), p. 223.
31. Smith, *Mostly Murder*, p. 157.
32. *Ibid.*, p. 158.
33. Information from HH Judge Alan King-Hamilton QC.
34. E. Jowitt, *Some Were Spies* (Hodder & Stoughton, 1954), p. 160.
35. Adamson, *A Man of Quality*, p. 327; NBT Fox, p. 3.
36. *Daily Mail*, 12 March 1930.
37. Information from HH Judge Alan King-Hamilton QC.
38. *Daily Mail*, 12 March 1930.
39. NBT Fox, pp. 59–77.
40. TNA: PRO DPP 1/90.
41. TNA: PRO HO 144/11771. Quotations from the evidence of Spilsbury, other witnesses and the judge are taken from the transcript of the trial.
42. Information from HH Judge Alan King-Hamilton QC.
43. Medical information from Professor Bernard Knight.
44. Information from HH Judge Alan King-Hamilton QC.
45. Medical information from Professor Bernard Knight.
46. *Ibid.*
47. Smith, *Mostly Murder*, p. 158.
48. Jowitt, *Some Were Spies*, p. 150.
49. TNA: PRO HO 144/11769.
50. G. Ridley with F. Welsh, *Bend'or, Duke of Westminster* (Robin Clark Ltd 1985), pp. 244–7.
51. TNA: PRO HO 144/11769.
52. R. Jackson, *Case for the Prosecution* (Arthur Barker, 1962), p. 171.
53. Information from HH Judge Alan King-Hamilton QC.
54. *Reynolds News*, 23 March 1930.
55. TNA: PRO DPP 1/90, opinion of Frank J. Powell.
56. TNA: PRO HO 144/11767.
57. *Ibid.*
58. *News of the World*, 23 March 1930.
59. Letter from Sir John Leslie Bt to the author, 19 March 1997 (Sir John also wrote, 'Alas! We thought S.F. was guilty').
60. TNA: PRO PCOM 9/280.
61. *Ibid.*
62. *Daily Mail*, 9 April 1930.
63. Perjury Act 1911, section 1(1).
64. Smith, *Mostly Murder*, p. 165.

Chapter Sixteen

1. FT Podmore, *passim*; TNA: PRO HO 144/12275–12281; TNA: PRO MEPO 3/1643; TNA: PRO DPP 1/93; H. Young, *My Forty Years at the Yard* (W.H. Allen, 1955); and Woodland, *Assize Pageant*.
2. TNA: PRO HO 144/2276.
3. CC Vivian Messiter.
4. Young, *My Forty Years at the Yard*, p. 140.
5. TNA: PRO HO 144/12275.
6. *Southern Daily Echo*, 4 March 1930.
7. B&T, p. 229.
8. TNA: PRO HO 144/12276.
9. Professor M. Green, *Is Sir Bernard Spilsbury Dead?*, in A.R. Brownlie, *Crime Investigation* (Scottish Academic Press, 1984).
10. B&T, p. 409.

11. TNA: PRO AIR 2/1247, and see generally for further detail of Spilsbury's role in this investigation.
12. NBT Rouse, *passim*; TNA: PRO HO 144/19178-19185.
13. *Daily Mail*, 28 January 1931.
14. CC 'Unknown'.
15. TNA: PRO HO 144/19185, deposition of Spilsbury, 15 December 1930.
16. *Ibid.*
17. NBT Rouse, introduction, p. xiii.
18. *Evening News*, 27 November, 13, 15 and 16 December 1930.
19. NBT Rouse, app. 1, pp. 293–4.
20. *Ibid.*, introduction, p. vii.
21. TNA: PRO HO 144/19178.
22. *Daily Mail*, 27 January 1931.
23. NBT Rouse, pp. 3–14.
24. *Ibid.* contains quotations from evidence of Spilsbury and other witnesses, and from the judge.
25. H.M. Hyde, *Sir Patrick Hastings* (Heinemann, 1960), p. 219.
26. TNA: PRO HO 144/19185, deposition of Spilsbury, 15 December 1930.
27. *Ibid.*
28. *Evening News*, 28 January 1931.
29. TNA: PRO HO 144/19179.
30. *Ibid.*
31. TNA: PRO HO 144/19181.

Chapter Seventeen

1. TNA: PRO HO 144/15018, *passim*.
2. *Evening News*, 5 June 1931.
3. TNA: PRO HO 144/15018. Quotations from Spilsbury and the judge are taken from the transcript of trial evidence.
4. Information from the late Sir Geoffrey Wilson.
5. TNA: PRO HO 144/16033, *passim*; MEPO3/787; TNA: PRO DPP 2/42; Fay, *The Life of Mr Justice Swift*, pp. 194–209.
6. P. Beveridge, *Inside the CID* (Evans Brothers, 1957), p. 134.
7. H.M. Howgrave-Graham, *Light and Shade at Scotland Yard* (John Murray, 1947), p. 100.

8. *Ibid.*
9. TNA: PRO MEPO 3/787.
10. *Ibid.*
11. *Ibid.*
12. *Daily Mail*, 16 September 1931.
13. TNA: PRO DPP 2/42, transcript containing quotations from trial evidence.
14. Fay, *The Life of Mr Justice Rigby Swift*, p. 201.
15. TNA: PRO HO 144/16033, opened to public inspection on 6 February 2006.
16. TNA: PRO MEPO 3/866 (partly closed until 2013). Quotations from witness statements and police reports; see also Hambrook, *Hambrook of the Yard*.
17. Information from Dr Ian Wilson.

Chapter Eighteen

1. Records in possession of Dr David Foster.
2. B&T, p. 195.
3. Smith, *Mostly Murder*, p. 192 and *passim*; see also B&T, pp. 181–2, 185.
4. TNA: PRO CRIM 1/598, *passim*; TNA: PRO DPP 2/62; MH, pp. 157–74. This extraordinary case is not cited in B&T.
5. MH, p. 158.
6. *Lincolnshire, Boston, and Spalding Free Press*, 12 April 1932, with author's interpolation.
7. *Ibid.*
8. *Ibid.*
9. TNA: PRO DPP 2/62 Pt 1.
10. *Ibid.*
11. *Ibid.*
12. MH, p. 159.
13. TNA: PRO CRIM 1/598, deposition of Spilsbury at committal, 26 January 1932.
14. *Ibid.*
15. *Ibid.*, deposition of Robert Churchill, 26 January 1932.
16. *Ibid.*
17. MH, pp. 160–1.
18. *Ibid.*, pp. 101–2.
19. TNA: PRO DPP 2/62 Pt II.

20. MH, p. 162.
21. TNA: PRO DPP 2/62 Pt II.
22. 'Gedney Dyke Murder Trial' (*Lincolnshire . . . Free Press*, 12 and 19 April 1932) contains quotations from trial evidence.
23. MH, p. 169.
24. TNA: PRO DPP 2/62.
25. *Ibid.*

Chapter Nineteen

1. TNA: PRO MEPO 3/1673, *passim*; TNA: PRO DPP 2/92; FT Barney; MH; Hyde, *Sir Patrick Hastings*.
2. B. Milton, *Paradise Mislaid* (Jupiter, 1976), p. 84.
3. TNA: PRO MEPO 3/1673.
4. *Ibid.*
5. *Daily Telegraph*, 5 July 1932.
6. TNA: PRO MEPO 3/1692.
7. *Ibid.*
8. *Daily Telegraph*, 5 July 1932.
9. *Ibid.*
10. TNA: PRO MEPO 3/1673.
11. CC Thomas Wm Scott Stephen.
12. *Daily Telegraph*, 6 July 1932.
13. MH, p. 189.
14. *Daily Telegraph*, 5–7 July 1932. Quotations from trial evidence are taken from these reports.
15. Hastings, *The Autobiography of Sir Patrick Hastings*, p. 153.
16. *Ibid.*
17. *Daily Telegraph*, 5 July 1932.
18. *Ibid.*
19. Hastings, *Cases in Court*, pp. 268–9.
20. *Ibid.*, p. 278.
21. *Daily Mirror*, 28 December 1936, quoted in FT Barney, app. 10, p. 126 and *ibid.*, p. 42.

Chapter Twenty

1. M-LS, *Medico-Legal and Criminological Review* (1934), pp. 1–13.
2. *Jersey Weekly Post*, 11 November 1933, *passim*; quotations from trial evidence

are taken from this report. See also Smith, *Mostly Murder*, pp. 197–204.
3. Smith, *Mostly Murder*, p. 202.
4. A. Bourne, *A Doctor's Creed* (Gollancz, 1962), p. 21.
5. Smith, *Mostly Murder*, p. 204.
6. ML-S, *Medico-Legal and Criminological Review* (1933), pp. 40–7.
7. *Ibid.* (1934), pp. 340–4.
8. TNA: PRO MEPO 3/1692, *passim*.
9. *Ibid.*, Spilsbury's report dated 4 July 1934.
10. *Ibid.*, Kendal to Roche Lynch, letter dated 21 June 1934.
11. TNA: PRO MEPO 3/1692.
12. H.M. Hyde, *Norman Birkett* (Hamish Hamilton, 1964), p. 396.
13. CC Violet Saunders (or Violette Kaye).
14. *Daily Telegraph*, 11–15 December 1934. Quotations from trial evidence are taken from these reports; see also Hyde, *Norman Birkett*, pp. 394–418.
15. Hyde, *Norman Birkett*, p. 397.
16. A.E. Bowker, *Behind the Bar* (Staples Press, 1951), p. 286.
17. Hyde, *Norman Birkett*, p. 417.
18. *Ibid.*, p. 418.
19. B&T, p. 207.
20. M-LS, 'Duties of a Practitioner in Criminal Courts', *Medico-Legal and Criminological Review* (1933), p. 261.

Chapter Twenty-one

1. T. Driberg, *Ruling Passions* (Quartet Books, 1978), pp. 101–4.
2. Quoted in B&T, p. 362.
3. TNA: PRO MEPO 3/1715, *passim*; also J.D. Casswell, *A Lance for Liberty*; I. Adamson, *A Man of Quality*.
4. Casswell, *A Lance for Liberty*, p. 131.
5. *Daily Telegraph*, 23 September 1936.
6. *Ibid.*
7. *Daily Telegraph*, 23–25 September 1936. Quotations from trial evidence are taken from these reports.
8. Casswell, *A Lance for Liberty*, p. 133.
9. *Ibid.*

10. Adamson, *A Man of Quality*, p. 176.
11. Casswell, *A Lance for Liberty*, p. 134.
12. NBT Nodder, *passim*.
13. TNA: PRO MEPO 3/877, *passim*; B&T, pp. 361–4; MH, pp. 220–6.
14. TNA: PRO MEPO 3/877, deposition of Spilsbury at committee proceedings, 22–23 April 1938.
15. *Ibid.*
16. *Ibid.*
17. *Ibid.*
18. D. Browne, *Sir Travers Humphreys* (Harrap, 1960), p. 332.
19. *Ibid.*
20. MH, p. 225.
21. *The Times*, 28 and 29 June 1938.
22. Bourne, *A Doctor's Creed*, *passim*.
23. TNA: PRO DPP 2/564 and *passim*.
24. *Ibid.*
25. *Ibid.*
26. Bourne, *A Doctor's Creed*, pp. 100–3.
27. Quoted in *The Times*, 30 December 1974.

Chapter Twenty-two

1. *Daily Express*, 4 March 1940.
2. TNA: PRO PCOM 9/872.
3. *Morning Advertiser*, 5 June 1940.
4. TNA: PRO HO 144/21444–5.
5. PW, pp. 316–17.
6. *Ibid.*
7. *Morning Advertiser*, 6 June 1940.
8. Official diary, St Thomas's Hospital, sent to the author by Dr Janet Jenkins.
9. B&T, p. 389.
10. *Ibid.*
11. M. Lefebure, *Evidence for the Crown* (Heinemann, 1955), p. 10.
12. Information from Molly Lefebure.
13. Information from Dr Hazel Baker.
14. R. Jackson, *Coroner* (Harrap, 1963), p. 188.
15. TNA: PRO CRIM 1/1397.
16. Hon. E.S. Montagu, *The Man Who Never Was* (Evans Brothers, 1953), *passim*; Jackson, *Coroner*.
17. Montagu, *The Man Who Never Was*, p. 23.

18. *Ibid.*, p. 24.
19. TNA: PRO ADM 1/25230.
20. Letter to Leonard Spilsbury, 18 September 1943.
21. MH, pp. 254–7, *passim*; P. Hastings, *Cases in Court* (Heinemann, 1949), pp. 279–91.
22. TNA: PRO CRIM 1/1583, *passim*; B&T, p. 401; Simpson, *Forty Years of Murder*, pp. 73–80.
23. TNA: PRO CRIM 1/1583.
24. *Ibid.*, statement of Detective Inspector Lamport.
25. Adamson, *A Man of Quality*, p. 242, noting also that 'Sir Bernard's belief in his own infallibility had grown enormously since Cassels had first dared question his opinion'.
26. Simpson, *Forty Years of Murder*, p. 77.
27. Adamson, *A Man of Quality*, p. 242.
28. Information from Molly Lefebure.
29. TNA: PRO CRIM 1/1583.
30. Simpson, *Forty Years of Murder*, p. 78.
31. Loaned by Professor Bernard Knight.
32. Information from Dr David Foster.
33. Letter to Leonard Spilsbury, 6 April 1945.

Chapter Twenty-three

1. Information from Molly Lefebure.
2. Alan Spilsbury's pocket diary for 1945, loaned by Professor Bernard Knight.
3. Gordon, 'Doctor Death', p. 89.
4. Letter to Leonard Spilsbury, 6 April 1945.
5. Discharge certificate with Spilsbury's 1944 diary, loaned by Professor Bernard Knight.
6. Letter to Leonard Spilsbury, 6 April 1945.
7. TNA: PRO DPP 2/1570, *passim*; B&T, pp. 403–6.
8. M-LS, *Medico-Legal Review* (1944), p. 194.
9. Quoted in B&T, pp. 404–5.
10. B&T, p. 403.

11. TNA: PRO HO 144/23402-23404, *passim*; B&T, pp. 406–8; MH, pp. 273–7.
12. *Daily Telegraph*, 29 April 1947.
13. *Evening News*, 5 May 1947.
14. MH, p. 277.
15. TNA: PRO HO 144/23402.
16. *Ibid.*
17. Information from Richard Whittington-Egan, from conversations with Bentley Purchase.
18. Information from the late Dr Philip Willcox.
19. B&T, p. 411; Jackson, *Coroner*, p. 192.
20. *Daily Telegraph*, 18 December 1947.
21. *Daily Mirror*, 18 December 1947.
22. Jackson, *Coroner*, p. 192.
23. *Ibid.*, p. 193.
24. MH, p. 277.
25. Letter from Dr Andrew Scott Reid, HM Coroner for Inner North London, 4 April 2006.
26. Information from the late James Surman, barrister's clerk, who entered legal service in 1922.
27. *The Lancet*, 27 December 1947.
28. *British Medical Journal*, 27 December 1947.
29. *UCH Magazine* (1948), no. 33, pp. 6–7.
30. Information from the late Professor Richard Cobb.
31. Information from Bryan Senior.
32. Keith Simpson, *Medico-Legal Journal* (1952), p. 31.
33. M-LS, 'Duties of a Practitioner in Criminal Courts', *Medico-Legal and Criminological Review* (1933), p. 26.
34. *Ibid.*
35. B&T, p. 361.
36. ML-S, *Medico-Legal Journal* (1948), p. 14.
37. e.g. the late Dr Philip Willcox.
38. Green, *Is Sir Bernard Spilsbury Dead?*
39. Smith, *Mostly Murder*, p. 204.

Select Bibliography

PUBLISHED SOURCES

Adamson, I. *A Man of Quality*, Frederick Muller, 1964
Allan, M. *The London Blitz Murders*, Collins, 1942
Anon. *Leamington Past & Present*, D. Sarney, 1884
Anon. *The Trial of William Palmer*, Ward Lock & Co., 1856
Anon. *Lord Darling and his Famous Trials*, Hutchinson, 1932
Bardens, D. *Lord Justice Birkett*, Robert Hale, 1962
Beales, M. *Dead Not Buried*, Hale, 1995
Beveridge, P. *Inside the C.I.D.*, Evans Brothers, 1957
Bourne, A., *A Doctor's Creed*, Gollancz, 1962
Bowker, A.E. *Behind the Bar*, Staples Press, 1951
——, *A Lifetime with the Law*, W.H. Allen, 1961
Browne, D. *Sir Travers Humphreys*, Harrap, 1960
Browne, D. and Tullett, E.V. *Bernard Spilsbury: His Life and Cases*, Harrap, 1951 [USA title *The Scalpel of Scotland Yard*]
Bruce, J.M. and Dilling, W.J. *Materia Medica and Therapeutica*, Cassell, 1921
Burt, Commander L. *Commander Burt of Scotland Yard*, Heinemann, 1959
Carlin, F. *Reminiscences of an Ex-Detective*, Hutchinson, 1927
Casswell, J.D. *A Lance for Liberty*, Harrap, 1961
Cornish, G.W. *Cornish of the 'Yard'*, John Lane, 1935
Cullen, T. *Maundy Gregory*, Bodley Head, 1974
Curtis-Bennett, S. *The Curtis-Bennett Chronicle*, Phillimore, 1998
Dearden, H. *Death under the Microscope*, Hutchinson, 1934
Eddy, J.P. *Scarlet and Ermine*, William Kimber, 1960
Fabian, R. *Fabian of the Yard*, Naldrett Press, 1950
Fay, E.S., *The Life of Mr Justice Swift*, Methuen, 1939
Felstead, S.T. *Sir Richard Muir*, Bodley Head, 1927
Firmin, S. *Scotland Yard: The Inside Story*, Hutchinson, 1946
Freeman, R.A. *Dr Thorndyke: His Famous Cases*, Hodder & Stoughton, 1929
Furneaux, R. *They Died by the Gun*, Herbert Jenkins, 1962
Gaute, J.H.H. and Odell, R. *The Murderers' Who's Who*, Harrap, 1979
Goodman, J. *The Railway Murders*, Allison & Busby, 1984
——, *The Seaside Murders*, Allison & Busby, 1985
Gordon, R. *Great Medical Disasters*, Hutchinson, 1983
——, *The Medical Witness*, Heinemann, 1971
Green, Professor M. *Is Sir Bernard Spilsbury Dead?*, in Brownlie, A.R. *Crime Investigation*, Scottish Academic Press, 1984

Grice, E. *Great Cases of Sir Henry Curtis-Bennett*, Hutchinson, 1937
Hambrook, W. *Hambrook of the Yard*, Robert Hale, 1937
Hastings, M. *The Other Mr Churchill*, Harrap, 1963
Hastings, P. *The Autobiography of Sir Patrick Hastings*, Heinemann, 1948
——, *Cases in Court*, Heinemann, 1949
Honeycombe, G. *The Complete Murders of the Black Museum*, Leopard Books, 1995
Howgrave-Graham, H.M. *Light and Shade at Scotland Yard*, John Murray, 1947
Humphreys, C. *Seven Murders*, Heinemann, 1931
Humphreys, T. *A Book of Trials*, Heinemann, 1953
——, *Criminal Days*, Hodder & Stoughton, 1946
Hyde, H.M. *Norman Birkett*, Hamish Hamilton, 1964
——, *Sir Patrick Hastings*, Heinemann, 1960
Jackson, R. *Case for the Prosecution*, Arthur Barker, 1962
——, *The Chief*, Harrap, 1959
——, *Coroner*, Harrap, 1963
Jackson, S. *Mr Justice Avory*, Victor Gollancz, 1935
——, *The Old Bailey*, W.H. Allen, 1978
Jowitt, E. *Some Were Spies*, Hodder & Stoughton, 1954
Lefebure, M. *Evidence for the Crown*, Heinemann, 1955
Lieck, A. *Bow Street World*, Robert Hale, 1938
Liston, R. *Great Detectives*, Platt & Mark, 1966
Lustgarten, E. *The Murder and the Trial*, Odhams, 1960
——, *Verdict in Dispute*, Wingate, 1949
Malcolm, D. *Family Secrets*, Hutchinson, 2003
Marjoribanks, Hon. E. *The Life of Sir Edward Marshall Hall*, Gollancz, 1929
Montagu, Hon. E.S. *The Man Who Never Was*, Evans Brothers, 1953
Neil, A.F., *Forty Years of Manhunting*, Jarrolds, 1932
Odell, R., *Exhumation of a Murder*, Harrap, 1975
Oddie, S. Ingleby, *Inquest*, Hutchinson, 1941
Oswald, H.R., *Memoirs of a London County Coroner*, Stanley Paull, 1936
Parmiter, G. de C. *Reasonable Doubt*, Arthur Barker, 1938
Pierrepoint, A. *Executioner Pierrepoint*, Harrap, 1974
Randall, L. *The Famous Cases of Sir Bernard Spilsbury*, Ivor Nicholson & Watson, 1936
Rhode, J. *The Murders in Praed Street*, Geoffrey Bles, 1928
——, *The Paddington Mystery*, Geoffrey Bles, 1925
Robey, E., *The Jester and the Court*, William Kimber, 1976
Rowland, J. *Murder Revisited*, John Long, 1961
Scott, H. *Scotland Yard*, André Deutsch, 1954
Shore, W.T. *Crime and its Detection*, 2 vols, Gresham, 1932
Simpson, Professor K. *Forty Years of Murder*, Harrap, 1978
Smith, Professor Sir S. *Mostly Murder*, Harrap, 1959
Symons, J. *A Reasonable Doubt*, Cresset Press, 1960
Tullett, E.V. ('Tom'). *Strictly Murder*, Bodley Head, 1979
Weis, R., *Criminal Justice*, Hamish Hamilton, 1988
Wensley, F.P. *Detective Days*, Cassell, 1931
Whittington-Egan, R. *The Great British Torso Mystery*, Blucoat Press, 2002
——, *The Riddle of Birdhurst Rise*, Harrap, 1975
——, *William Roughead's Chronicles of Murder*, Lochar Publishing, 1991

Whittington-Egan, R. and M. *The Bedside Book of Murder*, David & Charles, 1988
Wild, R. and Curtis-Bennett, D., *Curtis: The Life of Sir Henry Curtis-Bennett KC*, Hutchinson, 1937
Willcox, P.W.A. *The Detective-Physician*, William Heinemann Medical Books, 1970
Woodland, W.L. *Assize Pageant*, Harrap, 1952
Young, H. *My Forty Years at the Yard*, W.H. Allen, 1955

TRIALS

The following were published in the Famous Trials Series (Geoffrey Bles; various publication dates; trial dates in parentheses):
Herbert Patrick Mahon (1924), ed. George Dilnot, foreword by Edgar Wallace
Norman Thorne (1925), ed. Helena Normanton
William Podmore (1930), ed. H. Fletcher Moulton and H.L. Woodland

The following was published in the Celebrated Trials series (David & Charles; trial date in parentheses):
Elvira Barney (1932), ed. Peter Cotes

The following were published in the Notable British Trials series (William Hodge & Co Ltd; various publication dates; trial dates in parentheses):
H.H. Crippen (1910), ed. Filson Young
The Seddons (1912), ed. Filson Young
George Joseph Smith (1915), ed. Eric R. Watson
Field and Gray (1920), ed. Winifred Duke
H.R. Armstrong (1922), ed. Filson Young
Bywaters and Thompson (1922), ed. Filson Young
J.P. Vaquier (1924), ed. R.H. Blundell
J.D. Merrett (1927), ed. William Roughead
Sidney [sic] Fox (1930), ed. F. Tennyson Jesse
A.A. Rouse (1931), ed. Helena Normanton
Frederick Nodder (1937), ed. Winifred Duke

NEWSPAPERS AND PERIODICALS

Birmingham Post
British Medical Journal
Cosmopolitan
Daily Express
Daily Graphic
Daily Herald
Daily Mail
Daily Mirror
Daily Sketch
Daily Telegraph
Eastern Daily Press
Eastbourne Gazette

Empire News
Evening News
Evening Standard
Isle of Thanet Gazette
Jersey Weekly Post
Lancet
Law Journal
Leamington Spa Courier
Lincolnshire, Boston, and Spalding Free Press
Manchester Guardian
Morning Advertiser
Morning Post
News of the World
Punch
Reynolds News
St Mary's Hospital Gazette
Southern Daily Echo
Staffordshire Advertiser
Sunday Express
The Times
University College London Magazine

M-LS *Transactions; Medico-Legal and Criminological Journal; Medico-Legal Review; Medico-Legal Journal*

Index

'A', Miss 247–9
Ainslie, Dr William 89, 95–6
Aitchison, Craigie, KC 147, 149–50
Aitken, Maxwell ('Max') (Lord Beaverbrook) 241
Allen, Chesney 215
Allen, Dr 3
Allen, Nurse 87
Alness, Lord see Munro, Robert, KC
Altmann, Anton 222
Alverstone, Lord, Chief Justice see Webster, Richard Everard
Anderson, Sir John 109
Angell, Mr 81
Angell, Mrs 81
Archer-Shee, Col Sir Martin, MP 99
Armstrong, Major Herbert Rowse xx, 86–91, 96
Armstrong, Katharine (Katherine) 86–7, 89–91, 93–6
Asquith, Herbert, KC, MP 167
Astor, Nancy, Lady 74, 99, 241
Atkin, Sir Richard, KC, High Court Judge 67, 69–71, 74, 104, 141, 259
Atkinson, Sir Edward Tindal 182, 218, 225
Austin, Dr Cecil 169–70
Avarne, Dr Claude 229–32
Avory, Sir Horace, KC, High Court Judge 60, 70, 106–8, 112, 114, 122–4, 173, 197
Ayres, Herbert William ('Pigsticker') 199–200

Badcock, Col George 206
Bagot, Lady Theodosia 183
Baillie-Cochrane, Charles (Lord Lamington) 251
Bainbridge, Professor Francis 79, 142
Bainbridge, Hilda 79–80, 115–17, 128, 142–3, 147, 269
Bainbridge, Joan 79
Baker, Dr Hazel 254–5
Baker, Max 216
Baldwin, Ruth 222
Baldwin, Stanley, MP 137
Balzac, Honoré de xvii
Bankhead, Tallulah 225
Baring, Rowland (Earl of Cromer) 71

Barney, Elvira Dolores 221–8, 257
Barney, John Sterling 221
Barrow, Eliza 32–3, 35–7
Bates, Dr Stephen 43
Baumberg, Anton ('Count de Borch') 52–3
Baxter, Jeannie 41–2, 147, 173
Beard, ex-Police Inspector 121
Beauchamp, Earl see Lygon, William
Beaverbrook, Lord see Aitken, Maxwell
Beckett, Samuel 199
Bedford, Gilbert ('Gil') 264
Beerbohm, Sir Max 57
Belcher, George 163
Bell, Dr Joseph 15, 145
Bell, Dr Richard 144
Bennett, Alan 125
Bentlif, Dr Philip 230–1
Beron, Leon 54
Bigge, Sir Arthur (Lord Stamfordham) 110
Billing, Dr George 44
Billing, Noel Pemberton, MP 168
Birkenhead, Earl of see Smith, F.E., KC
Birkett, Norman, KC 193, 195–6, 236–9, 246–7
Blackwell, Sir Ernley xviii, 61–2, 70–1, 73–5, 88, 103–4, 108–10, 112, 124, 134, 137–8, 141, 153, 155, 161–2, 182, 186, 192, 197–9, 201, 218, 225
Blair Eric ('George Orwell') 241
Blair, G.K. 90
Blatch, Louise 43, 47
Blundell, Robert 142
Bodkin, Sir Archibald 19, 47–8, 88–9, 115, 138, 180
Bogarde, Dirk 265
Bonati, Bianco 154, 157
Bonati, Minnie 154–62
Bone, Dr Bertram Mayhew 213
Bontell, George 112
Bottomley, Horatio 71
Bourne, Dr Aleck 229, 231–2, 247–50
Bowen-Colthurst, Captain 99
Bowker, A.E. 26
Boyle, Miss 82
Brancker, Air Vice-Marshal Sir Sefton 188

Branson, Sir George, KC, High Court Judge 236, 239

Brazil, Angela 119

Brewer, Dr 112

Briard, Mr, Jersey Advocate 231–2

Bridgeman, W.C., MP, Home Secretary 109

Bridges, Chief Inspector 248

Broadbent, Sir John 12, 14

Brontë, Dr Robert Matthew 69, 128, 132–4, 136, 160, 162, 172–3, 177, 179, 181, 215–16

Brookes, Annie 1

Brown, Divisional Inspector 67, 73

Browne, Douglas xx

Brumby, Superintendent George 191

Bryant, Sir Arthur 260

Buchan, John 52

Buchowski, Lt Jan 256–7

Bucknill, Sir John, KC, High Court Judge 33, 38

Burnham, Alice 44–9

Burnham, Charles 44

Burrard, Major Gerald DSO 215–16, 218–19

Burt, Commander Leonard 153

Bush, PC 98

Byrne, L.A. 257

Bywaters, Frederick 99–101, 103

Cameron, Elsie 125–36

Cameron, Professor Sir Roy 267

Campbell, Helen 192, 197

Campion, DC 223–4

Camps, Dr Francis 254

Capone, Al 46

Carle, Dr 111–12

Carlin, Chief Inspector Francis 66–7

Carpenter, F.H. 236

Carraloucas, Louis 66

Casement, Sir Roger 70

Cassells, Sir James ('Jimmy'), KC, High Court Judge 122–4, 128–9, 131–3, 135, 174, 177, 236–8, 243–4, 259

Casserley, Ena 245–6

Casserley, Percy 245–7

Casswell, J.D., KC 243–4, 259

Cave, George (Lord Cave) 71, 74–5

Chamberlain, Joseph, MP 4

Chaplin, Edward ('Ted') 245–7

Cheese, Edmund 86

Chewter, Jim 214

Childs, Sir Wyndham 99

Christie, Agatha 206

Christie, Betty 143, 145

Churchill, Edward 13, 42

Churchill, Lady Randolph 167

Churchill, Robert xx, 41–2, 52–3, 77, 147–51, 209, 213–16, 218–19, 224–7, 256–7, 266, 268

Churchill, Winston, MP 30, 167, 241

Cienski, Lt Ludomir 256–7

Clarke, Beatrice 17, 19

Clarke, Sir Edward, QC 42

Clarke, Percival 157–60, 225

Clynes, Rt Hon J.R., MP 197

Cohen, 'Cocky' 81

Cohen, Sefton 109

Coke, Sylvia 222

Coldicott, Elizabeth ('Bessie') 126–7, 136

Cole, R.P. 203

Cook, Mrs 155

Cooke, John Parsons 1

Cooke, Private, 263

Cooper, Sir Astley 111

Copping, PC Harry 189–90

Cornish, Chief Inspector G. 155

Cornock, Cecil 264

Cornock, Rosina 264–5

Court, Jack 105

Courtneidge, Cicely 251

Coward, Noël 263

Creech, Mr 208

Crippen, Dr Hawley Harvey xix, xx, 21–30, 42, 53

Crippen, Cora (née Mackamotzi) ('Belle Elmore') 21–2, 24, 28

Cromer, Earl of *see* Baring, Rowland

Crooks, Will, MP 71

Cross, Arthur 165

Cummins, Gordon 255

Curtis-Bennett, Derek 246

Curtis-Bennett, Sir Henry, KC ('Harry', 'Curtis') 80, 91–5, 100–1, 103, 113, 122–3, 128–35, 173, 181

Curzon, George (Viscount Curzon) 109

Dane, Sir Louis 251

Darling, Sir Gerald, KC, High Court Judge xix, 57–8, 60, 70, 92, 94–6, 173, 181

Davies, John 86, 88

Davis, Superintendent 106

Deaman, Frederick ('Fred') 206–7, 210

De Antiquis, Alec 265–6

Dearnley, Drummer Albert Edward ('Pat') xx, 105–10

De La Mare, Elsie 230–1

Dennett, Sidney 207

Denning, Alfred, QC (Lord Denning) 67

Derrick, Linford xx, 242–4

De Valera, Eamonn 241

Dew, Chief Inspector Walter 22–3

Dodson, Gerald 216–17

Donaldson, Robert, Chief Inspector 235, 239–40

Donovan, Conrad 14

Dougal, Samuel 13

Doyle, Sir Arthur Conan 15, 80, 137, 145
Driberg, Thomas ('Tom') 241
Drought, Dr 101
Duff, Grace 164
Du Maurier, Sir Gerald 16
Dummett, Robert 107
Duncan, Ethel 120–1
Dundas, Lawrence (Marquess of Zetland) 251
Dunedin, Lord 67
Dunn, Reginald ('James Connelly') 98–9
Dunstan, Mr 35–6
Du Parcq, Sir Herbert, KC, High Court judge 187, 200, 248
Durrant, Dr Thomas 223–4
Dyer, General 251

Eales, J.F., KC 216–17
Eardley, William 18–19
Earengay, W.G. 203–5
Edmunds, Dr 41–2
Edward, Prince of Wales (Duke of Windsor) 82, 241, 263
Elen, Gus 26
Elliott, Dr Andrew 125–6
Ellis, Drummer James ('Tot') 105–10
Ellis, John 49, 96, 99
Elphinstone-Dalrymple, Horn 17–18
Elvy, Emily ('Nan') 79, 263
England, Cecil Lois ('Tony Mancini', 'Jack Notyre', 'Herman Nathan Gold', 'Luigi Pirelli', 'Antoni Luigi') 235–6, 239
Evrart, Georges 55, 61
Ewins, Ethel 73

Fabian, Acting Superintendent Robert 266
Farmer, Emily 14
Faulkner, Miss 45
Fearnley-Whittingstall, William 164
Finlay, William, KC (Viscount Finlay) High Court Judge xix, 128, 131, 133, 136, 138, 181
Finnemore, Douglas 193, 195–7
Flanagan, Bud 215
Fletcher, PC Thomas 65
Foster, Adelaide 183
Foster, Dr David 261
Fox, C.R., Chief Constable 201
Fox, Cecil 166, 169
Fox, Miss 78
Fox, Rosaline ('Rosie') 164–79, 181–3
Fox, Sydney xx, 77, 136, 164–75, 179–83, 187
Fox, William 166
Frampton, Ethelbert 205, 207
Franco, Generalissimo Francisco 255
'Frank' (Nellie Trew's cousin) 73
Freeman, R. Austin 163–4
French, Dr Frank 45

Freud, Sigmund 39
Fulton, Eustace 81

Gabe, Dr 55
Galt, Dr Hugh 134–6
Garbo, Greta xx, 241
Garden, Alban 217
Gardner, Dr Eric 255, 265, 267–8
Gathorne-Hardy, Hon Edward ('Eddie') 222
George V, King and Emperor 51, 71, 104, 109–10, 181
George, David Lloyd, MP 32, 39, 51, 167, 241
Geraghty, Christopher John 265–6
Gérard, Émilienne 54–61
Gérard, Paul 54
Ghandi, Mahatma 241
Gibbons, Stella 212
Gibson, Dr (in Dearnley case) 105–6
Gibson, Dr (in Cornock case) 264–5
Gibson, Dr Charles 128
Gibson, John 69
Giffard, Hardinge (Earl of Halsbury) 57
Gilbert, W.S. 26
Gillan, Chief Inspector 128, 134
Gilliatt, Mr William 250
Glaister, Professor John 16, 145–7, 149
Goddard, Ernest 261
Goddard, Rayner, KC 107–8
Godfrey, Sir Edmund Bury 245
Goodman, Jonathan 240
Goodwillie, Inspector 168
'Gordon, Richard' *see* Ostlere, Dr Gordon
Gore, Mr 165
Grant, Ernie 32
Greaves-Lord, Sir Walter, KC, High Court Judge 243–4
Greene, Graham 239
Greener, H.L. 216
Greenwood, David xx, 63, 65–71, 73–5, 104, 110
Greenwood, Harold 89
Greenwood, Jenny 65, 70
Greenwood, Samuel ('Sam') 65, 70
Greenwood, Mrs 65, 70
Grenfell, Joyce 119
Grosse, Inspector Albert 74
Grosvenor, Hugh (Duke of Westminster) 180
Günther, Robert 6
Gurrin, Gerald 235

Hailsham, Lord *see* Hogg, Quintin
Hall, Sir Edward Marshall, KC 26, 34–7, 42, 47–9, 80, 82–3, 92, 112
Hall, Julian 41–2
Hall, Mrs 223
Hallett, Sir Hugh, KC, High Court Judge 252

Halsbury, Earl of *see* Giffard, Hardinge
Hambrook, Detective Superintendent Walter 77, 164–6, 168, 172, 205, 208–10
Hamilton, Gerald ('Mr Norris') 168
Hamilton, Patrick 54
Hampton, Mary 73–4
Hanbury-Tracy, Richard (Viscount Sudeley) 248
Harding, T.J. 108–9
Hardy, Captain 99
Harmsworth, Alfred (Lord Northcliffe) 80
Harper, Dr Arnold 223
Harris, Dr Wilfred 39, 78–9
Harvey, Sir John Martin 16
Harvey-Wyatt, Dr Raymond 196
Hastings, Lady 225
Hastings, Macdonald 147
Hastings, Sir Patrick, KC, MP 112–14, 193, 197, 221, 224–8, 257
Hathaway, Harold 207
Hathaway, Mary 207–8, 210
Hathaway, Mrs 207
Hathaway, Robert 207
Hathaway, Thomas ('Tom') 207–9
Hay, William 73
Hayward, Frank 70
Head, PC 208–9
Henderson, Arthur, MP 51
Henry, Tom 54
Hermann, Marie 34
Herring, Bertha 251
Hewart, Gordon (Lord Hewart, Chief Justice) xix, 124, 136, 138, 181, 187, 197
Hichens, Robert 100
Hill, J.W. 136–7
Hincks, Dr Thomas 86–9
Hitler, Adolf 241
Hocquard, Philip 230
Hodder, Charles 64
Hodgson, William 85
Hogg, Quintin (Lord Hailsham) 236
Holcombe, Dr Roy 144
Holland, Camille 13
Holland, Lt-Col G.H.R., Chief Constable 213
Holland, Brig-Gen Percy 167–8
Holt, Mrs 154
Hopkins, Samuel ('Sam') 170
Hopkinson, Mary *see* Spilsbury, Mary
Hopper, Vera 169
Horder, Sir Thomas (Lord Horder) 249
Horton, Edith *see* Spilsbury, Edith
Horwell, Chief Inspector 201–2, 204
Howard, Brian 222
Humphreys, Judge Christmas, QC xix, 157
Humphreys, Sir Travers, KC, High Court Judge 18, 25–6, 33, 67, 197, 225–7, 246, 257
Hutchinson, St John, KC 173

Irving, H.B. 80
Inskip, Sir Thomas, KC, MP 101–2, 187
Isaacs, Rufus, KC, MP (Marquess of Reading) 4, 24, 26, 33–4, 36
Isherwood, Christopher 168

Jacobs, Hannah 82–3
James, S.T.T. 174, 182
Jeffery, Alan 209
Jeffress, Arthur 222, 224
Jenkins, Charles Henry 265–6
Jenkins, Ivy 192
Jesse, Fryn Tennyson 101–3
Jessell, Hon Edward 200
Johnson, Amy 241
Jones, Alfred Poynter 111–12
Jones, Mabel ('Mabs') 111, 114
Jowitt, Lady 173
Jowitt, Sir William, KC, MP, Attorney-General 166, 173, 175–6, 178–81
Joy, Maria 2
Joy, Martha 2
Joy, Thomas 2
Joynson-Hicks, Sir William, MP, Home Secretary 75, 137–8
Judd, Mr 157

Kaye, Emily xvi, 119–24, 157
Kaye, Violette ('Violet Saunders', 'Violet Watson') 234–9
Kempson, Annie 201–2, 204–5
Kendal, Norman, Assistant Commissioner, Metropolitan Police 234, 248
Kendall, Captain 23
Kent, Marguerite Sinclair 72–4
Kenworthy, Lt-Comm the Hon J.M., MP 108, 122
Kettle, Dr 78
Kindersley, Major, MP 122
King, John 5
King-Hamilton, Judge Alan, QC 174
Kitchen, George xx, 212–19
Kitchen, James 212, 218
Kitchen, William 212
Knight, Professor Bernard Henry 30

Lamington, Lord *see* Baillie-Cochrane, Charles
Lansbury, George, MP 71
Law, Andrew Bonar, MP 101, 104
Law, Mrs 155
Lawrence, Inspector James 189–91
Lawrence, Dr M.R. 251
Lawrie, Lt-Col Edward 18–19
Leahy, Dr 169
Le Crere, Dr 115
Lee, Gladys 106

Lefebure, Molly 254, 259
Le Feuvre, Sister 230
Le Neve, Ethel 21–3, 26, 30
Le Queux, William 52
Leslie, Lady Constance 167
Leslie, Sir John 167–8
Leslie, Sir Shane 167, 183
Leycester, William 18, 25–6
Lieck, Albert 15
Linklater, Eric 261
Littlejohn, Professor Harvey 16, 145–8, 161–2
'Little Tich' 57
Lofty, Margaret ('Mrs Lloyd') 44
Lombroso, Cesare xviii, 16, 45
Loughans, Harold 258–60
Lown, P. Sgt 213, 216
Luff, Dr Arthur 25, 27, 80
Lunn, Hilda 206
Luttrell, Col 256
Lygon, William (Earl Beauchamp) 179–80
Lynch, Dr Gerald Roche 90, 153, 166, 175, 186, 199, 234, 236–7, 239, 270
Lyon, M.D. 157
Lytton, Albert 71–5
Lytton, Tom 72–3

McCardie, Sir Henry, KC, High Court Judge 53, 104
McCawley, Faith 240
MacDonald, James Ramsay, MP 67, 112
McGill, Donald 44
McKee, Brigadier IRA 99
McLosky, A.E. 157
Macnaghten, Sir Malcolm, High Court Judge 245, 250
MacNaghten, Sir Melville, Assistant Commissioner 26
Mahon, Herbert Patrick ('Pat') xvi–xviii, 118–24, 128, 156–7, 166, 255
Malcolm, Dorothy 52
Malcolm, Lt Douglas 52–3, 77
Mallalieu, Edward Lancelot ('Lance'), MP 218
Malleson, Dr Joan 248
'Mancini, Tony' see England, Cecil Lois
Mann, Revd G.E. 209–10
Mansfield, William 216
Marshall, A.P. ('Archie') Marshall 193, 197
Marshall, Dr Thomas 27
Martin, Dorothy 88
Martin, Oswald 86, 88–9, 92
Mason, Alfred 51
Mason, Winnie 51
Massiah, Dr Edward 240
Mathews, Sir Charles, DPP 25, 33
Mattas, Dr C. 230–1
Maude, John, KC 259

Maugham, William Somerset 186
May, Leonard Morgan 57, 59–61
Mercier, Dr 17
Merrett, Bertha 143–7, 149–51
Merrett, Donald xx, 143–9, 151, 161, 203, 214, 261
Messiter, Vivian 185–8
Micklethwaite, St John, KC 203
Miller, Bruce 22
Milton, Dr Edward 64–5, 68
Montagu, Hon Ewen, KC 255–6
Moore, Garth 217
Moore, Miss 155
Morley, John (Viscount Morley) 4
Morrison, Stinie 54, 60
Morse, Charlotte 182
Morse (or Moran), Captain George 182
Muir, Sir Richard 24–30, 33, 53, 56–60, 81, 83, 104
Mullens, Lady 221, 223
Mullens, Sir John 221
Mundy, Elizabeth ('Bessie') 44–8
Munro, H.H. ('Saki') 215
Munro, Robert, KC (Lord Alness) 148, 211, 261
Mussolini, Benito 241

Nabarro, Dr David 134–6
Nares, Owen 16
Neil, Arthur, Chief Inspector 44, 47–8
Neil, Hazel 201
Newall, Tom 167
Newman, Oliver ('Tiggy') 199–201
Newton, Arthur 25–6, 29
Nichol, Dr Robert 171, 181
Nobes, T.H. 230
Nodder, Frederick 245
Normanton, Helena 135
Northcliffe, Lord see Harmsworth, Alfred

'O'Brien, James' see O'Sullivan, Joseph
Oddie, Stephen Ingleby xvii–xviii, 80, 98
O'Dwyer, Sir Michael 251–2
Oldfield, Dr Joshua 39
Oliver, Roland, KC 81, 249
Ormerod, Col C.M., Chief Constable 116
Ormes, Sgt Drummer Harry John 105–10
'Orwell, George' see Blair, Eric
Ostlere, Dr Gordon ('Richard Gordon') xiii, xix, 164, 263
O'Sullivan, Joseph ('James O'Brien') 98–9

Paling, Gerald 91
Palmer, Dr William 1–2
Peachell, Dr Ernest 71–3
Pearson, Dr xvi, xviii
Pegler, Edith 45

Pensotti, C. 174
Pepper, Mr Augustus 10–18, 23–5, 27–8, 30–1
Peregrine, Francis 200, 204
Peterson, Mrs 83
Pettifar, Mr 215–16
Pierrepoint, Albert xv
Pierrepoint, Thomas ('Tom') xv–xvi, 49, 138, 198
Pinero, Sir Arthur Wing 80
Pinter, Harold 156
Podmore, William 186–8, 248
Poland, Sir Harry, QC 42
Pollock, Sir Ernest, KC, MP 92, 94
Potts, Douglas 219
Powell, Frank 182
Primrose, Archibald (Earl of Rosebery) 261
'Prince' 213, 217
Prothero, Chief Inspector John ('Gentleman
    John') 81, 185–6
Pullin, Trooper Victor Lloyd 247–8
Purchase, Bentley, coroner 211, 255, 261, 266–8

Queen, Peter 211

Rattigan, Terence 99
Reading, Marquess of *see* Isaacs, Rufus
Reavil, Alice 45
Rees, DC 201
Rees, Dr 250
Reeves, Trooper Henry Richard 248
Reynolds, George 201
'Rhode, John' *see* Street, Major Cecil
Riddell, George (Lord Riddell) 183
Roberts, G.D. ('Khaki'), KC 82, 157, 243
Robertson, Professor George 147
Robey, Edward 60
Robey, Sir George 60
Robinson, John 155–8, 160–2
Robinson, Mrs 155
Robinson, Rose 258
Roche, Berthe 55–62
Roche, Martin 56
Rolls, Frederick ('Fred') 154, 157
Rolt, Terence 265–6
Roosevelt, Franklin D. 241
Rose, Dr 153, 157
Rosebery, Earl of *see* Primrose, Archibald
Roughead, William 143, 148, 150–1
Rouse, Alfred Arthur xx, 191–9, 226
Rouse, Lily 192–3, 197
Rouse, Mrs 54–6
Rowlatt, Sir Sidney, KC, High Court Judge 33,
    173–4, 181
Russell, Bertrand (3rd Earl Russell) 16
Russell, Florence 119
Russell, John (2nd Earl Russell) 16, 104
Rutherford, Lt-Col Norman 77–8

'Saki' *see* Munro, H.H.
Savage, Chief Inspector Percy 115–16, 118
Savill, Doris 235
Sayers, Dorothy L. 79
Schröder, Walter 44
Scott, Sir Walter xiii
Scrutton, Sir Edward, KC, High Court Judge 47
Seddon, Frederick 31–24, 37–8, 40, 45
Seddon, Margaret 37–8
Seddon, Maggie 38
Seton, Sir Malcolm 77
Seton, Miles 77
Seymour, Henry xx, 202–3, 205
Shaw, Dr Eric 190, 194
Shaw, George Bernard 16, 38–9, 241
Shearman, Sir Montague, KC, High Court Judge
    45, 47, 70, 100, 103
Shelley, William ('Moosh') 199–201, 204
Sheppard, P. Sgt 121
Shore, W. Teignmouth 142
Short, Dr R.H.D. 267
Sickert, Walter 4
Simon, Sir John, KC 53, 192, 218
Simpson, Dr Keith 116, 254, 258–60
Sinclair, Pridie 183
Singh, Uddam ('Mohammed Singh Azad') 251–2
Skeffington, Sheehy 99
Skeffington-Smythe, Denis 222
Skeffington-Smythe, Terence 222
Slater, Oscar 137
Slesser, Henry 67–9
Smethurst, Dr Thomas 2, 10
Smith, Frederick Edwin, KC ('F.E.') (Earl of
    Birkenhead) 26, 30
Smith, Corp Drummer George 107
Smith, George Joseph ('Mr Lloyd', 'Henry
    Williams') 43–9
Smith, H.E. Stanley 142
Smith, Mrs 201
Smith, Professor Sir Sydney 146, 151, 161–2,
    172–3, 178–9, 181, 183, 211, 215, 229,
    231–2, 254, 270
Smyth, Dame Ethel 38
Somervell, Sir Donald, KC, MP 249
Spear, G.F. 45
Spilsbury, Alan 41, 79, 251, 253–4, 261, 263–4,
    267
Spilsbury, Sir Bernard Henry *passim*: ancestry
    1–3; birth 3; personal characteristics 7–8, 14,
    79–80, 97, 141, 188, 254–5, 260–2; secondary
    education 4–6; at Magdalen College, Oxford
    6–8; studies at St Mary's Hospital, Paddington
    9–15; assists Pepper 10–13; Donovan and
    Wade case 14–15; Medico-Legal Society 16–17,
    39–40, 111, 141, 163, 172–3, 183, 229, 232,
    255, 261, 265; on infanticide 16–17; on status

lymphaticus 17–19, 123; Harrods death inquest 17–19; as witness 19, 29, 35–7, 42, 48, 59–60, 68–9, 77, 92–5, 107, 113, 122–3, 129–32, 147–50, 158–60, 175–7, 187, 193–6, 203–4, 217–18, 226–7, 231, 237–9, 243–4, 256–7, 259–60; 266; Crippen case 23–30; assists Willcox 31; Seddon case 31, 33–7; house at 31 Marlborough Hill 38, 79–80, 99, 254; President, St Mary's Medical Society 38; conservative opinions 14, 39–40, 48, 163, 249; Jeannie Baxter case 41–2; collaborates with Robert Churchill 41–2, 52, 77, 147–51, 213–16, 218, 224–7, 245–7, 256–7, 266; turned down for war service 42–3; Brides in the Bath case 46–9; Wheeldon case 51; Malcolm case 52–3; Voisin case 55–60; David Greenwood case 63, 65, 68–9; Dr Brontë on S. 69, 128, 173, 179; Rutherford case 77–8; leaves St Mary's and takes appointment at Bart's 78–9; takes flat in Gray's Inn 79; relationship with Hilda Bainbridge 78–80; involvement in Freemasonry 80, 219, 255, 261; Our Society 80–1, 142, 211, 219, 245; Starkie case 81–2; Hodgson case 85; Willis case 85–6; Armstrong case 89–96; conducts post-mortem on Sir Henry Wilson and fears IRA 98–9; Bywaters and Thompson case 99, 101–4; knighted 104; Dearnley case 106–7, 110; Lettsomian lecturer 111; Vaquier case 111–14; criticised by Avory 114; Mahon case 115–18, 122–4; conducts post-mortem on Mahon xvi–xviii, 124; Home Office refuses S. permission to keep section of Mahon's spine for demonstration purposes xviii; Thorne case 125, 127–39; controversy in the media 136–7; judge's doubt about murder conviction 138; S.'s secret meeting with Home Secretary 138; proposes institute of medical jurisprudence 141; death of Hilda Bainbridge 142–3; Merrett case 143, 147–51; Sir Sydney Smith on S. xix, 147, 151, 161, 172, 179, 183, 211, 231; Robinson case 153–5, 158–62; caricatured in Punch 163; literary inspiration 163–4; Croydon poisoning case 164; Fox case 164–6, 170–9, 181, 183; Podmore case 185–8; feigned dislike of being photographed 188; in R101 enquiry; Rouse case ('Blazing Car' murder) 189–91, 193–7, 211; Newman and Shelley case 199–200; Seymour case ('Oxford Murder') 201–5; Tarrant Keyneston shooting mystery 208–9; The Organon 211, 255; Peter Queen case 211–12; George Kitchen case 212–19; 'ghastly speculation' 217–18; Elvira Barney case 224–7; excluded from court 226; Jersey abortion case 229–32; Dr Aleck Bourne on S. 232; proposes Medico-Legal Institute 232; First Brighton Trunk case 233–4, 240; Second Brighton Trunk case (Mancini) 236–9; 'Public Favourite' 241; Linford Derrick case 243–4; takes Hellenic cruise 244–5; Nodder case 245; Casserley-Chaplin case 245–7; Armstrong Siddeley car 247, 261; Bourne case 247, 249–50; Uddam Singh case 251–3; loses against Willcox in civil case 251; suffers first stroke 251–2; death of Peter S. 253–4; bombed out of Gray's Inn flat 254; at Langorf Hotel 254, 267; Cummins case 255; 'The Man Who Never Was' 255–6; second stroke 256; Cienski case 256–7; Loughans case 259–60; Keith Simpson on S. xix, 259–60; third stroke 262; Cornock case 265; de Antiquis murder 266; suicide 266–8; obituaries 268–70; S.'s professional legacy 269–70

Spilsbury, Constance ('Connie') 3, 97, 247, 254

Spilsbury, Edith (Lady Spilsbury) 9, 17, 38, 41, 79, 116, 233, 254, 264, 269

Spilsbury, Evelyn (Mrs Richard Steel) 31, 38, 79, 233, 241, 254, 261–3, 267–9

Spilsbury, Gertrude ('Gertie') 4, 97, 247, 257, 262, 269

Spilsbury, Henry 1

Spilsbury, James (S's father) 1–7, 9, 13, 97, 247, 257

Spilsbury, James (S's great-grandfather) 1

Spilsbury, Leonard 4, 13, 247, 257, 262, 269

Spilsbury, Marion (or Maria) 2, 97

Spilsbury, Mary (S's grandmother) 1, 6

Spilsbury, Mary (Leonard S's second wife) 247, 257, 269

Spilsbury, Dr Peter 47, 79, 229, 245, 253–4

Spilsbury, Richard ('Dick') 78–9, 229, 244–5, 251, 253–4, 257, 263–4, 266–7, 269

Spurgin, Dr Percy 111

Stack, Sir Lee 146

Stamfordham, Lord *see* Bigge, Sir Arthur

Stanley, Oliver 218

Starkie, Dr Richard 81–3, 163

Steel, John Allistair 233, 267

Steer, William 206, 210

Stephen, Francis 221

Stephen, Thomas William Scott ('Mickey') 221–4, 226–7

Stock, Albert 265

Stopes, Dr Marie 163

Storey, Hilda 105–8, 110

Street, Major Cecil ('John Rhode') 164

Sudeley, Lord *see* Hanbury-Tracy, Richard

'Sunny' 210

Swift, Sir Rigby, KC, High Court Judge 78, 157, 160–1, 200, 203–5, 216–19, 227, 245

Sworn, Dr Henry 32

Sykes, Sir Percy 251

Talbot, Sir George, KC, High Court Judge 193, 197

Taylor, Dr Alfred Swaine 1–2, 47, 178

Taylor, D. Sgt 260

Telling, Dr Aubrey 196

Thesiger, Gerald 173

Thomas, Trooper David 248

Thomas, Dr J.C. 246

Thomas, Dr S. 185–6

Thompson, Edith 99–103, 113

Thompson, Percy 99–101, 103

Thomson, Sir Basil 61

Thomson, Christopher (Lord Thomson) 188

Thorne, Norman xiii, 125–32, 135–9, 154, 156, 159, 166, 179

Thornhill, Caroline 45

Thorp, Linton, KC, MP 216–17

Tinsley, Mona 245

Tobin, Alfred, KC 26–30, 34

Tolstoy, Leo 261

Toogood, Dr Frederick 94–5

Trapnell, Mr 187

Tree, Sir Herbert Beerbohm 80

Trenchard, Sir Hugh (Lord Trenchard), Commissioner, Metropolitan Police 233

Trew, Nellie 63–5, 68–73

Trew, Mr 63–4, 68

Troup, Sir Edward 62, 71

Tucker, Nellie 192

Tullett E.V. xx

Turnbull, Dr Gilbert 29–30

Tyler, Dr Margaret 74

Valentine, PC Robert 189, 191

Van Neck, Captain, Chief Constable 165–6, 176

Vaquier, Jean-Pierre 111–14, 127, 225

Vernon, Horace 7–8

Vine, Lawrence 157–9

Voisin, Louis 54–62, 265

Vonderahe family 33

Wade, Charles 14

Wade, Hugh 222

Wall, Dr Reginald 29

Wallace, Edgar 74, 120–1

Ward, Chief Inspector Alfred 38

Ward, Stephen 193

Warner, Jack 265

Warren, Miss 119–20

Watson, William, KC, Lord Advocate 145

Waugh, Evelyn 180, 221–2

Webb, Humphrey 89–90

Webster, Dr John 33, 37, 47, 51, 88, 90–1, 94–5, 101, 111–12, 245

Webster, Richard Everard (Lord Alverstone, Chief Justice) 25

Weeks, Elsy 206

Weir, Dr Henry 153, 157, 172–3, 176, 178

Weismann, Mary *see* Spilsbury, Mary

Welchman, Revd H. de Vere 165

Welham, Edward ('Ted') 205–10

Wensley, Chief Inspector Frederick 54–5, 100, 115, 121

Westminster, Duke of *see* Hugh Grosvenor

Wheeldon, Alice 51

Wheeldon, Hetty 51

Wheeler, Arthur 242–4

Wheeler, Kathleen ('Kath') 242

Wild, Sir Ernest, KC 80

Wilde, Oscar 25

Willcox, Dr Philip 267

Willcox, Sir William 11–12, 16–18, 23–31, 33–5, 37, 43, 47, 79–80, 88–91, 95, 252

Williams, William 104

Willis, William ('Bill') xvi

Willis, Dr Edward 85–6

Willshire PC 64

Wilsdon, Dr Ralph 267

Wilson, Sir Henry, MP, Field Marshal 97–9

Wilson, Dr Kenneth 208

Wilson, Mrs 208

Wilson Dr R.K., Captain RA 216

Windsor, Duke of *see* Edward, Prince of Wales

Winter, Inspector William 223–4

Witthaus, Dr 94–5

Wodehouse, P.G. 80

Woods, Dr 134

Wright, PC 167

Wright, Sir Almroth 12, 38–9, 164

Wyndham, Olivia 222

Yates, Major Peel, Chief Constable 208

Zetland, Marquess of *see* Dundas, Lawrence